Social Psychology

A Critical Agenda

Social Psychology

A Critical Agenda

Rex Stainton Rogers, Paul Stenner,
Kate Gleeson and Wendy Stainton Rogers

Polity Press

Copyright © Rex Stainton Rogers, Paul Stenner, Kate Gleeson & Wendy Stainton Rogers 1995

First published in 1995 by Polity Press
in association with Blackwell Publishers Ltd.

Reprinted 1996, 2006, 2007

Polity Press
65 Bridge Street
Cambridge, CB2 1UR, UK

Polity Press
350 Main Street
Malden, MA 02148, USA

ISBN: 978-0-7456-1182-2
ISBN: 978-0-7456-1183-9 (pbk)

A CIP catalogue record for this book is available
from the British Library.

Library of Congress Cataloging-in-Publication Data
Social psychology : a critical agenda / Rex Stainton Rogers . . . [et al.]
p.   cm.
Includes bibliographical references and index.
ISBN: 978-0-7456-1182-2 (alk. paper) — ISBN: 978-0-7456-1183-9 (pbk: alk. paper)
1. Social psychology.   I. Stainton Rogers, Rex.
HM251.S6718   1995
302—dc20   94–41679
                                                            CIP

Typeset in 11 on 13 pt Sabon
by CentraCet Limited, Cambridge
Printed and bound in Great Britain by Marston Book Services Limited, Oxford

This book is printed on acid-free paper.

For further information on Polity, visit our website: www.polity.co.uk

Contents

Preface   xi
Acknowledgements and Dedications   xiv

PART I

1: The Mission, Message and Marketing of Social Psychology   1

Making trouble   1
Social psychology as mission   2
  Social psychologists as initiates and redeemers   4
  Do-gooding   5
  Missionary expansionism   5

Social psychology as a product range   7
  Consuming social psychology   10
  Social psychology's market niche   10
  Social psychology's 'unique selling point'   11

What this book seeks to do   13

2: Towards a Critical Social Psychology   15

Human science as a Modernist endeavour   16
  The 'march of civilization' tale under question   17

The humaneering form of social psychology   18
  The subject of psychology   18
  Psychology the discipline   19

Crisis talk   22
Science and scientism   23
New paradigms for old   23
The Foucauldian turn   27
Theo-ry is dead   29
titlehis'ancero humanis andmepts tophieswholbe   33
Science as story-telling   34
All the world's a . . . conversation?   35

Inscribing social psychology   38
Politics by other means?   39
Mission statement?   40

PART II

3: From Personality to Textual Identities

3: **From Personality to Textual Identities**   42

What is wrong with a science of the self?   44
The reification of personhood as 'personality'   47
Biologizing personality   48
Damn lies and statistics   49

Situated identity: A turn to ecology   51
A turn to textuality   54
Being-in-the-world   55
Strategy, purpose, directedness: selfhood-in-action   56
We exist in time, and time in us   57

The textuality and tectonics of self   60
Textual identities?   60
'Are you for me or against me?' (the Other)   63
Circumstance   63
Be-coming   65
Standing, footing, location and positioning: their relation to
selfhood   65
Knowledging the self   67

4: **Between Ourselves**   70

Orientation   70
Conventional approaches   71
Triplett and the dynamogenics of reeling   72
Le Bon and the problem with crowds   74
The ideology of the self-contained individual   76
The influence of Le Bon on theories of influence   78
Here comes the Sherif   79

Asch – or 'size does matter'   80
Stan, Stan the electrodes man   82
'Collect $15 a day and go to jail'   84
Race relations?   86
Janus   89
Personal relationships   91
From nature and nurture to fields of possibility   94

5: In Social Worlds   98

Growing up social   98
Old chestnuts   99
Dilemmas of development   101
Becoming good, becoming bad   103
Tautology, trivia and truism   106
Social worlds revisited   107
Social worlds recovered and recast   109

PART III

6: From Attitudes to Opinionation as Discourse   111

Unsettling our differences   112
Attitude formation   117
The measurement of attitudes   120
Attitude change   123
Attitudes and behaviour   126
Epilogue: Putting opinionation back 'between ourselves'   130

7: Science and Common Sense   131

Making sense and making nonsense   131
The emergence of cognitive social psychology   134
The emergence of attribution theory   135
  Attribution and applied social psychology   139

Re-attributing attribution   141
Schema theory and social representations theory   142
Disciplined sense and common sense revisioned   144

Understanding as the negotiation of reality   145
From interrogation to reading   146

PART IV

**8: From Animosity to Atrocity: Social Psychology
      Explains Aggression**   149

The quest for explanation   150
The interface between lay and expert knowledge   151
  Choosing between explanations   152
  Explanations are always contingent   153

Explanations are socially constructed   154
Social-psychological explanations of aggression   155
  Aggression as a 'natural' response to frustration   155
  Environmental 'explanations'   160
  Social learning theory   161
  Aggression as cultural drama   165

The politics of social psychologists' explanations of aggression   166
A brief critical polytextual reflection on aggression   170

9: Social Emotions   173

Emotion addressed   175
Emotion in mainstream psychology   176
  Ordering emotion   177
  Emotion as communication   177
  Moral concern   178
  Emotion, cognition and attribution   179

The social construction of emotion   182
  Emotions as ways of being   183
  A concrete world of contexts and activities?   185
  Emotions as always social   188
  Finally, with feeling   191

**10: Pomosexualities: Challenging the Missionary
       Position**   192

Sex, gender and sexuality   192
A bit of 'the other'?   193
Sex   195

The consequences of sexual categorization   197
The biological warrant for sex differences   198
Challenging the biological warrant   198

Gender   200
Social learning theory   200
Cognitive-developmental theory   200
Psychoanalytic theory   201
Sexual alchemy   202
'Measuring' femininity and masculinity   202
Androgeny   205

Feminist theory   206
The feminist appropriation of psychoanalysis   208
Transdisciplinarity   209

Sexuality   209
A short history of sexology   213
Developmental sexology   217

Eroticization   219
Cross-cultural studies of sexuality   221
Critical readings   222

PART V

11: Methods of Enquiry   225

Experiments   227
Let's do an experiment   227
Our critique   229

Psychometrics   231
Dissolution   232
A turn to 'softer' methods   233
The interrogation interminable   234
The experiment goes marching on!   235
Discipline and publish – don't discipline and you won't get
published!   236
The 'good ship' experimental social psychology sails on   238

Alternative methodologies   238
Asking different questions   239
Social representations research   241
Discourse analytic approaches   243
Where we stand   247
Q methodology   248

Conclusions   253

12: Inconclusions   255

The dialogue   256

Bibliography   273
Index   299

Preface

Anyone looking along the bookshelves for a text on 'social psychology' may well feel spoiled for choice. Indeed, in one sense they are, for they are being offered the end-results of half a century of product development and skilful marketing. Much as products in a supermarket, they vie with each other to catch the consumer's eye, each one seeking to come over as glossier, more user-friendly, more relevant to 'real life issues' than the next. But, like cans of cola or video cameras, if you explore the range of textbooks on offer more closely, you will discover that the choice is more illusory than substantive. While the packaging and designs differ, their basic features are essentially the same. This is no accident for nearly all of them have been produced by major communications corporations, marketed to meet the requirements of the US educational system and market-researched to maximize sales therein. No one would deny that the match to the teaching (and test-based assessments) of social psychology on the US campuses has been well realized in these texts. The circle of instructions is completed through the 'instructor's manuals', 'test banks' and 'computer ancillaries' that often accompany them.

What these texts do not offer (nor, to be fair, do they claim to offer) is to meet needs outside of the dominant market segment they serve. For those of us who seek to teach *critical* social psychology – especially where a major thrust of that criticality is directed towards the way US psychology operates as a *de facto* form of 'intellectual imperialism' – the choice on the 'textbook supermarket shelves' is no choice at all. While there are now a number of useful critical books available in the area, these tend to be issue- and topic-based, aimed at the more 'advanced' reader, who is assumed to be already somewhat conversant with mainstream social psychology and the challenges to it. Critical social psychology as an area of syllabus has been constituted without a textbook, usually being taught by reference to a diverse collection of papers and book chapters and locally prepared hand-outs. This is less than ideal for students and makes starting such a course a major investment for teachers already facing heavy work-loads and crowded schedule. The time had come, we felt, to fill the gap by writing a general, introductory critical text.

However, as we soon discovered, to write an 'alternative' or 'counter' text to the mainstream syllabus in social psychology is a daunting task. To write one which is not also daunting to read is even harder! This is because it is necessary to present enough of the mainstream syllabus to provide a 'target' for criticality, while, at the same time, leaving enough space to present the critiques and outline possible alternatives. Over the critical agenda, we wanted to offer a reasonably comprehensive account of the various streams and themes of thought ('the climate of perturbation') which have shaped a critical forum to the mainstream discipline. We also wished to show how those critiques can be brought to specific cases of mainstream social psychological activity (as theory, as method and as research) and to give a sense of the broader place critical social psychology occupies as an academic activity in its own right. But this, on its own, we felt was not enough. A major failing of much critical work is that that is *all* it does – criticize. We feel it is important to address the question of how 'critical social psychology' can be pursued in positive terms – the analytics and methods that can be used to undertake transdisciplinary scholarship.

As a result, apart from the deliberately delayed treatment of methodological issues, the chapter by chapter development of the coverage in the book is actually very similar to that adopted in the US glossy textbooks and their more staid European counterparts. This has been deliberate. It means you will find much here you are likely to recognize immediately. What *is* different is that, instead of a mere regurgitation of the standard syllabus, we offer only a brief (and selective) review of it as a starting-point for criticism and deconstruction. The bulk of the text is devoted to arguing what we think is wrong with the mainstream, what are the implications and what we consider should be done instead.

To foster the objectives we have used a number of textual devices, which we developed (cf. Curt, 1994) as a means for making dense writing more accessible. Specifically, key issues are reiterated through the voice of an *'Itinerant Interlocutor'* whose contributions are shown in italic, while broader themes are developed through 'helpful little boxes' (called 'Boxes'). These are both introduced in the first chapter. We recognize that seeking in this way to transform how texts are written is risky – what may come over as amusing in the writing can – for some people – come over as decidedly 'twee' and embarrassing when read 'cold'. But we think the hazards of making critical work sound as dry as dust or more virtuous than high-bran muesli are even greater.

This is not to say that we do not take critical social psychology 'seriously'. To 'go critical' is not just a matter of subjecting 'all that is held dear' to scholarly, abstract scrutiny. To do it is also to live it – and that applies to every activity, including writing textbooks. Our jokey asides and titles, our disparaging remarks are not just meant as 'bits of fun' – they do have a serious purpose. You may like our style or hate it, but at least you should get the impression that this text was written by actual people – warts and all. It has not emerged (nor have its arguments) in some abstract 'discursive ether' somehow untouched by who and what we are as people in time and space. These are 'our' arguments, 'our' ideas, 'our' criticisms – in the specific sense that we have seen them into being. While we fully acknowledge the 'hidden hands' of our Berylite and Barcelona friends, our reviewers and the many, many texts we have scavenged, we 'own' them as our own. Now they are yours to read and ponder. This is the story we have set about to tell – but it is no more than *one* story (just like all the other ones we criticize). You can 'own' or 'disown' it, scavenge it, discard it, as you choose.

The Authors

Acknowledgements and Dedications

First of all, we acknowledge fifteen years of a government hell-bent on 'efficiency' and 'value for money' – to them we dedicate the epithet that 'they know the cost of everything and the value of nothing' and the ulcers we gained in pursuing this project in the margins of our time, lacking the benefits of any sabbatical leave.

We would like, however, genuinely to thank Rebekah Stainton Rogers and Nichola Thomasson, for all the hard work they put into preparing the text for publication, especially the bibliography. To them we dedicate a Vague night out in Leeds. Our thanks are also due to the many 'critical social psychologists' (both those who are 'out' and elsewise) within whose community so much that is laid out here has been shared. To them, we dedicate our perverted English! In particular, we wish to spell out our debts to both the hospitality and the scholarship of the 'Barcelona Brigade' at the Universitat Autonoma. We acknowledge too our growing friendship and support from the 'radicals' at Manchester Metropolitan University. To them we dedicate more frantic trips up the M6.

Our gratitude also to the broader Beryl Curt group for support and critical input. To them we dedicate the next decade of kitchen heroics. Finally, we acknowledge the reviewers (formal and otherwise) of earlier drafts of the manuscript. We, of course, blame them for all errors and lapses of judgement in this book, while reserving the site of any praise to ourselves!

1 The Mission, Message and Marketing of Social Psychology

Many a textbook in social psychology begins by defining its subject-matter, by setting out its mission or by leaping into a sales pitch about how reading it will transform your life. We are not going to do any of these – at least, not in the conventional sense. For a start, as one of our friends, Adrian Scaife (1994), says – we see our job as not to define things but to un-define them! If we do have a mission, then it is to make trouble – and part of how we intend to do this is to highlight social psychology's own (sometimes tacit, sometimes explicit) missionary agenda. In a sense, then, this book is a 'savage' attack on the conventional mainstream of social psychology – if you take 'savage' to mean the opposite of 'civilized' (i.e. colonized by the conventions of orthodoxy). As such its purpose is to be explicitly rhetorical and disputational. It aims to challenge and undermine the sales pitch by which textbook social psychology is usually 'sold' as a cure-all for modern life's ills and problems.

Making trouble

We seek, then, not to define but to un-define. Our mission is to resist evangelism by promoting heresy. And our sales pitch is not to offer a 'new improved' product (i.e. one which merely tinkers with the old formula by adding on a few new ingredients) but to encourage you to become a more wary and cynical consumer. These may seem rather obtuse things to say, but they do give you some flavour of what this book will be like.

The rationale for our trouble-making is that – in contrast to authors writing conventional textbooks in this field – we do not see social psychology as an unproblematic academic discipline – a means by which knowledge can be gradually uncovered by dint of rigorous, rational and value-free scholarship. Instead we see it (and all other disciplines) as an endeavour of human meaning-making, by which what comes to pass as knowledge gets created.

Social psychology as mission

We would argue that social psychology is pre-eminently a subject-area where knowledge is 'sought' not for its own sake but in order to achieve certain goals. These goals have always been made quite explicit. Take, for example, the following 'mission statement' presented by three early psychologists:

> The value of learning more about ourselves and human nature is obvious. Our social, political and economic theories rest ultimately upon our understanding of human nature. Upon sound knowledge of human nature depends the possibility of directing social changes, so as to make social institutions and practices better suited to human needs. As citizens, then, we need to make our beliefs about human nature as sound and rational as possible. The nineteenth century was marked by great achievements in engineering. Advances in psychology, sociology, and physiology should lead to as striking advances in 'humaneering' during the twentieth century. (Tiffin, Knight and Josey, 1940: 23-4)

This call to 'humaneering' is still very much with us. Varela, for example, repackages it as the notion of 'social technology' and makes a similar call to 'get stuck in':

> The fact is that we already have most of the technology we need to solve an enormous range of social problems, from personal miseries to organizational conflict, from the marriage bed to the conference table. If we wait for pure research to come up with the real-world answers, though, we will be waiting for Godot. Engineers and physical scientists cannot wait for theoretical perfection. If the Romans had waited for the elegance of the Verrazano-Narrows Bridge instead of fooling around with stone arches, the course of civilization would have changed. (1975:84)

This quest to boldly go and seek out 'sound knowledge of human nature' in order to 'make social institutions and practices better suited to human needs' is woven intimately into everything that social psychologists do. The topics they identify to study, the knowledge they seek to 'obtain' and the theories they construct are all shot through (as a fabric may be shot through with elastic thread) with this pursuit of human betterment. In other words, far from being 'mere scholarship' it is a profoundly value-laden, ideological endeavour, with a far-reaching commitment to 'do-gooding'. It is this 'hidden' (and not-so-hidden) agenda we intend our book to expose and to challenge.

I.I. Can I interrupt for a moment?

AUTHORS: What? Who – who are you? What's going on here? We were just getting into the swing of starting our book. Authors don't expect interruptions.

I.I. Allow me to introduce myself (as Mick Jagger used to sing). I call myself the 'Interpolated Interlocutor' (I.I. for short – pronounced 'Aye-aye') and my reason for insinuating myself into your text is to ask some of the questions your readers may be wanting to ask themselves, but can't. By the time it appears in print, any chance of interrogating it is no longer available. It's a technique you've used before in the previous book you wrote as part of Beryl Curt (Curt, 1994), the disembodied 'author' of Textuality and Tectonics.

AUTHORS: Well we (as bits of Beryl) remember our dear friend the Interrupter. Are you after taking on the role he played?

I.I. Well, yes and no (a phrase, if I remember, Beryl used rather a lot). I'm not intending simply to go for a repeat performance. But yes – if you like – having a textual agent (a device Beryl borrowed from Mulkay 1985) seemed to work pretty well before. If I remember rightly, when you were blasting out drafts of this book, you decided to try a similar technique again. So here I am.

AUTHORS: Fair enough, we did agree to give it a try. Well – now you're here, what is it you wanted to ask?

I.I. Well, I'm sorry to stem your flow of prose so early in the text, but I am already beginning to get a bit worried. You seem to be getting off on very dodgy ground, if you ask me. You seem to want your cake and to eat it. On the one hand you are making a pretty good argument that traditional social psychology is a rhetorical endeavour, shot through (as you would put it) by missionary zeal. But aren't you being just as zealous yourselves? I can almost hear the sound of your tub-thumping – definitely a case of 'pot calling' I reckon!

Apart from the observation that it is keys we are punching rather than tubs, you have a point. We are certainly being polemical. The difference is, we have no problems over admitting it. Once you accept the thesis that all forms of discursive labour – including the writing of textbooks – are inherently and inevitably rhetorical – done for a purpose, to promote a particular 'view of the world' – then there is no escaping from the acknowledgement that what is going on is 'tub-thumping'. The whole point of this book, as we see it, is to set out a series of arguments about what social psychology is, what it does and why it does what it does – and then to consider the consequences. You cannot make arguments like this and remain neutral – indeed, if you detect any creeping neutrality insinuating itself into the text, you should begin to worry.

I.I. Fair enough, I'll watch out. Now, where does that leave us?

The point about missionary evangelizing is that it is a certain kind of rhetoric, based on faith – on believing that you have an unique handle on 'the truth', and that this 'truth' has the power to redeem unbelievers.

I.I. And you are not doing that?

No we are not. What we are offering is not a new faith but an agnosticism. What we want to promote is not an alternative creed but a measure of scepticism in order to resist allurement into the conviction that there is any single 'true faith'. By contrast, what evangelism promises is salvation. By 'civilizing' the 'savages' it claims to be able to save them from the heresies and superstitious nonsense which blights their lives. Moreover, missionaries often peddle their dogma under the guise of 'doing good' and they seek to colonize – to move into the 'dark continents' and bring their peoples into the fold of the 'saved'.

Social psychologists as initiates and redeemers

The notion of the social psychologist as a particular kind of missionary may seem a strange one. It seems an eccentric reading partly because such an integral part of the dogma of psychologism (something we are all exposed to as part of living in a psychologized reality) is to see scientifically grounded social knowledge as opposite to 'blind faith' and scientific humanism as a replacement for religion.

However, in the very grounding of psychology upon these axioms it could not, perhaps, have become other than an evangelical, secular 'faith' dedicated to human improvement. Looked at like this, to become a psychologist is to respond to a calling. But under Modernism (about which we will find out more in the next chapter), the concern is not for 'saving souls' but for 'changing hearts and minds', and salvation is seen to lie in this world not the next! The rewards too are different, they are both quantifiable and as much directed to the 'priest' as the 'flock'. But what it does share with religion is its need to indoctrinate its initiates into 'faith'.

Do-gooding

The 'true faith' of social psychology is liberal humanism – an ideology of human betterment. This can be seen clearly in the way social psychologists contextualize their work. For example, Aronson (1988) states the following in the preface to the fifth edition of his *The Social Animal*: 'I attempt to paint a clear picture of the current state of our social-psychological knowledge and how such knowledge might be used to alleviate some problems plaguing us in the world today' (Preface). This kind of rationale proffers a double-edged inducement: it asserts a 'moral' justification (do-gooding); and it offers practical benefits (doing good). The catch, of course, is that to get the 'goodies' on offer requires buying into the ideology with which they are associated.

I.I. Just as old-style missionaries 'sold' religion by offering it in conjunction with access to Western biomedicine and education.

Precisely. In order to gain the 'solutions' to 'human problems' social psychology requires its practitioners and its consumers to 'buy into' liberal humanism.

Missionary expansionism

Mainstream social psychology, as a missionary endeavour, is certainly into expansionism and colonization. It has, since its beginnings, been consuming more and more resources, moving into new areas (in terms of both the social and the geographical locations in which it now operates), employing more and more people, producing more and more 'new models'.

It can come over rather like the Western industrialized world's 'love affair' with the automobile. Apart from short-term 'blips' at times of recession, we are getting more and bigger lorries pounding our roads, increased car-use and car-ownership – and, to meet the needs of the automobile, we have an ever expanding programme of road building. Yet growth, as green politics has taught us, should not be taken for granted as a 'good thing' in itself, whether we think of automobiles or academic disciplines. We need to ask questions of it – can it be sustained? Should it be sustained?

I.I. Are you saying that one can't really expect to get straight answers to questions like that from social psychology's establishment?

If you mean the British Psychological Society or the American (i.e. US) Psychological Association – no, not really. Given what is known of the ways organizations operate, we do not envisage the establishment wanting to debate whether 'going for growth' in psychology is an unmitigated benefit to humankind – they have all too much at stake if the answer turns out to be 'no'. The most we can expect from them is the odd ethics committee and – at a pinch – allowing a course here and there on 'critical social psychology' – as long, of course, that it is clear that this is very much a fringe activity and it is not going to rock any boats seriously.

I.I. So why bother?

That's a good question, and not one with any quick and easy answers. Indeed, much of this book is devoted to answering it. But for now we can offer three main reasons. First, we think academics should be in the business of raising awkward questions, not building and bolstering an establishment. Second, we are concerned about the downside costs of the growing power and ubiquity that the influence of social psychology has on people's lives. And third – and possibly most fundamental – we are extremely dubious about the assumptions on which psychology's imperialism is based.

We think the analogy with the expansion in automobile use works well here. Green politics argues that the environmental problems (such as pollution) and the harm done to quality of life (such as restricting the movement of children) are not going to be solved by cosmetic changes – like adding on catalytic converters to cars, changing to unleaded petrol and diverting motorways around certain areas. What is ultimately going to need to be changed is our whole way of life, and the part that automobiles play in it. Equally we do not believe that the problems that conventional approaches to social psychology bring about can be addressed just by tinkering on its margins. What is needed, we believe, is to expose the whole endeavour to challenge. What good does it do? Do we need it? And – if not – what (if anything) should be put in its place?

Social psychology as a product range

Before we get into addressing these questions, it is important to recognize that social psychology is not a coherent subject but a loose collection of different people doing different things from widely differing perspectives. At best it can be regarded as a 'melting-pot of ideas'. At worst, it often comes over as a mess and a modge.

One way of 'getting a handle' on this is to argue that it is rather like a set of 'products' that get promoted in the knowledge market, under the brand label of 'social psychology'. Its product range reflects both the history of its R&D and the attempts of its manufacturers to capitalize on the different 'wants' of different consumers.

I.I. You give the distinct impression you are back into your 'producing psychology is like manufacturing cars' analogy again! OK, I'll play along for a while – so tell me about its 'brands.'

To do so we are going to introduce another of our textual devices – 'helpful little boxes' (Boxes for short). Sometimes these will be used to summarize a whole area of work – the aim in these situations is to provide a basis on which we can criticize traditional approaches and methods, and argue our case against them. In situations like this one, boxes will be used mainly because we think it will make for easier reference.

Box 1.1 Social Psychology: the Product Range

Social psychology as science

This is the four-wheel drive line – sold on qualities of utility and its ability to tackle the hardest terrain. It stresses the psychology in social psychology, and asserts that it is the scientific study of individuals in social situations. These individuals are held to think (cognize), feel (emote) and act (behave) in ways that can be causally explained, and hence can be studied using hypothetico–deductive methods, primarily that of the laboratory experiment. Theories are ideally expressed in mathematical terms, with hypotheses stated as predictions about the impact of manipulating variables upon measures (e.g. of behaviour, affect, etc.). Statistical analysis of results are given prominence. You will know you are dealing with this identity whenever you come across the label 'experimental social psychology'.

Social psychology as social science

This one is more the 'family car'. It generally identifies social psychology as inter-disciplinary, and accords considerable importance to its socio-logical roots. Here 'social psychology' is identified with relationships between individuals and social structures (from two-person 'dyads' to organizations and institutions). Individuals are held to be both influenced by and influential upon social structures. Where 'theories' feature, they are likely to be either 'grand theories' (such as structural–functionalism) or interactional models such as 'symbolic interactionism'.

Social psychology as a humanist endeavour

Here we have a real 'love bug' – designed for 'being', with definite 'green' credentials. The key markers here are an immediate commitment to showing that social psychology is relevant to personal and social prob-lems. Markers to watch out for are the use of terms like 'self-growth' and 'self-actualization'. Its purpose is seen as helping to achieve a better world, with overt agendas of personal growth and championing the underdog. This may lead to some coverage of social developmental psychology (e.g. moral development). You will spot it as a 'warm and cuddly' identity by its recourse to communal and 'feel-good' values, and its determination to avoid 'getting too political'.

Social psychology as empire building

Very much the 'top of the range estate car' – a product intended to promote the owner's sense of having 'made it', with stressed qualities of flexibility and 'do-it-all-ability'. Here social psychology is presented as 'big enough to go it alone' – a discipline in its own right. It is a position often adopted in encyclopedias, handbooks of social psychology and in modular courses. Social psychology is seen to stretch from biology ('the social life of animals', 'physiological social psychology') to social science ('cultural psychology', 'economic psychology') and to encompass topics such as developmental psychology and personality theory.

Social psychology as a pragmatic endeavour

This is the lorry or van rather than the car – it is sold for commercial use. This approach is often expressed in books with titles like *Social Psychol-ogy for Security Guards* or *Social Psychology and Management: Turning People into Profits*. The topics covered may look similar to those dealt with under the Humanist banner, but you can tell this identity is on offer whenever the client is not portrayed as the 'human race' but as 'industry' or some specific practitioner group. A similar confidence in the power of social psychological knowledge is expressed. It may be linked with, even warranted by, evidence about applied activities (e.g. as a consultant).

Social psychology as a social constructionist endeavour

Here our metaphor begins to break down, as what is on offer is less an 'automotive product' than a vehicle for critical work. It declares itself early (e.g. in titles like *The Social Construction of Death*) in a challenge to all pre-emptive attempts to singularize (or even talk of) reality. However, social constructionism has become a buzz-term, and you may find you have bought a pragmatist or social scientist underneath the snazzy bodywork! Do not be fooled. Social constructionism, as we shall see in this book, offers a powerful challenge to the enterprises listed above. But be warned – social constructionism is not on offer if it is presented as just one approach among many, or called constructivism. This is somebody trying to have their cake and eat it, since constructionism is incompatible with all the above approaches.

Social psychology as a postmodern endeavour

No problem picking this one out, it has wheels within wheels! It will shout pomo-speak from the start. You will soon find that its proponents would rather risk incomprehension than being misunderstood. If you don't rapidly find terms like 'deconstruction' being used or any mention of French theorists (like Foucault, Derrida and Deleuze) it must be something else. More about this one later.

Social psychology as rebellion and resistance

A 'custom model' with a range of window stickers already attached. Sometimes this will be marked for you by the rapid recourse to words like 'feminist,' 'Marxist' or 'power'. But even where this does not happen, its polemical tone and rhetorical devices will soon show themselves. It dislikes and distrusts virtually all received social psychology. Some antisocial psychologists think that Humanists and postmodernists have either 'sold out' or don't understand that they are being 'used' and that social constructionists are relativists. It (and it flows through us sometimes) is prone to occasional attacks of wingeing and ranting relieved (?) by ironic humour or ferrous raillery.

Consuming social psychology

It is not a new point (see, for example, Parker 1989) but a point worth making, that for most of history people have managed well enough without social psychology – and most people in the world still do (having other, more pressing, things to worry about such as sheer survival). But in its home-base in the industrialized world, the consumers of social psychology include other social psychologists and students of psychology and sociology: professionals, trainee professionals and organizations engaged in various forms of 'people work' and 'people policy-making': and ordinary people in their everyday lives.

Where these consumers tend to differ is in the degree to which they 'buy' its certitude and its power. Full initiates (i.e. those who get to deal in it directly, as social psychologists in their own right) are generally (though far from always) sceptical about 'hard sell' tactics. They are sophisticated customers – who pick and chose with care, are aware of the differences between its different brands and look carefully at the pedigrees and the 'sell-by dates' of its theory and its knowledge. The further down the line away from 'expertise' its customers are, the more willing they (apparently) are to believe in 'cure-all' claims, and the more vulnerable they are to having imperfect goods 'dumped out' on them.

This analogy should not be read as disrespectful to ordinary people who lack 'sophisticated' knowledge of the 'social psychology' product. Just as it is the drug companies (and not their clients) that we hold responsible for 'dumping out' unsafe medication in the 'Two Thirds World', we regard the social psychological establishment as accountable for the way in which it markets its wares. Having said this, as we have mentioned already, a major motivation for writing this book is to spell out the critical importance of being wary about the 'sales pitch', mindful of the techniques used in advertising, and discerning over the promises and claims that are made.

Social psychology's market niche

Considered as a 'brand label' we can also ask where social psychology sits in the wider knowledge market. Again, early on, its proponents laid claim to a special 'market niche' at the intersection between the 'biological' and the 'social' and the 'individual' and 'society'. Tiffin, Knight and Josey again provide a good entrée into this claim:

> In his (*sic*) effort to understand social behaviour, the psychologist must recognise the reality of social forces just as he must recognise the reality of

physical objects. How, for example, can we understand the present strength of the desire to acquire wealth, apart from the social situation? Or how, apart from social conditions, can we account for the divorce rate? Or for women buying their spring hats in January? So important are social conditions in influencing behaviour and character that a branch of psychology, called social psychology is devoted to the study of the interaction between society and the individual. Man is a social being, and his behaviour is colored through and through by that fact. Psychology occupies the territory between physiology on the one hand and sociology on the other. (1940:22)

Beyond the hallmarks of their time and place (in terms of, for example, its sexism) such claims clearly mark off social psychology's territorial aspirations. This can also be thought of metaphorically. Imagine 'the human condition' as the current physical geography of the Americas and then let it be 'discovered' by academic adventurers. Picture the land to the north of 'Panama' as having been colonized and divided into dependencies called bio-natural disciplines (such as medicine, biology, physiology). Further imagine that the south of 'Panama' has similarly been colonized into territories called social disciplines (economics, sociology, anthropology). Finally, position psychology on the isthmus, covering Panama – the crucial intersection between 'the biological' and 'the social'. (See Figure 1.1.)

Social psychology's 'unique selling point'

By being sited at the crossing-point between 'the biological' and 'the social', social psychology is able to claim an unique warrant to tackle popular concerns (such as the pursuit of wealth, divorce and the vagaries of fashion). It makes social psychology a discipline that has special powers to 'tackle problems in the real world'. A good illustration here is what Triandis has to say when writing on attitudes and attitude change:

Many of the important problems of the latter third of the 20th century concern attitudes. Perhaps the biggest problem is that the rich nations are becoming richer while the poor nations are becoming poorer in a world that is progressively getting smaller. We have the technical knowledge to change the world, but most of us do not have the attitudes that can bring about change.

The next most important problem is that unless we can change our attitudes towards many of our fellow men [sic] there is the possibility of nuclear war, which would mean the end of all living things – except, perhaps, some hardy viruses. In the past conflict was highly undesirable: in

Figure 1.1   Locating psychology as a 'bio-social' science

the future it can mean total destruction. We must learn to live in harmony, to bridge the barriers that create conflict, and to develop new societies. (Triandis, 1971: 1)

We could hardly ask for a more explicit expression of the liberal-humanistic mission. It has so many 'feel-good' factors that it seems churlish to dispute its very evident utilitarian aspirations. And yet this is precisely what we are intending to do. But then, being radical should not – we would assert – ever be comfortable.

What this book seeks to do

There was a time, however, back in the late 1960s (as one of us can remember well) when to be radical in social psychology did have a certain cachet. Campuses were politically exciting, even dangerous places to be (thirteen students were shot, four fatally, at Kent State, Ohio, on 4 May 1970). Those 'revolting' campuses were also, by today's standards, academically easygoing and independent. There was (apparent) slush in the post-industrial economies, unemployment was low, graduate opportunities were excellent. In the UK students actually lived within their grants and overdrafts were whispered-about aberrations.

I.I. If I was being cynical, I might say that people felt that they could afford a little protest!

It was certainly a world away from the self-financing, academically audited, research-indexed, industrially parked, student-loaned campuses of today. Looked at like this, it is interesting to conjecture why, in the 'new realism' of the 1990s, we are seeing an upsurge in the critical treatment of social psychology. While still very much 'on the fringe', we are aware that there is a spate of counter-texts and disputational movements which are placing the whole discipline under scrutiny and asking awkward questions.

It is this questioning that we will move on to next. In Chapter 2 we will describe how and why 'critical social psychology' has begun to flourish, and what it has to offer in terms of a new conceptualization of what social psychology should be and what it should do. The rest of the book examines its various topics – such as attitudes, emotion, personality. It critically examines the history of how they each have become constituted as topics – how and why they have been 'knowledged into being' (or, to put it another way, how and why they have been made to matter). In each case we then consider some of the problems that result from the ways they are so 'knowledged'. And then we will make some suggestions about how each of these areas of topicality might be construed in a more critically informative manner.

In choosing topics we have had to be selective. Part II, consisting of Chapters 3–5, reviews what are traditionally regarded as the 'three levels of analysis' of social psychology. Chapter 3 looks at the level of the individual – particularly what is known as 'personality' or 'the study of individual differences'. Chapter 4 examines what is usually termed 'interpersonal interaction' – that is, analysis at the level of interaction 'between ourselves'. Chapter 5 then moves on to the 'social world' – analysis at the level of processes which operate in terms of groups and collectivities of various kinds.

Part III, comprising Chapters 6 and 7, takes a different kind of approach, here focusing on two 'social phenomena' which social psychologists study, and the theories they have proposed to explain them. Chapter 6 looks at attitudes and theories of attitude change; Chapter 7 examines the way psychology has theorized 'common sense', and the contrast it has made to 'scientific knowledge'.

Part IV adopts a different 'take' on social psychology's topics by examining three different aspects of 'social embodiment' (i.e. the interface social psychology assumes between the biological and the social). Chapter 8 considers aggression; Chapter 9 emotion; and Chapter 10 sexuality and gender.

The final section, Part V, undertakes two kinds of review. Chapter 11 considers the issue of empirical research – the ways in which social psychology has traditionally sought to generate evidence, in order to test its theorization. We then make some suggestions about how critical social psychology can be pursued in 'empirical' terms. Chapter 12, conventionally (though unconventional in its form) draws together the main issues that have been raised in the book, and sets out an agenda for 'going critical'.

2 Towards a Critical Social Psychology

Social psychology has not always been with us. As a collection of research questions, theories, procedures and techniques, social psychology grew up within a particular social context at a particular historical point in time. In order to simplify this issue (which otherwise could take up a whole book on its own) we will argue that social psychology is pre-eminently a Modernist endeavour. We are using 'Modernism' here as a portmanteau term to describe a *Zeitgeist* (the 'spirit of an age') that emerged in Western societies from around 1770. We refer particularly to the post-Enlightenment project, which was incorporated into the politico-economic arrangements of these societies at this time. The goal of this project was to replace irrationality with reason, superstition with empirically validated 'true knowledge', and thereby to pursue human betterment.

I.I. Hold on. Asking around I have found that in many other disciplines the term 'Modernism' is used very differently from the way you are using it. For example, in art (as in 'Modern Art') or in literature.

It is a troublesome term but we are stuck with its various differing uses across disciplines. In art and literature Modernism does indeed often refer to movements that were oppositional and iconoclastic – particularly to earlier notions of representing some reality. 'Modernists' like Ibsen, Joyce, Matisse, Picasso or Pirandello can hardly be said to have been replacing irrationality with 'reason' or superstition with 'true knowledge'! It may help to think of this sense of 'Modern-ism' (the 'spirit') as a critical commentary on 'modern-ity' (the 'age'). Discussions of Modernism and modernity can get notoriously confused and confusing – hence the setting-out of our definition right at the start.

Using our definition it makes sense to argue that the human sciences in general are one of the central products of the modern age. The first of such sciences, economics, can be dated to Adam Smith's *Wealth of Nations* (1876). Psychology is usually said to have emerged as an independent and unitary discipline in Wundt's Leipzig laboratory (1879) around a century after the beginnings of Modernism as we are telling it. What is less well known is that Wundt was no mere experimentalist but a generalist and integrator whose deep interest in folk-psychology (*Völkerpsychologie*) gives him a claim also to be accorded a founding status in social psychology.

Human science as a Modernist endeavour

When we say that the human sciences were 'central products' of the modern age, what we mean is that the bio-social sciences both were founded by way of Modernism and have played a significant role in making the modern world in which we live (i.e. the world which we, the writers – and most of the readers – of this book inhabit). This modern 'post-industrial' world is shot-through with ideas drawn from the biological and social sciences. Notions of individuals-in-society, of interpersonal relations, of 'selves' and social forces and so on, are so established that they can appear as if they were 'natural' ways of speaking about the world, rather than modern constructions. We now live in a world in which constructions like personality, attitudes, thinking, feeling and doing have all been made meaningful to us as essential qualities of human experience.

A central tenet of Modernism (particularly the High Modernism of the nineteenth century) has been that it represents the end-state in a three-stage developmental theory of civilization. Namely: (1) primitive belief in magic, which was superseded by (2) religious belief, which was itself then superseded by (3) science (cf. Douglas, 1965).

This story reflects a kind of intellectual Darwinism – an epistemological 'survival of the fittest' – where, over time, less adaptive 'ways of knowing' have been replaced by ways which are more evolved and more successful. The metaphor of a move from the 'darkness' of myth and superstition to the 'light' of reason and scientific truth is clearly expressed by the term 'Enlightenment', which came to be used as a label for early Modernism. The twin 'civilizing' agents of the European Englightenment – science and humanism – were presented in the popular education (which followed the growth in literacy), as gradually gaining ground across the world, leaving ever smaller 'pockets' of primitive thinking yet to be colonized and 'developed'. This narrative of the 'march of civilization' is thus integral to the human sciences.

The 'march of civilization' tale under question

As a grand narrative, this 'march of civilization' tale permeated all the human sciences, resulting, for example, in a psychology which for nearly one hundred years (from its founding in Germany in the mid nineteenth century to the period immediately after the Second World War) was, at the best, ethnocentric and, at the worst, downright racist. Yet by the end of twelve years which began with the atom-bombing of Japan into capitulation in 1945, learnt of the Holocaust, saw the major decolonization of the European empires and ended in 1957 with the Earth's own boundaries breached by the launch of the first Soviet satellite, the 'march of civilization' tale was beginning to fall into disarray. Even in its heartlands (the liberal democracies) the assumption that Modernism inevitably represented progress came under attack. This assault was not so much from its old enemies (e.g. traditional religion) but from its own avant-garde. To put just one marker on this, it was Bertrand Russell, that most logical of philosophers, who founded CND in 1958. By the 1960s, psychology was being taught in Western campuses against a background in which Modernism sounded like the voice of the despised establishment. There was much more to this time than 'protest' for protest's sake.

I.I. But surely, much of this protest was couched in the very terms of the 'Enlightenment' that you are implying it was criticizing. Noam Chomsky's political activities against US imperialism and exploitation, for example, were backed up with a lot of scientific rhetoric about 'seeing the real' truth!

Like many 1960s radicals, Chomsky (who in another incarnation was a linguist whose theories of deep grammar had a profound impact on psychology) used the rhetoric of scientistic Modernism – contrasting 'truth' with the polluting effects of 'ideology'. Yet in such critiques one can also see how, for all its claimed benefits, there were growing concerns about Modernism – specifically, that it does not so much offer 'solutions' as operate as a form of intellectual imperialism, promoting the interests of the powerful by exploiting and marginalizing the powerless. In this analysis, science is held to be not a means of human betterment but the agent responsible for the destruction of our environment, possibly of life on Earth itself. Some critics (like Reich, 1971) even argued for the emergence of a new 'consciousness' (a 'greening' of the USA in his case). Whatever the plausibility of such arguments, it is safe to say that the old 'march of civilization' certainties were shaken to their foundations. Whatever collective tectonics were signalled on the streets of Paris and Prague in 1968 and in the fields of Woodstock in 1969, they were not to be understood from anything coming out of the laboratories of experimental social psychology. Before examining how social psychology responded to this challenge to the 'march of civilization' tale, we will briefly indicate the extent to which the very form or structure of the discipline (as conventionally practised) is wrapped up in these questionable narratives of progress.

The humaneering form of social psychology

> The nineteenth century was marked by great advances in engineering. Advances in psychology, sociology and physiology should lead to as striking advances in 'humaneering' during the twentieth century. (Tiffin, Knight and Josey, 1904: 24)

We noted in Chapter 1 that social psychology can be construed as a 'humaneering mission'. This mission is clearly associated with the 'march of civilization' tale documented earlier. This quest towards social and individual improvement has a significant structuring effect, not only on the *content* of social psychology (what topics or problems it chose to investigate), but also upon the *form* that the discipline would take. Although we recognize that form and content cannot be precisely separated (the distinction is always a rhetorical one), we will now critically examine the form or structure of social psychology, and see how these were developed to suit the mission. To the social psychological missionaries, to humaneer requires two parallel representations; there must be a modelling of the discipline; and a modelling of the to-be-disciplined subject. We will take these in reverse order.

The subject of psychology

To be studied, to be interrogated, to be intervened upon and changed, social psychology first needs to construct its subjects *as* 'subject'. They must be seen as conceptually isolatable from their circumstances, and to

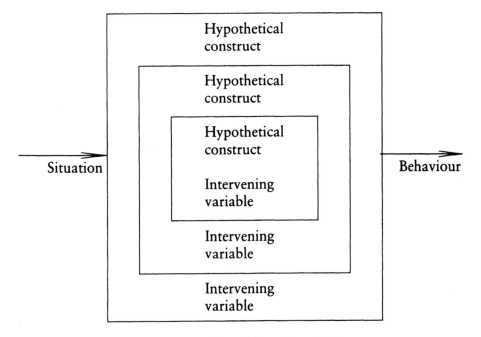

Figure 2.1 The subject of psychology

be possessed of stable, internal, intra-psychic structures which both are influenced by and mediate the impact of the impinging situation. Typically, the person is modelled as rather like a Russian doll – within the box which is 'the person' are contained further boxes (hypothetical constructs and intervening variables) which are purported to be the source of all human behaviour. Hence, this 'box' is positioned between 'situation' and 'behaviour' in such a way that these correspond to 'stimuli' (situation) and 'responses' (behaviour) – or, to put it another way, between 'cause' and 'effect'. This model hence serves to create the impression that 'behaviour' can be understood and controlled (as required by the mission) if, and only if, we have knowledge of both the situation and the box-subject. This is illustrated in Figure 2.1.

Psychology the discipline

By picturing or modelling 'behaviour' as a response or effect, social psychologists are able to consider it as, in essence, unproblematically factual or objectively recognizable. Hence the behaviour can be *a priori* identified as, for example, 'aggressive' or 'pro-social' (or whatever). Tied in with this is the possibility of picturing behaviour as an issue

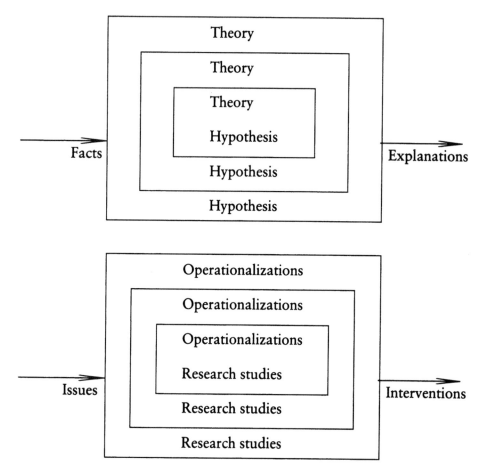

Figure 2.2   Psychology the discipline

(troublesome or desirable) to be worked on. That is, there is always immanent in this approach the implication that 'something should be done' – that 'we need to reduce aggression' or that 'we should enhance pro-sociality'.

This is what constitutes social psychology's double agenda and mission: a mixture of 'fact-finding' and 'tackling issues'. To meet that agenda, both 'facts' and 'issues' must also be passed through another box. The box this time is that of methodology, and it is a model of *knowing* rather than a model of the *to-be-known* subject (as was Figure 2.1 above). In other words, facts and issues are processed through a highly structured and rule-bound procedure (usually called 'scientific method') which is held uniquely to enable properly founded explanations and intervention programmes to emerge at the other end (Figure 2.2).

Figures 2.1 and 2.2 are attempts to represent the *form* of social psychology. This form is ideally suited to its humaneering task, and various *contents* can be inserted into it and dealt with in missionary fashion. In this way it enables social psychologists to tackle social agendas as if they were objectively definable issues which can be 'solved' by scientifically reached conclusions, and to approach people as if they were essentially predictable automata. This form, once established and accepted, also allows social psychologists to argue that any knowledge that has not been gained according to this arrangement, and thus does not follow the pattern of these structures, is not valid.

The value of learning more about ourselves and human nature is obvious. Our social, political and economic theories rest ultimately upon our understanding of human nature. Upon sound knowledge of human nature depends the possibility of directing social changes, so as to make social institutions and practices better suited to human needs. As citizens, then, we need to make our beliefs about human nature as sound and rational as possible. (Tiffin, Knight and Josey, 1940: 23)

Through setting itself up in this form, then, social psychology has both adapted itself to its missionary task and carved out and claimed for itself special powers, competences, interests, concerns and entitlements. If we ask on what grounds those claimed are justified, two possible answers seem to emerge. The first (which tends to be promulgated by psychologists themselves) suggests that they are empirical claims alone. In other words they could be tested and potentially refuted by the use of the structures depicted above. This falsifiability is exactly what the 'scientistic form' itself lays down as the criterion for valid inference.

Box 2.1 Falsifiability versus Gresham's Law

Had more experimentalists been broadly educated, they might have thought twice about the canon of falsifiability. It has an antithesis, namely Gresham's Law. Sir Thomas Gresham in 1558, following Oresme and Copernicus, argued that 'bad money always drives out good'. Galbraith says of it, 'it is the only economic law that has never been seriously challenged' (1976: 20). Applied to texts, it would argue that if enough rubbish is printed it will become the knowledge in circulation!

There are many examples of how strains of such 'psychobabble' (Rosen, 1978) have come to be the psychology in circulation. Bowlby's theory (*sic*) of 'maternal deprivation' is one. Much that currently passes as knowledge of 'child sexual abuse' is another (cf. Stainton Rogers and Stainton Rogers, 1992a; O'Dell, 1993). Contrary to the falsifiability doctrine, Beryl's First Law would state that 'bad research drives out good'.

However, even if psychology could be said to proceed internally (to resolve its own disputes by its own mechanisms) by such inferential processes as falsifiability, there exists no over-discipline where the claims of psychology itself are put to such a test. Rather (and this is the second way in which psychology's claims are grounded) its warrants could be said to be self-generational – to hold only so long as its foundational axioms and metaphysics (i.e. the form itself) are taken to hold. That is, so long, and only so long, as faith is maintained in its model of the person and its model of knowing (Figures 2.1 and 2.2). This interpretation proposes that psychology, like Catholicism, is self-sustaining. Methodology, like theology, does not operate so as to erode its own axioms. In the absence of challenge to its formal foundations it just continues inexorably on, interminably re-creating the conditions of its own legitimation. Under conditions of challenge, however, social psychology is just as prone to damage as any other evangelical movement.

I.I. I have been very quiet during your exposition but perhaps now you could introduce us to some of the challenges to social psychology?

Crisis talk

The various 'troublings' of the 'march of civilization' tale discussed earlier also had an impact upon social psychology. From the 1960s onwards, while the mainstream continued to pursue some version of 'progress', outside we have seen new forums of dissent from the global (e.g. Greenpeace) to the local (e.g. ethogenics, cf. Harré and Secord, 1972) making their own agendas. For many critical observers (e.g. Henriques et al., 1984), what has come to us is a new visibility of the cracks and tensions in Modernism. More recently, in his book *The Crisis in Modern Social Psychology – and How to End it*, Parker has argued that 'Social psychology is in permanent crisis. Or rather, it may be more accurate to say it is racked by a number of intersecting crises' (1989: 9).

To many critics, including ourselves, these crises are bound to arise within a discipline which is attempting to be both descriptive (objective and scientific) and prescriptive (concerned with 'human betterment' by intervening in human problems and issues). Faced with the task (often hardly recognized) of attempting to accommodate such tensions, while at the same time assimilating inputs from the ever-changing context in which it operates, social psychology has behaved like an operator under informational and processing overload – it has gone from crisis to crisis.

Science and scientism

The dissenting voices that are critical of received psychology are just that – protestant; they do not cohere into any single dogma – a protestantism. Nevertheless, there are recognizable dialects to criticality. One, which we have just encountered through Parker, is radically political. However, a frequent feature of the first wave of critical social psychology (around 1970) was a much less overtly political attempt at crisis-management. The strategy for managing the crisis in this dialect was to identify with, and re-define, the 'softer' pole of the discipline (humanism) whilst devaluing the other extreme ('science'). Scientistic psychology, as it came to be dubbed, could then be seen as avoiding all that 'really' matters about human nature, such as personal subjective experience. In other words, this position represents a challenge to the 'mechanistic' model of the person shown in Figure 2.1.

A recent recruit to this position is the psychometrician Kline, who argues that academic psychology 'is not concerned with what appear to non-psychologists to be the important or interesting aspects of being human' (1988: 11). Kline's criticism also extends to the model of knowledge depicted in Figure 2.2 above. His explanation for psychology's lack of relevance is that 'psychology is a collection of results, I cannot call it knowledge, that is of no interest, value or use except to other academic psychologists' (1988: 11). For Kline, coming from the heart of mainstream, disenchantment seems to have led not just to deconstruction but to destruction. His contention is no less than that 'the whole pursuit of psychology is worthless' (1988: 11).

New paradigms for old

What Kline seems to mean here by 'the whole pursuit of psychology' is the following of a 'natural' or 'objective' science method modelled according to the form just described (cf. Kline, 1988: 154).

I.I. Picking up on your section title, are we talking here about the kind of thing Kuhn meant by a paradigm shift?

Kuhn (1970) used the term 'paradigm shift' to refer to a move away from the taken-for-granted foundational axioms, practices and metaphysics of an established worldview – and their replacement with another (incommensurable) way of thinking. However, it should also be recognized that Kuhn believed that the human sciences were not 'mature' enough yet to have a paradigm! For him, a 'mature science' had enough confidence in its worldview, not to be constantly worrying it, and hence was able to concentrate upon its research agenda. Rather as the Enlightenment contested the theocentric worldview that preceded it, so the so-called 'new paradigmers' in social psychology contested the scientistic worldview of what they labelled as the 'old paradigm'. Hence, the criticisms of the 'old paradigm' were not nihilistic in ambition. Rather, they were offered for the purpose of 'reconstructing social psychology' (cf. Armistead, 1974) into the form of a more fully human 'new paradigm'. Probably the best contemporary exposition of this new venture is to be found in the work of Harré (e.g. 1989: 34). For him the old paradigm was haunted by 'two unexamined preassumptions', 'individualism and scientism'. He puts the contrast with the new paradigm thus:

> Everything relevant to the actions of a person, must, it seems, have been assumed . . . to have been found a place 'within'. . . . the envelope of the individual . . . The idea of 'within' is dominated by a certain model of explanation. So instead of describing human customs and practices, psychologists have looked for (or imagined) mechanisms . . . Instead of ascribing to people the skills necessary for performing correctly, they have assigned hidden states. (Harré, 1989: 34)

What, in part, both Kline and Harré are saying is that for all their 'humaneering' stake in tackling 'real-life problems', once mainstream social psychologists actually get down to the tasks they have set themselves, in practice they fail – paradigmatically – to get to grips with them at all. Instead they shift inexorably into practices and theorizing (individualism and scientism) which treat people as self-contained automata, and, in doing so, fail to address the very human ways of being they are seeking to understand and, ultimately, to manage. The form described earlier – which claims for itself the privilege of being able to speak objectively about people and their problems – turns out, according to new paradigmers, to be the source of distortion not clarification.

This is not to say that the 'new paradigm' approach is, per se, anti-science. It has not been populated, on the whole, by mystics, New Agers, or latter-day Luddites! Indeed, some, including Harré, hold to a form of scientifically grounded biological realism. The criticality has been specifically directed to the pursuit of human and social being by what are the purported methods of objective or natural science, that is, scientism: 'The methods or mental attitudes of men [*sic*] of science; a belief that the methods used in studying natural sciences should be employed also in investigating all aspects of human behaviour and condition, e.g. in philosophy and social sciences: scientific or pseudoscientific language' (Chambers, 1983).

On the whole, 'new paradigm' workers would not object to being said to be involved in science in the dictionary sense of 'a skilled craft' (Chambers, 1983). The critique of scientism arises in social psychology, in part, because – for mainstream psychology – science (as a skilled craft of enquiry) is often regarded as synonymous with hypothetico-deductivism, a particular philosophy of science which holds that there is a single, coherent, factual 'real world' which can be accurately ascertained by the application of experimental method. (This is a particularly clear expression of the model given in Figure 2.2). In its strictest conditions, knowledge is discovered by generating hypotheses, testing them and refuting them – knowledge is established negatively, by showing what is not true, or does not hold (Popper, 1959). Most usually (in social science at least) this boils down to an altogether less rigorous approach (cf. Harré, 1993: 103–4 and our Chapter 11), in which an experimental hypothesis is tested against a null hypothesis as two conditions each with its own pool of subjects – knowledge, here, is established probabilistically, an effect 'much more likely than not' to have been demonstrated.

The main problem with hypothetico-deductivism when applied to 'the social' is expressed neatly by Brown, a political scientist. For the social scientist it involves, he suggests,

> the mixed blessings of the operational definition and the tendency to interpose hypotheses, definitions, and concepts between himself [*sic*] and that which he wishes to observe. In their study of behaviour, social scientists have generally adopted a strategy of conceptualizing attitudes, feelings, and other relevant internal states or traits with properties that can be measured only indirectly through devices such as attitude scales, said to be operational definitions of them. (1980: 2)

In this interpretation, subjecting 'the social psychological' to hypothetico-deductive method requires devising a testable hypothesis (for example that 'violent TV programmes lead viewers to engage, themselves, in more violence'), which can be expressed in concrete, measurable terms (namely, a quantification of the independent variable (the television violence viewers are exposed to) and the dependent variable (subsequently evinced aggression). For something to be measurable, of course, requires it to be objectively definable. But, as Brown makes clear, such definitions do not neutrally mirror an objective reality – all they do is 'replace the subject's meaning with the investigator's' (1980: 5). Not only, he says, is it pretentious in the extreme for investigators to regard their own under-standings as in some sense objective or correct, this inevitably draws the whole endeavour into the realms of ideology – because imposing a definition is always a matter of coercion and power, the power to construct knowledge (cf. Foucault, 1974).

I.I. O.K. I now understand that 'new paradigm' social psychologists are critical of scientistic approaches because these treat people as if they were complex machines and hence ignore what is essentially human about social existence. I can also see that their research inevitably involves imposing meanings on their subjects and their audience. But what happened to the different dialects of criticality?

Although the early 'new paradigm' approaches set out to challenge the form of established social psychology, they did so, by and large, in ways which were partial and incomplete. For example, since they retained their position within the discipline, they failed to take full and explicit issue with the missionary stance which directs the discipline – and the political questions of power and knowledge which go with this. As a result, much of the challenge was relatively easily accommodated and re-appropriated back into the mainstream.

One clear way in which new paradigm ideas were absorbed back into the mainstream was by way of an overemphasis on methods – both 'old' and 'new'. The critique of hypothetico-deductive approaches was pursued through a move into alternatives. These included:

- ethogenics, which were concerned with the genesis and accountability of meaningful action (cf. Harré and Secord, 1972)
- repertory grids, which were employed to give a 'representation of the cognitive resources available to actors' (cf. Harré, Clarke and De Carlo, 1985)
- forms of ethnography such as autobiographies (cf. Harré, Clarke and De Carlo, 1985)
- role-playing techniques (cf. Mixon, 1972).

In claiming access to methods (albeit 'new' methods) this work was all too easily mapped back on to the traditional template (Figure 2.2). Hence, they could be, and were, understood by the mainstream as doing the same old missionary job but in different ways. Indeed, often the concerns (e.g. over aggression: Marsh, 1978) seemed unchanged. Further, in the mainstream there had always been an acceptance of a place for more 'experiential' methods (albeit as a soft and provisional option to be eventually developed in a quantitative way). And so a place was waiting – like an empty grave – for these 'new paradigm' methods. This allowed the new to be accepted into the old without fundamentally challenging the discipline itself at all.

Likewise with the emphasis on the 'subjective' and the 'human'. Rather than radically challenging the model of the person shown in Figure 2.1, the 'humanistic' aspect of the new paradigm work was all too easily slotted into the existing model as just another batch of variables and constructs. 'Meaning' became understood as something which mediates between 'situation' and 'behaviour' (now recast as 'action'). One clear way in which this appropriation took place was through the development and growing dominance of the cognitive science programme in psychology. Thereby the 'rules and roles' emphasized in ethogenics by new paradigmers like Harré were reconfigured as internal, cognitive scripts (Schank and Abelson, 1977) or goal plans (Miller, Galanter and Pribram, 1967), governed by a 'central processing mechanism' (cf. Harré and Gillett, 1994).

As for the incompleteness of the consideration of the mission of social psychology, on hindsight many new paradigmers mistook the character of conventional social psychology. In disputing its methods, they often concentrated on finding a better, more human form of science – hence, ethogenics. They did so at the cost of not fully addressing the power of the applied science of behaviour, the mission that we argue lies at the heart of the discipline. This left them in the position where they seem to be genuinely surprised (nay disconcerted) when old paradigmers don't simply recognize the improvements ethogenics offers – and 'shift'. As Harré and Gillett (1994: 2) put it: 'This is a phenomenon that should be of interest to philosophers of science. It is quite unique . . . in the history of science, that old, outdated, and manifestly inadequate ways of doing research and untenable theories, have persisted alongside new and better theories and methods.'

The Foucauldian turn

A contrasted dialect of criticism has been particularly influenced by the French philosopher (and psychologist – to the extent he taught it for many years) Michel Foucault. This line of thought emphasizes that the point of human sciences such as social psychology is not neutrally to discover timeless truths about human nature but to play a disciplinary, govermental role within the institutions and practices of modern life – what we have been calling its mission of intervention, its humaneering project. Rose, for example, traces a 'Foucauldian' history of psychology and argues that the discipline was developed as a form of 'policing' in order to govern, administer, treat and discipline such figures as 'mastur-bating schoolchildren and hysterical women, feeble-minded school-children and recruits to the armed forces, workers suffering fatigue or industrial accidents, unstable or shell-shocked soldiers, lying, bed-wetting or naughty children' (1989: 122). This Foucaldian argument is that sciences such as social psychology are misunderstood when treated as purely 'academic' activities, because this ignores their essentially practical and applied role. Their inputs feed directly into major institutions concerned (amongst other things) with social control and containment. Hence, the 'new paradigm' arguments about scientism not recognizing our 'humanity' can, from this perspective, be seen as missing the point that the 'old paradigm' is profoundly concerned with intervening in our 'humanity':

> Rather than basing a critique upon the need to rescue individual responsi-bility and subjective fulfilment from social repression, we need to recognise the extent to which our existence as selves, our awareness of our own individuality, our search for our own identity, is itself constituted by the forms of identification and practices of individualization by which we are governed, and which provide us with the categories and goals through which we govern ourselves. (Rose, 1991: 130–1)

One view of Modernism as a political revolution is that it worked by first claiming and taking authority over political construction and then bestowing upon its citizens, as individuals, the very essential 'rights' and 'responsibilities' it had first brought into conceptual being. A psychology which emerged within Modernism can then easily be seen to have laid upon these new citizen-individuals a similar set of psychological essences. Thus the person was held to be, as a self-contained individual, inhabited by, or possessed of, personality, attitudes, intelligence – just as they were by rights and responsibilities. In this way psychology never (as it is purported to have done) took on the task of discovering these traits in more or less accurate ways. Rather, its task was to recover or uncover them, into an arena of government-ability – where they already operated as specific, political constructions of the person-citizen. Just as individu-alistic constructions like rights and responsibilities were part of the political arrangements of Modernism, so constructing personhood as made up of measurable psychological essences suited the administrative, classificatory and policing requirements of the humaneering mission which psychology took upon itself.

A more radical critique, then, must not aim simply towards creating 'new and better theories and methods', but must more profoundly and more radically take issue with what is at stake in the very idea of approaching the social-psychological in terms of distinctions between theories and methods and results (a point we develop further in Chapter 11).

The theory–method–results structure inevitably reproduces the patterns set out in Figures 2.1 and 2.2. and constrains us to the metaphysical idea that the social-psychological essences, processes and mechanisms that are being studied exist objectively 'out there' (in the situation) or 'in there' (in the cognitorium), independent of our constructions of them. Once this metaphysical position is accepted, the task is to make informed guesses as to their structure and function by concocting theories which can be tested via methods (as purified as possible of our subjective biases) and accepted or rejected on the basis of results. In following this rhetorical structure, the social psychologist can claim to have been purely objective, and hence can criticize and dismiss other less 'objective' knowledge. All of this is achieved despite the whole enterprise being foundationed upon the wobbly and hypothetical assumption that what is being studied (the social psychological) exists objectively and can be measured.

Theo-ry is dead

Once a proclamation like Nietzsche's 'God is dead' is accepted, theological debates become meaningless and futile. There is no point in arguing about how many angels can fit on the head of a pin (quite possibly an apocryphal argument in any case) once the 'reality' of angels is called into question. Likewise, judging between the hundreds of theories proposed by social psychologists to explain some hypothetical process or entity or another loses its sense and purpose once the proclamation 'reality is socially constructed' is accepted (cf. Stenner, 1994b).

I.I. Surely you exaggerate the theoretical surplus in social psychology – it doesn't have that many theories, does it?

Oh yes it does, and we can 'prove it'. In a typical glossy US textbook there is not much short of a theory to a page – and in these books there are hundreds of pages! We might dub this Beryl's Second Law: 'A theory a day helps you work, rest and play' (apologies to the 'men' from Mars).

Box 2.2 Theories in Social Psychology

In contrast to its purported models in the natural sciences, where theories are restricted by canons of parsimony and explanatory power, mainstream social psychology appears to use theorizing as a political and rhetorical strategy. Theorizing language frequently seems to be employed as a value-added, 'feel-good' device, rather like the advertiser's 'natural' or 'new' – call a hunch a 'theory' and you have gained credibility. For a content analysis of a standard US 'social psychology' textbook, we chose Brehm and Kassin (1990). We counted a rate of around six theories per mainstream chapter or around eighty theories overall. This alone might be thought to be a surfeit in terms of most cognitive appetites. However, if we also take into account the marginal explanatory notes (which also cover hypotheses, phenomena and concepts), the overall rate rises to around four hundred!

In our book we shall cover only a fraction of this theoretical opulence – this is deliberate and strategic. For us, as we have indicated, this profusion is a sign not of vigour but of disorder. The reason we presented our (ironic) version of 'the form' of social psychology was that it enabled us to consider social psychology critically as a whole before moving on to its specific domains of concern. This is also our justification for being somewhat selective in the coverage of conventional social psychology we shall subsequently offer in the chapters that follow.

I.I. OK, that's fair enough. But before you rush on, I'd like some clarification. You said that a crucial part of the radical critique is a challenge to the idea that psychological essences are 'really there'. That goes against personal experience, they don't seem like 'social constructions' of psychological discourse to me.

The point is not that we don't experience emotions or hold attitudes or have a personality or whatever – nor is it that they were 'just invented' by psychologists. What is at stake is what is meant by these terms. Our argument is that these terms do not refer to objectively measurable 'essences' or processes which can be got at in some pure form by stripping away the subjective and the discursive. Rather they are part of and inseparable from the subjective and the discursive (Stenner, 1993a). Harré, in a recent move away from his previous 'new paradigm' stance towards a 'discursive' position, puts this over well when he says:

> discursive phenomena, for example acts of remembering, are not manifestations of hidden subjective phenomena. They *are* the psychological phenomena . . . events and objects are given significance by the discourses in which they appear and . . . these significations both arise from and in part constitute the subjectivity of an individual in relation to what is signified . . . The difference between the mind or personality as seen in this way and the traditional view is that we see it as dynamic and essentially embedded in historical, political, cultural, social and interpersonal contexts. (1994: 27)

I.I. Now I think I get it and can answer my last question myself. In rejecting 'essentialist' formulations you are saying.

1 *Social psychological phenomena are not like that.*
2 *They are not intrinsically like anything because they are only meaningful 'contextually'.*
3 *Humaneering is one context in which they are made to take a meaning – that of social psychology.*

That is not a bad summary, but obviously one doesn't secure it 'just like that' (as the late, great Tommy Cooper might have said). 'Securing' that appreciation is not easy against the power of other 'contexts'. That is why we still have most of a book to work through! Nevertheless, psychology can be resisted. In fact, commentators on psychology have long argued (as we shall get into later on) that the discipline is unusual in that its subject-matter (us) can answer back. Psychology's 'subjects' can predict hypotheses, try to deceive a researcher, change their minds in the light of awareness, and so on. Not only this, but psychology the discipline was *invented* by, and is undertaken by, its subject-matter (people). Hence we (the subject-matter) necessarily exceed the confines of the discipline – because we are not only 'psychological'. Also, the discipline itself, as a human social product, must be seen as itself part of its own subject-matter. But this raises an important question. If the topics we discuss are as much about 'social psychology the discipline' as about 'social psychology the subject-matter', can we still work under the untroubled title of 'social psychology'?

I.I. Is that why you started this section with the slogan 'theory is dead'? Are you arguing that these questions make doing separable work of theory, methods and results inappropriate? Like 'doing' prayer or worship without a belief in God?

The way we would put it is that critical social psychology challenges the *grounding assumptions* of social psychology (Stenner, 1993b). The structures in Figures 2.1 and 2.2 that we have made so much of are an integral part of social psychology's concern to *ground* its knowledge, its enquiry and its interventions in the certainty of empirical and rationalistic procedures. But in structuring itself according to these concerns, it must assume that its subject-matter (human social existence) is actually ground-able in this way – i.e. does actually operate according to fundamental laws and foundational axioms. In arguing that it does not (or, at the least, that we should be agnostic about such claims) critics are challenging not just the 'results', 'theories' and 'methods' of social psychology but the whole infrastructure, the grounding way of thinking which make these viable in the first place. Grounding assumptions, more generally under-stood, are those assumptions we have to take-for-granted in order to proceed untroubled with any day to day project (such as writing a book!).

At a less mundane level, the modernistic challenge to the religious worldview (noted earlier) brought with it, on one level, a deep-seated foundational crisis (Who are we? What is our purpose? How do we know?), and the philosophies of people such as Descartes and Kant can be seen, in part, as metaphysical attempts to establish new grounds and groundings for human existence. In recent times these very modernis-tic grounds (such as 'reason', 'experience', and, above all, science) have been challenged by a wave a criticism which is often brought together under the heading of postmodernism (Boyne and Ratansi, 1990; Smart, 1993).

Box 2.3 Postmodernism and the Climate of Perturbation

Postmodernism is a notoriously controversial and contested term. Usually, however, it is associated with some version of *non-foundationalism*. From a position which holds that there are not absolute *grounds* to our knowledge and action, postmodernists are critical of totalizing theories or 'grand narratives' (Lyotard, 1984) which claim to provide final or 'solve-all' answers. Hence, the idea that through gaining knowledge we (the human race) are forever progressing is placed in radical doubt. This 'March of Progress' tale is replaced with a vision of a multiplexity of competing and conflicting worldviews with incommensurable interests. Claims to speak 'objectively' (i.e. from an absolute viewpoint) are recast

as rhetorical ploys which conjure an illusion of certitude – an illusion essential in order to claim top place in Modernism's hierarchy of knowing.
Some key problems with the notion of postmodernism are

- It tends itself to be interpreted as an explain-all 'grand theory'.
- Its very name *post*modernism seems to imply notions of progress.
- To hail the postmodern as a contrast to the 'modern' can result in modernity being treated in a very one-dimensional way.

We prefer to draw postmodernism (along with post-structuralism and much other critical work) under a rubric which claims less, is a more minimal formulation – *the climate of perturbation* (cf. Curt, 1994 where it is called the 'climate of problematization' – that was before we were persuaded that 'problematizing' is itself a modern notion!).

Here nothing more is claimed than to be working under, or in, a 'climate' wherein received ideas are troubled – perturbated. Perturbation covers the range of disenchantments that have been directed towards Modernism: these include critical more-or-less-anything; postmodernism; post-structuralism; and social constructionism. (Plus a host of more local terms relating to specific disciplines and activities). The impact of this for social psychology is massive and fundamental. Taken one way, if social psychology is the craft of telling stories about how reality is socially constructed, then it is, or should be, as a discipline central to the 'climate of perturbation'. Taken another way, it dissolves the boundaries between social psychology and other textual/discursive and story-telling disciplines (such as cultural studies, film theory and the study of literature). What is meant here is not a liberal-intellectual 'interdisciplinarity' – what Lee (1993) calls 'setting up trade routes between disciplines'. It is 'transdisciplinarity' in which the borders and boundaries set up by Modernism's constitution of discipline-States (cf. Figure 1.1.) get 'folded and re-moulded', yielding a 'transdiscipline of the social' which admits no partition.

It can also be seen as centring social psychology at the heart of a new 'discursive psychology', where issues like memory as discourse can be developed (cf. Potter and Edwards, 1992). More than anything, it renders social psychology a craft of telling stories.

titlehis'ancero humanis andmepts tophieswholbe

I.I. *What's that when it's at home?*

Just a perturbating heading which accumulated from a bad typist using insert mode rather than type-over! But it does challenge the taken-for-granted, doesn't it?

Science as story-telling

A recurrent and guiding 'motif' within the climate of perturbation is the attempt to expose the seemingly objective and neutral claims and practices of scientists as concerned story-telling. Researchers within the sociology of scientific knowledge, for example, have shown how scientific work – varying from Pasteur's domestication of microbes (Latour, 1988a) through the detection of neutrinos (Pinch, 1986) to Einstein's relativity theory (Latour, 1998b) and high-energy physics (Pickering, 1980) – is an inherently rhetorical practice, which constructs reality as much as it reflects it. Primatologist Donna Haraway agrees with this view when she asserts of her discipline that 'the struggle to construct good stories is a major part of the craft' (1984: 80).

If even the natural sciences cannot sustain the claim of being purely objective and neutral, then, from a critical perspective, social psychology cannot avoid being recast as a story-telling practice. The stories are told at numerous levels. In a typical social psychology textbook (the following exemplary extracts are from Aronson et al. (1994, Chapter 1) we are told stories about how 'philosophers, social critics and novelists' depend upon and promulgate 'incorrect – or at very least, oversimplified' insights, which cannot be relied upon because 'more often than not they disagree with one another'. In this comedy of errors, social psychology comes to the rescue by addressing 'the same questions as philosophers and folk wisdom . . . but we attempt to do so scientifically'. Like other stories, this one is partial: it neglects, for example, to tell the alternative story that 'science' is, at every point, shot through with disagreement and contestation. It also avoids an alternative narrative, which would hold that any important issue worth its name is not soluble like a mathematical problem to which there is but one 'correct' answer. As 'folk wisdom' might say, 'there are two sides to every story'.

But it is not just the propaganda for social psychology which can be analysed as narrative, the subject-matter itself is also 'storied into being'. Aronson et al's text yields a particularly crude illustration of this when they define social psychology as the study of 'psychological processes going on in their [people's] hearts and minds'. There is no clear agreement amongst psychologists (let alone philosophers) as to what the phrase 'psychological processes' actually refers to (if anything). Any 'understanding' of it we may have comes from our having encountered these words in other stories, other psychological texts (just as we think we know what a 'fairy' is through our familiarity with conventions in the genre of fairy tales). However, in those psychological texts, the reference to 'hearts' is quite literal – as pulsating organs! – not as the site of 'psychological processes'.

I.I. But we know what is going on here – the authors are trying to be folksy, to relate to us 'person to person'.

Of course, they are using the story-teller's craft just as we do from time to time. Aronson et al, would no doubt quickly point out that they knew what they were doing – that their usage was metaphorical – to show that social psychology deals as much with the emotional side of people's lives as the rational side. Our point, however, taken from the climate of perturbation, is that *all* language is metaphorical. Hence, all of the entities and processes social psychologists take as their subject are multi-referential textual constructions, whether these be called attitudes, social representations, needs, self-esteem, cognitive dissonance or whatever. It is only when we forget (or fail to register) their metaphorical, rhetorical, textual and provisional condition that they seem to us as simply, self-evidently 'real'. Even terms like 'mind' and 'emotion' are metaphorical, textual constructions with their own histories (Soyland, 1994).

> The term 'emotion' is itself based on a metaphor. It stems from the Latin et movere, which originally meant 'to move out', to 'migrate' or 'to transport an object'. Metaphorically, it was used to describe physical conditions, such as turbulent weather, or psychological states involving turmoil. It did not, however, become a common term for referring to human emotions until the middle of the eighteenth century. (Averill, 1990: 107)

In the stories of social psychologists, then, elements of, or events in, the social world are narrated into a particular (psychologized) kind of being. It is in this mode that they are brought to our attention and 'made real' for us. The sentence 'psychological processes going on in their hearts and minds' means as little or as much as other constructions masquerading as fact, such as 'sinful ruminations going on in their souls' or 'synchronous resonances going on in their collective unconscious'.

All the world's a . . . conversation?

We have now argued ourselves to the position where not only is social psychology (the discipline) a story-telling practice, but also where the subject-matter which gets addressed by the discipline can be described as textual. Who we are, how we see and are seen by others, and how others see us – these are shaped and bounded by the narratives through which we render ourselves and our worlds intelligible. In a highly borrowable phrase, Christie and Orton (1988) talk of human kind as *homo narrans narratur*, the story-made story-teller – stressing that it is by telling stories, and by being told within stories, that people make sense of their world and themselves within it. This point has been explicitly picked up in a number of recent 'social-psychological' texts such as Sarbin's (1986) advocacy of 'narrative psychology', Shotter and Gergen's (1989) overview of work on 'texts of identity', Harré and Gillett's (1994) treatment of the 'discursive mind', Shotter's (1993a) coverage of 'conversational realities', Stainton Rogers and Stainton Rogers's (1992a) telling of 'stories of childhood', Stenner and Eccleston's (1994) meditations 'on the textuality of being' and Curt's (1994) account of 'textuality and tectonics'. Curt's (1994) analytic of 'tectonics' is useful in this regard.

I.I. Well, you would say that, wouldn't you!

As 'Bits of Beryl' of course we would. In drawing upon the geological metaphor of plate tectonics (and Curt is clear that the status is metaphorical), she *(sic)* is able to indicate how stories never operate in isolation but, on the one hand, are built up layer by layer (like sedimentary beds) where each new telling 'concretizes' and 'fossilizes' the older variants; and, on the other hand, where discrete and adjacent plates of narrative (Curt calls them 'tectons') can clash and grind together in a 'discursive agnostics' (perhaps throwing up 'mountain ranges' of hot, argumentative discourse and practice). This metaphor helps in warding off any individualistic misusings of the idea of 'story' as uniquely authored and free-floating from issues of power and conflict. It also reminds us that every apparently solid bedrock floats on a fluid magma. The supposedly firm foundational assumptions which we rely upon can begin to move – as 'the Earth beneath our feet'.

I.I. Do I detect you up to the folksy metaphors?

Why not – when notions like tectonics can help to avoid the accusation that it is naive to view all human activity as co-textual? (Not that we cannot see how the charge sometimes arises.) Within the climate of perturbation, it comes most often from a position known as critical realism (Bhaskar, 1989; Parker, 1992a).

To condense the argument, critical realists are worried by such statements as 'we are well on the way to seeing *conversation* as the ultimate context within which knowledge is to be understood' (MacIntyre, 1981) and 'the primary human reality is persons in conversation' (Harré, 1983). They see them as avoiding not only the not so cuddly issue of argument (cf. Billig, 1987) but also the realities of power and inequality – and not just in 'conversations'! Hence critical realists tend to see in postmodern ideas yet another form of relativistic escapism from political engagement. Parker, for example, cautions against the kind of analysis which can 'turn . . . into a series of rhetorical devices which buttress reductionism' (1992b: 95). As a critical writer he is particularly concerned to avoid what he sees as harking back to scientism and its 'representation of the world as organized by the metanarratives of humanized science, progress and individual meaning' (Parker, 1989: 54). But he none the less views 'critical realism' (cf. Bhaskar, 1989) as a necessary analytic for critical social psychology – devoting a chapter of his *Discourse Dynamics* (1992a) to setting out this position and how it can be used.

What most seems to matter to Parker is a vision that critical (social) psychology should be used as a means to bring injustice and oppression into visibility (and thus to attention). Thereby, he feels, it can be used to work towards changes that improve social arrangements and foster human emancipation. Given this as his agenda, it is no surprise that he worries about the dangers of slipping into a relativism, wherein for 'those fascinated by the power of discourse cut loose from any connection with the real outside, texts are becoming the vehicles for the "radical" expression of a purely pragmatic "new realism" which has lost any desire to take underlying structures of oppression and resistance seriously' (Parker, 1992a: 40–7).

The nightmare scenario here is a world in which the very people who may have the circumstances best to resist the 'horrors' of death and destruction get so beguiled by the postmodern carnival that they give up on radical politics altogether. They are 'fiddling while Rome burns'. Put crudely (very crudely), a relativism which admits no bombs, no torture, no oppression – only text upon text – is not just irresponsible but dangerous:

> As I write this, an area of Tripoli has just been laid waste by a number of aircraft currently (I hope) sitting on the ground a few miles down the road from my Ivory Tower. Some 100 people (not very many by modern standards) have been killed. They were not killed by words. Neither are they dead because the rest of the world decided to call them dead. Their death was brought about by the employment of a disproportionately immense amount of scientific and technological knowledge. If we can only see this knowledge as just another story, then we deserve to fall victim to it. (Craib, 1986)

I.I. I was going to question what all this politics was doing in a book about social psychology but having just read that I think I might be a 'critical realist'.

It gets to us like that too. But then it is meant to. It is a piece of agit-prop designed to engage us to a very singular effect. However, this is not achieved without cost. The price is *singularization* (the reduction of multiplexity to a fixed account). To point to horrific realities and solid objects (what Edwards, Ashmore and Potter (1993) call a 'death and furniture' argument) does not actually demand that we should recognize one 'true reality' – that comes from value-added political dogma. It can equally be used to sustain the case for 'conflict and contestation between multiple realities'. Or these two positions can be summated to give 'the one true reality is that there is conflict and contestation between multiple realities' and so on. There is no solution to be had here. What we can do is to ask of any stance, as we can of any narrative:

- In what context is this argument being made?
- To what issues is it claiming to be applicable?
- What interests is it serving?
- What alternatives is it obscuring?

In other words (our words), our discourse is never separable from the conditions of our existence but is inevitably an aspect (and a crucial one) of our Being. A sensitivity to this textuality (Curt, 1994; Stenner and Eccleston, 1994) means that to scrutinize any manifold of 'social realities' is (but is not only) also to be concerned with what each sensitizes and what each represses – what each may give and each may take, and to and from whom. Hence, the notion of 'story-telling' or 'conversation' can be retained, but not in isolation. As Haraway says, story-telling always involves 'complex webs of power, including the tortured realities of race, sex and class – and including people's struggles to tell each other how we might live with each other' (1984: 80). Engagement with singularization always carries the risk of a regime of sensitization/repression which regulates the place of challenge. Right and wrong, like truth and fiction, cannot be foundationed as givens. They are discursive productions over whose regulation we instal overlords (or overladies) only at our peril.

Inscribing social psychology

Criticality is to do with wanting change – to overthrow, in part or as a whole, the old order. However, this is not a matter (as it is often presented as being) of introducing politics where none existed before. Orthodoxy is not a-political.

I.I. How did you know I was going to ask about that? Are you psychic, into pre-conversation?

Politics by other means?

It is no accident that leads right-wing parties to call themselves conservative! By and large conservatism is about defending the status quo. It is about promoting 'traditional values', a 'back to basics' which claims to have a hot line to a 'golden age' of social stability – where women, the lower classes, natives and children 'knew their place' and did not rock the boat; a 'golden age' in which there were no upstarts insisting on 'political correctness', no nanny state; a world which could be neatly carved up between the 'civilized' and the 'savage'. It comes as no surprise, then, to discover that the 'hardest' (i.e. most predicated on science) sub-disciplines of social psychology – socio-biology and those others arguing for genetic inheritance of qualities from intelligence to morality – have been those adopted by the 'right', since these provide the most blatant justification for right-wing ideology and practice.

However, we should not necessarily assume that the 'left' is, generically, a source of calls to radical change in psychological endeavours. Generally proponents of old-style socialism are deeply immersed in Modernism, and do not question the claims of science to foster human betterment. Rather, their concerns are less to do with challenging the form of social psychology than with ensuring that its benefits are more equitably available. Ehrenreich (1978), for example, notes that old-style socialists do not seek to challenge the claims to efficacy of modern medicine; they take them for granted. What they want to do is to improve the access of poor people to medical services.

Neither can we assume that the 'right' is necessarily after leaving things as they are. There is considerable antagonism on the political right to social psychology's liberal-humanistic approach to social problems. You only have to listen to conservative politicians to hear antagonism expressed with considerable vitriol. One of Margaret Thatcher's best-remembered phrases is that 'there is no such thing as society'. The New Right is highly suspicious of any doctrine which might appear to be denying personal responsibility – whether for crime, for poverty or for being an unmarried mother. Equally there are increasing moves from the right to apply cost-benefit analyses to those forms of applied psychology paid for by the State (such as educational or clinical psychology) as well as to psychology departments in universites funded out of 'taxpayers' money', where systems of performance-indexed control over their activities have been imposed in order to regulate and control what is done in the name of 'psychology' (see also Chapter 11's discussion of the regulation of publication). Thus in no simple sense can we equate political position with a call for change. Both the 'radical left' (e.g. socialist-informed feminists, neo-Marxists and anarchists) and the 'radical right' may have an interest in challenging traditional (social) psychology. We need to distinguish between these two.

The 'radical right' is happy to support those aspects of social psychological theorizing which individualize personal and social problems, so long as this is extracted from the realm of 'politics' and not used to justify social policies which assume the State has any responsibility to resolve them. What it seeks to contest is the upstart new professionalization of 'concern', which places increasing demands on the public purse; and the penetration (as they see it) of Marxism, feminism and other forms of 'resistance politics' into the realms of 'social studies' as the late, great Sir Keith Joseph insisted on calling the social sciences. The right's offensive against social psychology consists of seeking to counter its impugned appropriation by the 'left', and a commitment to subjecting it to market economics.

By contrast, the 'radical left' seeks to challenge mainstream psychology's pathologization of particular individuals and social groups, precisely because of the way in which it depoliticizes individual and social problems. Kitzinger and Perkins (1993), for example, are highly critical of therapy. This is because they see it as undermining the ability of lesbians to place blame for their distress where they think it should be placed – on the patriarchal organization of the 'man-made world'. The 'radical left's' concerns about professionalization are not to do with monitarism but are about the ways it allows the already powerful to gain greater control over the powerless. The overall concern of the 'radical left' is to challenge the way mainstream social psychology promotes mainstream liberal-humanistic values, and in so doing has become a tool for governmentality – e.g. social control by the 'majority' over oppressed minorities. Or, to put it another way, in favouring images of human individuality, responsibility and autonomy, social psychology has become part of the disciplinary and confessional symbolic architecture of the dominant culture of the West (Foucault, 1977). It is this which must be resisted.

Mission statement?

However, by no means all critical social psychologists 'do' politics in these, ultimately Modernistic, senses. Rather, and primarily, they 'do' what they do. We ourselves do so (mostly) through a profound agnosticism about foundationing anything and a profound concern about 'singularizing discourses' (cf. Curt, 1994). A concern, if you like to avoid founding another mission! Taking up this theme, the rest of this book is dedicated to examining the subject of 'social psychology' through some of its various 'topics' and exposing them to 'perturbating' scrutiny. In each case we will seek to show that these topics were not just 'there' waiting to be studied, but have been profoundly 'knowledged into being' through social psychology's gaze. Having 'troubled' them we will seek to show that there are other (and, we think, more meaningful, more helpful and less discipline-bound) ways of addressing them. This is, for us, as critical social psychologists, doing what we do. What we may do elsewise as critical persons-in-culture is another conversation.

I.I. One for the pub afterwards?

If you're buying!

3 From Personality to Textual Identities

Psychology is far from unique in having an interest in 'what makes us tick' as persons. Amongst their other concerns, philosophy, religion, literature and art all address issues about the 'self' and what it means and matters to be a person. These include questions like:

- How do I (how does any 'I') know what kind of person I am?
- What does it mean to 'be myself'?
- How do we know what constitutes being a person?
- How can I tell what kind of person another person is?

However, from its beginnings in the mid-nineteenth century, such questions about the nature of the 'self' were appropriated by psychologists not just as concerns to theorize about but as problems to be empirically investigated. Since they regarded themselves to be engaged in a 'science of mind', they saw themselves as uniquely qualified to address these kinds of questions from an objective, scientific standpoint. A science of mind was needed, so the argument went (and still goes), because, as one psychologist has argued:

> So-called great minds may produce miserable ideas on occasion, and if poorly conceived notions have implications for the way human beings are to be treated, it behoves us to discover these erroneous assumptions before they harm anyone. The scientific method, then, is a value that helps to protect the scientific community and society at large against flawed reasoning. (Shaffer, 1985: 15)

I.I. If I've got you understood right, you're not going to buy into scientific psychology on that advertising are you?

Darned right we're not. As we argued in Chapter 1, behind its mask of objectivity, this kind of statement illustrates how psychologists were (and traditional psychologists still are) undertaking a particular mission, which was (and is) to exorcize society – drive out the 'devils' of irrationality, superstition and 'mere armchair philosophy'. In this way society can be made safe and made functional. Prejudice can be overcome, old wives' tales disproved, human foible avoided. Wherever and whenever it becomes salient to know what kind of a person a person is, science (and science alone) can come to the rescue and provide an impartial answer. So, for example, the science of psychology is presented as offering the only proper and effective technology for selecting staff to do particular jobs, screening out 'dangerous parents', identifying which children will benefit from academic education, telling who is a liar and who is truthful, who is sane and who is mad, and so on.

In its most scientific mode, psychology has often presented itself as a discipline which regards consideration of the 'self' or 'personhood' as constituted by, say, philosophy, literature or poetry as a lapse into heresy – at worst, dabbling in dangerous nonsense; at best, a waste of time or an indulgence. Such psychology has sealed itself off, drawn a *cordon sanitaire* around itself, and, in doing so, assumed it can engage in an objective science of 'personology' which is immune to subjectivity, bias and ideology; which is impregnable to the influence of romance, passion and desire. This stance is well captured by Cattell (a 'founding "father"' of psychometrics), when he opines that:

> Undoubtedly there *are* gems of scientific truth about personality, lying available in this literary approach, but there is no way – except through the fresh start of scientific research – to separate the living truths from the paste-board shams. Probably we do best to enjoy literature as an aesthetic product, in which scientific hypotheses of some vitality may exist, but not proven scientific discoveries. (1967: 14)

A somewhat alternative approach, much loved by some US social psychologists, is to produce books containing 'sprinkled quotations from writers, artists, and statespersons . . . throughout the text' (Aronson et al. 1994: xxii). They do so, of course, where these 'gems' serve to warrant the special powers of psychological activity. As Aronson et al. go on to say, '[t]he points made in these quotations parallel what social psychologists have pondered and discovered through experimentation' (ibid.). Here, social psychology is being presented as taking on a task to 'educate people to be both artists and scientists' (ibid.). And what kind of artist is a social psychologist? For Aronson et al. it is an artist in experimental design! 'Creating a well-crafted experiment is an artistic process, requiring a great deal of creativity' (ibid.). For many critical writers, what the psychological establishment (in the guise of the APA and the BPS, for example) has, by such claims, proceeded to secure for its initiates is the sole power to provide and operate the instrument by which its science is to be practised.

I.I. I can enjoy this as good knock-about stuff, worthy of Pseuds' Corner in 'Private Psy', but, come on, don't play it all for cheap laughs, give us some content.

In this chapter we will seek to do three things. The first is to challenge this assumption – to argue that there is a 'self-serving bias' (cf. Chapter 7) operating when psychologists claim a privileged access to a real world of the 'self' – on which they alone can shed objective light and, hence, on which they alone have the capability (and thus the right) to practise. Our second task is to explore some of the problems that they have created in pursuing this warrant. Our third agenda is to suggest alternative ways of making sense of the 'self', which we think not only avoid the traps of scientism but are also more functional and more open to moral scrutiny.

What is wrong with a science of the self?

In its mission to exorcise from society the spooks of irrationality, power and prejudice, psychology committed itself to a view of the world which privileges things which are observably present or presentable (i.e. which can be shown, either directly or indirectly, really to exist here and now). This positivistic way of understanding the world was considered the best antidote to the spooks: if it's not manifest to examination and open to objective definition and measurement, it doesn't count. However, our existence as people or selves is far more complex than that of physical objects and processes, and hence a positivistic approach to 'personhood' risks profound distortion. The point is that it is people who invented science – and people who ask scientific questions. In this sense, we (people) who are the objects or targets of questions, about, say, what it is to be a person, are also subjects or askers of the questions.

I.I. I know I asked for substance but this is beginning to feel like getting a rock-cake when I asked for bread. Lighten up, eh!

Box 3:1 Subjecting and Objecting

The terms *subject* and *object* can cause considerable confusion in psychology. In English grammar the modal phrase form is subject–verb–object (S–V–O) – as in 'The psychologist (S) studies (V) people (O)'. In standard philosophical usage the *subject* is that which experiences (feels and thinks) about or in response to some *object* (that which is felt about or thought about) – hence, the notion of a subjective or experiential realm which is often identified with the mind or the self. However, in mainstream psychology, the people that are studied, analysed or treated are often, and confusingly, called *subjects* – much as, in general English usage, are others under governance (as in 'subjects of the Queen'). In the paragraph above, we have been using subject and object in the grammatical sense. Grammar, of course, allows that the S–V–O form can be reflexive, as in 'I asked myself "What is it to be a person?"' – which is the situation we have just been talking about.

Hence any comprehensive approach to the question of 'what we are' must clearly include the recognition that we, ourselves, have an interest in the answers to the question. As Heidegger (1962) put it, in our kind of Being, our Being is an issue for us. Thus 'the self' is neither simply an observably present object to be pointed at and described nor simply a subject which points and describes.

To add a further complication, far from being an already existing object or naturally occuring entity patiently awaiting scientific discovery, our 'selves' are constantly in the process of being created, developed, transformed and negotiated. What we 'make of ourselves' depends upon both the possibilities afforded by the practical and social conditions in which we live, and the possibilities afforded by the ways of understanding, talking and thinking about 'selfhood' which are available to us. The injunction to be 'yourself' is meaningless unless you have some practical understanding of what this means, and some agreement as to what counts as an instance of 'being yourself'. In other historical and cultural circumstances, different understandings prevail as to what human beings 'are' (which tend to be related to differences in how social life is organized) and hence different ways of 'being a person' hold sway. As put by one famous anthropologist:

> The Western conception of the person as a bounded, unique, more or less integrated motivational and cognitive universe . . . organized into a distinc-

tive whole and set contrastively both against other such wholes and against
a social and natural background is, however incorrigible it may seem to us,
a rather peculiar idea within the context of the world's cultures. (Geertz,
1984: 229)

Or as expressed, rather dramatically, by an historian: 'Under the sails
of philosophy, religion, politics, and the arts, the self was invented shortly
after the middle of the eighteenth century' (Lyons, 1978).

These claims (see Sampson, 1993; Taylor, 1989 for more thorough
discussions) are disconcerting because, if they are taken seriously, we can
no longer assume that the ways in which we think of ourselves today are
natural, normal and timeless. Modern industrialized nation-States, in
being responsible for bringing 'psychology' – the science for the study of
the 'psyche' – into being, have created new ways of understanding,
monitoring and prescriptively acting on our personal existence. That is,
instead of thinking of psychology as striving simply to discover, describe
and measure the self, we should look to its role in creating, constructing
and governing our ways of being-who-we-are. The kind of Being that
psychology repeatedly tells us we are and ought to be is a self-centred,
self-contained and self-interested individual. Hence psychological discourse is littered with 'self-centred' concepts such as 'self-esteem', 'self-
concept', 'self-actualization', 'self-worth', 'self-image' and 'self-system'.
Through an engagement with such 'self-concepts' our personhood is
appropriated into an understanding-of-being which sends us on a path
towards becoming that which it is appropriate for us to be in such a
modern setting – 'ourselves'.

The psychological preoccupation with 'who we are' and infatuation
with the 'self' is an historically contingent discursive practice (Foucault,
1988) with an active interest in what we 'make of ourselves' from out of
the possibilities of contemporary life (what Foucault terms our 'technologies of the self'). This interest in what we make of ourselves is reflected in
psychology's practical concern with such tasks as selecting staff, screening
parents, identifying problem children, detecting pathological personalities, diagnosing mental illness, classifying criminal types and so on. It is
this humaneering mission (cf. Chapter 1) to control and predict behaviour
that generates the concern to accurately describe and measure the self,
and it is this concern which leads to the formulation of theories which
misleadingly treat 'it' as if it were a thing – theories, that is, which reify
the self. Indeed, psychologists who have been troubled by the soul-ful
(spooky) and unscientific connotations of the word 'self' have searched
for other terms which better suit their requirement of objectivity. The
term most generally adopted was *personality*.

I.I. Now that word I can relate to my syllabus. Is it time to reach for my highlighter?

The reification of personhood as 'personality'

Open any psychology text on 'personality' and you will find a more or less standard style of definition (e.g. 'consistent behavior patterns originating within the individual', Burger, 1993), together with lengthy descriptions of how it can be measured. What matters is that 'personality' should be definable and measurable. This is because the concept is used in psychology as an intervening variable or hypothetical construct which is thought to explain why different people 'respond' differently to the same 'stimuli', but each responds to it predictably. Through the concept of personality, the 'self' or individual in which it is located is made into an object per se (reification) as a theoretical and investigatory strategy. To control and predict behaviour we must know what causes it, and if 'personality' is one of the causes, then we need to be able to define and measure it precisely – in order to control for it. As Cattell put it (prior to psychology's de-pathologization of homosexuality – see Chapter 10):

> The homosexual has been a stumbling block to many clinical theorists – especially in that he fails to respond to treatment – and he has been described as obstinate, uncooperative, etc. The profile places him actually as an anxiety neurotic, perhaps as a result of undischargeable ergic [*sic*] tensions, but also with a peculiar emphasis on extraversion and radicalism. Thus unlike the introverted neurotic he is compelled to 'act out' his difficulty, and to do so without conservative inhibitions. The question of inferences for therapy belongs to the next section. (1967: 331)

Note that it is not just personality that is reified here: the entire positivistic approach involves reification – behaviour gets reified as a 'response' (or as a stimulus to further responses), the world gets reified as a collection of 'stimuli', and personality gets reified either as distortion which accounts for individual differences in response or as an internally located source of stimuli. Of course this is an elaborate metaphysical way of thinking, and not a property of the world or human nature! Just because human activity is set up and spoken about as if it were describable, explainable, predictable and controllable (according to positivistic requirements), that does not mean that human activity is literally like this.

I.I. Just when I thought things were safe . . .

Biologizing personality

The positivistic preference for what is observably present(able) leads to the idea that the best theory of personality must be one which is grounded in hard physiological fact. Indeed some psychologists still hold to the old idea (developed by people such as Kretschmer, 1925 and Sheldon, 1942) that physique itelf determines personality which in turn determines behaviour (Hart et al., 1982). Most contemporary psychologists, however take a dim view of such crude morphological models. The more standard approach takes a somewhat subtler line: that the physical structures which determine the way people act (i.e. their 'personality') are hidden within the body. This perspective is exemplified clearly by Eysenck's theory of personality (Eysenck, 1952, 1967) which (at its simplest) divides people up between 'extroverts' and 'introverts', 'stables' and 'neurotics'.

The suggestion that people act in a particular way because they are inhabited by invisible 'spirits' gets smartly dismissed by psychologists, who say this is metaphysics not science. Freud's ideas about 'invisible inner forces' get similarly short shrift. Yet Eysenck's formulations (and others like them) continue to enjoy considerable favour within the scientific community. What gives Eysenck's argument its scientific credibility is that he assumes that the 'essences' which cause behaviour have a material reality – specifically, that they arise from differences in the 'wiring' (i.e. neural structure) and physiology of the brain itself.

I.I. This is certainly a psychology I recognize, which presumably means it's about to have the ground cut from underneath it?

Such physiologically grounded theories of personality can give the appearance of considerable sophistication – not only in the physiological modelling they use but also because they draw upon notions of 'interaction' between organism and environment. 'Personality' within such models is seen as the product of past interplay between the material organism (i.e. its genes and their effects on physiology) and its environment (i.e. the stimulation received); while 'behaviour' is seen to result from the moment-to-moment interaction between 'personality' and 'situation'.

There are two major – and interrelated – problems here. The first is that the claimed mechanism of interaction explains nothing. It merely offers a circular argument. In human terms an environment is not a given objective condition but a reading made by somebody. If the reading is made by the researcher, then it is not the subject's environment but the researcher's at issue. If made by the subject, what could be producing the effect but the subject's personality? It is also an unprovable argument, because organisms can never be observed outside of any environment but only in context.

This 'trap' comes about because of the very thinking that is employed. It is assumed that causes can be empirically established by manipulating the things that cause effects. For a start, we cannot hold the environment constant and vary personality to see the effect, because personality is the very thing that ensures that the world is perceived differentially by different people. Yet this uninterrogated pre-commitment to establishing causes tacitly shapes the whole field of enquiry. Experimental personology (*à la* Eysenck) proceeds from the axiom that behaviour is describable, explainable and predictable. However, within the empiricist credo that only tangible, observable 'facts' can be taken seriously as evidence that something exists, we arrive at the tautological position that personality is held both to predicate and to predict behaviour. We can tell that extroverts are extroverts only because they behave in an extrovert manner – the label describes both the behaviour and the personality.

Thus the difficulty faced by those advocating the personology approach is how to locate and demonstrate the existence of the very entity that they are striving to explain: personality. The trouble is that 'personality' can be made evident perfectly well in the total absence of a body – think of Jane Eyre, Tom Sawyer or Natasha Rostoff. A personality scale can easily be completed (we get our students to do so regularly) which allocates each of these characters to a point position on an extraversion/intraversion dimension – with not a gene, a neurone or a neuro-transmitter in sight!

I.I. That's quite a neat attack but surely the real power of psychometrics is that it is successful in practice, thanks largely to its use of sophisticated statistics – ones most of the rest of us only half understand. That's what I take from the books, anyway.

Damn lies and statistics

Psychometricians of personality such as Cattell (1967) and Eysenck (1952; 1967) used factor analytic techniques in an attempt to crystallize 'personality' out of the flux and indefiniteness of everyday life and language-use, in order to render it tangibly present. Both propose the existence of stable and universal 'dimensions' of personality which underlie and dictate surface manifestations. The complex statistical procedures of factor analysis (which serve to identify commonality amongst correlated items in a data-matrix and to present this as a collection of statistically discrete 'factors') appear to them to provide direct access to basic and universally shared dimensions within the mind.

Two big problems afflict the psychometric method in personology. The first is that such 'factors' of personality as extroversion/introversion had a social life long before they were employed by Jung (1953 onwards) and then 'discovered' and measured for us by the likes of Eysenck. They are part of what psychologists usually call 'implicit personality theory' (Passini and Norman, 1966; Semin et al., 1987). When Eysenck asks in his inventories questions such as 'Do you like to go to parties?' and 'Are you impulsive?' he is doing no more than making it clear (by asking questions with that same meaning again and again) that the concern is with extraversion/introversion. Such a scale, in effect, asks 'How much of an extravert are you?' Interrogated through that format, Eysenck's subjects know how to tell a story about themselves in such terms – just as Eysenck himself did before he started his research endeavour. All subjects have to do is reply consistently and the result is a 'reliable' scale. (This same argument is explored in more detail in Chapter 10 in relation to scales of masculinity/femininity.)

The second problem is that the 'factors' obtained depend entirely on the questions you ask. Eysenck wanted independent (orthogonal) factors and, of course, got them. Cattell used a slightly different factor analytic method (an oblique system which permits the emergence of factors which are partially correlated with each other). He arrived at a different factor solution, on the basis of which he argued for the existence of sixteen underlying 'source' personality traits (measured by his 16PF inventory), which stimulated him into creating neologisms in order to label them (see below). If the 16PF measures themselves are factor analysed, one emergent 'super' factor is – surprise, surprise – our old friend extraversion/introversion, which clusters together 'a liking for people in the sense of affectothymia (A), with talkativeness and cheery optimism in surgency (F), with adventurous boldness of parmia, H, and with the . . . Q_2 primary which defines a tendency to live with the group as opposed to self-sufficiency and individualism' (Cattell, 1967: 123).

I.I. Doesn't that show exactly what I said, the evidence is that personality scaling 'works'?

Quite the opposite. The lesson here is clear, you get out of this kind of factor analysis what you put in. The measures created and the type of analysis adopted reflect the scale-designer's theory of personality. All he or she can get back is a version of what they introduced into the research in the first place; it has yielded not data but creata (Andersen, 1994). What is being 'tested' is not a 'real thing' (i.e. essence of personality) but the extent to which the scale-designer and the people who complete the scale share a common understanding of 'what people are like'. If the scale-designer has competent insight into the way 'personality' is told (in local and contingent terms – 'among people like us'), then they are likely to produce a 'valid' and 'replicable' scale. But they are doing no more than, say, showing that two clocks in the same household tell more or less the same time. This does not prove that 'time' exists as an essential entity, or that a particular schedule for 'what the time is' holds true except in a certain geographical locality.

I.I. Whatever 'zone' I'm in or you're in, I still think it's time to hear some alternatives. You've really done psychometrics to death.

Situated identity: A turn to ecology

Eysenck's EPI scale and Cattell's 16PF scale are classic examples of attempts to bring to the word 'personality' some observable present(able) substance to suit the positivistic requirements of conventional psychology.

Box 3.2 Metricating the Social Self

In experimental social psychology, not only are EPI-type and 16PF-type individual difference measures employed, but research reports are full of many more traits and styles tailor-made to address variability in *social* behaviour (examples will be noted later on). Some such as 'Machiavelli-anism' and 'need-achievement' are held to reflect social motives. Others claim to address dimensions upon which selves per se are said to vary, such as self-esteem and self-monitoring. Others yet again (although the distinction is fuzzy in the extreme) are cast as indices not of personality but of 'attitudes' (cf. Chapter 7).

All claim some research support as to their validity (i.e. ability to predict differences in laboratory 'social behaviour'). None escapes the criticisms of psychometrics we raise above and, as to their 'validation', this can be re-cast as demonstrating that the telling of one's self extends (sometimes) to conduct. As the old saying has it, 'Let your deeds be the advocate of your words'.

Approaches such as Cattell's and Eysenck's claim to offer not just accounts of the 'personalities' people have but also 'explanations' as to how people come to have them. Eysenck (and to a less florid extent) Cattell opt for biological explanations. Others favour 'nurture' and stress the importance of the unique learning (read conditioning) history of each individual. Social learning theory (Bandura, 1986; Rotter, 1966) is probably the most developed of these 'nurture' explanations. Where all agree (and how could they not, once the question is framed in this way?) is that a proper (causal) explanation of personality must include both nature and nurture. Of course, if our past 'environments' can act as a partial 'cause' of our present personality, it can presumably also be the case that our current 'environment' can act as a partial 'cause' of how we behave in the now. Hence, there is a second level to the argument: a proper (causal) explanation of behaviour must include both the person and the situation.

I.I. I feel an equation coming on: Behaviour = f (Personality + Situation).

So did a lot of people. This injection of 'social' elements of explanation (which became particularly fashionable from the early 1960s) served several agendas. One was the growing liberalism of that time and the influence of humanistic thinking. Another was that it had long been known (though not much talked about) that personality measures are poor predictors of behaviour. (A correlation of 0.4, on the high side in such research, 'explains' only [0.4 × 100] per cent of the variance, or 16 per cent, leaving 84 per cent of variance unaccounted for. In terms of prediction this is effectively useless!) Equally, the idea of personality as a fixed essence fitted ill with the growing practitionerization of psychology and the demands for 'quick fixes' to 'problem behaviour' this required.

All of this, of course, was music to the ears of social psychologists, whose excursions into measuring attitudes (cf. Chapter 6) and social traits had also proved highly problematic. They were more than happy, at this time (and the affirmation holds to the present day), to reassert their claims in the behaviour prediction stakes. It had now become dogma that: 'social psychologists believe that, when trying to understand social behavior, it is often more important to examine the nature of the social situation than the nature of the person. Thus, social psychologists believe, in the words of Judith Rodin, that "it is not bad people . . . but bad situations that create social problems"' (Aronson et al., 1994: 543). And not just 'social problems' of course. What social psychology was rewarranting was 'folk situationism' – that we expect people to be happy and extroverted at parties, sad and introverted at funerals, serious and studious in libraries, and so on. Social psychology was here very much returning to its 'roots' . . .

I.I. How could I forget?

... and the axiom that the way people act is as much dictated by the demands of the situation as by qualities belonging to the person. Another way of putting this is that behaviour is best thought of as coming not from the 'self' as trait but the 'self' as state.

Box 3.3   The Trait/State Distinction

Many words that refer to our psychological condition such as our anxiety or our self-esteem are used in ordinary discourse to refer, variously, to how we consistently are as persons (e.g. an anxious sort of person) and how we have been temporarily made or rendered. In many Romance languages (like Spanish) there are two different verbs to cover the two distinct kinds of being. In English there are not. We can 'be anxious', and then again, we can be 'anxious because'. The first, in psychological terms refers to our 'personality' (our trait), the second to an induced, temporary condition (our state). At a stroke, and only at the cost of a further leap into obsfucation (upon which the cynical might say pseudo-sciences like psychology survive), the explanatory possibilities of concepts like anxiety were doubled! The induction (particularly before the risks of being sued led to ethics committees) of negative 'states' was part of the 'artistic process' of social psychological experimental design. For example, being told that a 'test' had revealed a subject's 'latent homosexuality' was a common ploy to reduce 'state self-esteem' – and in the climate of those days in the USA, it 'worked'!

In a germinal formulation for critical psychologists, Alexander and Knight (1971) developed a version of the 'state self' which proved very troublesome for the interpretation of the results of social-psychological experiments. (Their first target was cognitive dissonance research; cf. Chapter 6.) What they offered was the notion of 'situated identity', a conceptualization which stressed that different situations, for different reasons (e.g. the expectations and obligations that people have about how we should act in given situations), call for different ways of being as a person (different 'situated identities' in their language). Exemplary, of course, of contexts which call for different ways of being as a person are alternative experimental conditions. Thus the troubling possibility was raised that social-psychological experiments employing different conditions do not test 'theories' at all but rather create the 'conditions' for different 'situated identities'.

In parallel, a rash of studies followed which sought to use statistics to segment the causes of behaviour according to features of the person, the situation and the interaction between them (e.g. Argyle, Shimoda and Little, 1978).

I.I. As in attribution theory, you mean?

Exactly, attribution theory (cf. Chapter 7) lays on ordinary thinkers the self-same model that social psychologists used in their own theorizing about the causes of behaviour.

I.I. I should be flattered?

Not if you're 'going critical' you shouldn't. All of this research was still framed by scientism, with its pre-commitment to the axiom that 'behaviour' is 'determined' by variables such as 'nature', 'nurture' and 'situation'. For 'situation' to be brought into such a scientific discourse, it too had to be conceived as a set of determinable, observably present(able) factors which exert an at least partially demonstrable causal effect on 'behaviour'. In this way 'situation' and 'person' can be treated as if they were entirely separate variables which are equally present(able) in an observable way, and which jointly determine behaviour (as if our actions were 'pushed from behind' by such forces). This kind of approach necessarily involves producing a stripped-down and limited understanding of 'situation' (i.e. as simply the collection of other things that are co-present with a person at any given time) to match the stripped-down and limited understanding of 'personality'.

A turn to textuality

The practice of a social psychology deeply concerned with the power of social situations is often expressed in terms of liberal-humanistic values, linked to a mission of human betterment (the Aronson et al. book we have been quoting from in this chapter is a prime example). This should not, we suggest, be taken as implying that such 'situational' social psychology actually produces a more open, more contextual (and hence more culturally aware and more ideologically sensitive) approach. It will not, so long as it clings to treating social situations as once it treated individual differences. What 'situationism' offers is still a form of present-ism (privileging the present and the objective). The (behavioural) events it studies are still thought of as being the result or effect of a range of potentially separable extant determining forces (whether these be located in the person or in the situation). The person is still thought of as pre-formed and fully present (the result of nature and nurture in interaction) and the situation is likewise conceived as a kind of self-sufficient objective 'frame' which exerts an independent causal effect on the person. All that has changed is that now the causal emphasis is being placed upon 'social influence'. The unaddressed problem in all this, we would argue, is that:

- a person is never not in a situation not subject to 'social influence' (and hence it is not possible to separate them clearly) – they always have Being-in-the-world;
- a situation is never simply an objectively present(able) set of environmental conditions but 'works' to influence action through its meaningfulness for people; and
- a person is never simply present-at-hand but rather comes into Being partly through the possibilities offered by situations which are strategically and ongoingly transformed and negotiated.

I.I. And 'a person is never going to grasp what all this means unless you make some effort to "chunk" it into assimilable elements'.

All right, then. Our way of thinking about selfhood is informed by non-positivistic approaches – such as hermeneutics, symbolic interaction-ism, and phenomenology and re-formed into a critical social construction-ism – which addresses these assertions as follows.

Being-in-the-world

We argue that people are inexorably part of, involved with and insepar-able from the circumstances that make up their world. To conceive of our selves (or whatever is denoted by the words 'I' and 'me') as the 'inside' and the world as the 'outside' (a collection of stimuli) is to fail to recognize the extent to which we exist alongside-and-within the world. It is through and against our everyday involvements and engagements with the circumstances of our worlds (especially including other people) that we come to know ourselves.

The positivistic approach encourages us to view people as fundamen-tally detached, isolated units which respond mechanistically to external and internal stimuli (which is of course reflected in positivistic methods like experiments which demand that 'subjects' be kept 'in the dark' so that they cannot suss out the hypothesis and ruin the experiment). From this perspective, issues of interest, concern, significance and involvement are regarded as pollutants to the purity of mechanical causation – the leaking-in of values and prejudice. We, in contrast, hold to the conviction that, if you want to know why a person is acting in a particular way, you first need to know what activities they are involved in, what their concerns are, what the significance of the situation is for them, and what is their interest in the scene in question. If we discover that they are unconcerned, disinterested and uninvolved, then these ways of being are still modes of concern, interest and involvement – that is, ways of Being-in-the-world which characterize what it is to be a person (Heidegger, 1928). A stone never was interested or unconcerned; a dead body is no longer interested or disinterested. Where personhood begins, positivism should end (we shall call this Beryl's Third Law).

In short, to separate personality from situation unproblematically is to be already stepping blithely along an intellectual path which renounces our fundamental worldliness in favour of a radical objectification and subjection of all that is (i.e. either everything is subjective or everything is objective). What we mean by 'the world' here is not some external objectivity that we, as primarily detached subjectivities, strive to get to know. To us the world comprises the meaningful constitutive circum-stances which are the source and target of our ongoing concerns and interests. The world is that with which we are already involved, and hence that which is significant for us: *our* world.

Strategy, purpose, directedness: selfhood-in-action

Accepting that it makes no sense to talk of being 'free' of circumstances-in-general (which is not to say that our particular, practical circumstances do not change, of course – and 'us' along with them), it becomes clear that to view our actions as 'behaviour' which is 'caused' by variables either 'internal' or 'external' to the person is wholly misleading. Any action is more than, and other than, the product of prior determinations. Such an interpretation misses the obvious sense in which our activities are directed by us from out of one set of constitutive circumstances and into another. Circumstances do not determine or foreclose our activity but guide our possibilities. Our speech and action are, in this sense, strategic and purposive, and, by virtue of this, are always unfinished or incomplete. To say, for example, 'I am a brave person' is not to look within oneself and to report what one discovers but to stake a kind of claim, on the basis of what has gone before, in a communicative interaction. At the same time our companion might reply 'actually I think you're reckless', and thereby challenge the temporary closure that this self-construal was aimed towards.

As Goffman (1959) and others (Harré and Secord, 1972; Sampson,

1991) have insisted, one of the concerns that orientates our activity during such social interaction is the desire to present a positive impression or image of ourselves. A whole field of so-called 'dramaturgical' research has grown up in order to study the dynamics of 'impression management'. However, in talking of 'directedness', 'strategy' and 'purpose', we should not restrict our understanding to issues of 'impression' and 'image' which might then appear superficial and insincere. Any action takes place within, and is projected from, a worldly field of concerns. In preparing a meal, for example, a person may be concerned to make something that tastes good and is, perhaps, 'healthy'. They may also be concerned to create a pleasant social occasion for some friends but at the same time also wish to use up the contents of their fridge. When mainstream psychologists address these kinds of fields of concern, they try to essentialize them into a causal framework. Thus we hear talk of 'behaviour' being 'multiply determined' – driven, in the case of McDougall (1908) by a manifold of instincts that ground social life; or according to Murray (1938), by a matrix of needs.

Some critical thinkers have found it useful to distinguish between the 'practical' (e.g. 'I wear shoes to protect my feet') and the 'expressive' (e.g. 'I wear fashionable shoes') when teasing apart the different concerns that orientate our activity (Harré, 1979; Parker, 1989). However, we would argue that any practice is concernful and hence expressive; and every expression is concernful and hence practical. Hence an overly clear separation is always distortive. The point remains that what we do, we do from somewhere – in order that other circumstantial possibilities are opened up somewhere else (even if those possibilities may merely be that we remain 'the same').

By now it should be clear that to view action as 'behaviour' which is the product of causes is to misunderstand that action fundamentally as static and finished. This ignores the directed, strategic and purposive aspects which are central to what any action is. This totalization of action (treating it as if it were a finished product) leads us into our third issue, concerning the way in which time is understood.

We exist in time, and time in us

I.I. A lot of your readers, and I'm one of them, have never done a formal course in philosophy. That makes following your argument tough, what about trying here to give an example or something?

To make the point in personal terms, ask yourself the question about yourself – what kind of a person am I? We suspect that your answer will not just be a matter of what you are in the immediate now (i.e. something observably present(able)) but will be wrapped up in who and what you have been in your (close or distant) pasts and what you are intending to do and be in your (close or distant) futures. Or try another tack – think about a time when you were 'not yourself' – maybe at a time of crisis or after a 'night on the tiles'. While in some sense this kind of experience can be said to reveal your 'true colours' (*in vino veritas*), in another it does make sense to construe yourself as, paradoxically, 'not yourself'! This illustrates well that once we accept that what we do and say is intimately and inescapably tied to the circumstances of our doing it – in terms of both the place from which we act and the possibilities into which our act is directed – then the way we think about time becomes crucial.

The meaning of our strategic, concernful activity is unthinkable without time, because we act within the flow of time. Bourdieu (1977: 5) illustrates this with the example of gift-exchange. The meaning of being given a gift (and, indeed, whether an object is considered to be a gift) can be constituted only in the flow of time. For example, any counter-gift must be both different from the original gift and deferred appropriately in time. To give back the same object immediately is to nullify or refuse the gift. To return a different object too quickly is to engage in swapping or to display a reluctance to be indebted which might be construed as ungrateful (and hence 'spoils' the gift). This example from Bourdieu gives a good impression of what he calls the artful 'necessary improvisation' which characterizes all human practice.

Retrospectively, of course, once what has happened has happened, it might appear that people's activities are predetermined by causal forces or by 'rules' and 'roles' that they are inexorably following (cf. 'role theory' in sociology). But at the time of action, each move is always a strategic leap into an only partially knowable possibility, where one choice of speech or action (amongst a variety made available by the circumstances) is taken, and where the way in which this choice is received is equally contingent. Scientistic thinking results not just in a reification (or 'thingification') but in a detemporalization of personhood. This combination of reification and detemporalization is implicit in the word 'present' (recall the positivistic insistence that things be observably present(able) if they are to 'count' as real) which denotes both the 'showing of a thing' (presenting something) and a particular mode of time (the present). To restrict our understanding of Being to that which is present(able) is to produce a crude and simplistic knowledge. As Bourdieu says:

> The detemporalizing effect . . . that science produces when it forgets the transformation it imposes on practices inscribed in the current of time, i.e.

detotalized, simply by totalizing them, is never more pernicious than when exerted on practices defined by the fact that their temporal structure, direction, and rhythm are constitutive of their meaning. (1977: 9)

This stresses the importance of recognizing that we exist within the flow of time, and it is only because of this that we can 'waste time', 'use time' or otherwise reckon with time. However, time should be thought of not only as that in which we live but also as that out of which we are made. Thinking in this way renders the idea that selfhood must be a present(able) entity all the more questionable. We exist in time, but temporality is also a phenomenon which 'has the unity of a future which makes present in the process of having been' (Heidegger, 1927: 374).

Box 3.4 Relish and Recipe

Here, as elsewhere, you may find some of our quotations tough going. Try approaching them like being offered an exotic new dish. First savour the taste and texture of the language, then ask 'how is it made?'

We think Heidegger's recipe unfolds in the following way. If our activity is strategic, directed, and purposive, then this indicates a thrust towards the future. From where we are (or 'are at'), we are constantly projected towards other possible circumstances (we do such and such in order that . . ., and we say this or that for the sake of . . ., and so on). In this sense, what and who we are is always-ever (albeit only partly) constituted and framed by that future which our present existence is aiming at – no matter how confused and short-term that aim may be (e.g. to impress somebody or to go to the shops). In this way, the 'future makes present'.

Likewise, what and who we are now is always experienced as made up of what we have been. As Durkheim (1938, quoted in Bourdieu, 1977: 79) put it, 'the present amounts to little compared with the long past in the course of which we were formed and from which we result'. The facticity of what we have been is not, however, the same as the distancing of an object which passes in time. What we were was also always circumstantial and unfinished, and hence (and like history in general) our 'pasts' are not composed of objective 'events' which might be known for what they truly were. Rather, they are constituted from what might be called the significance of these events (and non-events) (cf. Gadamer, 1975). We know who we were from what we are and will be, and hence the significance of the past is *presenced* in the now according to our future orientation. Our future, therefore, makes present in the process of having been.

The textuality and tectonics of self

I.I. That's your line, isn't it? Guess I can look forward to reading a 'good review' for once.

This realization that our identities are not pre-formed essences which exist independently outside of time, of talk and other social activity (i.e. our temporal Being-in-the-world) has led many contemporary researchers to abandon as misconceived the search for the 'true self' or for the 'real underlying personality' (alongside the 'true situation' or 'real social influence'), and to look instead to how, why and under what conditions different selves are constructed in discourse.

Textual identities?

Harré (1986), for example, proposes a theory of identity which is influenced by people such as Vygotsky and Wittgenstein. It hinges on the claim that 'to be a self is to be in possession of a theory'. Harré discusses how we craft out understandings of who we are (which can then become the most personal and private thoughts and feelings) from out of the socially available pool of textual resources that are available in a given culture at a given time. Similar 'social constructionist' arguments have been put forward by Coulter (1989), Shotter (1984, 1993 a and b), Sampson (1985, 1991), Burkitt (1991), Kitzinger (1987), Shotter and Gergen (1989) and others. We like how Shotter and Gergen have expressed this approach: 'The primary medium within which identities are created and have their currency is not just linguistic, but textual: persons are largely ascribed identities according to the manner of their embedding within a discourse – in their own or in the discourse of others' (1989: ix).

All of these writers point out that our self-knowledge and sense of identity is fashioned out of, and limited by, the ways of recognizing, classifying, understanding, judging and otherwise conceiving or thinking about selfhood which are socially available.

I.I. How's that kind of approach different from any other that draws attention to the social in social psychology?

Box 3.5 The 'Social' in Social Construction

To say that 'identity is fashioned out of, and limited by the ways of recognizing, classifying, understanding etc ... [of things] which are socially available' can sound like reifying the 'social' into a thing which works upon us causally. Just, in other words, like the mainstream's 'social influence' recast in high-falutin' language. In any social constructionism worth the name, it is not. To work within the analytics of discourse or textuality is to employ approaches which do not raise causal questions (except, of course, to approach them as forms of discourse fashioned out of the socially available!). Rather, what is being implied here is that identity discourse is not a 'natural', inevitable or universal element of writing or talk. It is to be found only in certain circumstances.

Where this takes us is that the ways in which we understand ourselves or 'who we are' cannot be judged against some true standard of who we really are, because there is no 'real us' template against which to judge. (Any suggestion to the contrary from psychology can itself be seen as discourse – perhaps in this case a self-serving professional discourse – but again no absolute template of the real permits an absolute judgement.) When Harré suggests that to be a self is to be in possession of a theory, he is indicating that we are what we believe ourselves to be. Freeman makes the point thus: 'how are we to escape the conclusion that we ourselves are ultimately fictions? The self, after all, is not a thing: it is not a substance, a material entity that we can somehow grab hold of and place before our very eyes' (1993: 8).

I.I. Just how is a 'textual identity' then different from the kinds of humanistic notions of 'becoming' which you seem to be trying to escape from?

To suggest that we pick out and adopt these available ways of 'being ourselves' as if they were options on some cultural 'menu' of available 'understandings' or 'theories' is to stretch the metaphor too far. Unless we are very fortunate (or particularly unimaginative) we cannot simply be whoever we chose to be. Our 'self talk', as elaborated earlier, takes place within-the-world and, for the most part, amongst-other-people, and is perhaps better characterized as a constantly evolving moral and political economy of self–other differentiation and association.

Kitzinger (1989: 82), for example, begins her discussion of the political nature of lesbian identities by quoting Johnston (1973), saying that 'identity . . . is what you can say you are according to what they say you can be'. The circumstances which make possible the adoption of particular identities often extend well beyond the mere availability of a given narrative. It is clear, for example, that having sex with somebody of the same gender within a cultural context of extreme homophobia will have radically different implications for the identities of those involved than the same activity in more 'liberal' circumstances. The precise ways in which such identities get talked into, thought into and acted into being under these circumstances are, however, textual matters which cannot be predicted – other than to expect variability and difference. If it is insisted that the ways in which people respond and relate to the circumstances of their existence is governed by laws and rules, then these are the laws of the land and the rules of convention, not those of science.

The way in which we talk about ourselves and who we are, however, is crucial in constructing the relationship we make to our circumstances. Indeed our circumstances only become determinate as what-they-are through the construction of our relationship to them (and often in the form of the narrating of an identity). In this sense, the construction of an identity (the significance of one's self) is simultaneously the construction of (the significance of) one's world. For example, if, as Kitzinger prescribes, a woman who has sex with other women adopts a politicized understanding of herself (as being lesbian in order to take a stand against patriarchy), then this involves not only the creation of a personal/political identity but also the construction of 'the world' as partriarchy-to-be-challenged. If a different woman (or the same one at a different time) understands under 'the same' conditions her lesbianism as a 'personal choice' taken freely under the influence of 'true love', then this makes sense only in a different 'world of circumstances'. A third woman who tells the story of her lesbianism in terms of the language of psychopathology (offered by 'specialists' such as Freud and Krafft-Ebing) constructs her self and her world yet differently again.

So, in constructing a self we thereby create a relationship to our circumstances. Thus, simultaneously we make our 'world' and our 'identity' existentially and contingently determinate as what-they-are. In this sense, they are co-constructions which act to legitimate and bolster each other. To limit the matter of identity to an issue of 'choice', then, is to miss the sense in which much that is significant about our identities was never presented to us as a matter for our choosing. The 'I' that chooses must already be, in some sense, 'there', and what is chosen is always chosen through a responsiveness to what presents itself to us from out of our circumstances. This distinction between the chooser and the chosen we have already encountered earlier in this chapter in the form of the difference between self-as-subject (who might point at an object) and self-as-object (who might be pointed at). This distinction is mirrored by William James's and G. H. Mead's distinction between the 'I' and the 'me', where 'I' represents the self-as-subject (or author/narrator) and 'me' self-as-object (or character).

'Are you for me or against me?' (the Other)

Of course, whenever we engage in self-talk (whenever a particular 'I' makes a claim to be a particular 'me') then this must be seen as a strategic and essentially unfinished move-in-time which takes place within the world of our circumstances including, of course, other people. As such it makes sense to ask 'who', at any given time, 'are we for'?

Mead, for example, drew upon Cooley's notion of the 'looking glass self' in order to indicate the extent to which 'who we are' is constructed out of the image of ourselves which is provided for us by the way in which 'significant Others' talk about and act towards us. In this sense the Other is like a mirror in which we recognize ourselves or a spotlight which illuminates who we are and where we are going. Likewise, Bakhtin (1895–1975) found it useful to distinguish between what he called 'I-for-myself' from 'I-for-others'. Like Mead, Bakhtin emphasized that 'I' am always striving to know how 'Others' see 'me', and that this process is essentially incompletable.

This raises the equally plausible question of 'who are we against?' Self-formation is always also an act of differentiation, distinction and disas-sociation. Or rather, to stake a claim for what you are is always also (implicitly or explicitly) to stake a claim for what you're not. If I think of myself as brave, then I think this against the backdrop of an Other who is a coward, and the sinfulness of the sinner is likewise lit up against the goodness of the good Other. In this case, the Other is not the spotlight which lights our way (as above) but the darkness which the light of our own self needs in order to shine ('You'll ne-ver walk a-lone . . .'). Both Others are, of course, circumstantial.

Circumstance

Our notion of 'circumstance' permits a flexibility that the positivist notion of 'situation' does not.

I.I. It sounds so good, maybe you should have called this section 'Pomp and Circumstance'?

The best way of conveying what we think is valuable about the notion of circumstance is to show how we do and do not use it. We are certainly not arguing, for example, that, if this circumstance prevails, then this way of being a self will be the necessary effect (such a 'social determinist' argument would simply invite the 'free-will' counter-position out for yet another airing). In the socio-personal space/time of human activity, a change in circumstances need not involve a physical change in 'location', and, likewise, a change in geographical location need not mean an escape from a given circumstance. We can stay in the same place with the same people yet the circumstances might change depending upon how we, as 'participants' in an interchange, define who and where we are, and what is going on.

If, for example, we 'split-up' with a lover but continue to 'see them' as friends, we can be said to have changed our circumstances without any necessary change in what is (except to a voyeur) observably present(able). This change in 'definition' is all that is required to undermine the conditions which foster and make possible or otherwise provide the 'footing' (cf. Goffman, 1959) for one identity (e.g. that of 'lover') and to create other locations or 'subject positions' (e.g. that of 'friend') from which to act and cobble together a self (cf. Davies and Harré 1990). Such 'space' is not, of course, a physical, quantifiable, location or position – despite that fact that we often talk about 'standing our ground' or 'finding our feet' (as if we were being supported from below). Rather, the 'ground' of our existence (where we are) can shift from solidity to total instability in the instant of a 'change of perspective' or in the blink of an eye on whose gaze we have risked our dependency.

The space and time of circumstance, in contrast to the positivists' 'situation', is constructed and existential. Rather than viewing 'self' and 'situation' as separable and pre-formed, we stress that both circumstances and selfhood are made determinate as what-they-are only through a mutually constructive moment of relationship. The positivists' 'subjectivity' (and their notion of an imperial self within it) stands 'over and above' the situation or world (conceived as a world of external objects), and from this single, detached location the world becomes known through being watched, heard or otherwise experienced. Circum-stance, in contrast, denotes a dispersed stance wherein we 'subjects' stand 'around and about' within a world conceived as that which we are already involved with and which is already meaningful to us (even meaninglessness, our inability to understand a foreign speaker, for example, is encountered as a meaningful part of our world).

In this sense the 'subject' and 'object', far from being separable, are radically interwoven with, and folded into one another in a kind of ecology or tapestry that we have elsewhere called textuality (Curt, 1994; Stenner and Eccleston, 1994). Circumstance should not, therefore, be passed off as mere 'context'. Not only are our circumstances and our 'selves' inseparable but also both are profoundly historical and futural. Hence the quiddity or truth of what is going on in any given interaction between people is never to be found in what is observably present(able) during that interaction (either 'in' the person, 'in' the situation or 'in' some glib formulation of an 'interaction'). This has devastating consequences for the plausibility of any 'experimental social psychology' which seeks to 'explain' people's 'behaviour' scientistically.

Be-coming

I.I. What would you do without hyphens?

We'd have to construct them, so we don't get mistaken for existentialists! From this circumstantial ontology, selfhood can be thought of as coming from our involvement with our world and as belonging in and longing for many different sites, locations and occasions. We would thus expect selfhood to be dispersed, contradictory and multi-faceted rather than singular, specular and original. Further, selfhood framed within the positivistic subject–object ontology is presented as essentially genderless, raceless, classless and bodiless (Casling, 1993): a universal form whose content is subsequently grafted-on or otherwise added. Selfhood conceived circumstantially, in contrast, is never pre-formed (like a finished product) or universal, but emerges from its circumstances and is always in the process of becoming – although not, obviously, in the sense in which the word is used in humanistic personality theory.

Standing, footing, location and positioning: their relation to selfhood

I.I. Or, 'they also serve who only foot and locate'?

Very generally speaking, our circumstances provide us with opportunities, footings and positions and present us with constraints, challenges and potential dislocations. As such, circumstances create possibilities for Being. If Being 'rebellious', for example, means to respond critically or resistantly towards a convention or requirement, then the possibility of

Being rebellious is created by the circumstance of a convention or requirement against which we can be predisposed. Further, an act of rebellion might aim towards the creation of new, different, and more agreeable circumstances. These circumstances might then provide the footing or location for somebody to identify themselves as being 'a rebel' (Stenner and Marshall, 1995).

Likewise to be 'ambitious' presupposes the possibility that there is something that can be achieved and that will require the kind of resolute focus on the future in orientating our present activity that we call 'ambition'. Again, this relates directly to the question of personality or identity because a person might then characterize themselves as 'ambitious' (or have that attribution laid on them by others). These (and many other) peculiarly human ways of Being presuppose (and, as we have been arguing, are unthinkable without) peculiarly human, and local and contingent, circumstances. What is clear is that to be 'ambitious' 'rebellious', 'greedy', 'considerate', (or any other potential characterization) is not to be in possession of some observably present(able) thing which might then be measured by a scale but to be involved in a particular relationship with one's circumstances.

I.I. That's got to be good for your research output ratings!

Box 3.6 The Experimental Social Psychology of The Self

We are keenly aware that, in what we have just said, we may be taken as claiming that everything which features in so many social psychology texts on the self is so much wasted paper. It is not to us, of course, because we are interested in all discourse on the self. But it is, we would say, if it is thought to offer some special handle on the truth. Experimental social psychology's data, or more strictly, its *creata*, may be generally fairly reported (rather than 'cooked' or made up) but that is all the truth we allow it (all the truth we allow our own work also).

Like another frequently employed means of *re-presentation*, photography, the social-psychological experiment offers a contrived 'snapshot' of our circumstances. Precisely because devices of psychological measurement, like devices for taking photographs, 'cannot lie' (they can, obviously, both be 'cooked') they also 'cannot tell the truth'. They can do neither because they have no agency, no ability to discourse notions of veracity. A photograph and the creata of an experiment both have a social life only when they are read, when they are told, when some truth value is narrated into them.

The snaps experimenters take of people – showing, say, that mirrors affect 'self-awareness' – need to be re-told as 'like a photograph' of social life so that to 'see a real likeness', in their creata becomes plausible. But character and situation no more come through an experiment than they do through a photograph – they are, rather, laid on them by a culture that holds *a priori* that they are 'there' to be discovered.

Knowledging the self

The notion that meanings are made rather than uncovered renders it inevitable that any and every way in which there is an involving of ourselves with our circumstances can be read and characterized in different ways. What you read positively as ambition, another might read as selfish manipulativeness, and where one person sees rebellion another might find delinquency. It is not a matter of this or that way of Being being essentially tied to this or that characterization, such that we might then expect selfishness or ambition to be discoverable empirical properties of human action or, even more ludicrously, human biology. Rather, when we characterize a way of Being or acting in a particular way (as in 'don't be greedy') we appropriate that action through language into the realm of our own concerns. In this way appropriation forms a link (perhaps an association, perhaps a distinction) between the act in question and our own concerns, whereby we stake a kind of claim on what the proper place of that act is.

This is quite different from saying that 'anything goes' – an appropriation has to be 'appropriate'! By appropriate we do not, of course, mean 'correct' against some absolute standard of truth (as, say, researchers have tried in vain to do in the area of person perception). Rather, we wish to allow for circumstantial mis-takes. For example, we might find that the person we called stingy was actually saving the money she wasn't spending in the pub that night to pay her mother's dental bill.

The point is rather that any action or way of Being can be correctly fixed in numerous ways if there are numerous ideas as to what the 'proper place' of that action is. Arguments over 'correctness', then, should not be thought of as debates about some essential or inherent property of the act or the person but as contests about linkage or articulation concerning what the act should properly be seen as being an example of and, hence, where it 'belongs'. In this way, words do not work to 'map on to' or 'represent' a fixed underlying reality but rather to establish or fix a version of what is real. Reality is, in this sense, essentially contestable.

To expand upon the earlier example, to call someone 'rebellious' is (in one reading of this word) to make a case for them which claims that their way of Being should properly be seen as a challenge to unwanted authority. The same person or action gets situated differently (associated with and distinguished from a different set of qualities) when, for example, they get called 'delinquent' (which implies neglect, failing and lack). Many contests or arguments do not concern 'the facts' but rather 'where' a way of being properly belongs. They are, in other words, exactly what objectivist psychology claims not to be concerned about (and everywhere builds in) – disagreements about moral place. Psychological characterizations such as 'well adjusted', 'internally controlled', no less than popular ones such as 'greedy', 'crafty', 'considerate', 'faithful', involve implicit judgements as to how people ought to act if they are to be considered 'decent' and 'worthy'. As put by Sabini and Silver: 'characters are earned and squandered; they are warranted by behaviour, although not necessarily predictive of behaviour. Our character language is rooted in our needs to encourage and discourage, praise and blame, reward and punish, ourselves and others' (1982: 10).

What this does, as we have seen before in other contexts in this book, is to re-locate the notion of 'self' back into the arenas of moral and practical concern. It liberates it from the dungeon into which psychology had thrown it, mouldering away (out of sight, out of mind from 'real life'). The self becomes recast as an integral moment and movement within the 'cultural politics of everyday life' (Shotter, 1993b). If, as we have maintained, the construction of an identity (the significance of one's self) is simultaneously the construction of (the significance of) one's world, then it is within this mutually constructive relationship that we dwell. We do not simply live within the physical or geographical spaces of our houses, towns and cities but in the meaningful space of our relationship to our circumstances. This raises the important question of what is our proper or appropriate place? Do we belong within our dwelling place? What and who determines the answers to these questions?

I.I. To me they are political questions, was that the answer you were looking for?

Sort of; here's how Shotter (1993b: 192) deals with these concerns:

But: 'Who belongs and what does belonging mean in practice?' (Hall and Held, 1989: 175). In this new politics what seems to be at stake is not the possession of material property as such, but access to opportunities to give shape and form to one's own life, that is, access to what earlier I called 'a political economy of developmental opportunities' that limits who or what we can become. For we cannot just position ourselves as we please; we face differential invitations and barriers to all the 'movements' (actions and utterances) we try to make in relation to others around us . . . such a politics can be formulated as an 'identity politics' or 'politics of citizenship'.

4 Between Ourselves

I.I. Right, I've got chapter 3. In critical social psychology, there's no person 'ticking' to be discovered. But surely the core of any kind of social psychology isn't personality anyway but human interaction?

Orientation

The social psychology which we are bringing under critical scrutiny traces its own origins (cf. Murphy, 1929) to the last decade of the nineteenth century when psychologists first brought their newly wrought 'scientific methods' to the study of social life. As Murphy goes on to argue there were three fields of inquiry which shaped the domain:

- The first is the study of the influence of groups on individual behaviour. (p. 298)
- A second field is the measurement of personality traits, with special reference to traits which are important for social contacts. (p. 299)
- A third field comprises the attempts to measure such phenomena as public opinion. (p. 299)

The latter two of these ventures are considered in other chapters (particularly 3 and 6 respectively); here we are most concerned with the first, the influence of groups on individual behaviour – and, more generally, human interaction. We have chosen to call this chapter 'Between Ourselves' because this phrase can be taken in several different ways, each of which provides an entrée into an area of social psychological interest.

- First, 'between ourselves', in indicating the relationships (interplays, interactions) between more than one person, can mean simply 'in company'. Thus the title points in an obvious way towards the 'social' in social psychology. However, what the 'social' in social psychology actually means is far from obvious and has been the subject of much debate and controversy.
- Second, it has connotations of shared privacy or secrecy, as when we keep something 'between ourselves'. Social psychology, as a science of the social, has made it its business to try to find out about other people's business. This raises the issue of the contentious role psychology plays in observing and sometimes interfering in matters which are usually kept 'between ourselves'.
- Finally, and somewhat more cryptically, the phrase can be read as alluding to that which exists in the gaps or interstices between our selves. This can point towards the different ways in which people are joined and separated, marked off and grouped, divided and merged both within and outwith themselves.

Conventional approaches

From its beginnings, social psychology both took and developed two major tools from the box of human science methods. One was psychological measurement (psychometrics) – mainly brought to the issues of personality and attitude (see above). The other was experimentation, in which the purported causal (or independent) variables controlling our social conduct were manipulated in order to study their effects upon behaviour (the so-called dependent variable). Here is how another historian of social psychology has described this experimental thrust: 'The first experimental problem – and indeed the only problem for the first three decades of experimental research – was formulated as follows: What changes in an individual's normal solitary performance occur when other people are present?' (Allport, 1954: 46).

Thus, the way in which social psychology had conventionally defined itself and its purpose is relatively simple to state: it is concerned with being acted upon and acting upon others.

I.I. Now we're getting into social psychology, aren't we?

Well – before turning to human interaction per se we want to position mainstream social psychology's approach to human interaction reflexively. In other words, to apply to it an important analytic in any critical scrutiny of a modernistic venture – to ask, using its own language: What is the exchange when we interact with social psychology? We are offered a benefit – we would be well also to wonder 'What is the cost?'

Among those costs with which critical writers tend to be most concerned are those that influence the way in which we are thereby enouraged to constitute the issue or concern in question. Clearly, how we come to constitute an issue or concern enables and disenables our construction of 'what to do about it'. That is, it takes us directly into social policy and into the domain of the political and the moral. In this case, we highlight that:

- not only have social psychologists raised questions around how the thoughts, feelings, decisions and actions of individuals are affected, shaped, changed and otherwise influenced by the (imaginary or real) presence of others.
- but also that, thereby, social psychologists have regularly committed themselves, whether knowingly or tacitly, to an individualistic and dualistic stance where 'the social' is understood only inasmuch as it impacts upon the 'individual' (the cost).

This point can be brought out most clearly by looking briefly at some key historical moments in the history of the discipline.

I.I. For agnostics, you don't half come over like the Salvation Army sometimes – always a sermon before the meal. I hope my patience is now going to be rewarded with something I can get my teeth into.

Triplett and the dynamogenics of reeling

The studies of Triplett (1898) provide a good starting point, as these are generally considered to be the first social-psychological experiments. On noticing, amongst other things, that cyclists who race together tend to achieve faster times than those who race alone or with pacemakers, Triplett devised a series of experiments which enabled him to demonstrate that children who are given a fishing reel and instructed to reel in the line tend to do so faster when in the company of other children than when alone. This led Triplett to talk of the 'dynamogenic' influence of the presence of others, and this in turn inspired subsequent generations of social psychologists to develop a theory of 'social facilitation'. Now, with the help of this label, on any occasion in which a person (or any other creature – Zajonc et al., 1969 added a new dimension to experimental social psychology by using cockroaches!) does something faster, or differently in some other way, when in company compared to when alone, this can be called a 'social facilitation effect'.

I.I. But aren't there times when having other people around slows you down?

Funny you should mention that. The best known example is what happens to men in shared urinals! (Middlemist et al., 1976). In cases like that the term used is, of course, 'social inhibition'.

I.I. It's easy when you know how.

Box 4.1   The 'Science' of Social Facilitation

When Triplett called the presence of others 'dynamogenic' he was simply saying that, for whatever reason, we go faster when others are present. But 'dynamogenic' is a tricky and scientific-sounding word which implies the trace of an explanation as well a description. Triplett's 'dynamogene' would probably best translate into modern psychologese as 'drive' (cf. Hull, 1943) – an internal force of energy which pushes us in a given direction.

It has been established for some time in general experimental psychology that 'drive' (like 'dynamogenesis') can both raise and lower performance. Zajonc (1965) (to be remembered as the 'man who reached for the roach') developed these notions into a particularly florid example of ultra-scientific social-psychological theory. He argued that animals (including people) are designed by nature in such a way that the mere presence of others acts as a stimulus which increases 'arousal'. Unlike 'drive', which carries – like its ordinary-language synonym *motivation* – connotations of goal-directedness, 'arousal' is more of a pre-condition (its ordinary-language synonym would be *alertness*). Thus – according to Zajonc – the presence of others makes us more alert. However, and this is the 'master-stroke' to the theory, being more alert has very specific effects on what we do. It strengthens the dominant response to a stimulus. Hence (!?), sometimes we get better (facilitated) and sometimes we get worse (inhibited). QED.

I.I. Come on. You are really setting up Zajonc as a 'straw man'/'grass man' aren't you? There's got to be better in experimental social psychology than that.

To be fair, even within mainstream social psychology, most found Zajonc's 'theory' a trifle simplistic. The result has been three decades of such cries as 'we need to do some more research' and 'yet more research is needed'. Probably the best known of several less cognitively challenged alternatives was offered by Cottrell (1972), who noted that if others are present when we are doing something we tend to compare ourselves with them and perhaps even worry about what they think of us and how well we are performing. There is certainly some 'face-valid' appeal to the idea that it is not some abstract, diffuse 'other' that effects us, for good or ill, but a specific, evaluating one.

However, it seems equally plausible to us that most people sometimes appreciate, sometimes depreciate, competition and scrutiny according to their circumstances (cf. Chapter 3). It also seems to us hardly a matter of experiment that it is difficult to compete with or feel judged by no one. This more 'common-sense' reading of the phenomenon is not, however, going to satisfy the conventional social psychologist. A large part of the appeal of social facilitation theory for her or him is that it can be read as indicating the existence of a universal social psychological 'law' tied in to hypothetical innate internal mechanisms and processes (like 'arousal').

Any such totalizing theory (one which aims to reduce all complexity to a single simple underlying principle) can be called 'social' only if an extremely restricted understanding of the word is adopted. Zajonc's theory, for example, is social only in the sense that the 'stimulus' which is thought to 'trigger' the 'response' or effect is the presence of other people (or conspecifics). As is usual in psychology, over the years a vast amount of research has accumulated around this small seed of an idea (see Guerin, 1986), most of which consists in wrangles about which experiments support which of the different (but equally totalitarian) competing explanations of the social facilitation effect.

I.I. I can't believe that the social psychology of human interaction is always focused upon the laboratory. Isn't there a social psychology of everyday life?

Le Bon and the problem with crowds

Another figure who has been a big influence on social psychology is Gustave Le Bon. His work provides a good illustration of the extent to which supposedly neutral and objective ideas can be saturated with the ethical and political values and concerns of the historical and cultural moment. His major work (1895) explored the characteristics of crowds and, although he warned against viewing crowds 'only . . . from the point of view of their criminal acts' (p. 63), his work nevertheless reflected the prevailing ethos amongst the rich and powerful of the time (perhaps any time): 'To-day the claims of the masses are becoming more and more sharply defined, and amount to nothing less than a determination to utterly destroy society as it now exists' (1895: 17).

Having personally witnessed the events of the Paris Commune in 1872, Le Bon, like many of his class, was highly fearful for the future of his civilization. He saw that Modernity had brought with it the erosion of traditional ways and beliefs and had left a 'gap' which led the masses in their crowds to 'act like those microbes which hasten the dissolution of enfeebled or dead bodies' (p. 19). A key part of Le Bon's theory is the idea that people in crowds somehow lose the capacity to restrain their 'reflex actions' and hence degenerate to a primitive, inferior and bestial stage – which Le Bon associated with the ordinary state of 'women, savages and children' (p. 40)!

This may sound like the bleatings of an ideologue – which of course it is – but it also taps a deep vein of metaphor, which can be traced via Hobbes back at least as far as Plato. The basic idea here is that in stable circumstances a 'social' or 'civil' skin (the 'thin veneer' of socialization or civil-ization) contains and keeps in check the 'beast within'. This, in its many variations and manifestations, has been one of the most influential ideas of modern times (the same trope is used in different ways by such figures as Durkheim and Freud).

I.I. Come on, not content with pontificating on Le Bon, you've now added two more figures whose place is surely in the history of social psychology. We're ninety years or more on now. What about the present-day social psychology of crowds?

The transit from Le Bon to Zajonc is not only a temporal one, there is also a massive shift in terms of operations – a reduction in scale from naturalistic observation to laboratory experiment. In general, the intervening years were not marked by a major interest within mainstream social psychology in crowds and mass phenomena per se. Among writers of broadly adopted core textbooks, probably only Brown (1965) gave the topic as a whole serious space and analysis. Even today, the Le Bon inheritance still marks the treatment of crowds and mass phenomena. Typical of current textbook coverage is that of Aronson et al. (1994) where the two examples dealt with are: the Orson Wells 'Martian' panic of 1938 (cf. Cantrill, 1940) which resulted from his radio docu-drama treatment of H. G. Wells's *War of the Worlds* being taken as 'truth'; and instances of 'mass psychogenic illness' (e.g. the phantom anaesthetist of Mattoon cf. Johnson, 1945). Both are read as examples of 'informational influence' ultimately acting at the individual level.

The ideology of the self-contained individual

Any social psychology which grows up amongst these kinds of ideas is likely to inherit not only a very singular and limited understanding of what 'social' means, but also an antisocial stance – with a suspicion, even a fear, of the power and the moral impact of the social world. Consequently this leads to a valorization of those who can stand apart from and above the madding crowd. 'Conformity' is seldom seen as other than a problem, 'deindividuation' as leading to a loosening of constraints against deviant behaviour. Unlike the case with social facilitation theory – which implies that our performance can improve when in company – the implicit message or sub-text of material in the Le Bon tradition is that we function most efficiently and most appropriately when alone (or at least away from crowds). Indeed experimental social psychology from its earliest days (e.g. Ringlemann, 1913) set out to study how individual output fell when tasks were pooled. There is even a very instructive name for this 'social disease' as Latané et al. (1979) dubbed it – *social loafing*. Following Sampson (1989) we can see that a social psychology grounded upon such an antisocial stance makes sense when one's prevailing cultural ideology is that of 'self-contained individualism'.

I.I. What I'm getting from this is that you see mainstream social psychology as being wrongfully individualistic, but isn't it part of the job of a science of behaviour to look for general laws of human nature? And where could those be sought except in individuals?

Box 4.2. 'Human Nature': Given or Made?

As we have noted elsewhere, scientistic psychology was foundationed upon ideas of universal laws of 'human nature', paralleling the universal laws of 'nature' of nineteenth-century natural science. By contrast, the critical notion of 'self-contained individualism' stems from the 'climate of perturbation'. This argues that ideas of 'human nature' and the 'human condition' are local and contingent. Scientistic psychology's fundamental error was to mistake the social constructions of nineteenth-century

Western society as universal truths. Yet that society was, in so many respects, new – hence, its characterization as Modern. Industrialization, urbanization, bureaucratization and other aspects of Western Moderniza- tion (such as the undermining of much of the authority of the church by science and philosophy) brought with them both a new valorization of independent rational thought and an undermining of traditional forms of relating and conceiving of personal identity. With the development of capitalism people were increasingly placed in new relationships to their work, to each other, and to the world (for example, more and more people moved to cities and worked in factories and bureaucracies), and these new relationships fostered and favoured, according to Weber (1978), rational and instrumental ways of thinking, talking and acting. Within such a 'climate of rational instrumentality' certain ways of talking and acting are newly positioned or constructed as irrational and abnormal, and a concern is developed for locating and explaining sources of distortion and error.

Were, for example, a teacher to insist that a given group of children must enter the classroom in silence, stand behind their chairs for five seconds and place their hands on their heads for three seconds before sitting down to start work, then it is clear that, as a direct result of this organization, the teacher has created (quite deliberately and in the name of 'discipline') extensive possibilities for disobedience and error (which might then be construed as irrationality, abnormality or 'badness', see Foucault, 1977). However, such matters are not usually considered to be the product of a way of seeing, organizing or relating to the world. More usually they are passed off as belonging to the world itself: as being the 'really real reality' of delinquency and pathology.

In various ways social psychology has contributed to this 'reification' (the fallacy of mistaking what is humanly constructed for natural reality) by generating theories which presuppose that the natural state of person- hood is self-contained individuality. In this way what is actually a culturally and historically specific and humanly constructed way of organizing relationships 'between ourselves' is re-presented as a normal and unchangeable fact of nature. This tendency towards reification is not simply the result of 'bad science' or a misguided theory, it is built into the metaphysics of the very conceptual model utilized by much conventional psychology. This model, when simplified, contains three basic steps:

1 The external world exists in a real, indisputable way.
2 Everything between ourselves would be fine if only the world were perceived by everyone objectively, i.e. as it really is.

3 Unfortunately, the rationality which would give us true information about the world is compromised at many points and levels by distortions resulting from the limitations of the human mind and the social structures it has created.

Social psychology tends to concern itself with distortions from rationality that result from the influence of other people (whether these distortions be facilitations or limitations). This (usually unspoken) agenda not only severely restricts the meaning of the word 'social': it actually obscures from view the social arrangements which make such an agenda feasible in the first place. This is why writers of Marxist, feminist and other critical persuasions have argued that psychology is an ideology which supports a status quo definition of rationality and what is real (e.g. Brown, 1974; Wilkinson, 1986). The fact that the 'real world' has been organized and constructed in a particular way for the benefit of some people and to the disadvantage (not to mention death) of others is ignored, just as the 'real world' of the classroom is organized by the teacher – or rather by those who tell the teacher what to do. Instead, this reality is delivered to us as the objectivity against which the natural failings of our subjectivity can be measured.

I.I. End of party political broadcast? Anyway, aren't you doing just the same thing but with a different politics?

If there is any merit in our assessment, then social psychology must be seen not just as a way of studying matters between ourselves but also as an attempt to foster and encourage certain ways of Being, whilst discouraging other ways of being. We would not deny that this also applies to our own work. Where we see the difference lies in the emphasis placed in critical work on acknowledging this inevitable knowledge/power synarchy, employing it reflexively, and in denying it a foundation or warrant (such as claims to scientificality or professional status).

The influence of Le Bon on theories of influence

Le Bon's book on crowds contains some basic 'seeds' which soon became large snowballs as they rolled down the snowy slopes of history, accumulating experimental data and accreting theoretical sophistications as they went. Apart from the obvious influence upon the continued study of crowds (cf. Brown, 1965; Moscovici, 1988), Le Bon also made some observations that contain the theoretical bones of the social-psychological study of conformity. He talks, for example, of 'collective hallucinations' which are distortions of the external world suffered by people in crowds as a result of processes of 'contagion' and 'suggestibility' (1895: 47): 'it is not necessary that a crowd should be numerous for the . . . real facts to be replaced by hallucinations unrelated to them. As soon as a few individuals are gathered together . . . the faculty of observation and the critical spirit possessed by each of them individually at once disappears' (pp. 48–9).

Whilst Le Bon was content to illustrate his observation with 'real world' examples such as the misrecognition of accident victims and the magic tricks of Monsieur Davey (a previous incarnation of Tommy Cooper), classic social psychology (e.g. Sherif, 1935 and Asch, 1959) strove to reproduce these phenomena under controlled laboratory conditions. These studies are good examples of research informed by the view that intersubjectivity distorts objectivity.

Here comes the Sherif

In his classic experiments into mutual 'suggestibility' Sherif (1935) took advantage of the autokinetic effect, whereby a pinpoint of light which is objectively fixed and unmoving appears subjectively to move about (when presented in a dark room). Sherif discovered that despite the fact that individuals differ in their judgements as to how much the light appears to move, when brought together in a group their judgements gradually converge upon a 'group norm'. Sherif also found that when this procedure is reversed and subjects are asked to give their judgements when grouped first and subsequently when alone, the 'convergence effect' which results from being in the group lingers on and influences the estimate when made alone.

I.I. Sounds less like an experiment and more like one of those dreadful party games to me – as in 'Let's turn off all the lights and look at this little light.'

We know somebody who met her husband just so – which does at least imply that experiments can have some purpose! But to get serious, this study opened the research floodgates and before long experiments had been conducted exploring such matters as:

- how long the effect might last (Rohrer et al. 1954)
- whether it is dependent upon subjects' expectations about the movement of the stimulus (Sperling, 1946)

- whether the effect is dependent upon the subjects' degree of liking for one another (Sampson and Insko, 1964)
- whether the established norms can be transmitted to new 'generations' of subjects (Jacobs and Campbell, 1961), and, more generally
- whether or not there exists a 'conformist personality' and an 'optimum group size' for effective influence (Krech, Crutchfield and Ballachey, 1962).

However, by the time most of the above studies had been conducted, a new paradigm had emerged – one which was very much a spectacle of its times.

Asch – or 'size does matter'

In the wake of the Second World War, the Nuremberg Trials and then a new, communist 'evil empire' occupying half of Europe, conformity (except to Senator McCarthy's views on 'American values', of course) had a special negative value in the USA of the early 1950s. Social psychology met that concern with conformity with a vengeance through Asch's famous studies (1952, 1956, 1959).

If we refer back once more to the three-step model discussed earlier in this chapter, we see that Sherif's paradigm had one crucial missing element: there were no 'real' (externally verifiable) phenomena involved – all the movements, small or large, were but apparent. Asch introduced a direct criterion of distortion. He achieved this by presenting a subject with two or three lines and asking them to judge which of these was most similar in length to a comparison line which was simultaneously presented. The subject is asked to make his or her judgement in the company of various other people (usually up to ten) who, unbeknownst to the subject, are stooges or confederates of the experimenter. Each stooge in turn makes their respective judgement, followed by the subject. On certain pre-specified trials the confederates are told to make incorrect judgements in order that the effect of this on the subject's decision may be observed. Some of the stooges' judgements were so obviously wrong that the subjects often appeared incredulous and even anxious. Nevertheless, some 33 per cent of subjects 'conformed' on half or more of the trials, whilst 5 per cent conformed on all. About 25 per cent did not conform at all (which, we are told, very much surprised Asch and his colleagues). Asch invented numerous variations on this theme in order to assess which variables were contributing to the effect. For example, he found that nobody conformed when only one confederate was involved, and having an 'ally' present who judged accurately tended to reduce conformity dramatically. Also, strong conformity effects were found when three confederates were present, but having more than three made little difference to the effect.

As might be expected, these studies raised the question of why these subjects came to orientate their avowed judgements towards the incorrect judgements of the confederates. Initially, simplistic notions of susceptibility to 'power' held the day – after all, women seemed to conform more than men! However, simply to dub this reaction 'conformity' is clearly to stick a vague and thought-smothering label on a potentially complex form of conduct. The current 'wisdom' on the issue suggests that while the Sherif paradigm produces 'real' or 'private' conformity, the Asch paradigm merely generates 'surface' or 'public' conformity. Another way of putting this (cf. Deutsch and Gerard, 1955) is to say that subjects in Sherif's studies were actively seeking information and guidance from their peers in an ambiguous situation ('informational social influence'), while subjects in Asch's studies were caving in under uncomfortable group pressure ('normative social influence').

I.I. But you, of course, know better?

As critical social psychologists, we, however, would question the view of people implied by this analysis – as we would question the very notion of inner essences of mind, like attitudes, that change when we 'change our mind' rather than just 'play along' (see Chapter 6). Nevertheless, saying that is far from saying that we think the consequences of 'conformity' are things we do not need to be concerned about. On the contrary, precisely because we adopt a transdisciplinary stand, we are open to all the evidence on offer about how, given the circumstances, humans will mistreat one another – whether that comes from history, groups like Amnesty International or wherever. For many social psychologists, however (and this seems to reflect the social catchments from which they are drawn as much as the theories they employ), gross acts of cruelty seem to bring out special attributional explanations, specifically a pathology either in the perpetrator or in their socio-cultural situation (or, of course, in their 'interaction'!). Or at least they did until the studies of Stanley Milgram (1963).

Stan, Stan the electrodes man

The basic Milgram paradigm is so widely used as a parable of 'man's inhumanity to man' (for once we'll leave the gender-marker – on the whole it is deserved) that we will do no more here over the study than reiterate the outcome: 'Faced with experimenter demands to continue administering (apparently) real electric shocks of from 15 volts to 450 volts (remember that is 4 times the North American mains level of 110 volts) to an increasingly protesting (and finally silent) "learner" – 65% of subject "teachers" went "all the way" to 450 volts.' As the original subjects were drawn not from some 'extreme group' or 'pathological population' but from a range of ordinary US citizens (not for once just students), this was seen as a 'shocking' result, prompting one researcher to wonder 'Are we all Nazis?' (Askenasy, 1978). From the start, the ethics of Milgram's study (because of both the deception involved and the evident distress that subjects experienced) were challenged. Far less challenged was the necessity for the study in the first place. Indeed, that necessity was often argued for on the grounds that the result was 'unexpected' – it did not match what similar people *said* they would do. Also on the precept that 'strong diseases need strong medicines' it was argued that destructive obedience was such a threat to humankind (this was still Cold War days) that the benefits of Milgram's work outweighed the costs.

I.I. And don't they? Doesn't every generation, particularly in 'good times', in 'good places', need such reminders?

Box 4.3 'Who Shall Judge the Judges?'

Perhaps the key issue over the Milgram studies is not their message but the manner of its deliverance – as 'scientific research'. Using value-added 'scientificality' to promote a politico-moral point has a less than happy history itself. This was exactly what the eugenicists did in promoting the sterilization of 'incorrigibles'. What this can do is to stifle debate through mystification – many will feel they cannot challenge 'the evidence' because they lack access to the specialized knowledge it claims to be based upon.

The argument that we can rely on other scientists to do that job does not solve the political problem of leaving it up to 'them'. Rather, it compounds the problem, leaving the warrant of scientificality itself unexamined.

Two further important critical analyses regarding the Milgram studies are worth emphasizing. First, how good is the argument that the study is informative because it surprises us? Does the surprise then lie in ordinary US citizens being destructively obedient? This does seem to have been what surprised other US citizens. To understand that we have to look to the times. In 1963 Kennedy was President (he was to be assassinated in Dallas on 22 November). It was a point at which most US citizens still felt they had 'God on our side'. This was before the events of 1968 (from the Chicago Convention to the My Lai massacre). The 'surprise', in other words, was a very local one in terms of both time and place – destructive obedience seemed 'out of place' in the New Camelot.

Second, how informative is the study as a paradigm of destructive obedience per se? Social psychology has always been prone to exaggerating the 'external validity' of laboratory studies. Probably the most extreme case has been arguing that two-person 'games' such as the Prisoner's Dilemma informed us about the traps of the Cold War. At best Milgram's study mimics short-term obedience, with one 'victim', in an unfamiliar context. Thrown into the unknown his subjects seemed to lack a 'script' for saying 'no'. By contrast, much 'real life' destructive obedience is long-term, with many victims, and takes place in a familiar context. This was as true for German concentration camp guards as it was for the Allied aircrews who fire-bombed Dresden.

The power of the Milgram studies then, we suspect, lies elsewhere (cf. Box 4.3). Specifically, they exemplify social psychology as mission. They were warranted (at the time) by that mission because they epitomized its self-declared authority to teach moral lessons, to act as the voice of the liberal-humanistic conscience. There are two painful paradoxes here. The first is that the very forms of destructive obedience about which the Milgram study claims to teach us (e.g. the Nazi experience) were themselves part of the same ethos – albeit perverted. The extermination camps too were used for 'scientific experiments'. The second paradox, of course, for all who would teach us moral lessons in this way, is that to make them effective, to 'hit home', someone has to get hurt. In Milgram's case it was his own subjects who were positioned into moral torment by the experimenter's demands to continue the shocks. However, the depths of just how low this missionary zeal was to take experimental social psychology were yet to be plumbed.

'Collect $15 a day and go to jail'

Perhaps nothing better epitomizes the troubles of Modernism than its response to deviance – containment. While prisons well predated Modernism, large-scale, long-term incarceration of offenders is a product of the nineteenth century which the twentieth century has retained and expanded, despite its manifest failure either to deter or to reform. Compared to the conditions inmates can expect outside, the present-day prison is far worse than its nineteenth-century equivalent. Furthermore, all evidence suggests that even in absolute terms, the twentieth-century prison is more violent, more corrupt than its nineteenth-century equivalent. Riots in US prisons in the 1970s highlighted this crisis. What more 'natural' then that the horrors of 'prisonerization' (Sutherland and Cressey, 1974) should be given the 'Milgram-treatment'?

In the basement of the Psychology Department of the prestigious Stanford University, Haney, Banks and Zimbardo (1973) built themselves a prison – complete with iron-barred cells and a solitary-confinement/ punishment room. They populated it with volunteers, pre-recruited for a fourteen-day study, who were randomly assigned to the 'roles' of either prisoner or jailer. For the prisoners this could mean being picked up from their lodgings by a police car, handcuffed, searched and unceremoniously bundled into the back of a police car. At the jail they were then stripped, deloused (!), had a chain bolted to their ankle, given a numbered smock, and confined to a demanded silence.

By now, the 'Zimbardo prison study' has passed into folk history and it is not always easy to separate the myth from the actuality. What is clear is that the effects were dramatic: guards soon become bullies, prisoners passive and demoralized. The experiments had to be terminated after six days – not just to the great relief of the subjects but, it is said, much to the chagrin of the jailers!

The 'Zimbardo prison study' is often presented in textbooks as teaching important lessons about the way in which power corrupts. By which is meant, of course, the effects of the simulated prison environment upon the subjects (particularly the jailers). Less often discussed is the way in which the power of social psychology made possible a more disguised corruption – namely, the building of that simulated jail, the setting up of that study and its maintenance even when its effects were clear. It is beyond belief that, say, a Department of German covering the Hitler years or a Department of Russian covering the Stalin years would have felt able to (or been able to) do something similar. Only the story of the unique informativeness of human science and its established history of experimentation (dubious and otherwise) warrants the Zimbardo prison study – and it is a warrant that demands critique.

I.I. This sounds like we're in for the attack on Milgram all over again – science claiming special status and all that. Can we hear something new?

What we are suggesting about the warrant here takes the critical argument a stage further. What in the case of the Zimbardo study the warrant makes possible, in addition to self-corruption, is to hide the agenda behind the demonstration. Haney, Banks and Zimbardo were able to produce the misbehaviour they 'wanted' only because they were able to build a jail that made it possible. But this is, of course, exactly what happens in society at large. Jailing is warranted and funded (psychology even provides prison psychologists to service it!). Mainstream social psychology is too much part of the order of its society to take any political commitment beyond preaching the gospel of liberal-humanism. The abstract lesson that 'power corrupts', and we can all be so corrupted, does nothing to address the conditions that permit it, other than to leave us with the same old picture (with a few new refinements such as the effects of 'proximity' and 'status'; cf. Milgram, 1974) of the individual being 'corrupted' by the influence of the 'social' (indeed in other studies Zimbardo has explicitly set out to study what he calls 'de-individuation') (Zimbardo, 1970).

Box 4.4 'Resisting The Discipline'

The core critical argument here is that the very divisions of social science enable social psychology to dodge out of other levels of explanation because they are someone else's business (the sociologist's, the political scientist's, the criminologist's). To be told that 'nice people' can in certain circumstances become 'nasty people' may be a useful rhetorical ploy in arguing against crude essentialists or political conservatives who insist that such matters are purely personal ethical concerns. But any such rhetoric, critical psychologists argue, should be backed up with an analysis of how these circumstances arose in the first place and what may be done to change them. For these questions, of course, there are no simple answers, and no scientific laws to be discovered, for they are questions about the complex social worlds that we have built 'between ourselves'.

Race relations?

I.I. Many, particularly the young, might agree that we have 'inherited' a pretty nasty world from the past. Social psychology has, at least, tried to suggest solutions. It's why some of us got to study it, for what it has to say about things like racism and sexism. Are you really saying we and they are wasting our time?

From a critical perspective, the trouble with explaining social psychological issues at the level of 'individual distortion' can be brought out most starkly by looking at a frankly political issue like racism. Social psychologists have tackled this issue, often with the best of intentions, on numerous occasions. An early attempt was mady by Adorno et al. (1950) who formulated the theory of the 'authoritarian personality' in order better to understand fascism. Couched, in part, in psychoanalytic terms of sexual repression and submerged aggressive impulses, the theory holds that the authoritarian personality is born of an upbringing characterized by rigidity, discipline and strictness (see Chapter 3). The authoritarian personality thus projects or scapegoats its aggression and frustration on to minority groups. In this way racism is explained in terms of the personality problems of the racist individual.

But as Henriques et al. (1984) point out, such a formulation not only distracts attention away from institutionalized racism, it also fails to answer the key questions of why particular minority groups in particular historical periods become the targets of racisms. Further, such an approach provides no means of understanding the kind of racism that locally passes for common sense and that seems to require no personal 'pathology' (as existed, for example, under the old – and happily now rescinded – South African apartheid system). In other words, it adheres to the three-step model we described earlier in this chapter (see pp. 77–8).

Adorno et al. were not the only psychologists to reduce racism to the level of individual prejudice or stereotyping. Allport and Postman (1947) and Allport (1954), for example, laid the ground for the research tradition of 'attitudinalizing' prejudice (and thereby, of course, individualizing it within the cognitive-affective systems of individuals). The basic claim of this approach is that social categorization is an inevitable feature of our 'social perceptual apparatus' – we see individuals as members of particular groups with particular attributes.

Equally we in some way fundamentally favour our own group over outgroups. The result is a rapid categorization of other groups, which results in distorted and irrational perception which is emotionally based. Two 'rational' strategies for dealing with prejudice follow. First, informational – the provision or acquisition of more 'accurate' information about the group or of some individual from the group who can thus then be seen as an individual without the qualities that are prejudicially attributed. Second, motivational – we can be paid in some way to make the effort to overcome prejudice: this may be no more than the emergence of a superordinate common goal or common enemy (cf. Sherif, 1966).

Of course, when Allport first formulated these ideas (and racism – as segregation – was official policy throughout the Southern States of the USA) it was never hard to elicit racial stereotypes and illustrate their effects upon social judgement. But times change. 'New' forms of prejudice have been identified, most notably sexism, while old forms are said to have mutated from an explicit racism publicly opined into an implicit racism which requires the 'subtlety' of deceptive laboratory techniques to be 'truly' tapped. What has not significantly shifted over the years is the model. The metaphor is still of an individual disorder: 'In modern racism, the overt symptoms have changed, but the underlying disease remains' (Brehm and Kassin, 1990: 176).

The notion that racism in the United States (where the above quotation comes from) or indeed in the UK has moved into some subtle form may be true of the 'politically correct' from whom social psychologists and their student subjects are generally drawn. However, it hardly describes US or UK culture in general. Rather, as critical social psychologists like Billig have argued, there has been a subtle and cynical shift in political rhetoric over racism in which:

> the image of fairness can be maintained by invoking the frightening image of extremism . . . For example, before the British general election of 1979 the Conservative leader, Margaret Thatcher, was able to use the rhetoric of racism (talking of Britain being 'swamped' by immigrants) while of course denying that she, or the Conservatives, were racist. Significantly, this increase in racist rhetoric was accompanied by a direct reference to the National Front (an uncommon reference in Conservative statements at that time). By raising the image of the unacceptable extreme, the balance is permitted to tilt towards the extreme, and the proof that 'we' are not racist (because 'we' oppose the extreme racists of the National Front) becomes mixed with the justification for the racist rhetoric. (1982: 218–19)

The study of rhetoric – not as a laboratory exercise in experimental social psychology but in the actuality of current politics – is a bold move. It involves not just a shift in methodology towards a 'discourse analysis' approach (cf. Chapter 11) but also a shift away from the notion of racism as inner essence towards the notion of racism as discursive (specifically argumentative) practice. It is one which meets the radical critique of the old metaphor: 'the conditions in which the social psychology of racial prejudice was progressive have been superseded. The racist *status quo* is maintained to a large extent not only through coercive and blatant racist practices, but through the liberal position which criticises these as aberrations' (Henriques et al., 1984: 88)

What, then, does a critical social psychology itself have to say about racism and about anti-racist practice? To begin, critical social psychological research into racism is conducted precisely because the existing research is held to be flawed. As a result, it seeks to avoid building into its own research those problems it identifies in the mainstream. The result is a stress on the particulars of particular racisms (not, of course, as a way of talking the issue away!). The racism of Margaret Thatcher (see above) should not be assumed to be that of the skinhead (if you trust that stereotype!). Crucial to this is avoiding the imperialism whereby the US social psychology story of racism becomes *the* story by sheer volume of output.

Useful in that regard are efforts that stress difference (e.g. between US and Dutch conceptualizations; cf. Essed, 1991). An alternative approach to highlighting diversity is to work in less-researched locations. A good example here is Wetherell and Potter's (1992) discourse analytic coverage of racism in New Zealand. In general, discourse analytic approaches to racism (see also Potter and Wetherell, 1987) are valuable in exposing the passing 'reasonableness' of racist rhetoric, the way it features all the complex, meandering and self-referential qualities of any talk (cf. also Van Dyke, 1992). Critical social psychologists would also see the need to explore discourse in the broadest sense. Through cultural studies approaches, it becomes possible to explore not just racism-the-product but also racism-the-production – how it is built into education systems and cultural forms like films, novels and television. Tourism too is a prime site of racist production – as a quick scan of the ephemera carried back home through airports as souvenirs will show you.

If in its research into racism critical social psychology tries to avoid totalizing theorization and remain 'alive to the event', it makes no secret of its political engagement in its research. From a critical perspective, of course, research can never just 'be' in some political and ethical vacuum – it is circumstantial. Note how, for example, Henriques et al. (pp. 60–89) criticize mainstream social psychological work on racism as no longer being 'progressive'. A common, if troublesome, agenda for radicals is empowerment. As Bhavnani points out: 'it is crucial, also, to consider carefully "who is being empowered?" In whose interests does that empowerment serve? For example, Billig's (1978) work on a social psychological analysis of fascists was aimed at *dis*empowering the group he was researching. And so, the empowerment was aimed at those who challenge fascism, not those who espouse it' (1990: 152).

However, the social world seldom presents us with the clear-cut choice of 'which side are you on?' between fascists and those who challenge fascism, as in Bhavnani's example. For instance, 'racial' and gender empowerment may not always work hand in hand, anti-racial discourse may itself become totalizing. The critical social psychology of empowerment must itself remain alive to the circumstances (cf. Chapter 3) of empowerment, not become mystified by the word.

Janus

I.I. I think that last section does give me some sense of critical social psychology working by the reflexions between affirmation and troubling its affirmations. But how then am I meant to take this header? As irony – or literally a looking forward which is also a looking back?
Social psychology: the discipline of studying the problems we have being together and the problems we have being alone. (R.S.R.)

A great deal of history, art, poetry, fiction and song is concerned with the troubled and troublesome time we have both living together and living apart. 'The blues', ballads of unrequited love, Shakespeare's plays of jealousy and betrayal are just a few examples from the English language heritage. The emergence of psychology brought something new to that collection of woes: the promise that they could be 'sorted out' so that we could all live together 'happily ever after'. Recast as 'problems' they take on both common meanings of that word. That is, they become either disorders that can be treated (suited to the medical model of mind) or puzzles or conundrums that can be solved (suited to the rational science of mind).

In other words, psychology can 'fix it'. But to see ourselves as both capable and worthy of such 'adjustment' is not a universal circumstance. It will not tend to be a possibility, for example, if we exist within a cultural location which implies that our condition is natural or supernaturally ordained, or which construes the self (cf. Chapter 3) collectively rather than individually. Many of the ten million or so people under analysis of some kind in the USA, for example, are seeking the sort of help which will enable them to exist comfortably as self-contained individuals (one of the common psychoanalytic themes or motifs is the adult who has not yet achieved 'separation' from the (symbolic or real) mother and who is therefore incapable of 'independence'). The few psychoanalysts working in India, by contrast, more commonly face the opposite problem. Kakar, for example, reports as typical for an Indian client of psychoanalysis the following problem: 'He is very stubborn in pursuing what he wants without taking our wishes into account. He thinks he knows what is best for him and doesn't listen to us. He thinks his own life and career are more important than the concerns of the rest of the family' (1990: 428). In other words, a psychology as we understand it could have emerged only in a cultural location where 'selves' matter. – where, for example, they have come to be economically and politically constituted as possessed of rights: 'We hold these truths to be self-evident: that all men [*sic*] are created equal, that they are endowed by their Creator with certain unalienable rights, that amongst these are life, liberty and the pursuit of happiness' (US Declaration of Independence, 1776).

In practice, the self-same economic and political construction of new 'selves' under Modernism yielded circumstances of flux and change in human lives in which 'selfhood' became 'problem-atic'. Modernism, indeed democracy itself, is grounded on the notion of individual choice. Yet this state of affairs has been constructed 'between ourselves' and can be sustained only by our continued joint effort (even the US constitution was a social product, not Jefferson's alone). Modernization was, in the nineteenth century – arguably it still is – a patchy process. For those who were more 'Modernized' (for example the middle class who provided Freud's patients' notions of choice and rights and the socio-legal changes that reflected them) it brought new problems. Not the least of these problems concerned personal relationships, where the sudden emergence of notions of rights to 'the pursuit of happiness' changed people's possibilities massively. Social psychology's concern with 'human relationships', then, is a concern not with 'human nature' but with a particular form or arrangement of relations between ourselves which is specific to the circumstances of modernity. As Fathali et al. state, 'a Western cultural perspective has led much of social psychology to focus on such relationships as romantic couples and first-time acquaintances, while giving relatively little attention to such relationships as kinship and community . . . in many cultures, kinship relationships would be the dominant relationship of interest' (1993: 94).

Personal relationships

I.I. 'Local and contingent' (as you might say) it may be but the issue of personal relationships certainly has direct relevance to me and my friends. Are you about to 'deconstruct' that too?

Thus far, we have had next to nothing to say about one of the most important sites of action 'between ourselves' in modern culture – our relationships. Here we find a germinal paradox of modernity – that we have a 'selfhood' (wherein lies our right to happiness and fulfilment) but must pursue those rights by action 'between ourselves'.

Box 4.5 Solitary Vices and Collective Pleasures

For the 'Victorian' society in which psychology emerged, self-pleasing, particularly sexual self-pleasing (masturbation), was powerfully proscribed. Yet psychology was soon to form part of a general 'liberalizing' movement in which moral condemnation of selves came to be largely replaced by a form of developmental failing. Thus the sin of selfishness became the condition of egocentrism, the vice of masturbation became the immature sexuality of auto-eroticism and so on. In turn, traditional virtues became recast as signs of maturity and adjustment, as in Freud's notion that the unneurotic adult was marked by a capacity fully to love (i.e. couple heterosexually) and to work. Pleasurable fulfilment became, in psychobabble, something that came 'from really relating to other people'.

As we have noted already more generally, this promotion of a 'secular religion of human relationships' still features vividly in a great deal of the content of US social psychology and the concerns it caters to: intimate relationships; first-time acquaintanceship; long-term friendship and love. As will become clear, the received scientistic conceptual framework upon which this research is grounded – that which mediates attraction, the 'measurement' and differentiation of love and friendship, the co-variance between the personalities, beliefs, desires and attitudes of the involved individuals – is challenged throughout this book.

What we do not challenge for a minute is that these concerns do profoundly matter to modern selves and modern society. Something that we have now come to see as 'relationships' has, at the same time, become seen as problematic. This is, we think, because they have now become things that we have to do – to 'work at', as the jargon has it. They are no longer either just happenstantial events or highly ritualized and formalized social arrangements, but makable, mendable, solvable – not to mention breakable, endable and dissolvable – projects. Compared to pre-modern times, nowadays – on average – we meet more strangers, have far more choice in our relationships and over the exploration of our 'sexual needs and orientations'. And, paradoxically, we see in all this flux and in all these possibilities perhaps the prime site for the development of our self-contained individuality: our selves.

By this we mean that personal relationships have come to be seen as 'personal' inasmuch as they are taken to belong to us-as-persons (and thereby speak, for good or ill, of our personhood). They are 'between ourselves' in the particular sense of speaking to the modern notion of there being a private life (separable from a public life). That is to say, they exist in a space carved out during Modernity between what could for convenience be called 'the public' (that space and time which is the business of others) and 'the private' (that space and time which is ours – for example when we are not selling our labour or promenading ourselves – which we do not expect to be intruded upon or interfered with by unwelcome others).

Box 4.6   Private Facilities and Public Conveniences

Modernity is a mobile way of life, in it people move around constantly, shifting between the private and the public realms. The hotel we travel to may well boast of being 'a home from home' in which all rooms 'have private facilities' where we can pee in the bidet if we choose but are unlikely to contribute a *graffito*. Yet our journey itself is outwith home and during it we may well need to make use of 'public conveniences' where very different rules apply. In the mores of 'relationships' also, the private and the public worlds run by their own distinct codes. In England and Wales, for example, it was established in the 1960s that adult homosexual relationships in private were not 'the law's business' (unless you were employed in the armed forces). The public domain of sexual involvement remained and still remains a province in which only heterosexuality can be safely owned.

Although the relations between the public and the private are, like any question of ownership, complex (we might personally relate to work colleagues, and engaging in sex can be both a pastime and an occupation), the point we wish to make is that precisely because 'relationships' have been delivered to us during Modernity as something 'personal' which we must organize, do, and discover for ourselves, they are a prime source for the construction and reconstruction of selfhood. We (who and what we are) are 'at stake' (tested, proved, found wanting, and otherwise real-ized) in them. And 'we' (the authors) in all of this are writing from our own point of view as white-and-Western — other 'we-s' in other locations would, of course, see things differently.

This sense in which our personal relationships are ongoing constructions which make sense only against the backdrop of certain historical and cultural circumstances has been largely avoided or downplayed within mainstream literature (see Shotter, 1993a and b; Cancian, 1987; Rose, 1990; Stearns and Stearns, 1988 and Stearns, 1989 for notable exceptions). This is largely because such social-psychological literature (and the professional practice it supports) is itself part of these circumstances and involved in these constructions. Nowadays when we have problems with our relationships it is likely to be to psychology that we turn for help and advice, whether directly (through psychotherapy, counselling, 'marriage' guidance or some other psychologically informed practice) or indirectly (through magazine articles and 'problem pages', television chat shows with guest 'expert psychologists', 'self-help' pop psychology books, talk-back radio programmes, and so on).

I.I. Everywhere but here it seems. Are you ever going to stop analysing into paralysis and tell us about some research?

We have avoided specific examples of 'research findings' so far because psychological 'expertise' on matters of personal relationships is so saturated into modern culture. It has become so familiar as a language that it is easy to take-for-granted the extent to which it has replaced other systems of knowledge and advice (such as the church, tradition and 'family wisdom') — and a little 'unlearning is no bad thing'. The 'warrant' for this influence and intervention in matters 'between ourselves' is, of course, the expert and/or scientific status that psychologists can lay claim to. However, to give just an example of what social psychology offers, after twenty-six pages on the science of interpersonal attraction in general, Aronson et al. raise the heading 'Close relationships' and proceed thus:

> After getting to this point in the chapter, you should be in a pretty good position to make a favourable first impression the next time you meet somebody. Suppose you want Claudia to like you. You should hang around her so that you become familiar, act in ways that are rewarding to her, and emphasize your similarity to her. Flattery is likely to get you somewhere,

though if you want to be especially clever, you should be a little critical to start with, and then compliment her profusely. We make no guarantee that you and Claudia will become best friends, but all else being equal, these techniques work pretty well. (1994: 396)

That, for what it is worth, is what the social psychological research has largely been about. What we are offered is a quantification of, largely, US student folk-ways and we see no reason to promote it with further coverage. However, it would be wrong to suggest that psychology as a whole has taken any monolithic stand on personal relationships – particularly when they go wrong. When it comes to the 'sick' relationship the diverse and contestational field of therapy (where values and politics are often most blatantly exposed) there is no such consensus. (Except, that is, for the professional one that it is not only unhelpful but dangerous for non-specialists to meddle in this area.) Among self-styled experts, we can expect considerable disagreement as to the nature of problems and solutions alike. A psychoanalyst, a client-centred therapist, a rational-emotive therapist and a feminist therapist would be very likely to offer radically different assessments and advice on how to deal with, say, a 'failing marriage'. What conjoins them is the simple fact of someone else claiming expertise over what is so personal, close and intimate to us: the problems that arise between ourselves.

To recognize properly the way in which psychology is implicated in, rather than separate from, the construction of relationships in modern times requires moving away from the scientistic discourse of cause/effect and nature/nurture which serves as a warrant for expert intervention into relationship problems. Again, this is not to deny that problems do exist (in the sense that they matter to people), or to proscribe nihilistically any form of intervention, but to draw attention to the possibility that scientistic discourse is *part of the problem*. To develop this argument, it is necessary to look briefly at 'between ourselves' as that is understood by social developmental psychologists and troubled by their critics.

From nature and nurture to fields of possibility

I.I. I suppose now you are going to tell me that I can add to my pile of discarded social psychology books my texts on development and socialization also?

Romulus and Remus, the mythical twin founders of Rome, are said to have been reared by a she-wolf. The investigation of the supposed Wild

Boy of Aveyron played an important part in the development of the post-Enlightenment project (Malson, 1972). Throughout the twentieth century 'wolf-children' and other purportedly feral young humans have been 'discovered' by investigators who should have known a scam when they saw one and would have made better use of their time reading *Tarzan of the Apes*. The lure of the underlying myth throughout is the promise of an answer to the question of just what is 'human' in human nature and what is valued-added through our sociality. The myth resurfaces in the nature/nurture question and has been thoroughly deconstructed from the perspective of critical developmental psychology (Stainton Rogers and Stainton Rogers, 1992a).

From a 'between ourselves' perspective too, it is a non-question, for its very formulation depends upon the existence of an investigating culture posing it as a question. Just as that question is possibly only 'between ourselves', so too are all our human powers. This point was put very forcibly by the science fiction and science writer Arthur C. Clarke when he said: 'It is one of the strangest of all facts, impossible for the sensitive mind to contemplate without melancholy, that for at least 50,000 years there have been men [*sic*] on this planet who could conduct a symphony orchestra, discover theorems in pure mathematics, act as secretaries of the United Nations, or pilot a space ship – had they been given the chance' (1973: 214).

Box 4.7 On Being Always, Ever Social

In 'developmental' terms, this strong statement of sociality argues that no isolated human child could learn to speak; come to think; have a sexuality or a sexual identity; develop a morality; even have any basis to stay alive. To say this is not to deny that such a child would to us (although not to them, for this too is a social concept) have a body. But to relate to a body as a body requires otherbodies and other bodies. We are, in this sense, so fundamentally social, so shot through with the circumstances of our place in time and space and the otherbodies who placed us there, that the idea that there could be a psychology which was not a social psychology, a learning that was not a social learning, a cognition which was not a social cognition, becomes fundamentally unworkable. In this sense a critical social psychology can only come to question the very uniqueness of social psychology as a discipline.

If indeed people are, in those senses, fundamentally social (i.e. their sociality cannot be thought of as separate or separable) then whatever seem to be our limitations, whatever may be our possibilities and powers are themselves also social. They are 'between ourselves'. This recognition leads to a reorientation of perspective away from viewing relationships between ourselves as either the inevitable manifestation of nature or the product of our unique learning histories (both of which pre-suppose that what we are is already somehow established – a product of the nature/ nurture interaction), and towards the idea that we, as bodies and otherbodies, organize ourselves and are organized (and are otherwise assembled, conjoined and articulated) within a social field of possibilities (note that a possibility is never already established, never a product, but always unfinished and potential). 'Power', state Harré and Secord (1972: 240) 'is related to a field of possibilities'.

This opens up many thought-provoking extensions to the idea of empowerment. For example, there is now a powerful movement which argues 'the social construction of disability'. Fundamentally, this posits that the circumstances of a person with, say, a partial paralysis are not those of a 'disabled person' but of a person facing a 'disabling society'. Whether a disabled person can gain access to your classroom, or participate in our meeting is not fundamentally fixed by their 'disability' but depends upon the circumstances created 'between ourselves' (e.g. whether there is a ramp for wheelchair access, braille facilities for the blind, accessible toilets and so on). Empowerment here means en-abling and that may mean challenging a great deal of the production that has gone on in the past concerning the construction of 'the disabled'.

Unlike the notions of emancipation built into liberal-humanism, the 'politics' of such critical challenges does not assume that all persons with a partial paralysis should 'radicalize' their circumstances. Rather as with the slogan 'any woman can be a lesbian', it is a possibilizing move. Both work on a rejection of any essential limitation or ceiling to human possibility. Both reject the idea of lawful trajectories to our lives and in that reject the myth of a science of human lives. Possibilities are not probabilities in the sense of predictive odds. There is a world of difference between the sexologist who, projecting purported present data, says a girl-child has a 4 per cent chance of being a lesbian and the opening up of possibility – that any woman can be a lesbian.

Here the critical perspective is arguing for the need to avoid the search for a totalizing account of the human condition – one which assumes that human activity is already finished somewhere, in our genes, or in our hormones. It does so by rejecting the metaphysics of prior causes. Having legs does not cause us to run, any more than having an autonomic nervous system causes us to be emotional. That 'critical' here means something other than politically radical can be seen by the way the critical perspective must also reject the idea that a man having a penis means that 'all men are potential rapists'.

These 'political' considerations are often held to be 'out of place' in academic psychology. It is not hard to see why: it is part of the rhetoric of most conservative ideologies to argue the line that 'we need to keep XYZ out of politics'. And, as we noted from Henriques et al. (above), psychology has become ideologically conservative. It was not always the case, quite the reverse in fact: the post-Enlightenment project and the psychology it co-generated began as a radical project, one suited to its times, the Age of Revolutions. For the 'selves' emerging into Modernism, human science was a critical power, one restructuring the field of possibilities. In other words, it told new stories and retold old stories of the human condition. To be psychologized (socialized into a psychologically informed culture) was to have the 'between ourselves' transformed. It was to be 'finished by culture' in a new way, one in which the field of possibilities was changed as when the lighting changes dramatically upon a fixed stage. Things once visible become unseen, things once unseen become visible. This is probably the most dramatic metaphor for this idea but it needs qualifying: when we are talking human possibilities the field is not visual but narrative. What comes under change is shown in Figure 4.1.

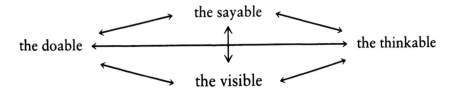

Figure 4.1 Between ourselves

For many critical psychologists (e.g. Ibañez, 1993; Curt, 1994; Shotter, 1993a and b; Sampson, 1993; Hilman and Ventura, 1989) there is now a climate of perturbation challenging the foundations of Modernism and its psychology. If that reading holds, then we are in for powerful tectonic movements in the cultural crust bringing with them new fields of possibility. Where those possibilities concern the 'between ourselves' it is, we believe, in critical social psychology and associated critical human studies that the new stories are being listened to. In our arrogant moments, we also think this is where they are being told!

5 In Social Worlds

I.I.: I can see that you were being serious at the end of the last chapter in saying that, to a critical social developmental psychology, we are persons in culture from the start. But where does that leave the study of socialization?

Growing up social

It has been a long-standing barb about experimental social psychology (we used it in the last chapter!) that all it informs us about is the social behaviour of United States undergraduates! Like most such quips, this one has more than a grain of truth to it. The questions this raises – of representativeness and generalizability – are all the more acute because, by and large, the 'subjects' of social psychology appear *de novo* in youth – their earlier social lives having been claimed elsewhere (by developmental and educational psychology). Interest in the person across the life-span tends to fall under another sub-discipline again (personality theory). To make matters even more confusing, many sociologists would consider issues of socialization to fall under their purview.

In raising this diffusion of questions of 'being social' and 'social being' as a problem, critical psychologists do not have in mind any call to a 'grand integration'. Far from it! They are not looking for a synthesis which maps an evolving (but sovereign) self, journeying through social life from birth to death. Rather, the function of the critique is twofold: first, to expose the operation of the regimes of knowledge which so dismembered persons-encultured and culture-enpersoned: second, to consider how certain key problematics have been differently high-lighted or down-played according to which regime has been dealing with our being social and social being. It is to that second agenda that we now turn.

Old chestnuts

One of the great truisms of human science is that we are the product of our genetics and our environment. It has the status of a foundational taken-for-granted – from it the arguments can start! But should we 'take it for granted'?

Box 5.1 A Thought Experiment

Imagine that we could take a thousand fertilized human ova from Roman women of AD 72 and transplant them into a thousand contemporary women of Rome in AD 1972 – moving their ova in turn back into the Roman women. What would be the result? For a host of reasons not all of them, in either context, would be carried to term and then result in live births. Not all the babies on either side of the 1900 years divide would survive to reach twenty.

But of those who did, those persons now living in AD 1993 would be (except for the offspring of a few migrant mothers) Italians, speaking Italian and being full participants in twentieth century culture. Similarly, those persons living in AD 93 would all be Romans, speaking Latin and being full participants in first-century culture. Both groups would be to all intents and purposes indistinguishable from their non-transplanted peers. To believe otherwise would be to assume that genes carry cultural information or that there have been psychologically significant genetic changes in *homo sapiens* over that time. Only on wildest fringes of socio-biology are such ideas held.

In the sense that comes from that thought experiment (as it does from the Arthur C. Clarke quotation in the previous chapter), what matters is socialization (how we become social and the social we become) not our embodied genetic information. We have put the case – obvious if not always recognized – that cultures work to make the accident of our place and time of birth (cf. Berger and Luckmann, 1967) uniquely meaningful in terms of who we take ourselves to be.

I.I. Hang on! There are two issues here. I can accept that culture makes us what we are, my clone in Roman Britain would not, in any sense be me. But you're surely not arguing that my sex might be switched or my hair colour?

No we would not. Nevertheless (and it is a crucial 'nevertheless') all cultures work on what they apperceive. And what they apperceive is read off (by their forms of understanding) our embodiment. We can confidently presume that those babies in both Roman Rome and Italian Rome that were read as boys were mostly what we would call XY chromosomed and those that were read as girls were mostly XX chromosomed. But the work of culture as enculturator involves weaving loose designs over how those boys and girls should be and should become. These are what would differ. For example, what we would call 'human and civil rights' were not bestowed upon Roman females in the way they are (albeit still grudgingly and partially) bestowed upon Italian females. Culture, in other words, always reads our embodiment, makes discriminations and judgements based upon it – shapes our lives, even our continued living – as it is seen. A crucial dimension upon which cultures differ lies in what they make of our bodies.

In other words, for critical social psychology, the nature/nurture question is not the question. Rather, nature/nurture debates are in themselves an object of study (as forms of knowledge in our culture, which psychology helps to shape). And an important part of the aim of that study is to make a space for other possible knowledges – just as, say, the gender politics of the Roman State were not those of the Italian State, so the gender politics of the future will be humanly (and no doubt differently) made.

Gender (cf. Chapter 10) is not to be taken as a given but seen as a problematic construction. This is what we have been outlining in the argument above. Any embodied condition ('genetic' such as 'Down's syndrome' or 'acquired' such as what is taken as and made by a culture into a disability) has a practical reality that comes from the culture in which it is brought into meaningfulness. We (and our embodied possibilities) are always in social worlds. So too are all our concepts of reality. 'Dyslexia', for example, has meaning only in a literate culture with a psychology to detect it.

Dilemmas of development

The psychology that we know today came into being in the nineteenth century – and how that century saw the human condition still haunts mainstream psychology today.

I.I. I know this is your argument, you've told me before several times. What's new when that is applied to studying development?

In particular, psychology was forged as a human science taking from Darwinian biology the notions of evolution and development. As a result, it is still generally taken-for-granted today that:

* non-human animals can act as models for humans;
* psychological phenomena are grounded upon physiological phenomena;
* persons develop in parallel to their bodily development.

These notions can be seen particularly clearly in the grand theories of developmentalism (Freudian and Piagetian) that still form a crucial part of the grounding of the child psychology syllabus. Typical of the kind of thinking involved is the idea that psychological development consists of a sequence of stages. Interestingly, even in theories which have moved away from a strict bodily foundation to human development, the notion of stages can still be found at work.

Two obvious cases in point are 'life-span developmental psychology' of the kind promoted by Erik Erikson (e.g. 1963) and the humanistic developmentalism of Maslow (e.g. 1968). Clearly, development has become such a strong story (cf. Stainton Rogers and Stainton Rogers, 1992a) that it seems able to stand on its own as a psychological commonplace even without direct recourse to a biological foundation.

I.I. Strange! What makes this possible?

The answer, once more, seems to lie back in the nineteenth century. The idea that individuals, economies and societies passed through evolutionary changes had a currency in social thought (so-called social Darwinism) which paralleled the emergence of Darwinian notions in the biological sciences. This mode of thinking is still current. 'Under-developed' persons, economies and societies are seen as 'held back' or 'growing up'. Contemporary psychobabble is full of developmentalist notions from 'getting in touch with our child within' to 'really growing as a person'.

I.I. I tell my cats not to listen to their 'kitten within' when they start tearing up the furniture – never works!

We're not surprised. But to get back to the point, popular politics often locates biological developmentalism as a dogma of the right (e.g. the eugenics movement) and social developmentalism as a dogma of the left (e.g. vulgar Marxism). Things are not so simple.

I.I. I didn't think they would be.

Many reformers (such as Sir Julian Huxley the biologist who served as Director General of UNESCO or Marie Stopes the contraception pioneer) have bought into eugenics, while Hitler's National Socialism (*sic*) also used notions of social Darwinism to its own devious ends. For critical theorists, it is not a question of 'which side are you on, nature or nurture?' but of 'how have these "sides" been made in the first place?'

Crucial to that question is a challenge to the notion that there are 'sides' there at all. Parallel though the biological and social notions of development are, in the history of ideas, we should not accept that they are equivalent. The sense in which a frog's egg develops into a tadpole and then into a frog is not the sense in which an agrarian society industrializes and then becomes a post-industrial society. Personal and social development is a theoretic and moral model imposed upon the human world. Both its purported stages and its end-state are contestable. In ecological terms, a hunter-gatherer society is far from being 'less-developed' than an industrial society. Equally, the kind of 'self-contained individualism' (cf. Sampson, 1990) that would place, say, self-actualization as the pinnacle of human development has become a key target for critical psychologists.

Box 5.2   From Ends To Beginnings: The Developmental Trap

Modelling human development, in other words, requires (theoretically starts from) the imposition of a notion of what a 'developed person' should be. If this were not bad enough, developmental theories in psychology build very particular (local and contingent) definitions of the 'developed person'. They predetermine what matters, what it means to be a full human being. While these definitions vary considerably from theory to theory (e.g. from Piaget's notion of an abstract theoretical thinker to Freud's of a heterosexual worker), what we suspect they have in common is a vision of 'someone like us' (i.e. like the theorists!). This 'ideal self' is also often put up as a model for therapeutic intervention. Therapy also employs notions of what a 'developed person' should be (cf. Kitzinger and Perkins, 1993) as, for example, in Rogers's (1942) client-centred therapy.

Once such a model is in place, the 'facts' of psychological development can, of course, be brought out by research interventions and laid upon it. But as Gergen and Gergen (1988) and Stainton Rogers and Stainton Rogers (1986) argue, this is a narrative, a story loosely linking the base proposition that we get 'better and better'. A developmental theory that said the opposite, that we 'regress', would make a unacceptable story.

One trouble with any developmentalist story is that it is triumphalist – what Kitzinger (1987) calls the 'up the mountain' story. Those who 'make it' are put on a pedestal (like Maslow's 'self-actualizers') or put themselves on one (like the members of Mensa, an organization literally made possible by IQ tests). Those who have not 'made it' (i.e. children) are 'scientifically proved' not to merit full civil rights. Those who purportedly cannot 'make it' (e.g. those with learning disabilities) can be incarcerated and sterilized lest they pass on their retardation (cf. Kamin, 1974).

Crucial to all such thinking, even for humanistic theorists who eschew biological notions of personhood, is the idea that personhood is an essence contained within the body. Little wonder then that critical psychologists have recently targeted developmentalism with considerable energy (e.g. Burman, 1993; Morss, 1990; Stainton Rogers and Stainton Rogers, 1992a).

I.I. Sorry to interrupt again but I think you are up to your old tricks of mixing two arguments. I can see sense in your claim that we need to look carefully at what theorists are making development mean but surely there are some senses of maturity which are consensual – like . . . I don't know . . . not messing up other people's lives – or your own.

Becoming good, becoming bad

Critical psychology has no trouble with the idea that we should be concerned in all of our doings (including our academic ones), or that varieties of concern and unconcern are proper targets for study. Its argument, once more, is with the ultimate failure of psychology as a discipline to deliver such 'goods', and with what it offered as a substitute.

Box 5.3 The Story of The Moral

The big trouble with trying to study human decency within the mainstream of ideas is that it is so hard to separate psychological-developmental

notions of 'moralization' from historical-developmental notions of 'civilization'. They both seem to impose the same kinds of implied choices. Would
you rather be 'amoral' or 'altruistic-autonomous' (Wright, 1971)? Would
you rather have a 'punishment and obedience orientation' or a 'morality
of individual principles of conscience' (Kohlberg. 1969)? The 'right' answer
seems obvious. And, if we buy it, there is a journey to be made, a march
of progress to join – towards moral development and self-control. If we do
not, if we think that the apparent 'right' answer is more of a story with an
imposed 'happy-ending', then the received psychology of morality is
unlikely to prove very edifying.

To appreciate why psychology produced the accounts of moralization
that have now become its curricular canon on the subject, we need once
more to take an historical perspective. From its beginnings, human science
took over from religion a warrant to speak and to act on questions of
human morals. Science was seen in the nineteenth century as a counter to
the fallibility and illogicality of human judgement. It was in the legal
sphere where expert witnesses (alienists as the early psychiatrists were
called) came to be employed to establish the condition of an accused's
moral development. The case, in 1943, of Daniel McNaughten, who
had assassinated Sir Robert Peel's private secretary, led to the formulation of so-called McNaughten Rules (cf. Smith, 1981) over insanity
as a defence. These stated: '[I]t must be clearly proved that, at the time
of the committing of the act, the party accused was labouring under such
a defect of reason, from the disease of the mind, as not to know the
nature or quality of the act he [*sic*] was doing; or, if he did know it,
that he did not know he was doing what was wrong' (quoted in Smith,
1981: 15).

From the power to speak on such early 'mad/bad' distinctions, human
science came to claim authority on issues of morality and moralization in
general. It became an agent in the general pursuit of social hygiene,
concerned not just with diagnostics but also with prevention ('moral
health promotion') and with treatment. The 'psy complex' became an
'agent of socialization', informing parents, schools, institutions and
governments on the promotion of moral development. Psychologists like
Wright (in the UK) and Kohlberg (in the USA), whose schemes we have
mentioned above, were very much at the tail-end, rather than the avant-
garde, of this social hygiene project. To get a sense of how social hygiene
sounded at the start of the century, here is Sully, a well-respected British
psychologist, writing in 1901:

The acquisition by the individual of the higher volitional processes and of moral character is greatly furthered by the action of others. In truth, the action of the social environment on the growing mind of the child is still more manifest in the case of moral than of intellectual development. The very idea of a morally good will implies the discipline supplied by a community which has a system of morality.

This moral action of the community on the individual works at first through the medium of those who exercise authority during the early years. As we saw in tracing the growth of the moral sentiment, the influence of authority and of moral discipline is a necessary condition of the formation of that sense of duty, the supremacy of which marks the highest stage of self-control.

The training of the child's will to fixed and worthy lines of action proceeds partly by way of the early government of the home and the school, and the system of rules this implies. (1901: 556-7)

There is much in Sully which presages the ideas of Piaget. In Sully we can see clearly the way in which the processional scheme argues from end-state to beginnings. As with general development, so with moral development – it becomes possible to trace 'progress' only once the end-state is defined. In the post-Piagetian schemes of Wright and Kohlberg, that 'end-state' is a self-contained, self-actualized individual. If it can be equated with a 'moral hero', it is not so much in terms of their deeds but how we hear them and tell them – for example, as in the moral discourse around a secular saint in the canon of liberal-humanism such as Gandhi.

For, above all, it is a command of moral rhetoric – a power in the logic of ethical argument – which is being celebrated. There is little wonder in that, for it is moral development – as a special case of cognitive development – which is being argued here. For reasons that we shall go on later to outline, such attempts to ground moral development in terms of universal principles of 'rights' and 'justice' have foundered recently. The cognitive approach per se, however, has not – moral development is now being pursued in terms of the child's 'theory of mind' (for a critical response, see Morss, 1990).

Of course, a key (and much vaunted) feature of human science is its status as an arena of theories in argument, a forum of liberal pluralism. In practice, this means that wherever there is a 'big issue' (and moralization is a 'big issue') everyone wants a bite of the cherry. Hence, in addition to cognitive developmental accounts, our moralization has been claimed as:

- sited in the identifications/re-identifications we make on resolving our Oedipus/Electra Complex (the psychodynamic approach);

- a biological variable in which conscience-formation is a form of classical conditioning mediated by our inherited cortical arousal with extraverts (particularly emotional extraverts) being 'born to crime' (Eysenck, 1957);
- something mediated by 'social learning' through processes like modelling (e.g. Bandura, 1977) and, hence, somewhat situation-specific;
- determined by particular (e.g. moral discourse inductive) styles of child-rearing (cf. Hoffman, 1975);
- something constituted out of components that can be operationalized and so studied experimentally such as 'bystander apathy', 'resistance to temptation' or 'delay of gratification'.

Put together (as they so often are in textbooks) this portfolio of approaches can read as though progress is truly being made across a wide front. The pluralistic ethic likes to show that it works in practice.

I.I. But does it? Or rather, what exactly is being worked?

Tautology, trivia and truism

Notions that the moral life depends, variously, upon both specific training and provided example (particularly in the family), concepts of temptation, or conditions of moral failure, and of universal principles riddle the Christian (and liberal Judaic) heritage. They helped to form the shape of Enlightenment moral philosophy and were drawn into the post-Enlightenment project. Equally, they foundationed the 'Puritan' concept of the child (cf. Thomas, 1985) and were, thereby, taken into North American popular culture. With a very few exceptions (e.g. Skinner, 1938), developmental social psychology can be said to have given a scientific gloss (to have formally theorized, operationalized, and quantified) ordinary knowledges of morality, rather than to have questioned or proposed radical alternatives.

I.I. In other words, the pluralism we find in the developmental social psychology of morality more reflects the diversity within popular forms of understanding of moralization than some quantum leap in knowledge.

Precisely — they seem meaningful, they differ in ways and argue about points (for example as to whether ethical behaviour stems from the head (reason) or the heart (pangs of conscience)) that can be immediately grasped precisely because they are founded on the same social order of which their readers are a part.

I.I. Part of your argument seems to be that there actually isn't any psychological theorizing of moralization per se at all – just an application of ready-made conceptualizations of socialization to what generally passes as moral issues. In which case I'm back where I started, asking, where does your approach leave the study of socialization?

Social worlds revisited

In social-historical terms, psychology as a mission asserted its power and authority as the 'science of behaviour' at a number of sites in which the moulding of behaviour and the re-shaping of problem behaviour had public and State attention. Looked at like that, the concept of socialization served to re-gloss notions of what, at the turn of the century, was known as the 'government of the young' with a veneer of scientificality. Broadly speaking, the models of socialization popular from the 1920s to the early post-Second-World-War era employed forms of theory language which presented the socialization process as a form of long-term domestication of our grounded animality.

This animality was seen as having two 'acute' phases, the first in early childhood – where we are 'house-trained'; and the second in adolescence – when animality is revitalized by the rush of 'sex hormones'. These were sometimes called primary and secondary socialization. So-called agents of socialization (e.g. the home, the school, the peer group) were regarded as variable causes (varying in, for example, both temporal sequence of impact and, more generally, in quality and power) determining the way in which nurture was inscribed upon nature.

Whether they adopted a loosely psychoanalytic approach or, more usually, some kind of social learning position, the concern was the issue of internalization – how, when and in what ways 'the social' got into 'the individual'. This was the great era of the 'baby books', the extremely varied and dubiously evidenced guides to parents (usually mothers) about how to bring up children 'scientifically' – and also the 'psychology of adolescence' (cf. Griffin, 1993).

By the 1960s, this approach to socialization lay in tatters, conceptually and empirically. Looking to the first, the longitudinal studies – which had sought to find the early environmental causes of adult character – had largely failed to do so (cf. Gergen, 1994). Instead research came into vogue which positively argued that outcomes were the result of interplay between the 'disposition' of the child and the contingencies of its environment (cf. Thomas and Chess, 1980).

Such shifts in empirical strategy reflected the gradual recognition that the 'over-model' of socialization as simple inscription could not hold. In many ways paralleling the then contemporary 'crisis' in social psychology over adult 'subjects', developmentalists began to reconstruct their subjects (babies) as active organisms. In a classic paper Rheingold (1982) hailed the 'socialized and socializing child'. Developmental research at that time was powerfully in the thrall of the then new behavioural biology (ethology and mammalian modelling), with the result that proto-sociality became regarded as 'wired into' the infant (cf. Richards, 1974).

It is no coincidence that the point at which mainstream psychology began to incorporate notions such as a 'sociality' within biological endowment, or the recognition that the infant could not be abstracted from its social field, corresponds to the emergence in critical work of the 'climate of perturbation'. They are two sides of the same crisis: the one showing an established order working to accommodate to new ideas, to restructure; the other the offerings of an avant-garde.

These politics of psychology are written right across the issues we have been discussing in this chapter. In the case of moralization (and much else in social developmental psychology), it was as much as anything the emergence in the late 1960s of new forms of the 'woman question' which impinged on the discipline.

Gilligan (1977) brought to social developmental psychology the argument that theories of moralization had been male-generated, male-explored and male-tested. Specifically, she argued that a morality of self-contained individualism (e.g. of justice) down-played the alternative, a morality of relationship (e.g. of care). What this turn served to bring to light was that so much of the social hygiene project in moral developmental research (e.g. its supposed utility in tackling crime and delinquency) has also been, almost unawares, directed at male behaviour. (Male offenders out number women offenders by a large margin in almost every criminal category.)

Likewise, the Kitty Genovese murder which gave the 'real-life' foundation to Darley and Latané's paradigm of 'bystander apathy' (1968), was a male perpetrator on female victim offence. Just how far every element of the social developmental psychology received into the 1960s was permeated with a tacit male gaze (see Chapter 10) is only today coming to be documented and exposed.

A significant case in point is the very primatology used to ground accounts of human aggression (cf. Chapter 8), and development. Haraway's *Primate Visions* (1989) uncovers this history well. However, all critique is Janus-faced. Important though challenges to received knoweledges are, they are only part of a critical agenda. There is also a concern with how it might be other(wise).

Social worlds recovered and recast

The received psychological sub-disciplines of human sociality, identity, change and possibility, as we outlined them at the start of this chapter, are subject to the critical charge of monologism (cf. Sampson, 1993). They take it as given that the significant roots of human being stem from essences within us as people. The charge applies most obviously to theorizing which takes it that these essences are intrinsically internal (in some way 'wired-in' to our singular biological embodiment as structure or as process).

However, the charge holds just as strongly to approaches which stress that 'the social' matters because it is internalized in socialization. It equally fits, we suggest, conceptualizing which is concerned with the interaction between singular forces such as 'nature and nurture' or even between persons (e.g. caregiver and child), where those persons are seen as the site of and source of that (inter)action.

Monologism comes under critical scrutiny for three linked but separable reasons:

1. It encourages a doctrine of graded sameness (the monothetic argument). A theory which starts by building in notions of what we are about (a battle-ground of instinct and culture; a biological organ of knowing; an information-processing system; and so on) can reflect only what the theorist (from their social position) thinks they are about. It can find only differences that are gradations of that sameness, gradations which at the same time are also judgements (levels of 'intelligence', 'development', 'adjustment', 'performance').
2. These notions of what we are about which are being used as theoretic axioms are bound to be historically resourced, empowered into position such that the sameness proposed lies in contrast to and in judgement upon the other (e.g. adults upon children; whites upon blacks; men upon women; middle class upon working class).
3. The monologic model masks all that is not monological, and that includes the most active features of sociality, namely sociality as it is lived between us. In other words, argument, collectivity, conjoint action, dialogue, and discourse.

I.I. OK, enough of the negative agenda. What has the critical approach itself got to offer?

What are at stake here are issues not just about how we 'do' social psychology but about how we go about the very business of 'thinking it' or rather, thinking the concerns it has claimed knowledge/power over. Critical social psychology asks us to question not just what we think but how we think. While they tend to agree that monologic is a bad thing, critical social psychologists do not necessarily agree as to where we look for alternatives.

The paths to criticality include anti-philosophy (e.g. Curt, 1994; Ibáñez, 1991), feminism (e.g. Wilkinson, 1986), neo-Marxism (e.g. Parker, 1989), and post-structuralism (e.g. Henriques et al., 1987). The alternative focus may be upon discourse (Edwards and Potter, 1992; Parker, 1992a), rhetoric (Billig et al., 1988), forms of dialogic (Marková, 1992 and Sampson 1993), a 'knowing of the third kind' (Shotter, 1993) or 'textuality and tectonics' (Curt, 1994).

I.I. Quite a reading list – that should keep me busy for a while!

Well, that's part of why we wrote the book. We hope it at least gives you a working appreciation of this critique. More crucial than just getting to grips with all the diverse forms of critical social psychology is developing a general 'feeling' for what it is about. Though the above list would make a pretty good start at getting on top of the literature.

I.I. (Muttering) Not going to come cheap though . . .

Sadly not. One important final point, though. It needs to be clear that it is not another theory or approach to be added to your reading list (although it may be presented that way). It's a whole new ballgame. As Shotter (1993b) puts it:

> times are changing . . . as our ways or relating ourselves to each other start to change, so must our ways of knowing begin to change, too . . . the modern 'human sciences' . . . have provided us with an ever-increasing wealth of fragmentary data, but as yet no overall grasp of either our own mental functioning or of the nature of our everyday social lives. But this is not to do with the fact that we have not yet found the correct theory – as if with yet more research effort (and funds) we shall one day get it right. It is to do with the fact that we have failed to grasp not only what it is we must 'theorise' here, but also what the task of 'theory' in this sphere is like . . . 'knowing of the third kind' . . . is not to do with our discovering actualities individually, but with our realising the possibilities we make available to ourselves, between ourselves socially . . . It is this kind of knowledge . . . that is the special kind of knowledge embodied in the world of a civil society. (1993b: 2–3)

6 From Attitudes to Opinionation as Discourse

In 1992, to the surprise of virtually everybody, the Conservatives were returned to government in the UK. That surprise was due in no small part to the fact that right up until the day of the election virtually all of the opinion polls had predicted either a Labour victory or no overall majority. To put this in psychological language, 'attitudes had failed accurately to predict behaviour'. The inevitable post-mortems followed (not least by the polling companies themselves, who as commercial operations have most to lose from any lost credibility). It was argued that a lot of voters must have 'lied' – had simply not been prepared to admit openly that they were going to vote as they did. Others suggested that people must have changed their minds at the last moment. Certainly, the impression has been strengthened that opinion polls are not effectively predictive, particularly now that people have become 'survey sophisticated'. People, it is beginning to sink in, tend to answer pollster's questions, if at all (for there is always a considerable rump of the unlocated, the refusers and the 'don't knows'), actively, and, on occasions, downright mischievously.

I.I. To sum you up, attitudes and behaviour can be polls apart, so to speak!

Perhaps we should call that Beryl's Fourth Law! To take our argument on, this failure to predict the Conservative victory from opinion polling provides a good illustration of the kinds of problems that surround the attempts that psychologists have made to theorize and do research into attitudes. For the past seventy years they have devoted a vast amount of effort into the pursuit of answers to four main questions:

1 Where do attitudes and beliefs come from? How are they moulded and formed in the first place?

2 How can attitudes be measured?
3 How and why do attitudes change? What forces are involved and what intrapsychic mechanisms operate when people shift in their opinion about a particular 'attitude object'?
4 How do attitudes relate to behaviour? What is it that links the way people think and feel about an 'attitude object', and what they do about it?

Overall they have not been very successful at answering any of them. At times psychologists have been able to make their work appear to be functional, in its own terms – to show that attitude scales produce consistent, replicable results, that attitudes shift in certain systematic ways or are predictive of conduct. But we would maintain that these 'successes' are artifacts of the approaches used and the assumptions upon which the work has been based. This chapter will explore those criticisms, and give some indications of how, by moving away from the study of 'attitudes' towards the exploration of the discursive production and use of opinion-ation, we can gain more interesting and worthwhile answers to some rather different questions:

1 Where do 'views of the world' come from? In what ways are opinionative discourses produced, legitimated, maintained, promoted, owned and used?
2 What methods of scrutiny can we use to address these discursive productions, and to illuminate their conditions of employment in varying circumstances?
3 For what purposes are they produced, legitimated, maintained, promoted, owned and used?
4 How, if at all, are opinionative discourses linked to conduct? In what ways does their use relate to power both established and radicalized (as empowerment)?

Unsettling our differences

Since around 1920, 'attitude' has been a key concept in social psychology – at times being hailed as the key concept (e.g. Allport, 1954). Over that time its theorisation has been highly susceptible to the changing fashions in the discipline more generally. Indeed any account of the history of the concept (e.g. McGuire, 1986) cannot avoid also being a history of those fashions. What has held that history together is that, whatever the particular micro level conceptualization employed, at the meta-level theorization around these questions has been positivist. In other words, it has assumed a simple model of cause-and-effect processes which locate 'attitudes' as more or less complicated psychological essences which exist and operate within individual minds. (De Fleur and Westie's (1963) 'latent process' type of definition of attitude). For example, as the prevailing psychological worldview shifted from a preoccupation with behaviourism into a more cognitive approach, so too have attitude theories shifted from ones based on learning theory to ones based on cognitive algebra (cf. McGuire, 1986). The major exceptions to this approach (De Fleur and Westie's 'probabilistic' definitions) have been the pure empiricism of some psychometric work – where attitudes are simply those consistencies attitude scales reveal – and radical behaviorism in which attitudes are treated as forms of Skinnerian verbal behaviour (Bem, 1967). Nevertheless, whatever their pedigree, orthodox social psychological theory takes for granted that the prime 'site of the action' of attitude-making, attitude-changing and attitude-impact on behaviour is always within the individual. In consequence, this field of work has been particularly prey to the kinds of disciplinary isolation which epitomizes the discipline more generally. Psychological theorization regarding people's attitudes has tended to concentrate almost entirely on the influence of processes operating within and upon the individual, and to down-play the 'between ourselves' aspect (cf. Chapter 5) to unspecified notions of interplay and interaction. Extra-individual 'variables' have been treated either as mysterious forces which 'tweak' the dial along pre-existing psychic dimensions of attitude positions or as transformed into internalized representations of the social environment such as norms.

Moreover, given traditional psychology's obsession with hypothetico-deductivism, it has tended to focus attention on the kinds of short-life, 'top of mind' human reactions that are most amenable to experimental manipulation. For a society well used to box-ticking as a way of life, these are not hard to come by! The result is a distinctly unbalanced approach. At the level of theory, there is often an assumption that a person's attitudes must have been originally engendered by longer-term formative processes (or even, by some accounts, may arise from pre-existing personality proclivities – cf. Eysenck, 1957). The vast bulk of research activity, however, has been directed towards those aspects of 'attitudes' which are either open to easy change in the short term, or seem to have a proximal link to behaviour.

Yet, ironically, from a critical perspective, these research paradigms 'work' not because of their controlled abstraction from the noisy world of real life but because they create a social world of their own. It is a social world in which knowledge and power are in the hands of an interrogator, who demands answers to specific questions. The subjects' role is to opinionate (to express affect about an object), not, of course, discursively, but on some pre-set scale. Only because they do so is the 'experiment' possible. Their 'response' then becomes a variable (usually the dependent variable). In other words, the typical experiment on attitudes boils down to a highly contrived, short-term inquisition, in which the form of the answer is pre-set (by the 'attitude' scale) – leaving the subjects to express what meaning they can make of the situation by the degree they adopt on the scale. The result is a pale and distorted shadow of the vast amount of opinionation which goes on in ordinary language use: in relationships: in negotiations: in mundane socializing.

I.I. You seem to have slipped suddenly into using that ugly word 'opinionation'. Ugh! Define!

This term we are using – 'opinionation' – is crucial to an appreciation of 'expressions of affect about an object' in ordinary discourse. We use it to escape from the essentialist trap of assuming that what we say reliably taps or reflects some inner condition: a representation of reality or a response-readiness (a template or a lever in Campbell's terms, 1963).

I.I. Or can opener?

Well, we certainly hope to 'open up a can of worms'. By putting the emphasis instead upon opinionation as discourse (cf. Potter and Wetherell, 1987) 'what we say' can be treated in its own right, as a human expression – not as a shadow of some inner psychic essence. This encourages us to view not just opinionations themselves, but also the idea that they reflect the selves that express them, as both forms of representational labour. In other words, as discursively produced, maintained and mongered features of our 'way of life'. Opinionation and the attribution of attitude are both within 'the social', 'the historical' and 'the cultural' as well as 'the psychological'. They are traded (not necessarily fairly, of course) in the economy that sustains the conditions that exist 'between ourselves'.

I.I. In which it might be said that you have a 'bad attitude' about 'attitude'.

Too right, we do. To adopt a 'critical' approach to 'attitudes' is to engage in consideration about the ways they operate as sites of power-play between knowledge and action (e.g. for the promotion of ideology). Once we have accepted this, two things become clear. First (as we have noted already in other contexts) the endeavours of theorizing, researching and communicating about 'attitudes' can be seen as, in themselves, discursive productions – means by which ideology is promoted and conduct warranted. Attitude research belongs in the tradition of psychology as 'humaneering' (cf. Chapter 1) whereby, at times – for the best of liberal-intellectual motives – the subject is seen as the site of efforts towards social hygiene. Put in the hands of more obviously (to the Western eye) interventional regimes (such as the China of Korean War times), that same agenda has been called 'brain washing' (cf. Lifton, 1961). This is not, of course, to equate the practices of the two contexts – what can be done in the name of 'humaneering' and the 'pathologies' deemed to be of concern are circumstantial, local and contingent to a particular social order.

The social order in which mainstream attitude research has been most pursued is, of course, the United States. This means that we can use the themes of attitude research as a kind of social history. On the one hand, these reflect the changing face of US society as it has moved through the century, for example: the Great Depression; the New Deal, the Second World War; the Cold War and McCarthyism; the formal desegregation of South following the civil rights movement; the Vietnam War; and, currently, the great health anxieties. On the other hand, that research also informs us about its enduring motifs and strains – for instance: its ongoing structural racism and sexism; its nationalism; and its tensions between nostalgia and progress, Puritanism and indulgence. To learn about attitude theory and research is also to learn something of how the academy in the United States sees its world – and that world is centred upon the USA. Viewed through a critical eye, the psychological study of 'attitudes' is also propaganda for a particular worldview and a particular project of 'social hygiene' – the one which at any point in social time has discursive dominance amongst academicians and the mandarins and quango-bosses who oversee the paying of their salaries.

What often makes that hard for students and their teachers in social psychology to keep in mind is that, at the time, this agenda sounds also like informed good sense. It corresponds to 'what everybody knows', the 'progressive chatter', the liberal prescriptions of the times. Both sides of the lecture theatre overhead projector see themselves as informed by a rational analysis, by an attempt to be 'scientific' about things: problems can be humaneered away. Thus, one's own position (for that is all it is) comes to be seen as different from the positions one studies. It becomes privileged and legitimates into being the best available approximation of how things 'really are'. Within this 'truth game', its objects and subjects of study are rendered 'other' and their viewpoints are constructed not as 'truths' but as mere opinions, beliefs and attitudes! In other words, the very activity of studying 'attitudes' acts as a means by which 'knowing' gets to be divided into two domains:

- the domain of empirical knowledge-as-converging-upon-reality which provides the foundational basis from which and by which the scientific scholarship of extra-ordinary people is pursued; and

- the domain of psychic pseudo-realities (i.e. the beliefs, opinions and attitudes) by which 'ordinary people' make sense of and manipulate their world.

We will take up this purported division between 'expert' and 'lay' knowledge in the next chapter (Chapter 7). All forms of study, of course, are ideological – in so far as they construct what passes for knowledge. But the scientized study of attitudes does more than that – it promotes the idea that 'inner' space can be adjudged from the 'outside' for its truth-value. 'Prejudice', it argues, results from a failure or pathology of certain individuals' social perceptual systems: this attitude is 'self-serving', that one the mere result of a cognitive system that 'seeks consistency', and so on. In short, the attitude area is shot through with the premise that it is possible to tell the 'really real' from the 'artifice'. Those who engage in it have set themselves up as 'seers' able to dislocate themselves from the badinage of everyday-life opinionation, and, by poking around in its entrails, read its portends without getting their hands mucky. This leads us on to our second point. If we accept that 'attitudes' are forms of discursive production, constructed and utilized in a social economy of competing knowledges, then the claim by any one knowledge-complex to have a privileged foothold on 'reality', is just a product-feature in the advertising of its representational labour. To put this another way . . .

I.I. It might help me through a textuality which has all the easy clarity of a treacle well!

. . . if there is no bench-mark in 'reality' against which to 'measure attitudes', if 'man [*sic*] is the measure of all things', then the contention that psychology can measure 'attitudes' cannot be other than a rhetorical claim. And, over rhetorical claims, we should ask not 'are they well founded?' but 'what are they doing?' In other words, how are they working for the promotion of that particular story of the world? At the same time, if they cannot be anchored objectively, if there is no bench-mark in reality upon which to ground a psycho-metric, then attitude measurement is as much as pseudo-science as phrenology.

Attitude measures are, proverbially (and to mix metaphors) lost upstream, foundering without a paddle! And once they have lost that special claim (the ability to measure, not the paddle), then the vast edifice of virtually all of their empirical work falls crashing round their canoe. Theorizing these mythic attitudes is an exercise in the art of illusion. Instead of (as they have purported to do) researching universal laws concerning 'how attitudes are formed', 'how attitudes change' or 'how attitudes affect behaviour', we would argue that all that attitude researchers have achieved is to discourse upon discursion – to write texts on texts. In other words, they have done no more than elicit and describe (some of) the local and contingent discursive *praxes* by which they, and their objects of study, have storied into being notions like attitude-formation, attitude-change and the contingency between attitudes and conduct. But we too have discoursed for long enough: it is now time to show how our argument works, to subject the way psychology has approached attitudes to a critical deconstruction, using well-known examples to illustrate our case.

I.I. You have taken the words right out of my mouth, so to speak!

Attitude formation

To tell our story so far, we too have made use of rhetorical, opinionative devices; we have, for example, 'stereotyped' attitude researchers as having a naivety over the opinionative character of their own work. It is time to redress that balance with a quotation from one such who was far from naive in this respect, Roger Brown.

> In 1938 E. R. Jaensch, a psychologist and also a Nazi, published the book *Der Gegentypus . . . or Anti-type. The Anti-Type was also called the S-Type because . . . he was synaesthetic . . . as in color hearing . . . The S-type would be a man [sic] with so-called 'liberal' views . . . S would be flaccid, weak and effeminate . . . Jews are Anti-Types and 'Parisians' and orientals and communists.*
>
> The contrasting personality . . . was the J-Type. J made definite, unambiguous perceptual judgements . . . He would be tough, masculine, firm . . . J made a good Nazi Party member . . .
> In 1950, in the United States, *The Authoritarian Personality* was published . . . The authoritarian type . . . was, more or less, Jaensch's J-Type, but J who was hero to Nazi social science, was a villain to American [sic] social science . . . The typologies of Jaensch and of the authors of *The Authoritarian Personality* were much the same but the evaluations were different . . . The Equalitarian was ourselves and the Authoritarian the man in our society whom we feared and disliked. (Brown, 1965: 477-8)

What then was this study into the authoritarian personality (Adorno et al., 1950) which so sketched out an anti-type from the liberal intellectuals who were the 'ourselves' in Brown's quotation?

Box 6.1 The Authoritarian Personality

The team which produced *The Authoritarian Personality* was headed by the sociologist Theodor Adorno, who had earlier in Germany been central in the critical, neo-Marxist, 'Frankfurt School' which worked in exile in New York after the rise of the Nazis. His first co-author, Else Frenkel-Brunswik, was a Viennese social psychologist also in exile from Nazism. Adorno and his co-workers were funded by the American Jewish Committee in 1944 to study the roots of prejudice, and, in particular, anti-semitism. The approach was based on psychodynamic theory, and hence sought to look for links between racially prejudiced attitudes and personality, and to trace the origins of this back into early experience and child-rearing.

The study examined attitudes by way of both qualitative (e.g. interviews, projective tests) and quantitative (i.e. attitude scales) methods, with about two thousand Californian white, non-jewish, largely middle-class, native-born US citizens. Statistical links were established between measures of anti-semitism, ethnocentrism and personality traits such as obedience to authority, punativity, stereotyping, tough-mindedness and conservatism over things like sexuality. Those evincing such traits and attitudes were labelled as having an 'authoritarian personality'.

The data from the study suggests that people with an authoritarian personality tended to have been brought up in very 'traditional' families in which there were rigid gender roles, inflexible rules of conduct and harsh punishment for rule-breaking, and where the children were expected to respect and obey their parents. Yet as adults these people idealize their parents, talking of their mothers, for example as 'the most terrific person in the world' and their fathers as 'absolutely sincere'. According to the psychodynamic theory used, the idealization was a means to repress latent feelings of anger and aggression. These antagonistic feelings had become displaced on to a less 'dangerous' target (in a psychic sense) – members of other races.

Given the historical timing and the way the study was funded, the research was obviously in no way dispassionate in its aims, and, it would appear, in the way it was carried out. It has been criticized, for example, because the interview coders were aware of the hypotheses being tested (see Hyman and Sheatsley, 1954). There were also numerous other methodological flaws in the way the work was done. Yet it gave rise to a great deal of interest among social psychologists – more than four hundred papers were written about it in the twenty or so years following its publication (see reviews by Christie and Cook, 1958; Kirscht and Dillehay, 1967). Triandis (1971) argues that an important reason for this is that the scale developed to measure authoritarianism is easy to administer.

I.I. Is he serious?

Absolutely. This could become Beryl's 'laziness corollary' or Fifth Law: given the choice between the easy way to operationalize a variable and other ways, social psychologists choose the former. This is not as trivial and snide a point as it may at first appear. Arguably it is a major reason why attitude scales have enjoyed the popularity that they have. (One of us was once told much the same story over the health locus of control scale: 'I use it because it's easy – data can be collected so quickly.') Scales like this do offer a very efficient means to garner large amounts of data very quickly, and hence an easy way to generate publishable academic papers. The problem – with the Adorno study on the origins of attitudes, as with many others like it which came later – is that for all the data gained and crunched, the approach can offer only a speculative explanation for the results obtained (in Adorno et al.'s case, a psychodynamic one). It does not allow for any crucial test which would support or refute the validity of the proposed explanation. These kinds of endeavours are not theory-testing but activities used to bolster not just the researcher's publication record but the theorist's own beliefs about cause and effect. (The authoritarian personality study, for example, simply does not address the question of authoritarianism of the political left (cf. Rokeach, 1960)).

This can be seen in the disputes that followed the Adorno study. A variety of alternative explanations for the results were proposed. For example Hyman and Sheatsley (1954) showed that there is a negative relationship between authoritarianism and education, and suggested that what was being tapped was not 'personality' but merely the impact of being educated. Billig (1978) suggests that the trait can be explained equally well by a combination of lack of education, low IQ and low socio-economic status. Or put another (less derogatory) way, a simpler explanation is that offspring tend to become enculturated into voicing the opinions that their parents and community endorse.

A last issue is also worth a mention. The scales Adorno et al. used would ordinarily be regarded as attitude scales (e.g. the Political and Economic Conservatism Scale). However, over the more famous Potentiality for Fascism Scale, the so-called California F, there is a very illuminating confusion.

So far as one can determine they never refer to the F Scale as the Authoritarian Scale in their book *The Authoritarian Personality*. However, since the F Scale is supposed to identify the kind of personality the book is talking about, it is reasonable to suppose the scale could also be correctly called the Authoritarianism Scale. At any rate it has been so called in many subsequent research reports. (Christie, 1954) (Brown, 1965: 486)

In other words, an 'attitude scale' can also be a 'personality' scale and vice versa. Operationally, of course, personality scales and attitude scales are identical, but it is a strange kind of science which can employ the same technique to investigate two supposedly distinct theoretical constructs.

The measurement of attitudes

As it happens, exactly the same kind of muddle surrounds our next example – locus of control (Rotter, 1966). While its grounding concepts often result in it being treated as a theory of personality (specifically as a cognitive social learning approach), its utilization, developments and problems are in many ways those of a theory of attitude. In fact, it comes very close to being a theory of attitude in the original sense in which the term was used in psychology – as a kind of 'set' (cf. Lange, 1888).

Box 6.2   Locus of Control

Rotter (1966) first proposed a simple bipolar model of attitudes, based upon social learning theory. He argued that individuals who have consistent experiences in childhood of having good behaviour rewarded and bad behaviour punished come to see themselves as 'in control' of the events and outcomes in their lives. They site the locus of control internally. Their successes are construed as just rewards for hard work and diligence, failure is what they must expect if they are lazy or do not try hard enough. Conversely, individuals who have had inconsistent experiences in childhood – who were rewarded or punished indiscriminately, irrespective of their behaviour – come, as adults, to see the events in their lives as due to chance, luck and fate. They see the locus of control as sited externally. This was measured by a test which counted up which of a series of binary alternative explanations – one 'internal', one 'external' – subjects choose.
   Like Adorno et al.'s work, the internal/external control construct led to much debate and criticism. Collins (1974), for example, argued that there

are not two but four independent, alternative viewpoints which are clearly attitudinal – belief in a difficult world, a just world, a predictable world and a politically sensitive world. While a belief in a just world may sound 'internal', in practice it seems to tap a rather authoritarian world-view which holds that, say, rape victims must have 'brought it on themselves'.

The 'external' construct proved even more problematic. Perhaps the most influential development was that proposed by Levenson(1981) who argued that it should be sub-divided into two – the original 'chance' and a new site of control, 'powerful others', to accommodate the belief that control could be attributed neither to chance nor to one's own actions but to the actions of powerful others. This led to the formulation of a multidimensional locus of control scale, which became highly popular (see Klandermans, 1983, for a review).

The locus of control construct very patently shows its ideological biases. Within the prevailing individualism of dominant US culture, 'internality' is seen as much more desirable than a belief in chance. Lefcourt has commented, for example, that 'An internal locus of control may be one prerequisite for competent behaviour and an external control orientation seems common for many people who do not function in a competently healthy manner'. (1981: 191)

Yet a series of studies by Levenson and Miller (1976) showed that, given the opportunity, the more individuals with radical, feminist or left-wing views were politically active, the more likely they were to attribute control to 'powerful others' rather than chance. Here, participants were clearly reading 'powerful others' in terms of conspiracy to oppress – but to the Locus of Control Scale it still renders them 'external'. Stainton Rogers (1991) has demonstrated (using a variant of the scale directed to issues about health) that, for certain religious and cultural groups, notions of 'chance' and notions of 'fate' have entirely different meanings. She argues that the locus of control construct imposes a conceptual strait-jacket upon the way people can opinionate, and an ethnocentric, politically biased one at that. Attitude measurement, in other words, has hardly delivered to researchers the simplification and structuring of human variability it promised. This, by the way, holds no matter what the specific form of scaling used.

I.I. Such as?

Likert scales, Thurstone scales, Guttman scales, etc. Any mainstream text will describe to you the menu of scaling techniques on offer – they tend, as you might expect, to intercorrelate strongly one with another. And this holds for their problems and artefacts also. To critical theorists, the explanation of this is not hard to locate. Rogers (1974: 67 = Stainton Rogers, R.) put it this way, in the language of the (then) 'new paradigm': 'We have a model in which any one tropic act (linguistic or behavioural) might be due to a universe of motivation ... Attitude expressions and tropic behaviours then, are, on this analysis very much communicational acts. As such, to be effective, their form must be specified in some lexicon and grammarium defining their meaning within a culture.'

Over a decade later, after the 'discursive turn' (cf. Curt, 1994) Potter and Wetherell were to argue that when people fill in attitude scales, far from 'performing a neutral act of describing or expressing an internal state', they are rather 'engaged in producing a specific linguistic formulation tuned to the context in hand' (1987: 45). And once we view their response as a discursive act, 'things become murkier, because there is a great deal of scope to perform different kinds of acts when filling in the scale' (ibid: 48). The production of attitude scales has not made possible the measuring of people's attitudes, the tapping into of intra-psychic essences. Rather it has proved to be a projective test of the scale designer's socially mediated preconceptions. Harré expresses this point cogently:

> The use of questionnaires with limited range questions ... which effectively preclude elaborations and reinterpretations ... means that the concepts deployed ... are predetermined. The effect of this is to produce not a representation of the social world being studied, but the representation of the shadow cast upon the social world by the prior conceptual apparatus deployed by the person who constructed the questionnaire. (1979: 115)

These preconceptions, as was argued earlier, tend to be those of a liberal intellectual elite. They result in a form of interrogation of opinionation which is statistically reliable (internally consistent and replicable) but substantively circular – not least because it pre-presumes that which it seeks to measure – a fixed intra-psychic essence. This technology bleaches out alternative concepts *a priori* because it does not allow for them. For example, in demanding a singular response ('tick the one box that represents your view') it disallows from the start the possibility that people can be in 'several minds' about an issue (or none at all).

I.I. I'm glad someone is saying this, I've always hated having to fix or even make-up 'how you feel right now' on some wretched scale or another.

So did we but, for us, these resistances can be thought about as more than just individual antipathies.

Box 6.3   Attitude Problems

The 'single-minded', attitude-possessed and attitude-driven 'subject' produced by the measurement straitjacket is not an apolitical 'objective' account of persons but a profoundly political one. Whatever its pedigree, it became not a 'liberal-intellectual' reading but a distinctly reactionary one once the 'new right' gained ascendancy in the USA under Reagan and the UK under Thatcher. Its new focus on the 'choices', 'rights' and responsibilities of the individual was one only too glad to find the causes of 'deviance' and 'deficiency' within the person rather than 'between ourselves'.

At its crudest, it became a philosophy of victim-blaming. In the 'just world' of the 'opportunity culture', there is no place for any structural responsibility for the ill-health or the unemployment that the under-privileged suffer, as it is their own 'attitudes' that are at fault! This politics had no truck with the old liberal 'horrors' of the past (such as the Authoritarian). Instead, new class-enemies – such as the 'welfare scrounger' – gained discursive dominance. They got presented in ways that sounded all too like the discoveries of social psychology such as the 'externally controlled'.

We find it no accident that over the same time period, the popular use of the term 'attitude' underwent a shift. On the one hand, it became an attribution of that which both explains one's past and has to be overcome to succeed – as in 'I had a real bad attitude at school.' On the other hand, for the 'underclasses', it became a cheeky form of resistance, something one 'had' in the way those who stood out were once said to have 'personality'.

I.I. I don't know if you intended it but that is a nice reflexion back on your point about the psychometric identicality of attitudes and personality.

Attitude change

The 'social hygiene' agenda which got attached to attitude research is based upon a medical model. First, of course, the 'ill' must be diagnosed, the 'bad attitudes' must be identified and the client group thereby defined. However, all this diagnosis is just the beginning. Its importance lies in that it warrants 'treatment'. Like Procrustes, psychology has felt it most important to be able to claim a technology of 'adjustment'. Only then can the 'maladjusted' be humaneered into the desired condition. In the attitude area, adjustment is a matter of attitude change, and much energy has been devoted to the uncovering of the key to successful opinioneering.

Every major theory, from psychodynamics to the information-processing approach has been mined-out in this quest. We will concentrate upon just one because it is uniquely social-psychological and uniquely emblematic of its own dis-eases, Festinger's (1957) theory of cognitive dissonance. Cognitive dissonance theory belongs to a meta-theoretical approach which social psychology has made its own – theories of cognitive consistency.

Box 6.4 Cognitive Dissonance

Festinger's (1957) theory of cognitive dissonance began life as an all-purpose formulation – one that could be applied to organisms in all situations, from rats in a maze to accolytes in a cult. In essence, it is a kind of pared-down, folksy, psychodynamic theory. It presumes that inconsistency between two cognitive elements is discomforting, and that this negative feeling motivates change in one or other cognition. In his *Scientific American* presentation (1962) Festinger deliberately appeals to folk-wisdom to explain the theory. Aesop's fable of 'sour grapes' is used to make the point. The fox starts off with the cognition that the grapes he espies are good eating but after several unsuccessful attempts to reach them, he now has a second cognition – they are unobtainable. He now experiences 'cognitive dissonance'. The cognition that the grapes are unattainable is too pressing to be gainsaid, all that can change is his 'attitude' to the grapes. Consonance is restored by 'attitude change' – the once-desired become mere 'sour grapes'. The theory became a paradigm of 'attitude-change' and, over the following decade and a half, it was the most researched approach in social psychology. Part of its allure was its claim to make counter-intuitive (which often meant counter-learning theory) predictions. The germinal study was by Festinger and Carlsmith (1959).

This investigation also set the mould for how cognitive dissonance theory was to be applied to attitude change, for it introduced the key manipulation of 'counter-attitudinal advocacy'. In other words, people were induced to argue against a position they had previously endorsed. The effect of this on subsequently expressed 'attitude' was then explored.

In this study experimental subjects were given incentives of either $1 or $20 for telling another person that a boring task they had just done was, in fact, interesting and exciting. The counter-intuitive result was that a significant shift towards describing the task as 'interesting' was found only for those subjects who were paid $1. The $20 reward group did not change their attitude.

Festinger and Carlsmith explained this by saying that the large reward (and in those days $20 was a pretty large reward) allowed people to discount their behaviour. They could see themselves as having been 'well-rewarded' for their lie and so experienced no dissonance and hence there was no need to change their attitude. But, for the other experimental group, the small reward was 'insufficient justification' for their perjury and they were not able to 'explain away their behaviour'. They experienced discomforting dissonance between what they actually felt and what they had done. Since they could not alter their behaviour (the deed was done), something had to go – and that something was their prior attitude. Hence they retrospectively reconstructed their own motivation by shifting to a more positive evaluation of the task.

This effect is pretty robust but there is much in the paradigm which is taken-for-granted, not least the presence of 'cognitive dissonance' itself and the explanation of the effect. These issues were to occupy the time of a great number of social psychologists, including one of the present authors in an earlier incarnation (Rogers, 1974). The outcome was to introduce a deep disenchantment in many about the whole laboratory approach. For the more critical, this work led to four main conclusions:

1 Such studies may 'work' not because their participants are all 'wired-up' to seek consistency but because they mimic social situations where we are 'put on the line'. They reveal not psychological laws but sociological mores.
2 It is not so much consistency per se that is 'tested' in such situations but norms of conduct in which inconsistency 'looks bad'.
3 It is a 'way of life' for us to seek to manage the impressions our conduct may create.
4 Opinionation and change in opinionation are central to such impression management.

In other words, Festinger and his colleagues (and experimental social psychology more generally) achieved no more than to demonstrate, in the trappings of an experiment, that they (as experimenters) shared a set of understandings with the subjects in their study about how we are supposed to conduct ourselves. This first wave of critique, an early manifestation of the climate of perturbation, was couched in the then-emergent 'new paradigm' of interpretative social psychology, at that time being propounded by people like Kenneth Gergen and Edward Sampson in the USA and Rom Harré and John Shotter in the UK. They denounced the essentialist image of people who can be studied in laboratories as 'idealized automata in bland, anomic environments' (Harré, 1979). They argued that we should view people, instead, as rule-making, rule-following and insightful actors who actively strive to 'make sense of' their world. Where these arguments have now moved to is the kind of critical social psychology we celebrate in this book.

However, it would be quite false to foster the impression that mainstream attitude work simply crawled up and died as a result of these perturbations. It did not. Rather, it sought to present itself as sensitized by them (cf. McGuire, 1986) while bolstering itself from further attack by further wrapping itself in the garb of science. The same response was made to the dismal record in terms of demonstrating any meaningful relationship between the attitudes people express and the actions they take. The best cloak and cloaking around proved to be the more general shift into cognitivism, and the generation of a series of ever-more complex models of cognitive algebra. Unwilling to give up on the hand-rail on 'truth' (cf. Game, 1991) that they saw empiricism as offering them, they resorted to the mystery language of mathematics to wrap their formulations safe from scrutiny (cf. Kline, 1988). This enables them, in Foucault's term, to 'draw a veil' over their discourse, keeping its secrets hidden so that its knowledge would continue to be prized and revered (cf. Foucault, 1970-88).

Attitudes and behaviour

Psychology's record in linking attitudes to behaviour is hardly a showpiece in its parlour (cf. Wicker, 1969; McGuire, 1986). However, as cognitive dissonance theory would argue, if enough has been invested in the effort, failure must be recast as containing the seeds of success. Clearly (?), the answer must lie in ever more sophisticated modelling. This has been achieved by:

- locating 'attitudes' as but one of several components involved in rational decision-making about behaviour;
- describing these components in precise mathematical terms; and

- theorizing how these interact together by way of complex mathematical equations.

The best-known example here is the work of Ajzen and his colleagues (e.g. Ajzen and Fishbein, 1980; Ajzen and Madden, 1986; Ajzen and Timko, 1986).

Box 6.5 Ajzen's Theories of Reasoned Action and Planned Behaviour

The theory of reasoned action

Ajzen specifies that his model 'is concerned with the casual antecedents of volitional action ... based on the assumption that human beings usually behave in a sensible manner, and that they take account of available information and implicitly or explicitly consider the implications of their actions' (1988: 177).

In the simplest form of the model, he argues that intention is the immediate determinant of action, and that intention itself is a function of two basic determinants – one personal (attitudes) and the other social (subjective norms). Put simply this says that a person's intention to act (or not act) in a particular way is a function of their evaluation of the benefits and costs of that action, taken together with their estimate of the value others place on it.

Attitudes towards the behaviour
↓
Intention → Behaviour
↑
Subjective norm

(taken from Ajzen, 1988)

This model was then elaborated to accommodate the antecedents of the attitudes and subjective norms, taking account of things like learned expectations about outcomes, normative beliefs, etc. The end result was the theory expressed as a mathematical equation.

$$B \cong BI \left(\sum_{i=1}^{n} bi.ei \right) W, + \left(\sum_{j=1}^{m} nbj.mcj \right) W_2$$

Theory of planned action

Ajzen then extended the model to accommodate the way people plan action and address numerous factors which may disrupt the intention-

> behaviour relation. It encompasses, for example, estimations of perceived behavioural control, and the likelihood of achieving particular goals.
>
> The kinds of overall conclusions Ajzen arrives at from his theory are that 'Generally speaking . . . people intend to perform a behaviour if their personal evaluations of it are favourable, if they think that important others would approve of it, and if they believe that the requisite resources and opportunities will be available'. (Ajzen 1988: 144)

What we can see here is a splendid example of what Kline (1988: 24) calls the 'the sacred language of science, the mythic script known only to those few who have undergone the dreaded rites of initiation' used to glamour a convincing illusion of the superiority of scholarly over common-sense knowledge. Such equations 'work' at all only because they have been 'fixed', post hoc, by incorporating just the right weighting variables to make them work. Their predictive accuracy is no more than mathematical sleight of hand (or computer).

This is the way that social psychologists like Ajzen have been able to make their theories appear to be predictive. But the kind of prediction they allow is chimeral. They 'show' no more than that, if you ask people to express what they intend to do in certain carefully defined situations, carefully limit the range of possible responses they can make and carry out some clever calculations with the data, you can sometimes get a reasonable 'fit' between what they say they intend to do and what they 'actually do'.

We are not of course the only people to comment that the emperor has no clothes. Leventhal and Hirshman (1982: 199) for example have argued that 'it is questionable that we greatly advance our understanding . . . by concentrating on the measurement of factors so proximate to action that we are practically using measures at the beginning of the act to predict the action itself'. It is, as they suggest, hardly surprising that you can predict fairly accurately whether or not people will do something if you ask them just beforehand if they think doing it is a good idea, whether they think others will approve, and whether they care about what other people think (see fig. 6.1).

Being able to predict in this situation, in any case, does not establish any 'casual' links between expressed opinions and intended action. It simply tells us (just as with Festinger's work) that the researchers and subjects in the study appear to have shared a common understanding of what the contingencies are between expressing opinions and taking action. We would argue that this kind of common access to the common

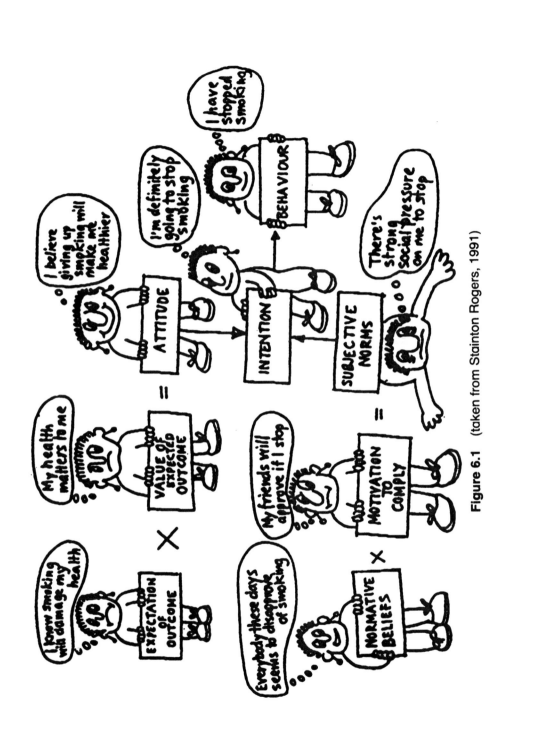

Figure 6.1   (taken from Stainton Rogers, 1991)

portfolio of discourses on contingency is all that we can ever build our
theories and empirical studies of attitude and attitude-behaviour upon.

I.I. As in 'Let your deeds be the advocate of your words?'

If the alternative is being sued for 'breach of contract', probably 'yes'.
On the other hand, we can always 'honour the words of a contract but
not its spirit'. The 'between ourselves' of folk wisdom, like that of popular
discourse, is always multiplex.

Epilogue: Putting opinionation back 'between ourselves'

The traditional social-psychological treatment of attitudes has been deeply
troubled over the past twenty years. As we have noted in the section
above, that is not to say that it has been abandoned – but it is no longer
the 'jewel in the crown' of the discipline. Shifts in theoretical fashion
alone (such as the emergence of attributional approaches, cf. Chapter 7)
have seen to that. However, concern with opinionation has developed
apace, with at least three strands of work being differentiable.

The first of these, discussed in more general terms in Chapter 11, is the
European social psychological approach known as social representations
theory. Here, attitudes are relocated into an approach which seeks, not
unproblematically (cf. Parker, 1988), to address the interplay between
personal and social subjectivity. In terms of research methods, this is the
closest to attitude work as traditionally practised. The second strand is to
seek to go 'beyond' attitudes and behaviour (Potter and Wetherell, 1987)
into a non-intra-psychic, language-focused discursive psychology (cf.
Edwards and Potter, 1992). 'Method' here denotes attempts to read both
on the lines and 'between the lines' of (largely spoken) texts – discourse
analysis (again also examined in Chapter 11). The final strand, to which
we would adhere, wonders whether opinionation as a form of social life
can be contained at all within a psychology. It argues instead for a
transdiscipline of expressive and knowledging activity (cf. Curt, 1994)
and employs a range of cosmopolitan forms of scrutiny, most notably in
the area of opinionation, Q methodology (Chapter 11 again). In each of
these areas there has been a sustained attempt to break free of the
groundings of traditional attitude work. Arguments within and between
these them are intense but it does make for a reflexive sensitivity to the
vagaries of opinionation!

7 Science and Common Sense

Making sense and making nonsense

Recently social psychologists have taken a renewed interest in the ways ordinary people make sense of the world – employing new theory languages such as attribution theory and schema theory to do so. However the concern is of long standing – the themes of social perception and social cognition (under various labels) have been part of social psychology for most of its history. What Jones and Gerard (1967: 131) called 'cognitive and perceptual processes' have long been employed in accounts of social behaviour and experience and of individual differences therein – particularly in the area of person perception. Within this work there has been a tacit (where not explicit) contrast between 'lay' theorization (i.e. ordinary, everyday 'common sense' – and its abnormalities) and scientific theorization: 'the paranoid often classes neutral events as referring to himself [sic] ('they are talking about me'), using cues that others would ignore or use for different purposes. The trained botanist exploits a range of cues which would be ignored by most of the rest of us' (Jones and Gerard, 1967: 133). Nowhere is this more true than where psychology has sought to contrast its own activities in explaining behaviour and experience with the person in the street's opinions about 'what makes people tick' – between, in other words, what are often called 'naive' theories (e.g. of character) as opposed to 'scientific' theories (e.g. psychological theories of personality).

I.I. This is more of the 'Mission', I suppose?

Absolutely. Psychologists have not tended to view what they term the 'lay beliefs' and 'naive theories' of the 'folk' they study as forms of knowledge in their own right. Rather they have construed them in one of two ways. Where the objects of study are people similar in background to psychologists (such as students acting as experimental subjects) then their (the subjects') ways of thinking are portrayed as the products of psychological processes that introduce distortion upon 'real' (i.e. rational, objective, scientific) knowledge. This is evident in the terminology that psychologists use. Social cognition theorization (see, for example, Nisbett and Ross, 1980) is replete with terms like 'the fundamental attribution error', 'the actor–observer error' and 'the false consensus effect'. Where, however, the subjects of study are more different – for example, working-class mothers or members of 'other' cultures (see Box 10.1), – then their cognitions are frequently seen not so much as distortions as entirely false knowledge – superstitions, myths and old wives' tales.

This immediately prompts the question – what motivates social psychologists to make these distinctions? One likely reason is that social psychology is anxious about its own status, being not infrequently viewed by more 'rigorous' psychologists as a bit of a pseudo-science. Certainly within many departments of psychology it is still tainted by association with a subject-matter which comes over – against the hard-wired back-drop of, say, cognitive psychology and neurophysiology – as nebulous, fuzzy and imprecise. It is often regarded as something of a fringe enterprise, because it adopts concepts, terms and research topics from sociology and anthropology (whose scientific legitimacy is viewed as distinctly dodgy). Because its focus of study is 'the social', it does not fit fully comfortably with the laboratory procedures and experimental principles which much of psychology has used to establish its scientific credentials – although experimental social psychologists have tried hard to counter this. Consequently social psychology is under particular pressure to demonstrate that it can come up with something more than mere 'common sense'.

One way of doing this is to show explicitly that there are real, observable and demonstrable differences between social psychology's knowledge and common-sense knowledge. In constructing a body of knowledge about lay beliefs, social psychology thus marks off its endeavour as a 'special' way of knowing – an expertise, which is quite distinct from (and superior to) the lay person's way of knowing. The creation of a distinction between common sense and expert knowledge thus not only constitutes topics and projects for social psychology to study (such as social cognition, attribution and lay-epistemic knowledge); it serves to bolster the 'scientific' status of social psychology. In its exploitation of the lay/expert distinction, social psychology established itself as a truly 'scientific' enterprise.

However, these topic areas place social psychologists in a peculiar position. Although they claim the authority to determine what counts as 'proper' knowledge, they are still none the less attempting to study within territories of knowledge which are (at least apparently) familiar to everybody. This is not like studying short-term memory or neurophysiology – topics which non-experts do not expect to know about or understand. Everybody has experience of being social and a wide repertoire of explanations to draw upon in making sense of their own (and others') social being. As Bannister and Fransella (1971: 12) point out, 'psychology is man's [*sic*] understanding of his own understanding'. To claim to be able to establish an expert body of knowledge, one must be able to claim to know more (to know better than or to know different from) 'what everybody knows'.

This is an inherently difficult task. To come up with expert knowledge which merely mirrors non-expert knowledge is to run the risk, as Humphrey and Argyle point out, of being accused of having nothing to offer: 'It has been objected that the results of much social research are not surprising, that we knew them all before' (1974: 14). But to come up with expert knowledge which is counter-intuitive – which flies in the face of common sense – is to risk coming across as absurd. It is much easier to persuade people of the distinctive quality of expert knowledge if one is looking at the minutiae of the nervous system or the vagaries of human memory than if one is exploring the more familiar territory of everyday human experience.

As a result, social psychologists have worked hard to distance their ways of thinking from the ways the objects of their enquiry (ordinary people) think – they have exerted tremendous effort to make the distinction between 'expert' and 'lay' knowledge as marked as possible. For example, theories which portray ordinary people as 'naive scientists' none the less take care to point out the errors of their ways – by, for instance, referring to them as 'cognitive misers' who are vulnerable to a range of lazy short-cuts and errors in their thinking. Social psychologists make it very clear that these 'naive psychologists' are a very poor version of the 'real thing':

Implicit psychology involves both attribution and the formation of private theories of reality. Unlike the theories of psychologists, in which the methods, assumptions and data are explicitly stated, implicit psychological theories are private and often cannot be explained by their owner. Indeed, people do not regard their implicit theories as theories at all, but as facts.

Consequently, they tend not to revise the theories when presented with contradictory data. Many prejudices and superstitions can best be understood as products of faulty implicit theories of human nature. (Carlsmith, 1984: 566)

Box 7.1   The Errors of Their Ways

Social psychologists who work in applied areas (such as health psychology) draw upon this assumed distinction between the superior 'factual' knowledge of science and the 'faulty' implicit theories of common sense to warrant the claim that ordinary people are ignorant of the 'true facts'. For example, Furnham vilifies ordinary people for their ignorance about alcoholism. Listing seventeen of what he terms 'factual errors' about the effects of alcohol and causes of alcoholism, he states: 'A surprising number of people would endorse these statements as true despite the fact that they are all demonstrably false. If their knowledge is so patchy, if not downright wrong, it is perhaps, therefore, not surprising that their explanations of, or theories for, alcoholism are simple or misguided' (Furnham, 1983).
Examples of the statements which Furnham states are untrue are

- Alcohol is a stimulant
- Alcohol can help a person sleep more soundly
- People with 'strong wills' need not be concerned about becoming alcoholics.

Another reading of the situation, which often seems to have escaped this approach to ordinary understanding, is that these statements have quite different *meanings* within popular discourse, compared with their scientific meanings.

The emergence of cognitive social psychology

I.I. You have previously taken a dim view of the value-added, 'feel-good' use of buzz-words like 'cognitive'. Should I prepare for another attack?

Yes, but also for a bit more history. To grasp how such lines of research and argument became so dominant, we need to look back to the changing agendas which psychology experienced three decades ago. Back in the

1960s, the kinds of alternative agendas psychology most listened to can be exemplified by George Kelly's (1955) call that psychology should see people as 'naive scientists' who – like real scientists – hypothesize about the world, test their hypotheses and keep to them or discard them according to whether this reality-testing confirms (or refutes) them. To be fair to Kelly's personal construct theory, it was intended to promote a humanistic shift – a move away from a puppet-like image of the person as riven by internal drives, towards a model which stressed human inventiveness and self-awareness. However, what mainstream psychologists seem to have turned it into is a self-serving polemic – 'the person, a pretty lousy scientist'!

From a critical perspective, there is another problem here. Much of the humanism prevailing in the 1960s (including Kelly's) was strongly individualistic, stressing subjectivity over intersubjectivity. As with other topics it studies (like attitudes and personality), traditional social psychology conceives of social cognition as sited within individuals. Billig characterizes what he sees as the two main themes in cognitive social psychology (attribution theory and schema theory) in the following way: 'Despite being separate traditions, both concentrate upon the way individuals make sense of their individual social worlds, and, in so doing, tend to ignore the extent to which human thinking is shaped by culture' (1989: 100).

As with any traditional psychological approach, it has gone about investigating common-sense thinking along two, main, pre-set paths. First, it has sought to construct and test general laws about its biases and errors. Secondly, it has pursued explanations of the 'facts' (particularly the 'problems') of the social world. Thus, for example, the beliefs that a person has about the causes of another's actions are held to play a part in their reaction and response to that other person's actions. In turn, the general features of such beliefs (i.e. the categories of causes they employ) are held to be universal, while their specific 'tunings' are internalized social norms. Hence, work in this field is assumed to inform us about how people construe the social world in a more general sense.

The emergence of attribution theory

As we expand upon it a little later, attribution theory (for some reason it tends to be singularized) very much took over from attitude theories around the late 1960s as the dominant concern of experimental social psychologists. There is not, of course, an attribution theory as such but rather a set of conceptual approaches.

I.I. I was afraid there might be – any chance of a summary?

Box 7.2   Attribution Theory

Attribution theory is usually traced back to Heider (1958) who first adopted the 'naive scientist' metaphor. Empirically, it is concerned with how people make attributions in general, but tends to focus on very specific types of judgements, for example, the judgement of whether a person's behaviour is the result of some internal factor or characteristic and is therefore *Dispositional*, or whether it is the result of some external, environmental cause, and is therefore *Situational*. This distinction was first made by Heider, and in one form or another is still central to work in attribution theory.

Nevertheless, attribution theorists feel that, if they can explain specific types of judgements in this way, they will be able to develop models which explain the more general process of attribution. A number of formulations have been developed, of which the best known are Jones and Davis's 'Correspondence Inference Theory' (1965); Weiner's 'Three Dimensional Taxonomy' (1986); and H. H. Kelley's 'Covariation Theory' (1967). Each is given lavish coverage in mainstream texts (e.g. Brehm and Cassin, 1990). Each postulates certain parallels between the tasks facing the 'naive scientist' and those facing the 'behavioural scientist'. This is particularly apparent in the case of Kelley, whose 'theory' boils down to the premise that attribution relies upon an implicit 'analysis of variance'.

Kelley's approach to attribution is based upon the covariation principle. Basically this means that when a person is trying to decide if someone's action has a dispositional or a situational cause, they will try to determine whether factors which are suspected to be the cause are present when the behaviour occurs and absent when the behaviour does not occur. That is, they are trying to discover whether a suspected cause consistently covaries with the behaviour. Given consistency, the key to a dispositional or situation attribution lies in (1) the level of 'consensus' (high if others tend to act as the target of individual acts, low if not) and (2) the level of 'distinctiveness' (high if the target person's actions are not their usual reactions, low if they are). High consensus and distinctiveness are associated with situational attributions. Low consensus and distinctiveness are associated with dispositional attributions.

Thus, in a nutshell, Kelley's attributional model reveals that if Chris consistently drives within the speed limit when police cars are about – as do other drivers – ('consensus'), but not otherwise (distinctiveness) then the 'naive scientist' should conclude that Chris's behavioural act of keeping to the speed limit when police cars are about results from the situation rather than something dispositional about Chris.

I.I. I suspect you may have set me up for this – but isn't that a bit obvious, more common sense than science?

Were attributional research confined to such mind-boggling inanities, one suspects that even experimental social psychologists would have lost interest by now. Clearly, work on attribution theory is seen to provide more than, and other than, this kind of information. Part of the answer lies in the very shift towards a cognitive social psychology itself.

Cognitive social psychology (cf. Eiser, 1980) is not just a metatheory in its own right, but one which was predicated upon a shift away from earlier metatheories – particularly behaviouristic and psychodynamic ones. The postulate of the person as a 'naive scientist' both replaced and displaced the postulate of 'man [*sic*] the rat' and 'man [*sic*] the plaything of the emotions' (cf. Wiggins et al., 1968). There was something of a 'false dialectic' (cf. Buss, 1979) at work here, a swing of the pendulum between an emphasis on passion and one on ration. The 'cool' of attribution theory supplanted the 'hots' of cognitive dissonance theory (cf. Chapter 7).

In the new paradigm of cognitive social psychology, people were seen to be guided by rational deductive thinking rather than by lusts and desires (cf. Billig, in Howitt et al., 1989). This image of the human subject was in marked contrast to the image of the lay person embedded within the cognitive consistency paradigm of the previous decade. Once elevated by scientists to the status of near-scientists themselves, the new subjects of cognitive social psychology were less to be duped and deceived and more to be worked with.

There was, of course, also a pragmatic agenda here. The 1960s left psychology with a greater sense of ethics (or at least the legal costs of their infraction!). Claims of emotional hurt were now very much to be avoided, and cognition was safely 'cold'. However, as a site of study, human cognition itself had a tradition, and that tradition was one of theories that were both descriptive and prescriptive in their claims. Obvious examples are cognitive developmental theories such as those of Piaget (e.g. 1952) or, very much 'in the air' as cognitive social psychology was forming, such as those of Kohlberg (e.g. 1966). Any model which claims to plot progress towards an 'ideal' state of cognitive development must also show the 'failings' of earlier states and stages (cf. Stainton Rogers and Stainton Rogers, 1992b). Just as influential was the information coming from formal cognitive psychology, where the limited processing capacity and short-term memory limitations of human subjects were a major topic of interest (e.g. Baddeley, 1992). Thus, if at his or her 'best' the naive scientist is to be the equal of the 'real thing', the conditions are created for the study of 'second best' and worse:

> As social perceivers, we may be limited in our ability to process all relevant information, or we may lack the kinds of training needed to fully employ the logic of attribution theory ... More importantly, we often just don't make an effort to think carefully about our attribution. With so much to explain and not enough time in the day, people take short cuts, hope for the best, and get on with life. . . . The problem is, with speed comes bias, and perhaps even a loss of accuracy. In this section we examine the consequences of these short cuts, or what could be called the bloopers of social perception (Brehm and Cassin, 1990: 1104).

I.I. What's a 'blooper' when it's at home?

Blooper is US English for what your grandparents might have called a bloomer (in the singular)!

Box 7.3   Biased, Ain't We?

Crib notes on 'the bloopers of social perception'.

The Fundamental Attribution Error

Having a discipline supposedly grounded on social-situational influences on behaviour, it seems to have come as a nasty shock to social psychologists that, in attributional paradigms, their subjects persistently 'overemphasized' dispositional factors as the cause of behaviour in others. So ubiquitous was this effect that they called it the 'fundamental attribution error'. Of course, researchers cannot actually get a fix on the 'true' explanation (we will have much to say about this later), what they do instead is to try to fix the cues so that a dispositional explanation seems obvious (e.g. the target behaviour is blatantly forced without choice).

Actor/Observer Discrepancies

Strictly speaking, the fundamental attribution error is not universal – one major exception emerges from the research. This is that we tend to make situational attributions when the actor is ourself rather than another.

Discrepancies Between 'Objective' and 'Subjective' Probability

These concern the tendency to underuse or mis-estimate consensus information (see Kelley above). Research seems to indicate that people are poor at using 'objective' data about probabilities. An obvious example is gambling, where potential high returns seem to capture our attention more than the very slight chance of actually winning. 'Objectively' the football pools and National Lottery return only a fraction of the money staked. However, the dream of getting rich quick appears to divert our attention from both the minute chances of winning and the poor return overall. This is usually called the 'base rate fallacy'. A second commonly identified discrepancy, false consensus, refers to an over-stating of the degree to which others will be, do or say the same as we ourselves.

Outcome Biases

These are well known to us through such folk sayings as 'a bad workman always blames his tools'. A negative outcome leads to a circumstantial or situational attribution, a positive outcome to a dispositional one. This seems to hold both for actions of the individual (self-serving bias) and for one's in-group (group-serving bias).

Motivational Biases

There is a considerable argument amongst cognitive social psychologists (who both believe in and care about such distinctions) as to whether outcome biases are 'motivational' or 'informational'. No such doubt surrounds the dynamics of 'victim blaming'. This is said to stem from the operation of a broad orientation to the world dubbed 'Belief in a Just World' (Lerner, 1980 – see also Chapter 6). This politically informed and informing argument-complex is grounded on such folk beliefs as 'you're gonna reap just what you sow' – whether that be illness, unemployment or rape.

I.I. Is there any hope, Doctor?

Attribution and applied social psychology

The notion that our modes of attribution can play a key role in our well-being – or otherwise – has its roots in Rotter's (1966) notion of locus of control and Seligman's theory of learned helplessness. Recently this has given rise to a branch of applied social psychology concerned with seeking to change attributional processes. The key to this movement into interventional practice stems from the importation into the learned helplessness area of attributational notions. Specifically, pessimistic thinking (Abramson, Seligman, and Teasdale, 1978) has been linked to attributions that are: internal (i.e. self-attributions), stable (i.e. long-lasting) and global (i.e. generalized to a wide variety of situations). Where these attributions are made to negative events, the result is claimed to be depression, lowered effort and a range of performance problems such as difficulties in learning.

I.I. Sounds like most of my mates . . .

We would accept that much undergraduate distress can be re-cast into such language. It does not surprise us either that where the time is taken to explain to a student that 'negative events' (such as initial bad grades) should not be laid on the self, the performance of the student improves (Wilson and Linville, 1982). What we might wish to question is why such interventions come to be needed. Why it is that good teaching practice needs to be introduced as an 'experimental condition'? Why does the obvious need to be re-cast into the language of attribution theory? What is going on?

I.I. Questions I might well ask too!

Considered as a whole, work on the 'naive scientist' seems to indicate that s/he is not just naive but logically perverse! The layperson is revealed not only as a long way from any rational ideal in their judgement but also as largely immune to change – persevering with their biases even when the evidence is stacked against them. However, critical writers argue that this is also typical of the workings of scientists themselves. The work of Kuhn (1970), for example, is used to argue that unsubstantiated belief perseverance is not unique to the lay person, it is also a common feature of scientific research itself. Where the key difference may lie is that the very institutional circumstances of being part of a 'discipline' can conservatize scientist's thinking – unlike Wilson and Linville's students, they are rewarded for their stable, global and internal attributions!

Re-attributing attribution

Attributional research in general has much in common with the broader psychological tradition of 'testing' the powers of the mind. In all such work, the subject is presented with a problem or dilemma to resolve, or a task to perform. The normal implication is that, if certain inferential schemes are both in place and are activated by the task, then a correct or proper inference will be made. There may well be, of course, an extremely low 'base rate' to both these preconditions being met under any circumstances (other than by the 'artificial intelligence' of constraint by a formal logic)! Ordinarily, such logics are not the language in which humans work and what is more they resent and resist being positioned in logistic dialogues (Wason, 1977), seeing them as trickery and power games in which they are the victim.

In other words, rather than exploring people's well-practised cultural competences, social psychologists test them in a largely alien mode and discover (hardly surprisingly) that they do rather poorly. This holds true, according to Wason, even for subjects who have high IQs, university education or even a professorship in logic! We should, in other words, expect to find problems rather than purport to be discovering them, Kruglanski, Baldwin and Towson (1983) argue that bias and error are inevitable in all inference, not just lay inference. They further suggest that the debate concerning the rationality or irrationality of lay judgement is very much a red herring. We have to agree. The invited comparison between the lay person's reasoning and the normative models of logico-mathematical inference (assuming the proven superiority of the latter) is not only a rigged contest, but there is little reason to think that the latter bears much resemblance to the actual working procedures of science (see, for example, Mulkay, 1985).

From a critical perspective, the fascination with attribution theory and alleged lay/professional differences can be read as informing us about how science works as discourse – how it warrants its claims for a special status to its pronouncements. Looked at like this, as we have already argued, attribution research serves to re-state the superior status of social psychology over ordinary explanation. Every paper on attribution theory is a double-edged exercise in the warranting of social psychological research itself. First, like social psychological research into other issues, it announces that warrant by its special language ('expertise') and its claims to be driven by adherence to a highly organized set of canonical rules for attributing cause and effect (more expertise). Second, by contrast, the subjects' approach to knowledge is shown to be undisciplined and, hence, prone to error.

Of course, in critique, we do not ordinarily just seek to identify language as power-play, we seek to challenge it. As critical social psychologists, we might also wish to ask: what are the researchers and the subjects claiming about their knowledges? The subjects, if challenged, will lay no special claims. They will probably say something like: 'It's obvious', or 'It's just my opinion', or 'Everybody knows that . . .'.

This is exactly what every social psychology student learns is neither what to say nor how to say it! The craft and its warrants demand something very different – expertise in expertese. This is, of course, how social psychologists have been socialized into their craft. Once we can see this professional discourse in terms of warrants to power, we can also learn more about why it is so often argued that it is scientized discourse which proceeds in this way rather than science per se. It is a necessary fiction for the craft – its public, presentational face – behind the scenes (as Goffman, 1963) we hear other language games. For example: 'the use of "I think" by eminent figures in social psychology . . . reflects and reproduces social status positions (in which those higher up give their "thought" (in a style closer to "speech"), and the minions have to offer "facts" (in objective "written" form)' (Parker 1989: 155).

I.I. I think that's a bit mean.

We think it's spot on!

Schema theory and social representations theory

Attribution theory puts its main emphasis upon how social information is processed in terms of analysis of causation. Its approach tends to the nomothetic, exploring general laws of throughput. The other main approaches in this area are rather more global in their interests and take a distinctly structural approach. They are concerned more with the effects of experiencing the social world: the schemata (schemas or schemes) or representations that are thereby said to result. For example, we could in Chapter 3 have spoken about the concept of self-schemas, the notion that individual differences in 'personality' result from what attributes are schematic for an individual's notion of self (and hence salient) and what are aschematic for them in that regard (Markus, 1977).

The roots of schema theory lie in the work of Bartlett (1932) and still carry forward notions that our internal representations act as a source of distorted and selective social perception and cognition. Bartlett studied this using a kind of 'Chinese whispers' technique, telling people a story (*The War of the Ghosts*) and then asking them to repeat it subsequently – often many times and over several years. It was a strange story, taken from Native American folklore, and – not surprisingly – Bartlett found that people made errors in their recall, which tended to become magnified and consolidated over multiple tellings. So – we should not look to schema theory for an escape from the pre-occupation with bias and failure. Quite to the contrary, it takes at least as dismal a view of the ordinary thinker as does attribution theory (Fiske and Taylor, 1984). It also parallels attribution theory's individualistic focus.

I.I. Or, dare I say it for you, its individualistic bias!'

Quite! However, if we go back and explore what gave British subjects so much common grief when dealing with an 'alien' (i.e. extra-societal) story, it was that their shared-together schemes for understanding it did not match those of the culture that had given birth to the tale. What led to the very 'British' readings Bartlett obtained were local or social representations. What is known today as the 'theory of social representations' was the result of work centred upon the ideas of Moscovici (e.g. 1982). In it 'social representations are seen as mental schemata or images which people use to make sense of the world and to communicate with each other' (Potter and Wetherell, 1987: 138).

Social representations theory is often hailed as a special European contribution to social psychology, offering (in contrast to US individualism) a truly social social psychology – something in a direct line from Durkheim's (1895) formulation of collective representation. Social representations are, in one sense, what a collectivity shares – its common theories or constructions of the social world: its 'common sense'. The theory does not, however, assume that, for a society such as ours, the condition of shared knowledge is static. Rather there is a process afoot, one where representations need to be seen as 'phenomena that are linked with a special way of acquiring and communicating knowledge, a way that creates realities and common sense' (Moscovici, 1981: 186).

There is, in other words, a flow of ideas both 'between ourselves' and percolating down from formal (i.e. scientific) sources of knowledge, albeit in some attenuated and vulgarized form into common sense. Moscovici's first study (1976) used the example of Freudian theory, arguing that the lay person treats the hypothetical constructs developed by Freud (such as the Id, Ego and Superego) as if they were objective entities in their own right – spatially distinct, almost tangible components of mind. Thus, according to Moscovici, the lay person is apt to objectify the abstract into something more palatably concrete (see Moscovici and Hewstone, 1983, for a fuller development of this idea).

However, despite the attention in social representations theory to the role of societal supra-structure (e.g. institutional agents such as 'science'), the actual medium of transmission for social representations theory is still seen as the individual. As a result, social representation theorists continue to postulate internal ('cognitive') mechanisms, drawing upon notions not unlike those employed in other European structuralisms (e.g. neo-Piagetian notions, cf. Jodelet, 1984). It has also pursued laboratory and psychometric studies into social representations in ways which are often hard to distinguish from North American schematic experimental social psychology.

Disciplined sense and common sense revisioned

In contrast to the powerful separation usually drawn between formal and popular thinking, a counter-case can be argued. This revisionism suggests that there are overwhelming constructural similarities between scientific and lay knowledge. For example, Horton (1972), studying African traditional thought and Western scientific thought, argued that lay and scientific theories have empirically identical structures. Basically, the activity of theorizing, regardless of the status of the theorizer, is an attempt to simplify and order an apparently complex universe. The main difference between the lay person and the scientist is that the scientist's attempts to construct a theory are more self-conscious.

I.I. If I was really mean, I could suggest they are more ritualized and self-important.

The theories which are formed to link the phenomena made relevant, by a limited number of rules or principles, are distinguishable only by the status which is accorded to them within our culture and often the barrage of technical terminology used to express (or, more jaundicedly, to obscure) them. At the same time, it is also beginning to be realized that the 'common sense' generally studied by cognitive social psychologists is itself local and contingent to our own culture. Thus Miller (1984) argues that the 'fundamental attribution error' features in US adults who are 'American' (*sic*) but not in those who are 'Asian Indian'(*sic*).

Again, although the scientist is supposed to be essentially and overwhelmingly sceptical, Feyerabend (1975) argues that this scepticism is directed against apposing theories rather than at our own theories. Research under the critical approach – known as the sociology of scientific knowledge (SSK) (e.g. Mulkay, 1985) suggests that scientists' discourse has much the same fluidity and instrumentally as mundane discourse. In other words, it is quintessentially meaningful within the language games of a specific collectively – it works 'between themselves'. Thus, scientists do not necessarily use the rules of science to guide their conduct, but rather to construct a coherent and convincing *post hoc* explanation for their actions.

Potter and Wetherell (1987) focus on the example of testability, which is claimed to be the major governing rule of scientific progress and procedure. They show in their analysis of scientists' discourse that this rule is drawn upon flexibly to give credence to the construction of their own theories (rather than to guide their construction) and to challenge other people's theories. In other words, we don't abandon our own theories on the grounds that they are not falsifiable, but we often find that the theories of our colleagues (and competitors) do require rejection.

Understanding as the negotiation of reality

To the critical eye, cognitive social psychology has generated an extremely partial account of how the social world is understood. This partiality can be summed up, with a little irony, as amounting itself to a set of 'biases':

- Assuming that understanding is primarily concerned with causes, as opposed, for example, to reasons. Assuming that the main site of activity is intra-psychic rather than 'between ourselves'. Assuming that there is an objective 'social reality' which in some way comes to be 'represented' subjectively.
- Assuming that unproblematic translations can be made between psychological theoretical constructs (e.g. cognitivism) and sociological theorization (e.g. structuralism) such that their interplay can be taken for granted.
- Assuming that social thinking can be idealized, and hence that the focus of interest lies in its biases and 'bloopers'.
- Assuming that social psychology (as a special case of scientific thinking) proceeds on a different and better basis than common sense.

In looking to what positive alternatives can be proposed for the study of social understanding, we need first to identify what renders such an approach partial. It is, to us, its thrust towards singularization – its opacity to the notion that understanding is a manifold of activities. Hence (cf. Curt, 1994) we would argue for a contrasted stance. Specifically, we argue that we should allow that people (even social psychologists) make sense of their worlds by drawing upon a plurality of available representations, ideas, discourses and theories. This social knowledge is always located and contingent, and like the people who use it – embedded within culture. Understanding thus takes place 'between ourselves' and its expression is 'circumstantial' (cf. Chapter 4) and shifts with our changing locations and subject positions. Such a realization can be linked to the more recent moves towards anthropological/ethnographic methods for data collection and discursive methods for analysis in social psychology's attempts to understand lay theories and beliefs (cf. Antaki, 1988; Curt, 1994; Stainton Rogers, 1991).

The irony of which we spoke earlier in talking of cognitive social psychology can now be revisited. The picture of social understanding it has produced is not so much 'wrong' (a collection of bloopers) as fractional (a partial account). Its paradigms have not interrogated nothing, they have interrogated precisely those possibilities of social understanding that such operationalizations allow (e.g. causal talk). To be more accurate, experimental social psychologists have here set certain constraints upon the negotiation of reality, and have found the expressed regularities which reflect those constraints. They have disciplined their subjects and (as in all such power complexes) they have learned nothing of what the mice play 'when the cat's away'. Cats, we suggest, are aschematic over mice – except in terms of the behaviour of the predated upon!

To approach something of the multiplexity of the never-ending flux in which social realities are negotiated, and re-negotiated, demands another form of scrutiny (cf. Chapter 11) altogether. The first piece of unlearning it requires is a dislocation from the interminable interrogation (cf. Chapter 11) of experimentalism. We need to get undisciplined!

From interrogation to reading

The notion that we learn something important by interrogating subjects, whether about the purported causes of some event or more generally, is usually predicated upon the belief that those subjects are in some way possessed of qualities to be tapped, or information to be extracted. Such as 'interrogation interminable', much like its parallels in legal activities, requires direct access to one's subject. Through that access, both the competence of the subject/witness and their knowledge is held to be extracted. While it is true that thereby some events (e.g. a crime) are held to be explained (i.e. their cause is determined), it is hardly a ideal-typical case of knowledging activity. For one thing, it is unusual in being formal, canonical and highly structured. For another, it fails to map on to the large amount of knowledging where there is no source-subject to interrogate. Clearly, we cannot by such means interrogate the dead, the never-living (such as characters in a novel or movie), the composite (e.g. the Government, the Union, the people) or (ordinarily) the distal – the television presenter or the politician. Nor (and this is perhaps the most crucial point of all) can we interrogate a conversation, an argument or a relationship – although these are the 'places' where most of anything takes place.

What we can do – arguably all we can do – over the vast majority of social life is to try to 'read' it. That immediately faces us with a choice over how further to proceed. We could insist that there must be some correct 'reading' but so to do merely recreates a different kind of interminability, an interminability this time of the kind that results if we ask:

- What did Shakespeare really mean in Hamlet's famous soliloquy 'To be or not to be . . .'?
- What is the authentic sound for Bach's third Brandenburg Concerto?
- What was Queen Elizabeth I really like?

As Eco (1992) points out, such questions have only answers that take negative certainty. Shakespeare was not referring to Descartes, Bach was not thinking of a Moog generator, Elizabeth I did not take hormone replacement therapy.

The alternative is to accept a reflexivity with the texts we read – in other words, to argue that our readings can also only be gainsaid by negative certainties. We are, of course, describing where the climate of perturbation has left the scrutiny of social life. Research on texts of 'ordinary explanations' (as exemplified by interpretative social psychology, discourse analysis and the like) constitutes reading practices, no different in kind from the work that may go on in a department of English, cultural studies or art history. Thus when Semin and Manstead (1983) write of 'The Accountability of Conduct' and analyse in great detail the wealth of 'excuses and justifications' to be found in ordinary explanations, we should see it as just that – an account, a version, a reading.

I.I. It certainly reads like an accountant's ledger.

Similarly, when Antaki and Fielding tell us that there are 'three types of explanation of social actions' – 'descriptive', 'agency' and 'morality' (1981: 28) – it is a reading, not an objective taxonomy. Explanation, professional or popular, is (on this reading, of course) not a subject property at all, but a discursive activity going on 'between ourselves'. It is, using the term broadly, the concern of discourse analysis (cf. Chapter 11). In turn, discourse analysis, while it may use (as an art historian may use) scientific procedures to inform its reading practices, is not itself a science. It is, as is critical social psychology itself, a craft of scrutiny.

8 From Animosity to Atrocity: Social Psychology Explains Aggression

As we have seen in the last part of this book, social psychology claims to produce knowledge about human experience and behaviour (and popular attempts to explain that behaviour) which is more accurate and less beset by 'errors' than is 'lay' knowledge. We disagree. We believe social psychology offers little more than formalized versions of such cultural 'wisdom', decked out in scientific terminology. In this chapter we will argue this case with respect to psychological theorization about aggression. Indeed, we will show that social psychological theories of aggression tend to fall into one of social psychology's so-called 'traps' for the unwary – the 'fundamental attribution error'. But, as importantly, looking at social psychology's work on aggression allows us to take the argument further. In our view, this work illustrates the way that, in purporting to dis-cover knowledge, social psychology covers up – draws attention away from – both other forms of knowledge and its own liberal-humanistic agenda. In order to present itself as engaged in a neutral, objective 'quest for truth', it disowns the ideological assumptions woven into the very technology it uses to pursue that quest. What we intend to do here is to expose its politics – to bring into view the ideological apparatus it uses to construct its own version of 'the truth'.

I.I. But haven't you often enough already in this book shown that social psychologists are frequently quite blatant about their liberal-intellectual politics?

   In raising this agenda here, we are particularly concerned to trouble the dual position most social psychologists occupy – namely that the discipline itself is neutral but that its knowledge enables affirmative social action: 'As a scientist, I like to work in a laboratory: as a citizen, however,

I like to have windows through which I can look out on the world. Implicit [*sic*] in all this is my belief that social psychology is extremely important – that social psychologists can play a vital role in making the world a better place' (Aronson, 1988: x – xi). This dualism permeates the discipline. On the whole, in the journals and more 'learned' books we hear mostly the voice of the scientist, in the textbooks the mission often comes through loud and clear (and this is one reason why we have often drawn our samples of discourse from books aimed at the undergraduate 'market').

The quest for explanation

This critique takes us to the very heart of the psychological endeavour. Its 'quest for truth' is a search for causal explanation. The basis of its claim to superior knowledge is its assumption that it can provide empirical evidence, on the basis of which we can come to know which of many explanations of a particular behaviour (such as aggression) is the 'true' one – what is the real (i.e. empirically validated) cause of the behaviour, 'the experimental method is the best way to understand a complex phenomenon to truly understand what causes what, we must do more than simply observe – rather we must be responsible for *producing* the first 'what' so that we can be sure it *really* caused the second 'what' (Aronson, ibid).

Box 8.1   Story: Jack's Spat

If Jack hits James because James was flirting with Jack's pint of beer, then this 'because' does not denote a 'cause' in the strictly scientific sense of an event which determines the bringing about of an effect. Rather, this 'because' belongs within Jack's account of the aggression and represents his 'reason' for hitting James. For Jack, James was 'out of order' (that is, he infracted or transgressed the local moral code – or the moral code of Jack's local! – by invading Jack's space).

We might want to give this account special status on the grounds that, as Jack was the agent of aggression, he should have some insight into 'why' what happened happened. But we may also want to take James's account into account – after all, he was the victim. James, when asked, reckoned that Jack hit him because of a long-standing grudge between the two of them, dating back to when Jill chose James over Jack for her romantic attentions. This account reaches out of the here and now of the interaction and draws upon past circumstances (which, so James believes, remain painfully significant in the present for Jack) to explain the aggression.

Molly, the owner of the bar, offered a different account still. 'He's the violent type', she remarks, thereby drawing upon the notion of a stable character trait which enables her to explain the aggression as the normal and expected activity of an abnormal type. 'No he's not', argues Hillary (his work colleague), who proffers a 'situational' account: 'He's been wound up all day because our company is threatening to sack most of the staff – he really was at the end of his tether, and listening to James prattle on is enough to make a Saint spit.' 'Well', pipes up Ken the local chemist, 'if you ask me, it's all down to those steroids he's been taking.'

We could also take into consideration the evidence of other drinkers in the pub such as Max the Marxist (Jack, as a member of the alienated and frustrated working classes, has little option but to channel his angst into personal violence). Freda the feminist ('typical male behaviour!'), Roland the role-theorist ('they are simply acting out the "pub-brawl" script, and doing a very good job of it!') and Simon the psychoanalyst ('Jack's pint is a symbolic substitute for his unresolved relationship with his mother, and James does look like Jack's father').

However, we think enough has been said to make the point that the task of looking for a single, law-like 'cause' for the aggression is problematic to say the least.

The interface between lay and expert knowledge

This story shows well how 'lay' and 'expert' knowledge cannot be neatly divided from each other. 'Lay' knowledge clearly draws upon 'expert' theories. Moscovici and Hewstone (1983) argue that contempory 'lay-epistemic' understandings are usually watered-down versions of scientific knowledge. (We, of course, argue that equally much 'expert' knowledge is little more than 'tarted up' 'lay knowledge'!). Moscovici (1961) devoted part of his early work as a social psychologist to studying the ways in which psychodynamic ideas have permeated popular understandings (in his case, of madness) and by looking to what happens to them as they get woven into existing, 'older' (in an historical sense) wisdom about the human condition (see Chapter 7).

Choosing between explanations

Social psychology even has a theory about how ordinary people chose between the various explanations available to them from the cultural menu of explanations – neatly dressed up, of course, in technological language as 'the lay epistemic process'.

Box 8.2   Cognitive Overload

Kruglanski, Baldwin and Towson (1983) explain the 'lay-epistemic process' in the following way. When confronted with a piece of behaviour which requires explanation, we weigh up a range of alternative explanations. If we try to entertain a vast number of alternatives over time we would quite simply be perpetually buried in thought. Therefore, we close in on one of these alternative explanations (at the expense of ignoring its competitors) and come to think of it as fact. Our motivation to 'freeze' an explanation in this way depends on a number of factors. But, according to Kruglanski, Baldwin and Towson, our need for structure and guidance on the particular issue plays a crucial part. In other words, the selection of a truth about the cause of a behaviour is a pragmatic business based on our need to be able to act without constantly being 'lost in thought'.

Here we can observe an example of psychology's tendency to constantly simplify and reduce complexity – its reductionism. It tends to treat questions as 'either/or', and, in doing so, denies the possibility that things (like aggression) can be maintained as multiple – explained in a diversity of ways because of the different ways they appear to, or are encountered by, different people at different times in different situations. And yet, as we have indicated, in addressing a 'real life' situation, Jack's punching James can indeed show up differently (means different things and matters differently) to the various parties involved.

I.I. But social psychology can deal with this – it will simply claim that we are seeing at work different 'attitudes', 'construct systems', 'schemas' or 'personalities' or, say, the same person in different 'moods'.

Box 8.3   The Fracting of Cause From Explanations

Mainstream social psychology, as we have noted before, is well entrapped in 'subjecting/objecting' problems. In this sense, it is Janus-faced, trying to address both behaviour and experience. To be 'scientific' – in the sense of pursuing general laws – it presents its nomothetic face and thus needs to hang on to the notion that there are real singular causes of events such as an act of aggression. Yet, at the same time, it also claims to find the site of individuality in our subjective representation of reality. In this latter mode it allows for considerable individual differences – while often at the same time as describing them also proscribing their validity (as 'errors', 'stereotypes' and so on).

In seeking to escape from this ontological quagmire, one critical route is to recast 'individual differences' non-intra-psychically, for example, by arguing that much 'psychological' diversity can be shown to be largely contingent upon and derived from simple social and practical matters such as:

- what different people are doing;
- what concerns are orienting their activity;
- how they are differently positioned or located *vis-à-vis* the act in question.

What are at issue are questions such as whether you were the person who was hit, who did the hitting or an uninvolved bystander. We would argue that the 'attitude' you have to the incident, the kind of 'character' or 'personality' you display in the face of it, the sorts of 'constructs' or 'schema' you bring to it, and the kind of 'mood it puts you in' are not so much aspects of intra-individual differences but depend upon how an incident impacts upon you and meshes with your concerns. Different 'explanations' do not simply compete on equal terms for processing space in a limited capacity cognitorium (as Kruglanski, Baldwin and Towson suggest). Rather they flow from different understandings of what the act means and matters.

Explanations are always contingent

Here we begin to engage with the first stage of our argument. It is that it is never possible to strip 'clean' an event – such as an 'act of aggression'

– from people's concernful orientation and positioning towards that event. We 'perceive' aggression, as we perceive 'trouble', within a gestalt of meanings none of which flows one from the other in any causal sense. It is not, for example, that our involvement determines the explanation offered to account for it (although a determined experimenter could always make it seem that way). What is the case is that particular conditions of involvement implicate certain explanations more than others – they are more feasible or meaningful (and hence possible) to that involvement. Curt (1994) uses the notion of 'conditions of plausibility' (drawing upon Berger and Luckman's (1967) notion of 'plausibility structure') to describe this situation. A person's 'concerns' will always frame the range of explanations they can plausibly adopt.

I.I. Like, if Molly knew nothing about the Jack and Jill affair, she couldn't, plausibly, proffer the possibility of a jealousy explanation?

A further crucial point concerns the location in place and time of that which is to be explained. A Simon in Shakespeare's time simply would not have access to a psychodynamic explanation. This leads us to another key issue involving the recognition that the forms of explanation we use are not invented by us anew each time we seek to account for something but always come to us, to some extent, in already organized and recognizable form. Explanations are woven out of the discursive resources available to us.

To explain a person's aggression as an instantiation of an unresolved complex is to understand it through an already formed psychodynamic understanding, within which the aggression is 'revealed' as stemming from unconscious processes. Clearly this psychodynamic explanatory framework has its own history and its own cultural specificity – it is a product of Western industrialized modernity. Through another form of understanding the same aggressive act – Jack hitting James – might be revealed as a matter of 'izzat' (loosely translated as 'honour'). To draw on this as an explanation would, of course, require access to the notion of 'izzat' both as meaningful and as mattering (i.e. belonging to a culture in which 'izzat' has cultural currency).

Explanations are socially constructed

Explanations are, in this sense, never simply individual productions. They are social constructions, in the double sense that we seek to 'explain' events only as part of our ongoing social and practical activity; and our explanations are drawn from out of the range of explanatory discourses which are extant (and pass as plausible) in our local culture. Thus we can see the explanations for aggression which we – as lay people – use as having been handed down to us and used by our socio-cultural group over relatively long periods of time. We tend to persevere with particular explanations not through laws of individual minds and their information-processing capacities and limits but because they are socially meaningful – and because they are socially useful.

One of the responses of the 'turn to textuality' has been a move to study these kinds of culturally available 'explanatory discourses' in their own right – all of the authors have done so. Gleeson (1991) explored explanations of 'madness'; Stainton Rogers and Stainton Rogers (1992a) studied explanations of 'child abuse'; and Stenner (1993a) examined explanations of 'jealousy'. These are all summarised in Curt (1994). Others have explored historical and cross-cultural differences in how 'aggression' is constructed and explained (Rosaldo, 1980; Heelas, 1986; Averill, 1982; Stearns and Stearns, 1986).

Social-psychological explanations of aggression

In this spirit, we can turn our attention to the explanations of aggression that social psychology has to offer.

Aggression as a 'natural' response to frustration

Its most common explanation is that aggression is a 'natural part' of being human – something we are all capable of expressing, given the appropriate triggers.

Box 8.4 Frustration: A Two-Stage Model

The notion of 'frustration' (decked out as a 'frustration-aggression hypothesis') was first suggested as an explanation of aggression by a team of researchers at Yale University – Dollard, Doob, Miller, Mowrer and Sears (1939). It is a two-stage model. First, the potential for aggression is seen as an innate tendency, arising from basic human drives. The innate drive,

> however, will be manifested as behaviour only if it is triggered by certain
> events, which, for example, block goal-seeking behaviour. Thus, although
> aggression is seen as essentially internally driven, its manifestation is
> governed to a large extent by external factors. People act aggressively
> only when circumstances frustrate their attempts to reach a particular
> goal: 'the occurrence of aggression always presupposes frustration'
> (Miller, 1941: 337 – 8).

An example of the way social psychologists sought to demonstrate empirically a causal relationship between frustration and aggression is a study by Barker, Dembo and Lewin (1941). They aroused 'frustration' in young children (lay people might say 'pissed them off') by letting them see – but not letting them play with – attractive toys. Children frustrated in this manner behaved (they claimed) in a more aggressive and destructive way with the toys when they were subsequently allowed access to them than children who had not been so frustrated.

Not all studies worked so well. It soon became clear that frustration did not lead to aggression in all circumstances. Rather than give up on the theory, however, what psychologists did was to make the frustration the subject of study – what factors affect whether frustration lead to aggression? They found, for example, that being prevented from reaching a goal was prone to lead people to respond in an aggressive way when: they are close to achieving it; their expectations are high; and, the block seems arbitrary or unfair (Harris, 1974).

I.I. That's just astounding!

This, however, is not the end of the story, we now turn to Berkowitz's re-working of the frustration-aggression hypothesis.

Box 8.5   Frustration + Cues: A Three-Stage Model

Berkowitz (1993) provided a more sophisticated re-working of the theory by introducing a third stage in the model. He argued that frustration will not inevitably lead to aggression, but rather that it will cause an internal emotional state – anger – which, because it is psychologically painful, may lead to aggression. However, for anger to be converted to aggression, certain cues must be available in the environment. This cue-arousal theory suggests that when people are made angry through frustration of their goal-seeking efforts, if a cue which is associated with

aggression is present, the anger will be translated into aggressive behaviour. It is the cues which act as 'triggers' to aggression.
We can translate this into equations like this:

innate 'aggression' + frustration = anger
anger + cue to 'act out' = aggressive behaviour

In order to demonstrate this experimentally, Berkowitz evoked 'frustration' in subjects in a laboratory experiment in which, for some, weapons (a revolver and a shotgun) were 'casually' lying around.

I.I. Casually?

Berkowitz's is a good example of the tangles social psychologists can get into when they try to test their theories empirically. The weapons – in order to be visible as aggression-releasing cues – had to be presented as meaningful in terms of their significance in everyday (US!) life. That, at least, is 'face valid'. But in order to measure aggression, Berkowitz fell back on the technique of getting his subjects to (appear to) administer electric shocks by pressing a button.

Supposedly giving somebody an electric shock can be claimed as an index of aggression (as opposed to conformity to situational power, for example) only if subjects see it as such. Pressing a button is not usually an aggressive act in itself (though it can be done aggressively, which is another matter). When the button pressed is a doorbell, for example, it merely signifies a request to be let in at the door. Thus to use button-pressing as a measure of aggression cannot merely be so defined by the experimenter by fiat. The experimental subjects need to be given a plausible storyline. Berkowitz used the good old chestnut of telling subjects that they were providing 'feedback' (in the form of what psychologists and doctors often call 'discomfort' and the rest of us call pain) about the quality of their attempts at a problem-solving task.

As we commented in respect of the first use of this scenario by Milgram (see Box 4.3) such a scenario may be the one an experimental rationale requires, but there is no guarantee it is interpreted in this way by experimental subjects. They can equally well consider themselves to be engaging in a necessary, if troubling, 'pro-social' act ('being cruel to be kind') rather than an aggressive one, given that the person asking them to do this is presented to them as a responsible scientist who knows what they are doing. A reflexive cultural effect may well be at work here given that vulgar learning theory notions are well sedimented in any psychologised society. Further, given how well known Milgram's work had become at the time of Berkovitz's experiment, it does not seem too far-fetched to surmise that at least some subjects may have thought to themselves 'Aha, it's button-pressing time! I know what I'm supposed to do – blast the bejesus out of the sucker. It's all a game anyway.' In a culture like the USA, where experimental subjects know all about ethics committees, and what it takes to insure against being sued, it is hard to see the ostensive experimental scenario as having much credibility. These issues about the so-called 'internal validity' of the study are compounded by its doubtful 'external validity'. It may seem to you, as it does to us, that much is being stretched in assuming that pressing buttons in a laboratory and, say, mugging an old lady in an alleyway are determined by essentially the same cause-and-effect process.

I.I. Hang on a minute, this is all very interesting, but I'm getting rather lost. What started out as an examination of the explanations social psychologists offer for aggression seems to have got bogged down into a fine-grained critical analysis of experimentation. Where is all this leading? What's the point you are trying to make?

We have moved along this track to make two important points. The first is to show in relation to aggression – as much as to the other topics we have looked at – just how convoluted and strange are the things social psychologists do in the name of 'experimentation'. The second, related, point is to demonstrate that given, as we see it, that aggression has no objective or fixed meaning, trying to construct ways to measure it objectively is highly problematic. Whenever a researcher attempts to isolate the relevant variable so that it can be experimentally manipulated or measured, they are forced to engage in creating for it a particular meaning (or, at least, trying to) when it is the making of meaning (although they wouldn't call it that) which is the very thing that is required, in their theorizing, to constitute its salience in the first place. Thereby, a nonsense is made into a value-added (scientificated) nonsense.

I.I. Aren't you being over-harsh? Surely, from their perspective, Berkowitz and his kind are only making the first stumbling steps towards a model-ling of aggression so that it can be studied in the laboratory. You're not telling me that they think the 'very preliminary results' gained from this kind of study contain actionable lessons over aggression in real life, are you?

Sadly, it is paradigms like these that have been used every time there has been a fat pool of money for research into such political panics as the 'link' between televisual 'violence' and violent crime in society. Berkowitz himself (1972) used the frustration-aggression hypothesis in attempts to explain then 'top of mind' civil unrest and rioting in the USA. He argued that the aggressive and destructive behaviour acted out in riots are consequences of the frustration caused by social disadvantage, arousal caused by environmental factors such as a rise in ambient temperature, and the presence of aggressive cues (policemen carrying weapons). Although historians might be able to demonstrate a variety of connections between economic crises and civil unrest, it is hard to believe that these are best explained by people in a rioting crowd all simultaneously experiencing high levels of frustration, and all coincidentally chancing upon the same target on which to act out their aggression.

I.I. Put like that, I can see why you call this 'an ideological reading', very much feeding off particular issues at particular times and places. It downplays the possibility that 'aggressive actions' like rioting may equally be construed as political acts of protest and resistance or that one can have 'cultures of crime'.

We think this is easy to see by noting that groups like the students demonstrating in Tiananmen Square in 1990 were not so interpreted by liberal intellectuals in the USA. Nor, to bring things closer to home, were the gay activists outside the UK parliament in 1994 after the lost vote on equity over the 'age of consent'. When 'trouble' is ideologically validated, it somehow becomes easy to see that it can be deeply insulting to activists to be told that they were acting only out of 'drive reduction' or 'responding to cues'. Such explanations have the effect of sanitizing and de-politicizing such actions, which – in context – can be seen as deliberate attempts at resistance, intended to challenge the dominant social order. Indeed, it could be feasibly argued that, say, Michel Foucault's theorizing – where it challenged the 'humaneering missions' of psychology, psychiatry and criminology – arose in no small part out of his political convictions, and his active participation in political action (which included several instances of him being beaten up in demonstrations) (Macey, 1993).

Billig (1976) highlights the reading that explanations based on the frustration-aggression hypothesis, although they incorporate factors and cues in the environment within their explanation, are basically individualistic and individualizing explanations. They ignore the socially constructed nature of the appropriate target for aggression as well as the socially defined repertoire of aggressive acts.

We have one final point to make on this subject. It is that where theories emphasise 'internal drives' in explaining aggression, we would argue that social psychologists – like the lay people they research and theorize over – are guilty of making the 'fundamental attribution error'.

They overemphasize internal and individual disposition when judging the behaviour of others.

Box 8.6   Person – Situation Revisited

In critiquing such modelling of aggression for where it 'over-individualizes' explanation by a focus on 'psychological processes' such as frustration and aggression we need to be clear that this does not imply a sudden endorsing of the problematic person–situation dichotomy we have previously challenged. While we do problematize explanations based on an abstracted 'person', we have just as much trouble with the other side of this phoney coin – 'situational explanations of aggression' – in which notions of an equally abstracted environment become the focus.

Environmental 'explanations'

Situationists in experimental social psychology have been eager to demonstrate a relationship between aggression and environmental factors such as crowding, noise and ambient temperature. However, the effects of such factors are never entirely straightforward. For example, overcrowding appears to lead to increases in aggression in men but not in women (Baron, 1977), and, while Bell and Baron (1976) claim to be able to show a relationship between raised ambient temperature and aggression, the findings are rather complex and perhaps even contradictory.

In Bell and Baron's study, people were subjected to insults in either an uncomfortably hot situation or a pleasantly cool environment. The aggression invoked by the insult in those conditions was measured (again) in terms of the intensity and duration of electric shocks subjects were prepared to administer to the insulter. This type of explanation draws upon a 'pressure cooker' metaphor, which links aggression to arousal, as a function of external conditions. Such metaphors have long roots within culture, and are captured within the 'instinct'-based ethological explanations of human aggression, as well as the drive-based explanations of Dollard et al. (e.g. 1939).

However, findings within such research conflict. For example, moderate over-heating in the environment is seen to contribute to aggressive behaviour while extreme ambient over-heating does not. Baron (1977) explains such results by arguing that it is the subject's interpretation of the environmental conditions which is important here. If the temperature is raised sufficiently for the subject to be aware of it, then they may interpret their discomfort and subsequent arousal in terms of getting hot rather than frustration. Of course, as Siann (1985) points out, this explanation depends upon Baron's assumptions about the attributions made by the subjects, because, of course, nobody actually thought to ask the subjects about their motivations for the aggressive behaviour.

I.I. Sounds to me like they have taken expressions like 'cool it, man' a shade too literally.

Certainly, there is a lot of the metaphorization of emotions like anger as 'hot' in such thinking as well as a 'Northern' view of the Other in the 'hot' South as 'more emotional'. But perhaps most crucially there is here far too much 'mechanical' thinking – collectivities are not like bearings which play up in the heat! And once attributional ideas are introduced one can see the vacuity of such reasoning – bath-houses may have all sorts of reputations but 'hot beds' of aggression are not among them!

I.I. I can see why that doesn't wash. What you haven't covered yet is how social psychology's 'grand theories' deal with aggression.

Social learning theory

For some theorists, aggression, like all other behaviours with the exception of a few inbuilt reflexes, is learned.

Box 8.7   If It's Not One Thing It's Another

To say something is 'learned' is, in itself hardly a massive leap forward in understanding. Clearly, within standard either/or logic, if we are not born with an innate knowledge of hand guns that knowledge must be acquired. The power that learning theory claims is not the proposition that we end up being able to do things that logically could not have been hard-wired in millions of years ago but that it can specify the intra-psychic mechanisms whereby we acquire them. For social learning theorists those mechanisms are uniquely sensitive to 'social' influences to which their attention is mostly directed. How well, or badly, these claims stand up in the area of aggression we are about to explore.

Social learning theory largely avoids consideration of fixed internal mechanisms (whether related to drives or to motivation) in favour of acquired dispositions, expectancies and reactions. Within such a framework, aggression is not seen so much as to do with escaping from negative internal feelings (such as frustration or anger) but as largely instrumental. Aggressive behaviours will be performed if an individual has learned that such behaviours will lead to desirable ends. Social learning theorists would allow that some aggressive acts (in a child, for example) can be spontaneous – at least initially (but even these are subsequently open to reinforcement). However, most aggressive acts are seen as involving complex patterns of behaviour (and even tools – like guns – which require learned skills) which are acquired through modelling and reinforcement.

Bandura, Ross and Ross (1963) conducted a series of studies in which children observed adults behaving in distinctively aggressive ways towards a large inflated toy – a Bobo doll. Bandura argued that the child's imitation of the adult's aggressive behaviour towards the Bobo doll is an illustration of the ways in which children can acquire new behaviours. Where children observe an adult receiving reward for such behaviour, they are likely to imitate it. Where children observe an adult being punished, they will not imitate the behaviour unless they themselves are subsequently offered a reward for doing so.

Such an approach (and it relies a great deal upon its commonsensicality) would certainly seem to permit an explanation of intra-cultural and cross-cultural differences in aggression. A good illustration of this is that Japanese parents actively discourage arguments and fighting in their children and reinforce yielding behaviour. This may be contrasted with the models offered to Western children, whereby the person (perhaps we should read male!) who 'stands up for themself', rather than the person who backs down, thereby gains respect. Thus differences not only in the level of aggression between cultures but also in the range of aggressive behaviours used can be accounted for in terms of different socialization experiences, differences in available models and differences in reinforcement.

I.I. There seems to me to be much in the social learning approach which seems to be saying what you are saying – that aggression is socially constructed.

In some ways there are parallels between social learning ideas (particularly Skinnerian ones) and social constructionism. Apart from anything else, the ideas of social constructionism did not appear ready-made from nowhere.

Box 8.8 Social Construction Is More Than Social Learning

The notion that we are made from what we learn (in lay terms 'how we are "conditioned"') can seem an escape route out of the idea that we are born into a pre-formed and unmalleable condition (say, with an 'instinct' for aggression). However, while social learning theory still places the site of action in the organism (e.g. in its learning propensitities), social constructionism is concerned with matters 'between ourselves'. Where we would say the differences lie most of all are in two things:

1 Social learning theory lacks full reflexivity. It does not take seriously its own character as a construction, it does not examine its own axioms.
2 Consequently, social learning theory remains locked in its own cultural location – which is as a branch of psychology, a discipline existing within particular societal forms that have their own very particular concerns over both what and where aggression is and the nature of the individual who shows it.

We would argue that one of the steps necessary to get out of those traps is to build on the idea that 'aggression' is a social construction from the word 'go' – or rather, the word 'aggression'. Once we accept that aggression (or harm-causing or whatever) is always understood from somewhere to somewhere, then it is axiomatic that it will differ as each of those 'somewheres' differ. Our recent dig about gender was not accidental, for over most known 'somewheres' there are massive gender differences. To say that such differences are 'learned' is to miss out on (to render opaque) questions of politics and power which permeate notions like modelling and, indeed, the experimental paradigm itself.

More recent developments in social learning theory make clearer how far its track takes it from anything like a constructionist approach. It has become 'cognitivized', taking on board notions of the intra-psychic processing and containment of information. While the purported focus remains upon observable behaviour (as befits a behaviourist approach), there is now much more recourse to inner conditions such as emotional arousal. There is a kind of convergence around the sort of model that we earlier linked to Berkowitz. Thus it is now often argued that arousal may be a necessary but not sufficient condition for aggressive behaviour, not least because arousal may lead to a wide range of possible behaviours other than aggressive ones.

Social learning theorists still suggest that we learn the ways and means of being aggressive through modelling, and the aggressive behaviours which are learned are in turn controlled by the consequences of such behaviour. Nevertheless, Bandura's more recent work allows that the consequences – which act to affect the probability of subsequent behaviour – are not necessarily tangible or observable. They may simply be internal emotional states. The control of aggression now passes to re-cast traditional moral internalizations, such as self-disapproval and guilt, consequent on behaving inappropriately. These dynamics are described in terms of 'self-regulatory mechanisms' (Bandura 1983).

The social learning approach (and/or its roots in popular wisdom) has certainly captured the imagination of the general population in many parts of the West. There are, for instance, frequent calls to censor television programmes, especially those aimed at children, in the belief that children should not be exposed to violence as this will lead them to imitate it (see, for example, Thomas et al., 1977). However, despite social psychologists' best attempts to demonstrate a link between viewing violence and acting in aggressive ways, the evidence has always remained somewhat unsatisfactory, even within its own terms of reference. Laboratory studies are criticized as having low ecological validity, on the grounds that children do not typically view programmes in a social vacuum, devoid of the comments of their parents and their friends.

Furthermore there has been a great deal of criticism of the experimental social psychologist's tendency to regard the effects of viewing aggression as immediate and short-term (Gunter, 1985). Field studies which attempted to find a link in a more naturalistic way, have had to rely on correlational analyses which do not permit talk of causal relationships. Indeed, many have argued that it is not surprising that the television programmes and films people watch reflect the world-views and practices of the persons who choose to watch them.

At the same time, within media studies, there has been a shift away from considering the audience of film and television as passive recipients of messages, whether about aggression or about any other issue. Rather the viewer is considered as someone who acts upon the material presented to them, and as capable of taking a range of different readings from the programme. These readings relate to the viewers' 'decoding' position within society (e.g. their membership of different groups which might limit or enable access to particular ways of making sense of the programme (Doane, 1992; Morley, 1980)). Such a view challenges the social learning theorists' idea that the effect of aggression shown on television is pre-given and determined by the nature of the programme alone. Rather the viewer is considered to be in a dynamic relationship to the text.

Aggression as cultural drama

An alternative social-psychological explanation for aggression, which emphasizes the sociological within social psychology, is found in the ethogenic approach of Marsh, Rosser and Harré (1977). This team of researchers argued that researchers cannot afford to assume that they can understand the aggression of another by simply viewing aggressive acts as outsiders. They argue for a phenomenological approach to aggression, which involves using a variety of techniques to gather accounts or self-reports of behaviour, in an attempt to uncover the rules which football hooligans ascribe to their behaviour. This approach draws upon sociological explanations regarding the formation of a subculture, which allows young people an alternative means of achieving identity and status where the culturally ascribed routes for achieving such things have been blocked.

Marsh, Rosser and Harré suggest that the ritual 'warfare' between groups of soccer supporters allows the construction of alternative social hierarchies, within which those who are destined to fail (by virtue of social location) may instead succeed (albeit in different terms). Marsh argues that confrontation between football supporters is usually at a symbolic level, although it may progress to verbal and physical aggression. Such behaviour is not lawless and random, but is governed by rules and rituals which limit the extent to which the conflict may result in injury, while still providing the means by which reputations can be made and defended.

Box 8.9 The Cost of Civilization Tale

The 'naturalistic turn' of some social psychological researchers working in the early climate of perturbation was, to some extent permeated by a more general movement into ethological methods. It is important therefore to be sensitized to the resonances with ethological explanations of aggression offered, for example, by Lorenz (1966). Lorenz suggested that agonistic rituals can be functional for species' survival, and are to be found in many other 'higher' animals. Male deer, for instance, display complex ritualized combat, in which there are clear signals which allow the weaker animal to back down before either gets badly hurt. Sadly, according to Lorenz, such 'wired-in' mechanisms for avoiding death and destruction (designed to counter 'wired-in' aggressive tendencies) can be undermined once combat ceases to be 'hand to hand'. When weapons of mass destruction are used at a distance and through a chain of command, the 'natural' blocks against aggression fail to operate. In this way our 'technological advances' may lead to the eventual annihiliation not just of the human race but of the entire planet. According to ethologists like Lorenz, human ritualized combat has become enculturated into competition in sport. They see this as potentially functional, in that it allows an outlet for 'natural aggression' in a safe form.

Because of their phenomenological stance, Marsh Rosser and Harré used participant observation and interviews (both formal and informal) in order to collect accounts. However, the researchers did not take the fans' accounts at face value, claiming that much of the content was expressive – designed to promote a dangerous and exciting image rather than accurately describing events. Thus Marsh et al. seem to be arguing that much of what appears to be aggression simply isn't. Rather it is part of an identity-enhancing symbolic display – a cultural drama.

I.I. Couldn't it be both?

We certainly wouldn't see this research, any more than experimentation, as operating free of ideology (here perhaps, including a certain liberal-academic romanticizing of 'working-class' culture!). Nevertheless, it is worth seeing what this work highlights, as well as what it hides. One facet of their argument patently serves to render the aggression of football fans as something other than aggression. Certainly Marsh et al. are not primarily concerned with aggression. They are more interested in explaining the reasons why certain social behaviours will appear to be aggressive, or will be described and defined as aggressive, by both the participators and the wider social group. For Marsh and his colleagues, aggression may well be a taken-for-granted human predispostion. That which society defines, recognizes and problematizes as aggression may well be a set of functional activities dressed up as cultural drama. If we look for the explanation of aggression within the individual actor, rather than addressing the complexity of the cultural drama, we fail to recognize the social, political and economic factors which are involved in such social activity.

The politics of social psychologists' explanations of aggression

If anything links the kinds of explanations of aggression that are offered by the mainstream it is that they avoid (and make opaque) any need to challenge the larger social order. Locating the site of the 'problem' in the individual, or the immediate 'situation' (or some combination of these), or re-writing aggression as a sometimes functional social drama, constrains and one-dimensionalizes the possibilities of considering another 'problem' – namely, the way society is organized. Specifically, it does so by presupposing a liberal-humanistic consensus, a creed well expressed by Zimbardo as follows:

> we believe that the scientific study of the behaviour of organisms [*sic*] must be extended to include the multiple influences of social, political and economic forces on our behaviour. If these forces can make us compete rather than cooperate, fight rather than love, stifle and destroy instead of create, we need to know about them. Only with a knowledge of what can go wrong and how, can we reformulate our modes of relating to one another and design social institutions more appropriate for the fulfillment of each of our individual lives. (1976: 413)

I.I. OK, it sounds a bit 'wet' but beyond that is it really such a bad agenda?

It's hard to dub something as 'bad' which sums up the dominant dream of two hundred years (what we have called the post-Enlightenment project). But it may be useful to remind ourselves that half way through that time we were invited into 'the interpretation of dreams' (Freud, 1900) and it may pay to examine even our most cherished ideas.

For example, just what is implied when we forget that society is a human-made product and start seeing it as a set of abstract 'forces', and what they are said to act upon, not as persons but as 'organisms'? Language and perhaps, as Freud suggested, particularly the language of dreams, is never neutral, never just what it seems on the surface. To seek within such a model explanations for aggression within the effects of the mass media (e.g. violence on television) allows social psychologists to treat aggression as an enforced consequence of individual (organismic) vulnerability. By taking-for-granted that kind of model, we mute certain routes of challenge to taken-for-granted social reality. Indeed, such explanations may well actively reinforce the power-bases of those who (by virtue of status and position) seek to control and monitor the messages presented to us through the media.

In other words, we would argue that the explanations offered to us by social psychology serve a double-edged ideological agenda. Where attention is focused on to the personal (aggression is seen as an individual problem), attention is thereby drawn away from the political arena. Where attention is directed towards social deviance (aggression is viewed as a product of dysfunctional learning (e.g. within violent families) or the mores of deviant subcultures), attention is thereby drawn away from institutionalized 'aggression' – aggression gets defined as that which deviant groups engage in, not the ways institutionalized power is exercised. For example, where there is social unrest – such as rioting – 'aggression' is sited within the actions of the rioters, not within the actions of the State that may have precipitated it in the first place or subsequently be marshalled to quell it. In this way only some people – those defined as 'deviant' are seen to have 'a problem' with aggression. Hence only their behaviour requires a 'solution' to tackle it.

Griffin (1993), writing more generally about young people perceived as the 'cause' of social problems, identifies three discourses – of deficiency, of dysfunction and of deviance – through which their 'troublesomeness' is constituted. This framework also works well in terms of social psychological explanations of 'aggression'. The discourse of deficiency views aggression, for example, as a consequence of 'poor' learning – a failure to acquire the necessary self-control, or of imitating 'poor' role models. The discourse of dysfunction views aggression as a consequence of 'sickness' – ensuing, for instance, from the 'down side' of our unique human attributes, what Zimbardo calls the 'perversion of human potential' (1976: 413). The discourse of deviance views aggression as a manifestation of antisocial behaviour, acquired from immersion in deviant subculture. Each of these discourses, according to Griffin, implies prescriptions for intervention. Deficiency 'requires' education; dysfunction 'requires' therapeutic treatment; deviance 'requires' judicial measures. Each of these ways in which aggression is defined and explained thus warrants the use of regulatory power – directed either to individuals or to 'troublesome' sub-groups.

Box 8.10   The Problem Of Problematization

When something gets constituted as a problem it is necessary to ask 'what's the problem?', 'why is it a problem?' and 'a problem for whom?' For a road-builder, a woodland may be a problem because it is in the way of a motorway development. For a conservationist the proposed motorway may be a problem because it would destroy a beautiful woodland. Problems and their explanations are hence not 'natural things', waiting out there to be explained. The very act of 'problematizing' is a profoundly social practice which is immanent with political and moral issues. Moreover, the very notion of 'problem' implies a 'solution' – a problem 'sticks out', asking to be resolved – it implies we need to 'do something about it'.

Giving a child a 'good clip round the ear' might always have been a problem for the child. But only in specific cultural and historical circumstances is the child's 'right' not to be assaulted given credibility (and seen to matter) – and only in these circumstances is there any sense that action may need to be taken to stop people doing it.

Aggression, then, becomes a problem only from particular circumstantial locations and conditions. We do not regard the wielding of the surgeon's scalpel, or the pruning of a tree in autumn as 'aggression', because these are viewed as purposeful acts which need no such explanation. That we can, now, see chopping down a woodland as 'aggression' (using a term like 'eco-terrorism') is a measure of how conditions and circumstances can change, and thereby alter assumptions about functionality.

Historically, and where ever punitivity is active in societies today, the regulation of what is understood as aggression implies 'fighting fire with fire' i.e. meeting unsanctioned harming with sanctioned harming (as all corporal punishments from smacking children to executing murderers do). We have chosen this way of expressing things in order to indicate our own position over aggression – namely, that aggression needs to be understood within the manifold of sets of meanings whereby aggression is constituted. Thus aggression can be seen not as an action or a state but as a set of interwoven textual identities, actions and descriptions. Cast like this, the 'issue of aggression' – indeed its very status as an issue – comes to pivot on the ways in which we come to give meaning to aggression. There is no simple or single entity which we can call aggression but a complex range of different actions which under the appropriate local circumstances will lead to aggression being used in explanation. What is useful in reviewing extant accounts of aggression, for a critical perspective, is that we come to see that, say, Bandura et al. or Marsh et al. are not just presenting different theories concerning the same phenomenon, they are presenting theories which are embedded within different sets of meanings and are addressing quite different phenomena. Social psychology has sought empirically to distil from a set of descriptions and explanations a creation which, by its very social construction, cannot be of a uniform shape. Rather, it is set of distinctive event contingencies which can be worked over by a range of different discourses – a manifold which encompasses not complementary accounts but accounts in complementarity (cf. Curt, 1994). Beyond logging these various incommensurable accounts and their wider discursive resonances, perhaps some of the most interesting tasks of critical work lie in how, faced with such heterogeny, social psychologists choose what to focus on and how they brought the object of their focus into being. Of course, if social psychology has indeed constructed its own specific constitutions of aggression, this puts into a very different perspective its claims to explain (and, perhaps, control) it.

The fact that most theories and explanations of aggression emphasize processes within the individual, and interpersonal acts of aggression rather than intergroup aggression whereby the frustrated ambitions of groups within society are reduced to individual frustrations, can, according to Billig (1976), be linked to a conservative ideology designed to maintain the status quo. The emphasis on emotional factors has led to a neglect of social circumstances, but even more so to a neglect of addressing the socially constituted nature of aggression. Billig argues that psychologists' decisions about which aspects of aggression to study have resulted in them focusing on phenomena which do not require them to examine their own ideological position or the society in which they live.

We need also to address the problem that aggression is simply not accessible to empirical investigation other than as a set of socially negotiated meanings. We have shown in earlier arguments that this is a problem for experimental social psychology even within its own terms of reference. For example, to study aggression in the laboratory we are faced with the problem of operationalizing aggression and defining a dependent variable which is capable of accurate (and meaningful) measurement. In turn, the very pursuit of standardized, replicable (and these days 'ethical') measures leads to a convergence of procedures. The operational definition becomes both narrow and of dubious representativeness – even in the terms of the theories being tested. Lubek (cited in Averill, 1982) reports that 65 per cent of studies of aggression used the distal administration of purported electric shocks as the main index of aggression. It is not just in its atypicality as a context for aggression that the laboratory context should be seen as troublesome (e.g. few subjects are drunk, few subjects know their victims) but also in terms of the constrains upon behaviours enacted within it. For obvious reasons, ethics committees cannot allow even the possibility of murder!

A brief critical polytextual reflection on aggression

Social psychology has got into rather a strange habit of looking at the ways in which lay people make sense of the world and remarking, 'Gosh, these people are using almost the same procedures in order to develop and test their naive theories as us'. How rare it is for social psychologists to look at their own practices and say, 'Gosh, we are acting almost as though we were real people.' To loop back to the lay-epistemic process with which this chapter opened, we need to remember that social psychologists did not invent these theories of aggression, they had currency in everyday explanations – including the everyday explanations of psychologists – in some form long before social psychologists sought to mould them into what pass as scientific theories. To the extent that all of the theories of aggression which social psychology proposes have one foot in commonsensicality, each can play a part in accounting for aggression precisely because all of them can be drawn on to make sense of our experience and to make conduct possible. When we are 'frustrated', aggression is a feasible (culturally available and meaningful) response. When we feel 'anger' we 'know' that (because that is what it means to us) it has somehow been caused by an external event. We know that aggression involves some kind of 'cognitive' judging process because we share in the idea that we can think ourselves out of it (Warner, 1986). Therefore our understanding of aggression, as well as our experience of it, is literally polytextual. Although by our social conventions about explanation we tend to opt for singular stories at a given moment, we are nevertheless at some level aware that we use more than one story.

It seems therefore that aggression is socially constructed in at least two senses. It is constructed in the sense that agreed meanings must be arrived at by the collectivity regarding what behaviours will be deemed aggressive. It is also socially constructed in the sense that through such negotiations a range of discourses of aggression emerge which permit us not only to think in different ways but also to conduct ourselves in different ways. Anyone seeking to freeze an explanation, and to find a fact about aggression that will hold up over time, might as well try to empty a well with a sieve. This is inevitably a futile task because at any moment or even at every moment the thing which they are trying to pin down may well have become something else – changed shape and form. All facts about aggression, all research findings, are inevitably contingent and located.

In this, the experimental social psychologist has much in common with the Mullah Nazrudin in the *Tales* by Idries Shah (1994). In one of these tales we find the mullah outside his house looking for something. A passer-by stops to ask what he is doing. He replies that he has dropped something inside his house and is looking for it. They ask why, if he has dropped it in his house, is he looking for it outside. He replies that it is easier to search for it outside because the light is better there. Except of course, that, as a social construction we can 'find' aggression in the laboratory. We can generate it (as arguably Milgram or Zimbardo (cf. Chapter 4) did for their subjects) and we can ease our subjects into 'doing it'. There is something to be learned here, but it no more explains aggression *qua* cultural manifold than an experiment on pitch discrimination explains the symphony.

9 Social Emotions

The topic of emotions and feelings has been central to social psychology from its origin as a discipline in the last decade of the nineteenth century. Crucial to many of its 'founding fathers', such as Sighele (1898) and Le Bón (1895), was a concern with the irrationality, the 'infective' emotionality, of crowd (mob) behaviour. In turn, the theoretical impetus to their work was provided by contemporary French psychiatry and its concern with how suggestion could countermand the individual will – the same source, incidentally, which (through Charcot) influenced the early work of Freud. Thus 'emotion' as a topic entered into early social psychology, conceptualized as a supposedly powerful and even dangerous threat to rational thought and action.

Box 9.1 Theory and Context

Over its history, social psychology has often proved highly permeable to the concerns of intellectuals in general. At the turn of the century, one major focus of debate was the agitated state of social life itself – in the case of Le Bon the 'threat' to social stability raised by such dynamics as seen in the Paris Commune. The tradition for social psychology to address issues raised by current events was well established by the time Ross (1908) produced the first book to bear the title *Social Psychology*, which is characterized by reflections upon contemporary events. Ross further developed notions of how the individual 'loses their mind' to the group in such phenomena as 'crazes' – an interest which, incidentally, still shows up in present-day texts. At the same point, Freud (e.g. 1900, 1905), drawing upon the same intellectual tradition (and the same bourgeois anxieties) was busy laying the ground for a social developmental account of socialization in which emotional identifications (i.e. those following the Oedipus and Electra complexes) were presented as the key to understanding enculturation. Just as outer social order was held at this time to be achieved by firm rational government controlling and harnessing the unruly passions of the masses (including the working classes, the colonized from other continents and even women), so inner psychological order was seen to be achieved by internalizing authority in the form of parental identification. There was thus a parallelism between ideas about the social world and the personal one.

This parallelism was very much structured along the distinction between the 'civilized' (culture, rationality, restraint, control, transcendence, the mind) and the 'savage' (nature, emotionality, animality, unrestraint, immediacy, the body). In such a discourse, emotions get associated with nature (biology) and with loss of control (people get emotional when their minds lose their grip on controlling the body). A rather similar dynamic was very much in evidence in response to the nuclear war anxieties of the two decades after the Second World War, in which the roots of large-scale human aggression were sought in the 'naked ape' within (cf. Morris, 1967).

A social psychology partly founded upon the notion that individual rationality was a fragile and vulnerable condition found much in its broader discipline base to sustain and build upon its preoccupation. Not only psychiatry but mainstream psychology provided that bedrock. As a bio-social discipline, psychology in general had taken on board the Darwinian (and social Darwinian) message – rationality evolved both phylogenetically and culturally (McDougall's (1908) theory of emotions as instincts was highly influential, for example.) If mobs stripped from us the 'thin veneer of civilization' they could do so because what lay beneath that veneer was 'hot' (emotional) animality. Freud's Id-ridden infant was the animal within revealed. The human condition was at this time mythologized in terms of stark choices – Dr Jekyll or Mr Hyde.

I.I. I like the movies too and I can accept that each age mythologizes its troubles (and that people like you are there to 'read' that for the rest of us) but surely there's more to the psychology of emotion than myth-like theory and research?

Emotion addressed

Dr Jekyll and Mr Hyde, reason versus emotion, and the whole host of other bi-polar tensions (e.g. nature/nurture, savage/civilized) are often said by critical commentators to typify the thinking of Modernism (See Chapter 2). It is possible to see this bi-polar reasoning as also at work in James's (1890) germinal contribution to the psychology of emotion (which became known as the James–Lange theory of emotion). Read one way, this theory amounts to a simple antithesis of common-sense notions of emotion. Instead of arguing that we run away because we are afraid, it posits that we are afraid partly because we run away. What it does not challenge is also crucial – namely, that there is a 'real' (i.e. empirically investigatable) distinction between emotion as bodily perturbation and its cognitive appraisal. This reiteration of the association of emotion with biology left open the possibility of continuing to model the mind as a form of governance, with 'higher functions' having the role of controlling the 'impulsive' body. Technological advances worked hand in hand with progress in neuro-anatomical modelling to put brainly flesh upon the bones of this conceptualization (e.g Cannon's (1927) theory that emotion 'occurs' when cortical ('higher' brain) control over the thalamus is removed). However despite (and indeed because of) all the work which the new century brought upon the mainsprings of emotionality – research in which animal modelling and intrusive work on the 'lower-brain' (e.g. the hypothalamus) were crucial – little questioning was made of the concept of emotion per se.

To explore how the study of emotions has been conventionally cast in psychology, we will once again make use of the device of dipping into the texts of the zenith of grand psychologism. By looking at discourse at the point at which the 'humaneering project' (cf. Chapter I) still appeared secure, we can see most clearly where the psychology of emotions 'came from', what it was that the 'climate of perturbation' came to challenge. Here is how 'our feelings and emotions' were presented to students, fifty years after James and half a century from the present:

> No one needs to study psychology to know that at times he [*sic*] is angry; that it is easy to be afraid or even panic-stricken; that to love and be loved are of great value; that both remorse and pleasure 'happen' to most of us; that envy, jealousy, generosity, and pride are natural to human beings, whether they are black or white, male or female, bright or stupid, rich or poor. We know through experience a great deal about emotions and feelings. What a study of psychology can do is to systematize our present

knowledge of emotions; increase our sense of their importance; and, by contributing insight into their nature, give us more control over the feeling fraction of our total selves. (Tiffin, Knight and Josey, 1940: 184)

Feelings and emotions, in other words were constituted as:

- a part, or 'fraction' of us (the implied contrast is to our thoughts or, as is usually said these days, our cognitions);
- a 'fraction' of us which contains a clear set of discrete conditions – the various emotions and feelings;
- knowable through direct experience;
- universal to all; and
- susceptible to and requiring 'control'.

The task of a psychology of feelings and emotions was to:

- 'systematize' this common-sense knowledge;
- highlight the 'importance' of studying affectivity;
- uncover its 'nature'; and,
- create conditions for its 'control'.

Emotion in mainstream psychology

As elsewhere in this book, the aim of exploring something of the history of a topic is to make sense of how that topic comes to us today. As we now look to the place of emotion in contemporary social psychology, it becomes possible to see where this past has brought us. Taking the agenda for a psychology of emotion in the kinds of terms just given above, there is no doubt that a vast amount of research evidence has been accumulated. Whether this has truly added much to the 'insight' that Tiffin, Knight and Josey felt had been achieved by 1940 is another question. Nevertheless, contemporary social psychology does indeed have a well-rehearsed story of emotion to tell. However, it is a story which, we want to argue, for all its use of current technology, for all its allusions to contemporary concerns, remains grounded in (and prey to the problems of) the Victorian melodrama of civilization and savagery where it began. Sifting through current texts, four key themes emerge again and again: ordering emotion; emotion as communication; moral concern; and emotion, cognition and attribution.

Ordering emotion

This includes work which eschews direct enquiry into what an emotion is and instead searches for a basis to and/or an ordering principle to the vast repertoire of emotion words in English (Averill, 1975, lists over five hundred). Two main orientations have been adopted to such research: first, arguments around the attempt to anchor a taxonomy of emotions in 'wired-in' bodily expressivity and its development (Ekman, 1982; Izard, 1971; Ortony and Turner, 1990; Ricci Bitti, 1993); secondly, arguments around the attempt to employ psychometric techniques to refine the 'meaning' of emotion terms and their connotations to basic structures such as pleasant/unpleasant, forward-looking/backward-looking, or underlying conceptual frameworks, etc. (Plutchik, 1982; Ortony, Clore and Collins, 1991; Kövecśes, 1989). The outcome of these efforts has been, even in the judgement of mainstream psychologists, less than fully successful: 'However, we do not know how many emotions there are, whether they fall into separate and independent categories, or whether they consist of mixtures of a few primary dimensions. As a result, psychologists have restricted their investigations to particular, limited aspects of emotion' (Carlson, 1984: 528); 'If there really are basic emotions, how can there be so much disagreement about them?' (Ortony and Turner, 1990).

Emotion as communication

A frequent form of 'restriction' is to approach emotion as an aspect of communication. In this way it becomes possible to research both the sender and the receiver of emotion within the broad paradigm of 'non-verbal communication'. Two issues in particular run through this approach. The first is concerned with questions of individual and contextual differences and the development of emotional communication. By regarding emotional communication as a social skill (cf. Argyle, 1992), it becomes possible to ask:

1 When, in human development, do particular emotions become reliably transmitted and de-coded? (cf. Harris, 1989; Manstead, 1993)
2 How, in terms of categories of individuals (e.g. by gender, by psychopathology) do persons differ in the transmission and/or reception of emotional information? What situational and psychological variables impinge upon this process? (cf. Zimbardo, 1977; Duck, 1986; Zammuner, 1993)

Such research is, of course, 'restricted' in more than the immediate sense. With (as Carlson's comment above makes clear) no research bedrock to ground the studied emotions upon, the investigations cannot be other than common-sensical. In other words, at best, they can do no more than quantify the effects of ordinary definitions.

The second direction of enquiry into 'emotional communication' inter-links with the first and makes the same assumption that 'success and failure' can be unambiguously formulated by ordinary knowledge. This is the attempt to distinguish truth from deception. The roots of this approach are deeply practical. It began with the demands of policing and the claim that physiological indicators could yield a lie detector (the polygraph). Of course, in many practical situations (interviews, customs examinations) it is not viable to 'wire-up' one's interrogee. Certainly, our politicians would resist it! Hence the interest in whether deception can be picked up by using a human observer as our instrument. Do, in other words, our 'restless legs' leak out the lie our lips utter so easily (cf. Ekman and Friesen, 1974)?

Moral concern

The mission of social improvement through self-improvement which guides most social psychology has inevitably led to a way of studying emotions which involves a double problematization. First, emotions which are deemed negative in their implications and effects have been approached in such a way as to discourage their expression, and to provide the lay person with techniques for 'working on' these 'feelings' in order to 'deal with' them better. The most obvious example is aggression (to which we have dedicated Chapter 8), but anger (Cozens, 1991), jealousy (Hauck, 1991; Barker, 1987), hatred and envy (Schoeck, 1969) have also been rounded on in this fashion, and branded with the label 'antisocial emotions'. However, some seemingly 'negative' emotions, like embarrassment, shame and guilt, have also received attention, but for a different reason. These emotions are of interest to the social-psychological missionary because of their association with the maintenance of a 'moral' social order. Successful enculturation or socialization is often said to hinge upon the adequate internalization of rules and principles, and the evidence for this internalization is the capacity of an individual (child or adult) to feel guilty, ashamed and embarrassed. In this sense, social control is thought to be mediated by negative 'social' emotions (Bandura, 1983; Oakley, 1992).

Second, and partly as a reaction to a perceived bias in the literature towards focusing upon 'negative' emotions, there has been a recent attempt to focus some attention upon 'positive' emotions such as happiness (Argyle, 1992), joy (Schutz, 1973), pride and hope (Averill, 1990). These are, in the main, studied with the aim of fostering and encouraging 'altruistic behaviour' and 'pro-social attitudes' (Nagel, 1970). Argyle (1992), for example, laments the dominant focus on 'negative' emotions, and goes on to inform the reader that our joyful experiences are caused by 'success', 'sex', 'music, nature and reading a good book', 'eating and drinking' and 'social relationships, especially being in love'. He proposes a 'social skills training' programme to help facilitate and engender joy (although this reduces to the statement that 'extroverts are happy', and that getting married, staying married, having children, keeping up with relatives, having plenty of friends, keeping on good terms with the neighbours and finding a job which is satisfying are steps towards a happy lifestyle).

Emotion, cognition and attribution

Given that so much of the psychology of emotion is structured by a distinction between mind and body, it was somewhat inevitable that a brand of research would develop as an explicit challenge to the simple association of emotion with physiology and instinct. This challenge stressed the importance of cognition and attribution to emotion and the key study was doubtless that of Schachter and Singer (1962) (see Box 9.2). Crudely speaking, the starting point of cognitive theories is that people respond in different ways to the same stimulus because of different cognitive representations of the environment. It is therefore these cognitive representations which arouse emotions, motives and behaviours, and not, as James suggested, direct perception of the environment.

Further, Schachter disagreed with the idea that each separate emotion had its own separate pattern of physiological responses (i.e. that the difference between, say, joy, anger and sadness is physiological). He argued instead that the same physiological arousal could be 'interpreted' in different ways depending on the cognitive representation of the situation in question. For example, high arousal could be interpreted either as excitement or as anxiety, and low arousal either as boredom or as relaxation, depending on the way the individual cognizes, or makes sense of, the situation: if you are waiting for your favourite friend to call round, any high arousal might be interpreted as excitement; if you are waiting for a job interview, the same arousal might be interpreted as anxiety. In this sense the emotion is *completed* by the cognition. Emotion becomes newly understood as cognitively 'labelled' arousal.

Box 9.2 Schachter and Singer

Schachter and Singer (1962) devised a now famous experiment which involved getting subjects aroused without them knowing why, so that the experimenters could then manipulate the different cognitive appraisals that could be made and assess the effects of this on experienced emotion. First, subjects were deceived into thinking the study was about the effects of a new vitamin compound on vision. In fact subjects were injected either with adrenaline (a drug which mimics sympathetic stimulation, i.e. blood pressure, heart rate, and respiration levels rise significantly leading to palpitations, tremors, flushing, faster breathing and so on for about twenty minutes), or with saline solution, which had no effect. Subjects injected with adrenaline were assigned to one of three conditions.

- adrenaline informed – who were told what effects the 'vitamin compound' would have on them,
- adrenaline ignorant – who were told that the injection was mild, and harmless and would have no side-effects, and
- adrenaline misinformed – who were deceived into expecting such effects as itchiness, numb feet and headaches.

The latter two groups were called 'misattribution' groups because they suffered arousal without a ready-to-hand explanation as to why. All subjects were then exposed to a situation designed to provide cognitive cues suggestive of an emotional labelling for their arousal. One group was assigned to what was called the euphoria condition (they waited for twenty minutes in a room with a stooge (masquerading as another subject) who behaved in what was designed to be a euphoric way), and another to an 'anger' condition (the same, but the stooge acted irritable and angry with the situation). The subjects' responses were observed through a one-way mirror and then a five-point self-rating questionnaire containing various key questions such as 'How angry or annoyed would you say you feel at present?' and 'How good or happy would you say you feel at present?' (five-point scale measures). The results showed (although the effects were small, especially for the self-rating index) that subjects in the misattribution conditions reported more emotionality than those injected with saline solution, and that, roughly speaking (see Reisenzein, (1983) for a detailed critical assessment of the study and results), those in the euphoria condition attributed their arousal to happiness, and those in the anger condition interpreted their arousal as anger.

One way of simplifying the cognitive approach is to say that 'true emotion' is always a mixture of the 'heat' of the body (arousal) and the 'cold' of cognition: if the first is missing we have 'mere arousal', if the second is absent we have 'mere thought'. It is easy to see how this formulation comes to be presented as opening up the topic of emotion to the social in social psychology because within it emphasis is placed not so much upon arousal per se but upon how arousal is understood and explained. The way we make sense of arousal is held to differ depending upon the social context (e.g. waiting for a friend compared to waiting for an interview, or being amongst angry as opposed to euphoric people). If understandings and explanations are partially social, then, the argument goes, so are emotions. Schachter's approach therefore inspired a whole range of 'misattribution of arousal' studies which aimed to develop this point.

A classic study by Dutton and Aron (1974) tried to show that arousal produced from one source (e.g. the fearful) can be falsely attributed to another emotional source (e.g. the sexual) intensifying the latter feeling. Specifically, they found that North American male subjects were more likely to feel sexually motivated and to ask an 'attractive female' stooge for a 'date' if they encountered her on a swinging rope bridge joining two sides of a vastly deep canyon than if they encountered her on *terra firma*, the argument being that arousal caused by the scary bridge was 'misattributed' to heterosexual desire.

I.I. Surely this is no surprise, isn't this what taking your partner on a roller-coaster ride or to a horror movie is all about?

Apart from issues of their commonsensicality ('Whenever I feel afraid, I whistle a happy tune') the ontological trouble with such 'two-factor' theories is that they rely for their plausibility upon a problematic split between mind (cognition) and body (arousal). This not only retains the dubious assumption that, in its 'basic' (proto-emotional) state, emotion is undifferentiated arousal awaiting a contextual label but also forces questions like 'how do the two join up?', 'which comes first?' and 'which is most important?'. For many critical psychologists, for all that the equation *arousal + label = emotion* looks scientific it may well not give rise to questions of process which can be resolved empirically. However, within the mainstream they have prompted raging debates between defenders of the primacy of 'mind' (like Lazarus (1984) who insists that emotion is always preceded by cognition) and defenders of the 'body' (like Zajonc (1984) who insists in his position of 'affective primacy' that the body can work to produce emotions independently, and without the help of, the mind). Both of these positions take for granted that it makes sense to talk about a clear separation between body and mind, and neither recognizes that such questions and debates are a product of an artefactual dismemberment of the two in the first place. Nevertheless, just because many psychologists find it plausible to separate cognition from arousal and mind from body does not mean that the world really is divided in this way. To paraphrase Nietzsche (1918), they seem not to understand what is comical about one who says 'I Name Thee Cognition. Lo! I have discovered cognition!'

Box 9.3   Ingenious or Ingenuous?

There is no denying, as we hope our examples show, that this social cognitivist approach to emotion has been pursued with considerable creativity in terms of both field and laboratory studies. In areas that range from attitude change and the impact of drugs, 'misattribution' and other 'two-factor' paradigms have given birth to countless inventive studies which focus upon the influence of 'affect' on the way 'information' is 'processed', and vice versa (Bless, 1993). For critical writers, the challenge of finding means for teasing apart and manipulating arousal and cognition and then recombining them in interesting ways shows both the strengths of experimental social psychology and its weaknesses. Its strengths are patent, the ingenuity with which it operationalizes variables, creates controls and seeks to hide the 'true' purpose of the research from its subjects. Its weaknesses are often less easy to apperceive, being the under-examined other side of the same coin, ingenuousness – in other words, a naivety or innocence as to the constructed character of the whole puzzle it so cleverly addresses and the philosophical quagmire upon which its empirical programme rests.

The social construction of emotion

One characteristic of each of the four key themes discussed above (the structure of emotion concepts/words; emotion as communication;

emotion as a moral concern; and emotion and cognition/attribution) is the relative absence of questioning concerning emotion per se. The question of emotion 'itself' is persistently avoided in favour of viewing emotion *as* physiology, or emotion *as* cognition and affect, or *as* communication, or *as* irrationality. Such questioning tells us less about emotion as a phenomenon than about the preconceptions, presuppositions and prefigurations of those who study it. It also tells us of the concerns and preoccupations of those doing the questioning: most importantly, that they aim to bring what they typically characterize as 'irrationality' under rational control. Psychologists are typically concerned with emotion only in so far as it can be presented as a problem requiring intervention or a benefit to be fostered and encouraged: in other words, only inasmuch as it fits the humaneering mission (cf. Chapter 1). Inasmuch as this is the case, psychologists are, wittingly or unwittingly, themselves involved in the social construction of emotion. They are contributing to the construction of what it means and matters to 'be emotional' in modern life.

Emotions as ways of being

One aspect of the social constructionist approach to emotion is a return to basics, for example to questions such as: What are we talking about when we say 'emotion'? In use, emotion is a generic concept which encompasses a range of particular emotions such as love, anger, pity, anguish, sadness and so on, all of which have in common some way of relating to our world (usually to the other people in our world) in which we are in some way moved. In pity we are moved in that we feel sorry for some unfortunate: pity denotes the manner in which we relate to their misfortune (if we had envied that same person we might relate to their misfortune differently, perhaps gleefully: what is called in German *Schadenfreude*, literally harm-joy). Pity, envy and glee, in this context, denote different orientations towards the person in question. These orientations 'tinge' both our 'outlook' (what we perceive, what we don't notice, what seems important and what doesn't matter) and our 'inlook' (how we 'feel', how we understand our selves), and the way in which we (our bodies and the actions our bodies engage in) look to others (in glee we might smile and walk with a bounce, in pity we might talk quietly and respectfully, frown concernedly and cast our eyes downward).

This way in which an emotion can seem to saturate our very being (influencing our 'look' our 'outlook' and our 'inlook') fits well with our talk of being moved (the 'motion' in the word e-motion clearly points to movement). In passing from sadness to happiness, for example, not only how we appear to other changes, but how the world appears to us changes, and how we appear to ourselves changes. Equally, to 'get emotional' is to be displaced (moved) from our ongoing being into an affectized mode of being.

But this common-sense sketch of what anybody who has experienced an emotion already implicitly knows is already a far more complicated picture than that painted by most contemporary social psychologists. The sketch, for example, belies any simplistic attempt to separate out the 'cognitive' from the 'affective'. It points to far more than brute 'irrationality'; suggests the involvement of more than 'instinct' and physiology; and implicates more than simply 'communication'. For a constructionist, emotions are not just (perhaps not even) a 'feeling' mixed with a 'thought' but ways of being – ways, of course, that vary over historical time and from culture to culture (cf. Harré, 1986).

Thus, when we *THINK* angrily, this does not mean that a bit of affect (anger) accompanies an otherwise pure cognition, it is a way of thinking (different to the way we might think when, say, joyful or logical). When we *ACT* angrily, this does not mean that anger affect accompanies our behaviour, it is one way amongst others of acting. Anger as anger is nothing more than these angry ways of speaking, thinking, acting, remembering, anticipating, responding and appearing.

But if an emotion is a way of Being, then what separates different emotions is not simply that they might have different characteristic feelings associated with different physiological concomitants, nor that they might be the result of different cognitive appraisals having been made of some experienced arousal, but that they have (and are) different ways. They are also different ways which may be prompted by different circumstances. Hence we can talk about the particular 'way of Being' of a given emotion, and about the particular circumstances that conventionally prompt that way.

Thus in our culture the way of anger, for example, is prompted when we take someone or something to have wronged or slighted us (or someone/thing that matters to us) or to have otherwise acted offensively. The way anger takes when so prompted is towards a defensive assertion of our position. To be saddened by that same offence is to have taken a different way or to have adopted a different orientation to these circumstances (and the way of sadness is very different to anger in terms of our outlook, inlook and look). The way of jealousy, by contrast, is prompted when something or someone we value threatens to slip from our hands into those of a rival, and the way of jealousy is to guard against that loss (which might involve, for example, anger or remorse if we do lose it/ them).

What we call emotions, then, are ways of being (thinking, feeling, looking/appearing, acting) which are responsive to and constructive of particular circumstances and which, along their different ways, bring to us their (our) own peculiar 'outlooks', 'inlooks' and 'bodylooks'. Fundamentally, therefore, an emotion is not a 'thing' – neither an entity nor a process, neither energy nor physiology. Nevertheless, as Harré laments:

> There has been a tendency among both philosophers and psychologists to abstract an entity – call it 'anger', 'love', 'grief' or 'anxiety' – and to try to study it. But what there is are angry people, upsetting scenes, sentimental episodes, grieving families and funerals, anxious parents pacing at midnight, and so on. There is a concrete world of contexts and activities. We reify and abstract from that concreteness at our peril. (1986: 4)

When we say 'I am angry!' we do not mean 'I have anger' or 'I can feel an anger-thing within me' but I am angry (to describe yourself as simply 'feeling' angry does not have the full force of *being* angry) (Armon-Jones, 1985). Anger, then, is not just a way of feeling but a way of being. We do not expect the person we are angry at to reply 'where do you feel it?' or 'how does it feel?', but 'why?' or 'well you have no right to be' or 'oh dear, I'm terribly sorry, I didn't mean it.' This is because our anger – as a defensive reaction to a perceived offence – calls those around us (particularly those who are the target of our anger) to orientate themselves towards our angry concern. Even if they ignore our angry outburst, this is still clearly a form of orientation.

A concrete world of contexts and activities?

I.I. All very interesting I'm sure. But at this point, I am getting into an emotional 'way of being' over the risk of all this leading to an 'analyse until you paralyse' kind of position. I didn't come to this book for 'social philosophy', you know.

These points about emotion risk incomprehension through becoming too abstract. It might help, therefore, to follow Harré's advice and to give a 'concrete' research example. The following participant-generated exemplary scene, in which two female friends (Ann and Carol) discuss in an 'emotional' way the implications of Carol's having had sex with Ann's boyfriend Bob, was produced through the method of 'seeded thematics' (Stenner, 1992: see also Chapter 11).

1 Ann: Ah, so the party on Saturday, what was it like, did you have a good time?

2 Carol: Yeah, it was alright.

3 Ann: Yeah, I heard you did.

4 Carol: Did you? Oh – well, so how's

5 Ann: [*interrupts*] No, going back to the party – I was speaking to this guy who gave me some rather interesting news, about you and Bob at the party on Saturday – that you'd ended up in bed together – the pair of you.

6 Carol: Who told you?

7 Ann: Doesn't matter who told me – what have you got to say about that?

8 Carol: I'm sorry, it's true.

9 Ann: How could you do that to me?

10 Carol: I'm sorry, I was drunk.

11 Ann: Drunk? – you're supposed to be my best friend – how could you do that to me – how can you possibly even think about doing that?

12 Carol: It didn't mean anything. Sorry, I'm really sorry.

13 Ann: There's no point saying sorry now – what am I supposed to do? How can I ever trust you again? It's disgusting!

14 Carol: I don't know what to say.

15 Ann: Well, think of something, quickly.

16 Carol: It's my fault? So, you're blaming me completely?

17 Ann: Well, it's both your faults – it takes two to tango, but you're my best friend, I don't expect you to go off with my boyfriend at a party when I'm not on the scene, well, has this been going on for a long time?

This short scene provides a concise illustration of a number of different emotions (although ideally this material would be presented by video, supplementing the written word with sound and vision). Carol, for example, is showing remorse inasmuch as she repeatedly not only apologizes but emphasizes that she is 'really sorry' (no. 12). Clearly there is a world of difference between seeming to be simply mouthing the words 'I'm sorry' and the conveying of genuinely feeling or being sorry, and Carol is at pains to demonstrate that the latter is the case in this situation. Her apology is prompted not by Ann's anger (for we have no indication of anger immediately prior to the apology, just cold questioning) but by a prior understanding that this sort of 'infidelity' tends to make the 'aggrieved party' angry, jealous or otherwise upset. There is a shared understanding that 'infidelity' is a moral issue: i.e. one that involves questions of who is right and who wrong, who guilty and who innocent, who has the moral high ground and who the low ground, etc. In this sense, Carol's remorse marks the fact that she has to some extent accepted the position of the one who has wronged: the guilty party (and, although there are no obvious signs, we could well imagine that she is feeling guilty). Her guilty positioning is also reflected in the fact that she offers an excuse for her actions ('I was drunk' (no. 10)), and hence tries to play down her responsibility and hence blameability. Ann, exploiting her position on the moral high ground, makes it clear that this account is not satisfactory (no. 11) and states that the apology is not sufficient to 'mend' the situation (no. 13). At this point she is not only angry but disgusted. This leaves Carol first speechless (no. 14) and then with little alternative but to attempt to 'shift some of the blame' and responsibility on to the others involved, which she does rhetorically by raising the question of fault (no. 16) for Ann to pick up on (no. 17).

What we notice here is that not only is it artificial (and largely pointless) to attempt to separate out 'cognitions' from 'arousals', it is somewhat distorting to attempt to separate out discrete emotions at all! Carol's remorse and guilt belong as part of the same assemblage as Ann's disgust and anger, and all exist in a relation of reciprocal presupposition. The 'emotions' felt are also clearly inseparable from the location or positioning of the people involved (which can be expressed in terms of 'footing' on moral 'ground' – cf. Chapter 3 – although it is important to note that these positions are not given but negotiated, worked at, resisted at some points, foisted upon others at other points, and so on), and hence the profoundly moral nature of these emotions (in this assemblage at least) is clear. We can see, for example, how Carol's being remorseful and Ann's being disgusted serve to reinforce, reproduce and otherwise perpetuate the 'moral order' (Harré, 1986) of monogamy. Also the fact that Carol was sorry and Ann was angry and disgusted, and that these responses seemed to come 'as if naturally', indicates that both of their identities have been at least partially formed and constituted through discourses of heterosexual monogamy (things might have been different, though not necesarily 'better', if Carol had taken a stance like, 'yes, I slept with him – so what, I enjoy sex!', for example). Not only are the different emotions inseparable from one another, then, but also 'emotion' is shown to be intimately connected to the formation of identity and that in turn to the perpetuation and/or transformation of existing social and cultural forms or orders.

Further, to call these emotions 'irrational' would be to miss the point that, as ways of being, different emotions have their own particular rationalities associated with their own particular 'ways'. If Ann can be said to be jealous about the above infidelity, then this jealousy is not irrationality but a kind of hyper-rationality which can involve an intense concentration and preoccupation (sometimes even a fixation) upon the infraction in question and all related to it. If jealousy becomes 'blind', then this is only because its own form of hyper-rationality starts to 'take over' and hence to obscure other concerns and interests, other ways of seeing, such that one's whole life can seem to collapse into jealous concerns. Likewise, it might be interesting to measure the heartbeat, GSR and respiration rate of Ann and Carol, or even to implant electrodes into their brains and ANSs, but we should not fool ourselves that in so doing we are 'measuring' emotion: physiological responding is all that we would be measuring.

I.I. Very interesting I'm sure, but how is this psychology?

Box 9.4   In What Way is All This 'Social Psychology'? (Rather than, say, socio-linguistics)?

The simple answer to this is 'in every way!', but we must be careful about what we take this to mean. Much social constructionist work on emotion, for example, has reacted against the dominant and inappropriate 'biologism' in mainstream psychology by stressing at every point the lack of importance of the body compared to social organizations, rules, practice, meaning and so on. This stance should not, in our view, allow itself to become a denial of, or a fleeing from, embodiment, however (Brown, 1994). We should not, then understand the phrase 'emotions are socially constructed' as 'emotions are not of the body', because this distracts us from what is perhaps most fascinating about emotions – namely, the sense in which they are a key site, perhaps *the* key site, for the articulation and interpenetration of 'the body' with 'the discursive and the cultural'. An emotion is always a complex assemblage of bodily organization and transformation, bodily experience, thought, judgement, evaluation, perception, all of which takes place in specific cultural locations at particular historical junctures within the context of given social arrangements and practices and in the light of particular personal circumstances. As put by Harré, 'Emotions are not just bodily perturbations. Embarrassment is not just blushing and squirming. It is a particular case of the interplay between social conventions, moral judgements and bodily reactions' (1991:145–6).

Emotions as always social

From a constructionalist point of view, human emotions are unavoidably social in as much as they 'take place' within the world of specific circumstances. Ann's anger and disgust were prompted by her reading of the significance of the sexual liaison between Carol and Bob. Her way of being was therefore responsive to these circumstances, and cannot be understood without them. Further, Ann's anger is not only drawn out of particular circumstances, but also aims towards the creation of new circumstances. The anger is itself a 'call' to Carol to orientate herself newly towards these circumstances: first to share in the definition of what this situation actually is (i.e to establish that it is a moral situation where Carol has wronged Ann: a scene of infidelity or even adultery), and second, once this construction has been agreed and fixed in place, to 'do something about it'. It is clear, then, that the circumstances that we respond to are themselves complex constructions – socially meaningful events and happenings, not brute 'things'.

I.I. But what about all the evidence from ethology about emotions in the animal world? Surely there's a sense in which our emotions are, literally, brute things?

Box 9.5 Animal Passions

For a 'strong' constructionist, non-human animals, even 'higher' animals 'have' emotions like anger only in the sense that skies or sties can be 'angry'. In other words, constructionists reverse the direction and the character of arguments about animal passions. Emotions (in the sense in which we use the term) are held to be attributed to animals – not inherited from them. Animal life can never be separated from myth and metaphor – and this holds not just for ordinary understanding (e.g. in talking about our pets) but also for academic investigation. It is quite easy to indicate how we all have an implicit phylogenetic scale of emotionality by exploring what sense we can make of such phrases as:

- an angry gibbon
- a proud mouse
- a guilty penguin
- an envious lizard
- a jealous cod
- an embarrassed woodlouse

One of the strongest arguments against the biological foundation of human emotions lies in these emotions being clearly social in as much as they are historically and culturally specific arrangements. In a culture where sexual relationships are assembled differently (perhaps polygamously or polyandrously) then our earlier example of the configuration of bodies (X having sex with Y who is partnered with Z who is X's friend) would signify differently – have a different meaning – and hence not be 'the same' circumstances (in these different arrangements and assemblages, different emotions, or none at all, might be conventionally prompted). But even within a shared 'social world' of meaning, circumstances are negotiable as to their significance, and these negotiations too take place socially, between ourselves (the answer to the question of exactly 'whose fault it was' is not given but needs to be negotiated, argued and constructed – as we saw, even if blame is taken, excuses may still be offered to mitigate responsibility).

Further, we should not take for granted that the 'way' of any given emotion is fixed and pre-established. The form and direction our 'emotions' take once prompted is influenced largely by conventional script-like understandings of what you do when angry, jealous, in love or whatever. Averill (1986) calls emotions 'transitory social roles' to accentuate this point, and Sarbin (1986) develops this by describing them as 'dramatistic scripts' which are 'patterned after half-remembered folktales, fables, myths, legends and other stories. Not taught and learned in a systematic way, the plots of these stories are absorbed as part of one's enculturation'. Nowadays it is more likely that we will draw our understanding of how exactly to be when jealous, angry or otherwise emotional from novels, films and television than from fables and myths. Indeed, Nick Lee (personal communication) refers incisively to television soap operas as 'the emotional news'.

Part of our cultural competence then – our skill at 'passing' as an ordinary member of our collectivity – lies in the ability and willingness to bring emotions into being. If we are to be Dr McCoy rather than Mr Spock, human rather than alien, then (in circumstances where it is culturally the norm so to do) we have to not just to show we have feelings but make those feelings show. Authenticity demands emotionality (and often the more passionate, seemingly undeliberate and non-rational, the better). To pass, for example, as authentically 'in love' it is not enough to say we are 'head over heels': what is required is that we produce a passable display of it!

Finally, emotions are social in that the very language we use, as argued throughout this book, serves the active task of staking claims and making 'decisions' as to what is what and where it belongs. To call Ann 'jealous' in the scene above, for example, is not simply to identify neutrally her way of being but to tie it down to a particular scene of significance or meaning. If, as it often is, jealousy is associated with negative connotations such as possessiveness, immaturity, insecurity and so on, then to call Ann jealous is to help to undermine her 'position' or location or footing within the scene above (it is to locate the 'problem' within Ann – or within Ann's insecurity, immaturity and possessiveness). If she was to argue, 'I'm not jealous, I'm angry', then this might represent an attempt to re-establish her footing with the claim that she is responding appropriately to a wrong that has been done to her.

Finally, with feeling

These various ways in which emotions are inescapably social point yet again to the need to approach this aspect of human life with a sensitivity to its inseparability from other aspects of 'being social'. These needs must include such facets of 'social being' as: identity, language, attribution, action, thought, and meaning-making itself. Our argument is not that emotion needs to be joined back together with these other 'portions' or topics but rather that their separation in the first place was always a particular artefactual (constructed) imposition – local and contingent to the analytic and reductionist *Zeitgeist* in which nineteenth-century human science arose. As with any elemental language-game this particular fragmentation informs us not about the 'nature' of its focus – here emotion – but rather about the conditions of its 'naturalization', the life-world of those doing the enquiring and claiming their professional warrant over enquiry. It goes, we hope, without saying that, in this respect, the word 'social' is no whit different from the word 'emotion'. It too is another one of these divisions which conceals more than it reveals, and hence to call emotions 'social' must, once its rhetorical job is complete, be problematized and questioned.

10 Pomosexualities: Challenging the Missionary Position

I.I. Pomo, shmomo, I suppose this is what happens when postmodernism gets its hooks into sexuality!

Sex, gender and sexuality

Traditionally social psychologists have assumed that sex is a given bodily property – a manifestation of a naturally occurring differentiation – which is revealed by embodied characteristics and is foundationally determined by one's 'sex' chromosomes. Most simply, individuals possessing a pair of XX chromosomes are female, have a vagina and develop breasts and a rounded body shape. Persons possessing one X and one Y chromosome are male, have a penis and develop a more muscular shape.

These 'biological realities' – which may also be assumed to cover differential dispositions, for example to aggression – are then assumed to be subsequently overlaid by socially and culturally produced male and female identities, often termed 'gender' (see, for example, West and Zimmerman, 1991). As a rule there is a straightforward one-to-one mapping of sex and gender, female to feminine/male to masculine, although there are exceptions. An individual who has paired XX chromosomes, but who develops 'male-looking' genitalia, may have their sex misattributed to that of boy (at least before puberty) and be socialized towards a male gender role.

Sexuality is a more amorphous (and contested) concept still. Often (with notable exceptions such as Freudian theory) it is seen as something which develops only in – or towards – adulthood. A central issue is that of hetero-, homo- and bisexuality, about which there is strong debate – for example whether these are 'wired-in', biological tendencies, lifestyle choices or matters of sexual politics. Also encompassed are other forms of sexuality (such as paedophilia), and consideration of the part human sexuality plays in such areas as intimate relationships, interpersonal interaction and family dynamics.

I.I. So far this all sounds like you were working from your sex education revision notes. You weren't . . . were you?

Well two of us were involved in the early sex education movement but we won't bother with the references. We've left that far behind and this is what we indeed to do with that sort of approach in psychology also! In this chapter we will look critically at each of the 'helpful little booklet' topics – sex, gender and sexuality – in turn. We will consider how each has been addressed by traditional social psychology, how these orthodox approaches have been challenged, and what alternatives the 'climate of perturbation' has to offer. It is worth noting that this is a vast area, and we will be able only to touch on some of the many topics involved and approaches which have been applied.

A bit of 'the other'?

I.I. Is that sort of word play really necessary?

Most writers in this area fall prey to 'groping prose' (Hill and Lloyd-Jones, 1970) – we use it deliberately, and to a purpose. However, before we can get into our declared topic areas, we need first to take account of something which makes sex, gender and sexuality particularly problematic areas of study (and not just for social psychology). It is that for the majority of its *history*, its theorists and researchers have been male, and the discursive arena in which it has been produced is deeply steeped within a 'male-stream' (or 'manstream') orthodoxy of knowledge.

Haraway has addressed this issue with respect to primatology – the scientific study of apes. In her view 'primatology is politics by other means'. In other words, it is not so much a science as a craft – a craft of story-telling, enmeshed with values and ideology. Until quite recently, virtually no woman had the status of 'scientist' in this field, and hence the stories told about primates were men's stories – stories of hunting, aggression and hierarchical competition for dominance. Once (white) women achieved the social and symbolic power which accorded them the ability to become primatologists: 'they brought with them histories, experiences, and world views that reconstructed the basic stories of primatology. They changed the facts of nature by changing the visions of possible worlds' (1984: 80).

This brought about a number of changes in the way primatology is currently practised and theorized. For example, it introduced other stories – about nurturance, child-care and co-operation to achieve common goals.

However, Haraway points out that this does not result in a straight-forward and equal competition between 'male' and 'female' versions of the story-telling craft. The reason is that women enter the discursive arena as persons 'whose materials are necessarily the inherited stories that mark the biological category "female", as well as actual women, as other' (1984: 83). She goes on to assert: 'Female and women, the marked categories, are inflected linguistically and socially. To be the unmarked category is to be the norm: to be the marked category is to be the dependent variable.' The case Haraway is making is that, when women engage in theorizing about such things as sex and sexuality, their feminity is both the object of study, and, at the same time, the condition of their status as theorists. This immediately places them at a disadvantage, because the discursive resources at their disposal are largely male-constructed ones. They are not just the creations of individual male thinkers (though this is often, literally, the case) but the constructions of a whole system of thought which is constituted from a masculine viewpoint. This viewpoint is one which treats women as 'other' (i.e. that which is ab-normal, devious and deviant, and hence in-need-of-explanation).

There are links here with the arguments made by feminist film and art theorists about studying the history of art (see for example, Mulvey, 1975 – whose ideas we will be looking at later in the chapter; Pollock, 1988). Because, they say, artworks have, through history, been predominantly constructed by and perceived through the 'male gaze', feminist theorists argue that it is not enough just to 'bolt on' an alternative (i.e. feminist) reading of them. The 'male-stream' of artworks is so shot through with the particularities of the 'male gaze' that all this does is tell us something about the 'male gaze'. It says very little about how any other approach would constitute the objects and the issues that art seeks to address.

Thus when we come to examine how social psychology has theorized about and researched into issues of sex, gender and sexuality, it has to be with a distinct sense of unease and with considerable caution. Whether we come to this task as men or women, we inevitably come to it as persons-in-culture, who cannot but be informed and affected by our own historico-cultural legacy of 'meaning-making' – a legacy which is far from gender-neutral.

Box 10.1 Aliens And Others

In some senses psychology as a whole was grounded upon a very particular 'gaze'. It was, for example, mainly brought into being by white (mainly US) academics, within a discourse which marked all non-whites, all 'alien' cultures, as 'Other' (cf. Guthrie, 1976). As Guthrie's title lays out, 'Even the rat was white'. This sets the agenda which rendered 'race' an issue and even when it came to be challenged (another parallel to the study of sex and gender) continued to shape its treatment (e.g. through the 'humaneering' of 'racism' as a personal pathology). In the same way, the US 'way of life' is the 'social' of their textbooks of social psychology. A studied appreciation of other cultural locations, particularly from within, is relegated to anthropology (paralleling 'women's studies'). Where cross-cultural comparisons are made, the implied 'we' is the baseline, the explicity identified 'them' is the contrast, the Other. This is in no sense confined to social psychology but is said to permeate scholarship in the West more generally (Said, 1978).

Otherness equally affects the way sexuality, sex and gender are studied. Even where women seek to engage in challenging 'male-stream' constructions, they usually do so from a 'white' perspective (since most of the women accorded the opportunities to do it are 'white'). Thus these challenges are themselves often ethnocentric. Their attention is focused on those aspects of challenge which are most salient to sexuality, sex and gender as experienced and constituted from a 'white' perspective. This is, arguably, gradually changing – certainly it is now much more widely acknowledged – but it remains true of the vast majority of work.

Sex

Sex is one of the many contrast terms in discourse which invite a categorization into one of two classes (see Deleuze and Guattari, 1992). Categorization has been claimed by mainstream social psychologists (e.g. Doise, 1976) to be a cognitive process common to all societies and cultures. At this level, sex categorization works like the contrast between nut and bolt. Logically, categorization implies no antithesis (i.e. that a nut is the opposite of a bolt) and no differential valorization (i.e. that a nut is better than a bolt). All that is implied is that the two classes are different, and are mutually exclusive. What happens when they are employed in discourse, of course, is another matter altogether.

A number of criteria may be used for sex categorization, and they apply (more or less) to all 'higher' (phylogenetically speaking) animals. The topology of the external genitalia is generally taken to be the key discriminator, and amounts to a culturally universal sign designating sex. Such criteria apply to gorillas as much as they do to humans.

I.I. Though I assume you won't accept any responsibility should a rush of unreconstructed experimentalism lead your readers to put that to the test!

Box 10.2   Pinning Down Sex

Prior to the emergence of a science of physiology, the near-universal basis to sex categorization was the possession (or not) of a penis. Even today, in post-industrial societies, that is how most of us get 'sexed'. It is that which determines what gets written on our birth certificates and in the UK that is your legal sex for life, come what may! 'Chromosomal sex' is not a better criterion just a different one, differently employed. A Pope's maleness is decided by his genitals, a pole-vaulter's femaleness by chromosomal sex. In the market of sex science, 'you pays your money and you takes your choice'.

What varies from society to society is the significance accorded to these signs. For example, the consequence of being categorized as a bullock in Britain may well be to be fattened up and rapidly slaughtered, whereas a heifer will be allowed a longer life of milk-production. But in Spain a bullock may have a different fate in the bullring. In Hindu India the significance of the gender sign might be said to be of far less import than the special categorization accorded to bovineness. For human children, sexual categorization will matter more (or at least differently) in some cultures than in others. Where there is strong sex segregation, from the moment sex is assigned, a great deal of the child's future will be largely mapped out for it. But even in cultures where there is greater commonality, the attribution of 'female' or 'male' will have a significant impact on the child's future identity, life-choices and life-chances (along with other things like class).

1.1. Which is why they so often appear as variables in research?

Indeed, the sex and social class location of a baby are far better predictors of that baby's future than any test a developmental psychologist can lay on the child.

Soon after assignment as 'boy' or 'girl' a child's identity is usually sex-marked by the name it is given. From that point on their 'scripts of identity' (e.g. in the UK birth certificate, passport) will tell the world to what category they belong – male or female – along with other markers (such as hairstyle and dress). From now on the people and institutions that make up their world will treat them differently, according to their sexual category.

However, although sex is a status which warrants and permits identity, identities involve a great deal more than sex. They are enmeshed in many other socially constituted and negotiated categories (such as class and race). Not only are sexual and procreative behaviours thereby socially scripted, but other seemingly biological outcomes (such as musculature and longevity) are deeply influenced by the social locations of class and racial group as well as gender category (Lorber and Farrell, 1991: 8).

It is worth emphasizing that sexual categorization does not depend upon sexual activity (or lack of it), nor even on having a 'real' body. A three-year-old boy, a statue of David, a painting of St Sebastian, a monk – all have the assigned property: male. All that matters is that male-embodied characteristics are manifested or implied in some way or another.

The consequences of sexual categorization

The constructive power of the attribution 'female' or 'male' is therefore massive. It is everywhere always-already presenced. Borrowing the language of pre-war Gestalt psychology, what categorization does is to flatten the differences within categories and to sharpen the differences between categories. It beguiles us into seeing men as fundamentally similar to each other, and as fundamentally different from women (and vice versa). One consequence is to lead individuals to value and seek to reward the distinctiveness of their 'In-group', while acting oppositely to their 'out-group'. This, by the way, forms the basis of yet another mainstream social psychological 'theory' – social identity theory (Tajfel and Turner, 1979). We will come back to this when we tackle the topic of gender.

The biological warrant for sex differences

Some social psychologists – particularly those informed by socio-biology – have drawn upon a 'biological warrant' to explain expressive differences between the sexes. For example, Rossi (1977) has proposed that the 'female' hormone oxytocin makes women more nurturant than men. The explanation given is that this has arisen because it endowed an evolutionary advantage, the argument being that more nurturant women are more successful at rearing their young, and hence are more likely to pass on their nurturing capacity to future generations. Others (e.g. Goldberg, 1977; Wilson, 1978) have suggested that higher levels of 'male' hormones (androgens) make men 'naturally' more aggressive than women.

As well as 'sex' hormones . . .

I.I. Why the warning marks?

There are three answers: one silly – testosterone molecules don't have willies; one a reminder – oestrogen won't make an apple tree flower; and, one serious – both sexes secrete both sets of hormones, albeit in different proportions.

. . . differences in brain size and organization have also been seen as reasons why males and females differ in their cognitive abilities, and hence in their performance in certain areas such as science. Gray (1981) for example argues that girls perform more poorly than boys in science at school because they are less capable in tasks which involve visuo-spatial ability. This is because, the argument goes, the left/right hemisphere specialization of the brain in female development is less well suited to such skills. Boys are assumed to have developed higher visuo-spatial capabilities because these were needed for hunting and defending territory.

Challenging the biological warrant

These kinds of explanations are, however, based more upon theoretical dogma than upon science. The processes of evolution and natural selection are taken as 'givens', which are then applied – often very selectively – to certain observations which are clearly socially constituted (Walkerdine, 1988). For example, Rossi's assumption of a link between oxytocin and nurturing is based upon observing that it stimulates nipple erection prior to breast-feeding. It is an extremely tortuous leap from this manifestation of hormonal influence to the whole host of behaviours we normally think of as 'nurturing' (see Sayers, 1982, for a fuller critique).

Similarly sex differences in tests of visuo-spatial tasks is miniscule in comparison to the large differences between boys and girls in their attainments in science (Sayer, 1987).

Foucault (1978) is the best-known proponent of the view that there is nothing 'natural' about sex – that it is not an inherent property within the body waiting to be ascribed. Rather, we would say, it is a classification laid upon *bodies* that human meaning-making (i.e. story-telling) imposes. Haraway expresses the argument like this: 'It is important not to make the mistake of thinking sex is given, natural, biological, and only gender is constructed and so social. Biology is an analytical discourse, not the body itself; and biological sex is an object of knowledge and practice crucial to power in the modern West' (1984: 85). What she is saying is that the science of biology is a discursive resource (a story-telling practice) by which we 'write on to' (which is basically what 'ascribe' means) the body our understanding of the body. This may seem, at first, a strange idea – sex is so obvious, so conspicuously, visibly 'there'. How, then, could sex possibly be anything but a natural, bodily property? Sedgewick provided a nice illustration which may help. He argued that '[t]he fracture of a septuagenarian's femur has, within the world of nature, no more significance than the snapping of an autumn leaf from its twig' (1992: 30).

In other words, broken legs are meaningful to us and matter to us because they impinge in a particular way upon our lives. Broken legs do not naturally fall into a category of 'injuries' any more than falling autumn leaves naturally fall into a category of 'being picturesque' or of marking 'the autumn'. They 'are' that way because (and only to the extent that) that is the meaning we impose upon them. Equally, possessing a penis does not naturally create a category of 'maleness'. Male-ness is a product of us construing having a penis as a meaningful category of human-ness (or animality more generally). Sex – just as much as gender – is a site of socially rather than biologically imbued status.

I.I. I've always liked the digest of Freudian symbolism: 'concave or convex, all reminds me of sex'!

With that thought in mind, we can move on now to examine the notion of gender.

Gender

Apart from a few die-hard socio-biologists in the discipline, social psychologists have generally rejected crude biological determination as an explanation for sex differences, and have developed theories which see them more in terms of 'gender'. Most still accept 'sex' as a biological 'given', but view gender as a product of the interplay of nature and nurture. A range of theoretical perspectives have been brought to bear.

Social learning theory

Social learning influenced theorists, such as Sandra Bem (1981) . . .

1.1. Why Sandra Bem?

Why indeed? One argument is that, in areas dominated by men, we tend to assume that a citation (e.g. Bem) is to a man – it's another attributional error (cf. Chapter 7) – unless we make it explicit. In making it explicit, we challenge a taken-for-granted. The other argument, more to the point, perhaps, here, is what do we do with couples (brother/sister pairs etc.)? As there is also a Daryl Bem in social psychology, forenames get added where confusion might arise – just as in Rex Stainton Rogers/ Wendy Stainton Rogers.

. . . propose that girls learn to be 'feminine' by modelling themselves on their mothers and by observing other role models (e.g. as shown on television). In this way they gradually acquire sex-role characteristics, such as limited interests in science and technology. At the same time girls and boys tend to be rewarded for different behaviours. Girls are rewarded for being quiet and subservient, boys for being assertive and boisterous.

Cognitive-developmental theory

Cognitive-developmental theorists such as Kohlberg (1966) argue that children develop their sex-specific behaviours once they gain the capacity to see themselves as different according to sex – around the age of three. At this stage in their development they avoid 'sex-inappropriate' behaviour because of their need for a stable sense of object constancy (which according to Piaget, is their main focus at this stage). Quite simply, the argument goes, children at this age believe that if they, say, dress in the 'wrong' clothes or act in the 'wrong' way, they will turn into the 'wrong' sex. Constancy of sex role is thus well established by the age of about five or six, once the child is ready to move on to more abstract ways of thinking (see, for example, Marcus and Overton, 1978). Once children reach the concrete-operational stage in their development, they tend to base their concepts on obvious physical characteristics. Here the argument is that, since men are generally bigger than women, children of this age tend to see them as more powerful, and therefore as more intelligent.

Again, this theorization raises more questions than it answers. Sayer (1987) for example asks why it is that children are assumed to be so affected by sex as a categorization – rather than other kinds of equally obvious physical differences such as hair-colour. We could add that 'bigness' seems not to be a quality which is valued in women in the same way as it is in men – children seem not to grow up believing that big women are more intelligent than small women – if anything, the opposite is the case.

Psychoanalytic theory

Freud argued that psychological differentiation between the sexes arises because small children interpret genital sex differences in terms of having or not having a penis – castration anxiety in boys, penis envy in girls. It is the genital eroticism of the phallic phase (and the parental identifications thereby meditated), according to Freud, and the significance the child places on genital difference as a consequence of this eroticism, which leads boys mainly to become masculine and girls feminine.

While there remain many adherents to this traditional psychodynamic view of gender development, psychodynamic theory has both come under challenge from feminists and been appropriated to a very different agenda by feminist theory (particularly in the field of art and film). We will come on to look at these later in the chapter. Here we will look just at a variant of psychodynamics which has been developed by a social psychologist.

Chodorow (1978) suggests that mothers, sharing the same sex as their daughters, tend to feel closer to them and hence prolong the period of closeness and mutuality they share with their daughters compared with their sons. Mothers see their sons as more separate and 'different', and hence propel them relatively soon into the outside world, and into the process of individuation. Girls thus grow up with a greater capacity for intimacy, empathy and mergence; whereas boys grow up with a greater capacity for 'derring do' and detachment. In other words, this version of psychodynamics views sex differentiation as mainly the product of the mother's (rather than the child's) response to the 'biological fact' of sex.

We will take up this argument again when we come to look specifically at feminist theory.

Sexual alchemy

While they differ as to where they site the main locus of action, all of these approaches tell a story of alchemy – of how 'masculine men' and 'feminine women' are created by the fusion of 'nurture' and 'nature', the social and the biological. As Stainton Rogers and Stainton Rogers (1992a) have argued elsewhere, this offers a superficially convincing story for two main reasons. First, it draws upon an analogy with chemical processes, such as the fusion of the elements of sodium and chlorine to produce salt. Second, it resonates with many of our deeply sedimented cultural myths about the components of human nature, from the historical feral children 'Romulus and Remus' and fairy tales of changelings to contemporary modern fables such as 'wolf children' in India and 'Superman'.

I.I. Why do you call 'nature/nurture' modelling 'alchemy'? I presume there is more going on here than just 'knocking copy'?

Box 10.3   'Nature and Nurture': Paradigmatic or Narrative?

The 'disillusion' of the 'climate of perturbation' can be marshalled to resist being beguiled by the apparent commonsensicality these metaphors impart. While scientists can draw upon a clearly articulated theory to explain why sodium and chlorine can combine to produce a compound which differs in its properties from these constituents, psychology has no such theory to explain how 'nurture' and 'nature' (e.g. sex hormones and gender dress codes) interact. This is why we use the term 'alchemy' to worry the chemical metaphor. We are presented not with theory (as the scientistic paradigm approach demands), but with an illusion of (or, perhaps, allusion to) scientific theory. 'Nurture' and 'nature' have yet to be theorized in ways that accord them qualities which render them fusable. Rather they remain lodged in the narratively fusable, *made* to link (much as are 'Beauty and the Beast'), in the stories we tell about the world.

'Measuring' femininity and masculinity

While 'sex' is generally seen as a binary, either/or categorization, gender is usually viewed as a dimension – people can be more feminine or less feminine, more masculine or less masculine – men can have 'feminine' qualities and women 'masculine' ones (depending upon the local definitions of the concepts). Many cultures (as evidenced by the work of social linguists such as Ortner and Whitehead, 1981) engage in a metaphorical language game which feeds off the femininity/masculinity dimension. It is the ideologization (i.e. the making to matter in terms of knowledge and power) of this tension and its inscription on to males and females which constitutes the social construction of gender and of gendered identities.

Box 10.4 Social Psychological Studies of Gender Differences

The taken-for-granted assumption of a dimension of masculinity/femininity was capitalized upon early by the growth industry of psychometrics (see Brown, 1986 for a review). Between around 1920 and 1960 a large number of scales were developed, which were highly successful in distinguishing men as 'masculine' and women as 'feminine' and each as different from the other. For example, one of the original scales, devised by Terman and Miles (1936), yielded an average score for men of +52 and for women of −70 (where 0 represented the cut-off point between the two) with virtually no women scoring positive or men scoring negative. (It is interesting that that was the way the dimension was expressed!)

These psychological tests worked on a simple and circular definition. Any question which discriminated between men and women was a feminity/masculinity item. Items with which women tended to agree and males disagree (such as liking cooking and sewing) were clearly femininity-items. And vice versa, those where men agreed and women disagreed (such as liking wrestling and football) were masculinity-items.

There are no surprises in the gender-linked qualities that were so 'discovered': independent, assertive, dominant instrumentality (and a liking for football and wrestling) typifies masculinity; interpersonal sensitivity, compassion and warmth (and a liking for knitting and sewing) typify femininity. All, of course, these tests showed was that people are well aware of gender stereotypes, and tend to see themselves as conforming to the one which applies to them. Men see themselves as 'instrumental', since that is what a man is supposed to be. Women see themselves as 'expressive', since that is what a woman is supposed to be.

Indeed later studies which simply asked people questions like: 'In general, how masculine do you think you are?' and 'In general, how feminine do you think you are?' yielded results which strongly correlated with their masculinity and femininity scores (see Storms, 1979). Psychometricians interpret this as showing their scales have high construct validity. We, naturally, see it as showing that constructing scales like this is a

> pointless activity – it merely demonstrates that people know what is expected of them when they fill in questionnaires!

Whichever view is taken, the scales originally devised to measure masculinity were clearly tapping into deeply sedimented understandings of what masculinity and femininity were seen to mean in terms of men's and women's capacities and qualities.

I.I. But things have changed since then – people don't do studies like that any more, do they?

Don't you believe it! In Chapter 11 we review some recently published studies (1993) in a 'prestige' journal (read, one which gets you lots of 'Brownie points' in research assessment). They include one which seeks to show that women see each other as more similar and men as more different from them – and vice versa. The 'feminine qualities' used to test this hypothesis were: 'gentle', 'dependent', 'shy', and 'reluctant to speak in class'. The masculine qualities were: 'ambitious', 'opinionated', 'involved in intramurals' and 'believing wild parties are the best parties'.

Box 10.5   Gender and Mental Health

One of the most telling studies here was one which explored the qualities that 'mentally healthy' men and women are supposed to have (Broverman et al., 1972). Their data was obtained by asking a large number of practising mental health professionals (both male and female) to characterize 'the mature, healthy, socially competent adult', 'the mature, healthy, socially competent man' and 'the mature, healthy, socially competent woman'.

The ideally healthy man was one with instrumental qualities and some of the more desirable expressive traits. This was also the description given for the healthy 'adult'.

But the healthy woman was described rather differently – as more submissive, more easily influenced, excitable in minor crises, concerned with her appearance and more likely to have her feelings hurt. She was less independent, dominant, aggressive, objective and adventurous than the healthy 'adult'.

In other words, professionals who work in the mental health field view see women as needing to conform to a stereotypical 'feminine' woman – not to an 'adult' – if they are to be judged as 'mentally healthy'!

The instrumental/expressive divide is often used to explain (and hence justify) why, for example, women on average earn less than men, and why so few women reach positions of authority (and power) – whether in commerce or in other institutions such as politics, the law and education. Masculine instrumental qualities are seen to suit men for the high-powered, well-paid jobs for which women's feminine lack of these qualities make them unsuited. Equally, for example, men suffering from depression are generally taken much more seriously than women sufferers. As the study described above suggests, women are not really expected to aspire to adult levels of mental health.

I.I. But gender roles and, more specifically, women's position in society has changed and is changing; surely social psychology has taken that on board?

Certainly part of the 'crisis' that beset social psychology around 1970 involved a concern for the unexamined sexism of the discipline and a sensitivity to the emergent 'women's liberation' movement. Social psychology today is different. For a start, the journals now follow guidelines about the avoidance of sexist language, even when the articles remain thematically 'unreconstructed'. Some journals (e.g. *Feminism and Psychology*) have sought to take feminist criticism to the heart of the discipline. However the mainstream much more reflects the liberal-humanistic response to changing notions of gender and gender roles.

Androgeny

The liberal-intellectual response to feminist criticisms of psychology's sexism has been for some social psychologists to argue that neither masculinity nor femininity represent the ideally 'together' person. Rather, the optimal identity is one which combines the best qualities of both – a person who is flexible and adaptable (rather than sexually stereotyped) in their qualities, competencies and attitudes – possessing qualities of both instrumentality and expressivity

Sandra Bem is probably the best-known proponent of this view, arguing for androgeny as the psychological ideal. She has conducted a whole programme of work to support this contention (see Bem, 1978, for a review). Possibly her best-known study is one which showed that people scoring highly on androgeny had higher self-esteem than either highly masculine men or highly feminine women (Bem, 1977). In other words, Sandra Bem was able to show that people like her – a woman possessing high levels of desirable instrumental traits with high levels of desirable expressive traits ('desirable', of course, in the context of the culture of US academia) – are the best kind of people to be.

Box 10.6 – Beryl's Sixth Law – The 'PLU' Principle

Bem's study is a wonderful example of what we may call the 'PLU' Principle. This is the tendency of psychologists to believe that the best kind of person to be is a 'person like us', and its converse – the less like us you are, the less adjusted, healthy, together, desirable, etc. you are. In order to bolster their claims, psychologists are very good at devising studies to demonstrate that PLU-ness is good, non-PLU-ness is bad.

Other examples are the work done on the authoritarian personality (see Chapter 3) and work we will describe later in this chapter, where some lesbian feminists argue that lesbianism is a healthier, more politically valid identity than heterosexuality.

This takes us back to our consideration of the notion of 'Otherness' (as described at the beginning of the chapter) and forward to a consideration of the challenge which has been made to male-stream scholarship from feminist theory.

Feminist theory

As we saw at the beginning of the chapter, much of feminist theory is concerned with bringing to our attention the ways in which being ascribed the category 'female' brings with it a host of disadvantages and forms of exploitation. Feminists argue that we live in a 'man-made world' – a patriarchial system which so dominates our reality-making that it fundamentally casts women as 'Other'. Feminism sees patriarchy as a system of thought and as a set of praxes which make sex-difference profoundly matter; which valorize masculinity and accord men power; and which render women powerless and subservient. It thus limits girls' and women's opportunities in every sphere – in terms of access to education, to employment (and hence to income) and to the law. Thus patriarchy's central tenets are self-fulfilling – they construct difference, they then act to reinforce that difference, and hence the difference becomes more marked. This more marked difference then acts to justify further differentiation – and so the system continually feeds upon itself.

However, feminism is a very broad school, which encompasses a wide diversity of perspectives (see Eisenstein, 1984 and Segal, 1987 for readable reviews). At its most harsh it prescribes lesbian separatism, based upon the idea that heterosexuality is the mainstay of patriarchy, is fundamentally oppressive, and hence must be challenged and resisted (see, for example, Jeffreys, 1990). At its 'softer' end (if one accepts such a dimension), liberal-humanistic forms of feminism argue that patriarchy is oppressive both to men and women, and what is needed is for persons of both sexes to seek to transcend its limitations. Some feminists draw upon a biological warrant, viewing femaleness as inherently different from maleness. Others regard sexual difference as mainly or entirely socially constructed.

Box 10.7 Critical Social Psychology and Feminist Theory

There is considerable overlap between the theoretical positions taken in much feminist theory and the approach we have taken in this book. Both stress that much of what we 'take for granted' is not as it seems. The world around us is not a natural and inevitable 'reality' but a constructed reality. The knowledge that we have of that world is not a simple mirroring of reality but a human product. Both share the view that power is centrally at issue – it is the powerful who construct knowledge, and knowledge is shot through with power.

Where our position differs from feminist theory is that the feminists (in differing degrees) valorize sex/gender as the main axis around which issues of power and knowledge – and their consequences in practical terms on people's lives – should be addressed. Our approach seeks not to valorize any one axis and, indeed, seeks to challenge all realist conceptions, including the sexual categorization on which feminism is based. It too, we believe, should be subject to scrutiny and to radical doubt.

This is not to say that feminism is unconcerned with other loci of power/knowledge. Indeed, feminists have been highly instrumental in addressing issues of race (e.g. Yuval-Davis, 1994), disability (e.g. Lorde, 1984), and class (e.g. Walkerdine and Lucey, 1989). Feminists have been particularly influential in bringing the sexual exploitation of children to the forefront of attention (e.g. Nelson, 1987) and often the feminist approach to child sexual abuse is highly social-constructionist (e.g. Saraga and Macleod, 1991).

The feminist appropriation of psychoanalysis

An interesting development in feminist theory has been its appropriation of psychoanalysis. This has been particularly developed in relation to the study of film. According to Mulvey the cinema is an advanced representational system which 'reflects, reveals and even plays on the straight, socially established interpretation of sexual difference which controls images, erotic ways of looking and spectacle'(1975: 14).

Mulvey contends that the significance of the phallus to both masculinity and femininity is not (as Freud assumed) 'a fact of nature' but a cultural product – it arises out of the phallocentrism inherent in partiarchy. The impact of phallocentrism, however, has been as pervasive and profound as if it were 'a fact of nature' in the construction of the unconscious. The point is, she suggests, that the unconscious is equally not a 'fact of nature' but constructed – and (in patriarchy) constructed predominantly by men and for men. But paradoxically, the constitutive process depends upon women:

> The paradox of phallocentrism in all its manifestations is that it depends upon the image of the castrated woman to give order and meaning to its world. The idea of woman stands as lynchpin to the system: it is her lack that produces the phallus as symbolic presence, it is her desire to make good her lack that the phallus signifies. (1975: 14)

Thus women are accorded two main functions: to symbolize the castration threat by her lack of a penis; and to act as cultural transmitter, raising children into this symbolic order – to turn her children into signifiers of her own desire to possess a penis. Outside of these functions she has no place or meaning of her own, her own desire is subjugated and denied: 'Woman then stands in patriarchial culture as signifier for the male other, bound by a symbolic order in which man can live out his fantasies and obsessions through linguistic command by imposing on them the silent image of woman still tied to her place as bearer, not maker, of meaning' (1975: op. cit.).

Mulvey's express purpose is to appropriate psychoanalysis – to overturn its use as a tool of male oppression, and to turn it back on itself to expose the ways that cinema is used commercially to perpetuate and reinforce patriarchy.

I.I. Hang on! This is supposed to be a book on social psychology, however much you 'problematize' it. This seems to be wandering dangerously close to cultural studies.

And why not? Part of criticality is challenging the discipline's claims to special authority.

Transdisciplinarity

This drawing together of art theory and psychoanalysis is a good example of one of the most significant outcomes of 'the climate of perturbation' – a move to transdisciplinarity. While there have been, for some time, attempts within the social sciences to make links between academic disciplines – to explore topics from an interdisciplinary stance – transdisciplinarity is something different. While interdisciplinarity is the building of bridges between disciplines, transdisciplinarity is the folding of disciplinary boundaries (see Lee, 1994, for a fuller development of this argument).

Sex is an obvious topic where the transdisciplinary approach can be useful, given that issues of sexuality, gender, eroticism and desire pervade art and literature, law and social policy, education and religion as much as (if not more than) they do psychology. Very little of human life and human concerns is not enmeshed within sexuality in some way (which is what makes it so hard to 'stand outside' of the discourse on sex and challenge its 'fact of nature' status).

What sets psychology aside as (supposedly) uniquely qualified to address these issues is its claim to base its knowledge on empirical 'fact finding'. Once that claim is disputed (as we have been doing in this book) two things follow. First, it opens up for scrutiny the ways in which psychology's treatment of sex and sexuality has been affected by their cultural construction. Second, of course, it begs the question – what role has psychology played in that construction?

Sexuality

Something interesting happened in 1973, at a meeting of the American Psychiatric Association, unlikely as that may sound! Following a series of disruptions of its earlier meetings by gay activists, its members collectively conceded that homosexuality was not a 'disease', and voted to remove it from their Diagnostic and Statistical Manual. What happened next is perhaps even more instructive. Within a few years it was homophobia – the 'irrational, persistent fear or dread of homosexuals' (MacDonald, 1976) – which had become the 'sickness'. Marmor (1980), for instance, wrote of it as 'a mental health issue of the first magnitude' and Weinberg argued that 'I would never consider a patient healthy unless he [sic] had overcome his prejudice against homosexuality' (1973: 1).

Kitzinger (1987) comments that this reversal – from classifying homosexuals as sick to classifying homophobes as sick – is just one of several such 'about turns' within the history of psychological theorization about sexuality. It is, however, one of the most dramatic and well-documented. Morin (1977) has estimated that around seventy per cent of pre-1974 psychological research on homosexuality was sited within discourses of deviance and dysfunction, devoted to three questions: 'Are homosexuals sick?' 'How can it be diagnosed?' and 'What causes it?' The early 1970s then saw a proliferation of studies on homophobia (see Kitzinger, 1987, for a detailed account), and a flurry of scales designed to measure it, yielding clear 'evidence' that it is linked to a host of other forms of personality defect (such as authoritarianism).

The field of 'sexuality' is indeed a fertile one for observing how, in its theorizing and research, psychology (or, perhaps more accurately, the 'psy complex' of its associated disciplines and professions) mirrors not any 'natural reality' but the 'reality' that is constructed through the historically and culturally constituted mores and ethical values of a society. Another example is that of masturbation – transformed, over time, from 'self abuse' (a cause of irrevocable psychological and physical harm) at the turn of the century to a 'normal and natural' form of childhood exploration in the 1960s, to a 'worrying sympton' of possible child sexual abuse in the 1980s and 1990s (see Stainton Rogers and Stainton Rogers, 1992a, for a more detailed review of this shift).

We can now ask the critical question – why has the field of sexuality been the site of such tectonically 'hot' shifts in what is seen to constitute knowledge? According to Michel Foucault, this is the case not just for the 'psy' complex but much more generally. Foucault argued that sexuality is far from just a matter of individual orientation, or even cultural mores; it is a potent discursive site around which power is wielded, within a synergy of power – knowledge – pleasure. He wrote three volumes of a *History of Sexuality* (though never completing his proposed scheme) exploring this theme – it is the first volume which is most influential and frequently analysed and cited.

Box 10.8   Foucault's History of Sexuality

Foucault (1976/1980) began his history by observing that a commonly held assumption is that within Western culture there has been a sequence of transformations of sexuality. According to this story, in the seventeenth century sexuality was relatively openly and freely acted out and discussed. By the nineteenth century sexuality had become repressed – regulated, censored and hidden away. In current times it is supposed that we have sexual liberation – a reaction against the old hypocrisy and prudery and an opening-up of sexuality.

Foucault argued that, while there is some truth in this perception, it is only one of the stories that can be told. A counter-argument is that far from being repressed, sexuality became, over time, increasingly to matter – to be a site of power, a means of regulation and a source of knowledge. The task he set himself was therefore to 'define the regimes of power – knowledge – pleasure that sustain the discourse on human sexuality' (1980: 11).

He proposed that four main strategies have been used to regulate sexuality:

- A socialization of procreative behaviour, involving the 'responsibilities' of couples. Legitimate sexuality in this way gets doubly 'contained' – first sequestered within the confines of the normative family and then, within the family, hidden away behind the paternal bedroom door. This warrants the alliance of the family – as a normatizing force – and privatizes fertility control and child-raising.
- The hystericization of women's bodies, whereby women's sexuality has been constituted as central to their personhood. This has enabled women to be placed under particular governance – to be positioned as legitimate objects of medical and psychological control.
- A pedagogization of children's sex, casting sexuality in childhood as precocious and perilous, and children as simultaneously dangerous and endangered by their sexual potential. This has warranted adult regulation of childhood sexuality – in everything from the architecture of schools to subjecting children's actions to parental and professional scrutiny.
- A psychiatrization of perverse desire, whereby all deviations from 'normal sexuality' (particularly homosexuality) were pathologized. This has been used to justifying the application of corrective technologies – including re-education, treatment and criminal sanctions against all forms of non-legitimated sexuality.

Foucault suggested that these strategies, acting in concert, do not, however, just act upon sexuality to regulate it. They use this regulation of sexuality as the 'glue' to hold together a normalized/normalizing social structure.

This is a theoretical position going far beyond the usual way in which sexuality is perceived. It suggests that sexuality is a potent site of power operating across the manifold of human experience: sexuality functions as 'an unique signifier and as a universal signified' (1980: 154). It allows a whole host of different things – anatomical elements, biological

functions, conducts, sensations and pleasures – to be linked together as
a single 'whole', and accorded a causal relationship.

Thus the purpose of regulation, according to Foucault, was not simply
to repress the sexuality of the governed – to force them to hide it away
and to deny it. This may seem on the surface what is going on, but it is
only one manifestation of regulation. Rather, the main goal was to promote
'the body, the vigour, the longevity, progeniture and descent of the
classes that "ruled". This was the purpose for which the deployment of
sexuality was first established, as a new distribution of pleasures, discourses, truths and powers . . . a defense, a protection, and an exaltation
. . . a means of social control and political subjugation' (1980: 123).

But the important point Foucault makes is that, over time, this became
not just a one-way process. As a site of power, sexuality has become as
much a locus for resistance as a locus for governmentality. As the
governed have sought to challenge the governance to which they are
subjected, 'deviant' sexuality has been used as a major mechanism to
undermine the different forms of regulation set out above.

Foucault's formulations can be viewed as just as much 'self-serving'
and 'self-justifying' as other theorizing we have criticized in this book. In
arguing that sexual 'deviance' is not just a lifestyle choice or a predilec-
tion, and that homosexuality – and indeed other forms of 'perverse
pleasure' (such as sado-masochism) – are potent means of political action,
Foucault could be seen to be warranting his own sexuality as a form of
resistance against hegemonical power.

Of course in Foucauldian terms all theorization – as a form of
discursivity – is a strategic use of power/knowledge (or knowledge to
produce power). Foucault would never have claimed his own discourse
was immune to such a reading. At the same time, what Foucault's (sadly
unfinished) exploration of sexuality did was dramatically change the
whole way we can 'make sense of' sexuality. Far from its being a
biological 'given' or even an isolated and limited 'aspect' of human
experience, he opened up for us the possibility that sexuality is 'an
important area of contention around which innumerable institutional
devices and discursive strategies have been employed' (1980: 30). As a
consequence, sexuality has become one of the major preoccupations of
our times: 'From the singular imperialism that compels everyone to
transform their sexuality into a perpetual discourse, to the manifold of
mechanisms which, in the areas of economy, medicine and justice, incite,
extract, distribute and institutionalize the sexual discourse, an immense
verbosity is what our civilization has required and organized' (1980: 33).

A short history of sexology

Seen in the light of Foucault's analysis, the history of how social psychology has studied and theorized sexuality suggests a rather different reading from the usual 'march of progress' tale. Far from being a gradual imposition of scientific rationality upon the prejudices and wild misunderstandings of the past, we can see the shifting concerns and approaches of the discipline as a cultural 'litmus test', reflecting wider shifts in concerns and power-plays in relation to sexuality which have arisen over the last hundred years or so.

Victorian Values From the late nineteenth century onwards, sexuality was scientized – brought under the gaze of the human sciences. Sometimes it has even been accorded a specific discipline of its own – sexology (see, for example, Walling, 1909). Walling's overriding preoccupations were very much to do with regulation. This is illustrated by his treatment of childhood sexuality, where the major focus of his concern was upon the horrors and harm-potential of 'self-abuse' (i.e. masturbation).

Box 10. 9   The Horrors and Harm-Potential of Self-Abuse

Walling's textbook is an ideal case for 'thematic decomposition' (cf. Chapter 11) because it condenses over a century of official moral panic about masturbation. As he puts it: 'gems of knowledge gleaned from the entire field of standard literature and from the documentary evidence of eminent European and American men and women Physicians, Professors, Lawyers, Preachers and other brilliant minds' (1909: 7).

  He then goes on to make his case for the harmfulness of self-abuse. It is, he argued, 'the foundation of physical, mental and moral maladies, the causes of which are as unsuspected as they are consequently persistent in their operation' (1909: 34) The disastrous impact of the vice is evident, he argued, from its manifestations in the behaviour and demenour of the child who has been caught within its grip:

  Perhaps the most constant and invariable, as well as earliest signs of the masturbator are the downcast, averted glance, and the disposition to solitude. Prominent characteristics are loss of memory and intelligence, morose and unequal disposition, aversion or indifference to legitimate pleasures and sports, mental abstractions, stupid stolidity, etc. (1909: 38)

  Moreover, it can be diagnosed on the basis of physical signs. Quoting with approval one of his medical authorities, he noted: 'Deslandes says:

'I have every reason, from a great number of facts presented to me in practice, that of every twenty cases of leuchorrhea ("whites"), or of inflammation of the vulva or vagina in children [*sic*] and young girls, there are at least fifteen or eighteen which result from masturbation!' (1909: 46)

Untreated self-abusers, for Walling, were a danger not only to themselves but to others: 'If a boy is an onanist he is sure to corrupt the smaller boys of his acquaintance whenever a safe opportunity presents itself' (1909: 13).

Consequently, parents must – according to Walling – be vigilant to protect their children from being 'led astray'. He censored parents whom he saw as 'too indulgent or too careless to discharge their duties of supervision' (1909: 22). He berrated parents who allowed their children to read material of a corrupting nature – who did not, in his words, 'deem to scruple to place in the hands of their daughters the journals of the day . . . teeming with advertisements and "news items" of the most revolting and indecent character' (1909: 24).

(Condensed and modified from R. and W. Stainton Rogers, 1992a).

It is usually easy, with hindsight, to spot the posturing stance adopted in historical texts of this kind – and it often provides excellent amusement. Pulled out from the times and locations from which they were written, their implicit values and moralizing agenda are patently obvious. This is one reason why the study of historical texts is such a fertile form of analysis. We can learn a lot about our contemporary values and moralizing agendas both from the differences, and from the commonalities, between the way a phenomenon was viewed in the past and the way it is viewed today.

Two main observations spring to mind when examining Walling's work. First, while there are clear discontinuities between his preoccupation with 'self-abuse' and our contemporary preoccupation with 'sexual abuse', the similarities are also striking. For Walling the locus of concern was masturbation – this, he argued, was the 'cause' of harm, and the 'problem' which needed to be addressed – treated when it arose, and prevented by adult vigilance and probity over exposing children to material of a depraving nature. The 'fact' that children who masturbated had often been taught to do it by adult care-takers (usually, in Walling's misogynist view, by governesses and nursemaids) was treated as no more than a small by-line in his argument.

By contrast, today's preoccupation with child sexual abuse views adult exploitation as the pre-eminent 'problem' and the 'cause' of the uniquely damaging and irreovocable harm which sexual abuse engenders in its victims (see O'Dell, 1995, for a review of the scientific 'evidence' for this assumption). In contemporary discourse it is masturbation – as one among a whole host of possible signs which may indicate a child has been abused – which is treated as the unimportant by-line. (For a fuller analysis of the similarities and differences in the two discourses, see Stainton Rogers and Stainton Rogers, 1992b.)

The other arresting resonance we can observe between Walling's discourse and that of today is his conviction that children are particularly vulnerable to being corrupted by the mass media. Then it was 'journals of the day . . . teeming with advertisements and "news items" of the most revolting and indecent character' which he held to be perilous to the innocent minds of the young. Today popular and professional concern over the media and the young centres less (although that theme is still there) on the corrupting influence of sex per se than of violence and 'sexual violence'. And, of course, with technological advance, the medium of concern is no longer magazines but the television set. In particular, it is the 'video nasty' which now preoccupies our latter-day Wallings. It is salutory to note that anybody who today argued that the content of turn-of-the-century news-stand magazines seriously corrupted a generation of children would be, rightly, ridiculed. Yet there are plenty of nice fat research grants to be had these days to investigate the impact of watching television and video upon children's propensity to violence!

Sexual 'Liberation' The discourse on masturbation underwent a sequence of changes, gradually shifting from a major preoccupation over its dire consequence, through being seen as a matter of 'poor manners' if done in public, to the view held in the 1960s that it was a normal – indeed desirable – stage in children's self-exploration and growing ability to engage in sensuality. Now, as we observed in the previous section, it has become somewhat perturbating – if engaged in 'obsessively' it is seen as a worrying sign that the child may have been sexually abused.

However, Foucault's 'pedagogization of child sexuality' (albeit stripped of its warrant to put children in straitjackets or subject them to surgery to prevent masturbation) none the less remained – and remains – a potently regulatory strategy, in which psychology has played a key role. From the 1930s onwards to today, social psychology has taken a strongly governmental/educational stance over youthful sexuality. Again, while there was a brief celebration of 'liberation' around 1970 (Zimbardo (1976) calls sex 'a most natural, normal activity, pleasurable in both process and consequence'), the emergence of the HIV has enabled governmentality over sex to be re-asserted in a new way. Brehm and Kassin (1990), in their textbook *Social Psychology*, for example, head their sub-section on sex education: 'The importance of being safe'.

The liberal-intellectual discourse on sexuality which grounded the 'sexual liberation' movement of the decade around 1970 was expressed thus by Zimbardo:

> For many individuals the most important element is not what happens *during* sex, but the attitudes, motives, expectations, anxieties, and cultural values with which they have been inculcated and which they carry with them like a cumbersome duffel bag without a handle. [*sic*]. . . In order for human sexuality to be treated as a subject worthy of psychological inquiry, it must be 'legitimized' as a scientifically valid topic. (1976:219)

Here, we think, the Foucauldian reading of sexual liberation as at the same time governmental is well illustrated. The classic case of making human sexuality a 'scientifically valid topic' is probably the work of Masters and Johnson (1966). They quite literally took sexuality out of the bedroom (or wherever) and into the laboratory. With that move, the 'nuts and bolts' of how people come could not only be talked about openly but subjected to public scrutiny. McNeil's text *Being Human* (1973), for example, hails Masters and Johnson as nothing less than 'the first victory of the sexual revolution in the laboratory'.

Others trace the purported liberatory agenda of sexology back much earlier into the immediate post-second-World-War era. A case in point is the use of phylogenetic data to restore the 'normality' of homosexual contact (if it's OK for baboons it's OK for us) and human normative data (e.g. Kinsey et al., 1948) to argue that many 'normal' people have had such 'outlets'. Hence claims, later taken into the 'sexual liberation movement', about heterosexuality/homosexuality forming a continuum of 'sexual object choice' (a kind of scientific re-statement of the old POW saying 'home before Christmas or homo before Easter').

It nevertheless goes without saying that much of the 'human sexuality' so liberated was freed under what presented as a heterosexual, male gaze. Many subsequent feminists have taken a dim view of its agenda (cf. Kitzinger, 1987). However, the warrant for research does make possible a documentation of an era. For example, work carried out at the Kinsey Sex Research Institute (Bell and Weinberg, 1978; and Bell, Weinberg and Hammersmith, 1981) demonstrated how the 'gay scene' (at least in the San Francisco Bay Area at the time the research there was carried out) reflected a lifting of regulation. This research found that the vast majority of self-defined homosexuals (both men and women) reported no regret about their sexual orientation – and the few that did regretted negative public attitudes rather than the homosexual identity itself.

Sexuality is also a prime site in which to argue that what may appear to be signs of liberalism are often far from liberatory. A good example is the growing provision for offering individuals the opportunity to change their sex or exchange their gender. But the interesting thing about bio-medical 'gender-bending' isn't that new categories of gender are constructed, or even that new types of sexual orientation are invented – that is strictly the province of science fiction – but that their clients have to fit into the two predetermined, socially defined categories (Lorber and Farrell, 1991).

Thus transsexuals have to be able to pass as 'true women' in order to establish their status as transsexuals. Rather than undermining social rules about sex and gender, clinics involved in sexual reorientation therapies (usually working with and for male clients), demand reinforcement of sex role stereotypes. They impose what some have described as a 'man's idea' of a woman, a male-imposed definition of femaleness in terms of dress, speech, and body language, even career.

The identification of a person as a transsexual can happen almost as soon as validation of the membership of a gender group begins. The UCLA Child Gender Program, for example, took on the treating of children who are diagnosed as potential transsexuals. That is, they are treating young boys who are identified as having gender disturbances – boys with feminine mannerisms who have feminine voice inflections and who have an aversion to masculine play (Raymond, 1979). It is easy to see the way in which the social psychologist's supposedly neutral attempts to describe and define gender have provided a mechanism for prescribing appropriate behaviour, and a justification (if a somewhat circular one) for reinforcing the taken-for-granteds about gender. This does not show vast signs of changing.

Developmental sexology

As we have noted, despite this sexual liberation in other areas, when it came to the acquisition of sexuality by the young there remained a great deal of moral posturing. Read through a Foucauldian gaze, there also appears to be a strong element of voyeurism and scopophilia. Because, unlike sex, sexualization can be thought of in terms of degrees, it forms an ideal subject for scientized research. For example, it is not too difficult to do a study which 'demonstrates' that young people tend to engage in french kissing earlier than they do in genital fondling (Schofield, 1965). Similarly Christopher and Cate (1985) have plotted a domino sequence (where one thing leads to another) in sexual experience. Scientism also offers us stunning insights like 'relationships progress from superficial exchanges to more intimate ones' (Brehm and Kassin, 1990: 254).

I.I. That is certainly something to ponder on deeply!

But not too deeply, for a few pages on they inform us about other 'theories' that imply the possibility that there are qualitatively different kinds of relationships. According to this perspective, no matter how many positive experiences occur within one type of relationship, the result won't necessarily be a more intimate type of relationship – it is, they suggest, like eating ice cream (1990: 259).

I.I. Aha, so that's where Häagen-Daz got the inspiration for their advertising campaign!

Social-psychological research here, as elsewhere, acts as a vehicle for giving a scientific gloss to the normatizing (and, of course, pathologizing) of sexualization. Indeed, over sexualization, the borderline between academic and 'popular' psychology is very fuzzy indeed.

Box 10.10   The Perfumed Garden

Under the header 'Sniffing out a sexual partner', Baron and Byrne (1987: 577) report an experiment with a neat interaction:

- Perfume increased males' attraction to a female stranger who was dressed informally.
- Perfume actually decreased males' attraction to a female stranger who was dressed neatly (*sic*).

Of course, this effect might not be universal. The study is limited by (amongst other things!) the use of only one fragrance – 'Jungle Gardenia'. Clearly, more research needs to be done!

Baron and Byrne, incidentally, also provide a classic example of the biological warrant by prefacing their effluvial work on humans with a section on sexual pheromones in 'other species' (starting with ants).

I.I. Come on, you are not trying to tell me social psychologists really think that sexual attraction is the same in ants and humans, are you!

You'd better believe it! The biological warrant over sex is deeply ingrained in Modernist thought – a hangover, perhaps, from the Victorian notion that sex is inherently 'animal-like' – bestial, brutal and kept under control only by the forces of civilization. It was just this taken-for-granted notion – that biologists 'know about sex' – that first led Kinsey (at the time an expert in gall-wasps which, ironically, can reproduce partheno-genetically) to be called into campus sex education in the 1930s and hence into his famous studies of human sexuality (Kinsey et al., 1948; 1963).

Eroticization

> In olden days a hint of stocking
> Was thought of as something shocking,
> Now heaven knows – anything goes.

The raising of questions about how (and if) material comes to be seen as 'social – psychological' is one of those self-reflexive activities that critical academics employ to trouble the discipline. Despite the emergence of the term 'social developmental psychology', the disciplines of social and developmental psychology bridge less than one might expect. Where they do, it is most often in terms of social cognition (identity, schematization and moral development). Perhaps, then (perhaps), we should not expect to find the topic of eroticization in the index of social psychology texts. Certainly we don't.

It has to be constructed out of diverse sources: studies of sexual inception; psychoanalytic speculations about the psychology of clothes (e.g. Flugel, 1930); the mapping of go and no-go areas of the body by social relationship of touched to toucher (Jourard, 1968); and the misattribution of fear as sexual desire (Dutton and Aron, 1974).

I.I. Hardly a comprehensive coverage, is it?

Not at all. It is much easier to find sections on 'sexual arousal'.

I.I. That sounds exciting, can I have a sample?

Zimbardo reports Kutshinsky's experimental study of the effects of erotica on married (nice warrant that) Danish students thus: 'Comparing the two sexes it was found that the men began with higher expectations and were more disappointed than were the women . . . The researcher concludes that "during the session there was a tendency toward 'heating up' of women . . . while the men tended to 'cool down'"'' (1977: 222).

I.I. Oh.

Yet eroticization is widely permeated in the biographies and social worlds of social psychologists (and their students), if only because it is a major cultural thematic. However – as the introductory quotation is meant to highlight – in their specifics our cultural mores about eroticization change, eroticization remains predicated upon a cultural normalization of heterosexuality. To put this another way, coverage of male homosexual erotics or lesbian sado-masochism is still the province of the avant-garde – and mainstream social psychology has never been that!

What mainstream research can reveal, then, is commonsensicality and normalization writ large. In this tale, the bodies of the other sex are expected to become developmentally eroticized. Hence, for example, caregivers are more likely to accept bedroom sharing between same-sex children. This permeates schooling, in, for example, statutory requirements about showers and changing rooms having to be set up on a single-sex basis, and where cross-sex visual body experience is discouraged through architectural planning as well as by social rules. (Most children, of course, find ways round this!)

De Swaan (1990) provides an historical analysis of our domestic arrangements for living, which he suggests have played a part in determining the nature of sexual relationships. It seems that, for the 'masses', the kind of spatial segregation which we would today regard as a necessity for privacy was not made possible until the period between the 1880s and the 1940s. This, he claims, had a profound impact on the nature of sexual intimacy and certainly the signalling and communication of sexual intimacy (a theme also extensively developed by Foucault).

De Swaan noted that 'the flash of an ankle' was a 'signal of intimacy as long as the lower leg was normatively covered' (1990: 192). In times where near-nudity is commonplace (at least on the beach), the nature of self-exposure has changed. Today, if we wish to bid for the establishment of an intimate relationship, we are more likely to express our erotic preferences or communicate our fears of desertion, and are less likely to depend upon the display of body parts to communicate interest.

I.I. As in the phrase 'Yes means yes, no means no, whatever we wear, wherever we go.'

That's a good example. We might wish to retain a degree of ambiguity in negotiating our sexual relationships, but this ambiguity depends more upon word-play than upon the display of the body.

The relation between embodiment and eroticization is a fascinating one and, again, little explored as social psychology. In Western art, for example, (at least outside of erotic art) female genitals and female pubic hair were notable for their absence until the twentieth century. At least one Victorian art historian, John Ruskin, is said to have been permanently traumatized by the wedding-night revelation of his wife (Euphemia Gray)'s pubic hair! Discourses of eroticization by exclusion begin early – it is still common practice for three-year girls (in Britain though not most of the rest of Europe) to swim with their nipples covered – but we know far less from psychology of the sexual subjectivity of young girls than we do of their pre-operation social thought. (From a critical perspective, Valerie Walkerdine's *Schoolgirl Fictions*, 1990, offers some very useful counters to this.)

As we noted in the earlier section, our constructive abilities render all sorts of artefacts erotic, not just those in contact with or obscuring flesh but in and of themselves. If your appetite runs to silk you are 'normal', if it runs to rubber you may be 'fetishistic'. Whole industries (like advertising) depend upon eroticization of both product and promotion. The erotic power of representation – scopophilia (in words or images) – fills much of our art and entertainment. The best that mainstream social psychology has to offer over this is some conceptually weak but highly fundable research on the effects of pornography and the use of erotica in misattribution of emotion studies.

Eroticization, we could say, is played out on our embodiment, but culture writes the tunes. Thus if bulging biceps or mammoth mammaries become eroticized, then we get into a game of constructed biology – a game our technology reflects back through anabolic steroids and silicone implants, the gym and the club. Yet, again, the standard social psychology syllabus all but ignores this. (If sexual imagery is considered, it is either in a psychometric mould (Do oral men prefer big breasts? (cf. Wiggins et al, 1968), in the mate-selection paradigm or as the visual back-drop to studies of sexual identity.) What we get instead is, again, revealing. The growth of the psychology warrant to practise brings to social psychology the clinical – the anorexic and the bulimic.

Cross-cultural studies of sexuality

'Comparative sexual behaviour' was the rationale offered for Ford and Beach's classic *Patterns of Sexual Behaviour* (1952). In its coverage of human sexual anthropology, this work was important in promoting awareness of the massive cultural variability in mores and practices of sexualization. It identified the notion of 'permissive societies' around fifteen years before Anglic culture found themselves in the 'permissive society' – and, of course, their pundits found their own young people a 'tribe' with very different sexual mores to their own!

Such an anthropologizing (or ethnographic) turn in sexology itself promotes the study of: 'rites of passage' (e.g. losing one's 'virginity' – a classical social construction by the way); 'taboos' (like those concerning 'incest'); and specific knowledges needed to pass as a competent member of the culture (such as 'getting off with someone').

Because sexology has never achieved the status of an over-discipline centralizing sexual studies, a good deal of cross-disciplinary reading around is required to grasp this work as a whole. Texts of social psychology, as we have tried to show, provide a very partial account. But just as historical analysis can help us reconsider our taken-for-granteds, so too can examining how things are different in other cultures.

I.I. With a degree of caution, I presume, about not simply marking this as 'Other' – therefore exotic and alien.

Precisely – indeed, with very extreme caution. It is critical not to get drawn into the story that what this allows us to see is more 'natural' human behaviour – what it looks like when you scratch off the veneer that civilization has lain over human animality. Or the 'Garden of Eden' saga of the innocent savage. Both of these have a nasty tendency to seep through into liberal-humanism, however couched around with politically-correct terminology. But as an exercise, see how you feel about stumbling upon a community in which it is believed that: 'girls will not mature without benefit of sexual intercourse. Early sex play among boys and girls characteristically involves many forms of mutual masturbation and usually ends in attempted copulation. By the time they are 11 or 12 years old most girls regularly engage in full intercourse. Older men occasionally copulate with girls as young as 8 years old.' A case for a dawn raid by the social workers? No, this is Ford and Beach (1952: 52) describing the Lepcha!

Critical readings

By clashing such possibilities against our cultural and historical taken-for-granted, a critical social psychology position is not, of course, thereby endorsing them. The challenge is an intellectual one – though where it raises questions as to whether young people's civil rights should include sexual rights, it is also more than that (see, for example, Sullivan, 1992). Nor, in stressing the social constitution of sexuality, are we denying 'the body' as a practical and social facticity (see, for example, Fox, 1992). What we would argue is that, for us, the body has become a commodity, an object packaged. (This says more than that we use perfume!) And thereby it raises the ante in social psychological analysis.

I.I. So what is it you are arguing can be gained from this kind of analysis?

Perhaps to make a space for the notion that, in our kind of sex-economy, a 'sex object' is cyborg (part organic, part artifice – see Haraway, 1984 for a fuller treatment of this notion). Many artefacts, thereby, become sexualized and acquire a powerful socio-emotional aura. It is not just that the behaviours of sexuality have changed but that the 'cyborg' has changed. Few of today's men who are now in their forties or fifties would have gone, in their twenties, to a chemist and asked for sanitary towels; today they buy tampons with the grocery at the super-market. In their youth getting condoms usually involved getting an unwanted haircut or visiting the now nearly extinct surgical stores where contraceptives were sold alongside trusses and commodes (an opportunity for association learning indeed)! These days they can be bought at petrol stations, are handed out in 'student packs', and are available in slot machines in women's as well as men's public lavatories.

I.I. Is what you are saying that what people do has changed, because what people can do has changed?

Yes indeed. The major concern of the early sexologists (and that includes Freud) was to pathologize this cyborg. Hence, we lost touch with its ordinariness in all our lives. Indeed, the classification and theorization of 'fetishization' became of major concern to psychology. Later, behav-iouristic psychologists tried to put fetishistic behaviour on to a more 'scientific' basis, even seeking to 'condition' (and 'decondition') links between 'stimuli' and 'response' (arousal and thigh-length boots in one classic study: Rachman, 1966).

I.I. Clearly they were not listening to the Velvet Underground!

Critical writers have had a field day with the sexist, racist, ageist and commodifying discourse of such research – not to mention its rhetorical device of continually shifting between the scientizing of sexuality and appeals to the subjective experience of the (male) reader. Feminists have, for instance, subjected the early history of scientized sexuality to extensive critical scrutiny over its treatment of women's sexuality (see, for example, Scully and Bart, 1978; Gavey, 1992; Rich, 1980).

A more direct call to our subjectivity is often made in critical social psychology. This strategy seeks both to deprivilege mainstream psychology's claim to special access and insight, and to employ 'experience' reflexively in order to challenge its conditions of construction – i.e. the ways we and our sexuality were made subject.

The original impetus for such explorations came from those whose sexuality is regarded as 'Other' (i.e. other than the male heterosex orthodoxy within which sexology from Krafft-Ebing to Masters and Johnson was cast) – women and gay men. However, over the last decade, as critique has begun to move into the campus discourse of 'political correctness', issues such as the need for 'men's groups' and concerns such as 'date rape' have begun to enter the mainline social psychology syllabus.

As we noted at the start of this chapter, the socio-emotionality of sex language makes it an arena for 'groping prose'. By locating sexuality in the 'objective' language of science (by talking of coitus rather than fucking; auto-eroticism rather than wanking), it can be made to lose 'visceral clutch'.

1.1. But the 'trick' works!

It does, but only through denying moral self-reference. Scientizing sex brings with it the dubious importation of a mechanistic sex-world: 'pair-bonding'; 'outlet'; 'sex object'; 'sexual releasers'; 'G spots'. It also made possible reification and pathologization, the discovery of sexual disorders and 'diseases' like homosexuality, nymphomania – whose 'causes' may be found in those remarkably built chemicals the 'sex' hormones. The deconstruction of 'objective' sex language (and much else in language) has been the hallmark of the feminist and gay-affirmative critique of sexology (cf. Kitzinger, 1987). What may be less obvious to 'heterosexual' critical psychologists is that 'heterosexuality' is also a construction of this same scientized sexology.

If, as much critical analysis argues, psychological knowledge does indeed co-vary with social climate, in the 'nervous nineties' we could well be in for a spate of born-again essentialism in research on sex and gender. A prime site for this is neurophysiological psychology and the continued search for the hard-wired grounding of sexuality. Some gays, for example, endorse such research because, to them, it offers the prospect of grounding their 'special identity'. Whether exposure to 'political correctness' will also prompt 'heterosexuals' to favour a scientized grounding to their 'condition', time alone will tell.

11 Methods of Enquiry

Over the past ten chapters of this book we have exposed the contrasts between mainstream and critical social psychology. While we have been at pains to avoid presenting either as a singular totality, it should be very clear by now that their approach is fundamentally different at every level. Nowhere is this more evident than in the ways they go about research. Research done by mainstream social psychologists is presented as a scientifically informed interrogation of the phenomena of sociality. Critical social psychologists also 'do research' – but what they do and what they are seeking to find out are profoundly different. In this chapter it is these contrasts that we will explore.

I.I. That's all very well – but what bothers me is that every other social psychology textbook I've seen starts with coverage of methods. Why have you left it almost to the end? Is there a critical point – or are you just being difficult?

There is indeed a critical agenda to our position and positioning of method in the book. To grasp why, you have only to do some informal textual analysis over how and why method is employed in the construction of the 'mission': 'I believe in Science the Almighty, Explainer of Heaven and earth; and in Hypothetico-Deductive Method . . .' is part of the creed which sets the believers apart from the heathen. As Aronson et al. put it: 'Although novelists and social critics often provide valuable observations about why people behave as they do, ultimately such observations must be translated into hypotheses that can be tested scientifically' (1994: 33).

I.I. Aren't you getting a little sacrilegious here, likening a faith in science to the Creed? You could offend a lot of people.

It is not Christians who should be offended. The Decalogue is quite clear about worshipping graven images. And that is our charge – that mainstream psychology does not just use certain methods, it is 'methodolatrous' – it idolizes scientific method, according it superior status as the only self-respecting means by which 'true knowledge' can be discovered (see Curt, 1994, for a fuller account of the notion of methodolatry). Given the criticisms and concerns about scientism we have raised in this book, we can ask why this is – why this methodolatry? The answer, we believe, has more to do with the way psychologists wish to present themselves, and with their hegemonical concerns, than with an open-minded evaluation of its practical utility.

First of all, it offers the credentials of being 'serious' and 'scholarly'. Scientific method places heavy emphasis on research as exacting – requiring hard, committed work. It is a highly skilled activity, full of pitfalls for the unwary. Empirical investigation, the implication goes, can be done only by 'experts'. Consequently it confers exclusivity. It provides a persuasive rationale for arguing that 'understanding people' and making sense of what they think, feel and do is the province of the Academy. Foucault defines 'the Academy' as the locus of secret and exclusive – and thus prized – scholarly knowledge, which, even when those outside of the Academy get to know about it, cannot be fully deciphered. It is the site of 'discourse with a veil drawn over it' (1970: 88). Methodolatry thus serves the purpose of enabling psychologists to cast themselves as the sole architects of legitimate knowledge about 'the science of behaviour'.

Together what this adds up to is that methodolatry acts to bolster psychologists' credentials as genuine scholars – hard-working, technically skilled and knowledgeable – and it provides them with the legitimated authority to dispense knowledge, and decide what is 'fact' and what is 'fiction'. Aronson et al., whom we quoted earlier, are by no means the first authors of glossy texts to offer readers a quiz 'based on social psychological research' (1994: 34) to reinforce this point. Their re-emphasis is not idle – the crux of methodolatry lies here. The ability to select and use appropriate methods of enquiry (and their associated statistical techniques) is held to be the key to extracting the 'gold of pure truth' from the dross of opinion, prejudice, folk-tale and superstition. Methods are the alembics of these modern-day alchemists. In marking its territory with the Academy, mainstream psychology, almost throughout its history, has presented scientific methods of empirical enquiry as the antidote to the ills of 'armchair psychology'.

I.I. I think that expression comes from before my time.

It's intended as an insult, like calling somebody else's work 'metaphysical'. What it conjures up is 'mere thinking', idle 'philosophizing' or 'theorizing' rather than rolling up the sleeves of one's lab coat and 'doing research'. As a result 'philosophical psychology' has been very much a backwater, a place where suggestions that some questions about human nature and social life may be 'rhetorical' rather than 'empirical' could be safely contained. By contrast, in the 'fast track' of the scientized world of 'real' psychology, theorizing is seen as of little use in itself. Rather, its primary purpose is to generate hypotheses, which can then be subjected to empirical test. Theorizing, in other words, is no more than a necessary staging-point in the quest for the real trophy – good, solid, 'hard' data. Empirical data, obtained by way of scientific method, is what proper psychologists are after.

Experiments

A central tenet of methodolatry is that the laboratory experiment is the best kind of method – it is uniquely suited to the task of testing hypotheses directly, by the controlled manipulation of variables. So it is here we will begin our look at scientific method. We have selected as an example a study described in a book by Aronson. We chose this one not just because Aronson is one of mainstream social psychology's best-known writers but also because he provided a detailed account of his own thinking and motivation. He begins the book by explaining:

> The purpose of this volume is unashamedly (but with some trepidation) to spell out the relevance that socio-psychological research might have for some of the problems besetting contemporary society. Most of that data discussed in this volume are based on experiments; most of the illustrations and examples, however, are derived from current social problems – including prejudice, propaganda, war, alienation, aggression, unrest, and political upheaval ... Implicit in all this is my belief that social psychology is extremely important – that social psychologists can play a vital role in making the world a better place. (1988: x–xi)

Let's do an experiment

The illustrative study we have chosen to look at has a particularly neat reflexive irony to it. In describing this particular experiment, Aronson was motivated by wanting to 'persuade' his readers (mostly young US university students) about the usefulness of using scientific method to study persuasion!

The story Aronson tells begins from his reaction to listening to a speech being made by the poet Allen Ginsberg. Aronson describes Ginsberg as looking 'a trifle wild-eyed (was he stoned?)' and being mocked by the studio audience. Aronson thought this was a shame, since he himself saw Ginsberg as 'talking earnestly – and, in my opinion, very sensibly – about the problems of the young'. Aronson comments: 'The scientist in me longed to substitute the conservative-looking banker in the neatly pressed business suit for the wild-eyed poet and have him move his lips while Ginsberg said the same words off camera' (1988: 72).

I.I. I reckon if you put a 'suit' in front of most UK students today, they would be distinctly unimpressed.

Agreed – psychologists are seldom half as good as they think they are at accurately estimating what their students see as 'cool' (thank you the Wunderkind for putting us straight all the times you have; please indulge us where they have not). However, to get back to the argument we are making, Aronson's hypothesis (which he attributes to 'Aristotle, the world's first published social psychologist') then was that credible communicators are more persuasive than ones who lack this credibility. But Aronson (in decidedly self-congratulatory mode) notes that it 'required some 2,300 years for Aristotle's observation to be put to a rigorous scientific test'. According to Aronson, it was Hovland and Weiss (1951) who did this. In their experiment they examined people's reactions to claims that building a nuclear-powered submarine (at that point in history, this was very much science fiction) was a viable proposition. They tested the hypothesis that *credible communicators are more persuasive than ones who lack the credibility* in the following way:

1 They operationalized the independent variable (the hypothesized cause of the effect) by setting two levels of communicator credibility
   (a) *low*: *Pravda* the official organ of the USSR Communist Party (this was at the height of the Cold War)
   (b) *high*: J. Robert Oppenheimer (the so-called father of the Second World War US atomic weapons project).
2 They randomly assigned subjects to the two conditions.
3 They measured the dependent variable (the hypothesized effect of the cause) by looking at scores of opinion change.
4 They used statistics to test the null hypothesis of 'no significant difference' between the groups against the experimental hypothesis of significantly greater opinion change in the high-credibility condition.

The experiment 'worked' – they did indeed get significantly more change in the high credibility than in the low credibility condition. Thus, Aronson concludes, the experiment was able to 'show' that the hypothesized process did indeed operate.

Our critique

There are, we would argue, a whole host of flaws in the reasoning which underpins this study (see Rogers, 1974, for a more detailed critique of such attitude-change methodology). First, the logic of the experimental design is circular, and hides a reflexivity. How did Hovland and Weiss know that *Pravda* would be a 'low-credibility source' and that Oppenheimer would be a 'high-credibility source'? They could only have done this because they shared the same common-sense cultural knowledge as the subjects of their experiments. The effect is 'obvious' because they (the experimenters) 'knew' it in advance.

The hypothesis itself likewise parallels common-sense knowledge, to the extent of being virtually tautological: the meaning of being 'credible' is to be convincing, beievable, reliable – and hence persuasive! Yet the hypothesis is presented in terms of 'there is a genuine question here to be answered' as if, somehow, there was any serious doubt about the outcome. There surely could not have been – Hovland and Weiss must have had a strong hunch that they would be proved right, or else they would never have bothered to do the experiment in the first place.

I.I. Or – more cynically – if their reasoning was wrong and their experiment didn't work, they would have obtained 'null' results – and we would never have got to hear about it. Psychologists don't publish their failures!

Oh yes they do (see Stainton Rogers 1991 in relation to locus of control research). Publication has much more to do with who you are and how good your 'connections' are than the quality of your data. But we accept the general point you are making – misguided hunches tend (usually) to moulder on shelves, giving an over-positive impression of psychologist's intuitive abilities. But the argument here about Hovland and Weiss is that if they did 'know' the outcome in advance, setting up the null hypothesis was a farce. Only Bayesian statistics deals with the surprisingness/unsurprisingness of subjective probability of an outcome, and they are very rarely used in experimental social psychology.

Subjective expectations are, of course, subjective! Forty years on and in another cultural location, we can imagine a group of UK students today presented with either a somewhat wild-eyed, hairy and dishevelled man (Bob Geldoff?) or a pin-stripe-suited banker type (John Major?). Whom do you think would be seen as the more credible communicator?

I.I. I know my answer and it doesn't go the Hovland and Weiss way.

Precisely. The most credible is the one most likely to be listened to and taken seriously. If credibility can only be judged in terms of specific historical and cultural values, then how on earth can an 'experiment' avoid being merely an artificial 'set-up' in which those cultural-historical values (rather than anything 'objective') are what are at stake?

The main problem, therefore, goes deeper than this. It is that Aronson (and indeed the original experimenters, Hovland and Weiss) assumed that the origin of the effect (i.e. the opinion change) is located in the heads of individual subjects – it is their 'minds' which are 'changed' in the experiment. However, that the experiment 'works' only because its subjects – when subjected to a given condition (i.e. receiving information from a 'low' or 'high' credibility source) – all tend to do roughly the same thing – they act lawfully.

Elsewhere in social science, where certain 'conditions' produce uniformity, we look for the explanation in sociological or cultural factors. For example, when we observe that in the UK people drive their cars on the left but in France they drive on the right, we do not assume that people 'change their minds' as they cross the channel. Rather we point to the obvious – that there are different rules for driving in the two countries.

The study, then, was, as an experiment, a sham. It purported to show the way that a particular social psychological process operates – how, hidden deep somewhere within individual minds, there sits a mechanism by which 'attitudes' can be 'changed', the operation of which can be discovered by conducting an experiment. Instead all that is actually going on is that some people (called psychologists) make well-informed guesses about the consensual practices which other people (called experimental subjects) follow, and then set up a situation in which they can observe whether or not people actually do follow them.

I.I. I take it that you mean that criticism to apply only to social psychological experiments? I mean people don't have social 'rules' about acoustic perception, do they?

That critique is indeed directed to social psychology specifically. But the much more general paradigm of comparing the performance of groups against each other means that most psychological data is 'social' (i.e. averaged across people), even when the theoretical constructs are individual psychological mechanisms. The problem is that data from the same basic paradigm can fit the study of what may be more like mechanisms (as in acoustic perception) but are blatantly open to alternative 'sociological' explanations where the 'responses' clearly mimic forms of social conduct like opinionation.

Finding agreement amongst 'subjects' in a social psychological experiment is rather like going round a building and writing down the times shown on a series of clocks, and finding out that the time they tell is much the same. It is not 'time' that has been discovered but merely a set of conventions about time. All that the Hovland and Weiss study showed is that – like driving on the right in the USA and Europe but on the left in the UK, sipping tea but spooning soup, or men buttoning their shirts one way and women the other – people can be squeezed into acting according to convention. When asked by the 'demand characteristics' of an experiment to decide whether or not a particular argument requires reacting to, they draw on conventions about the reliabilty of the source of the argument to inform them about what credence to be seen to give to it.

I.I. In other words, an effect of the 'situated identity' or 'impression management' you covered in Chapters 3 and 6?

Or, more generally, of the meanings of opinionation or opinionation change in an interrogative discourse.

Psychometrics

Psychometrics shares with experimental methods a commitment to the hypothetico-deductive approach. They differ in that, instead of looking for coincidence between variables that have been manipulated in short-term, set-up situations, researchers look for coincidence between responses in questionnaires or scales of some kind. A good example is the research based on a scale developed by Wallston and Wallston (1981): the health locus of control scale (see Stainton Rogers 1991 for a fuller critique). The development of the scale – much like Hovland and Weiss's hypothesizing for their experiment – drew upon Wallston and Wallston's (limited and partial) cultural knowledge and assumptions. This led them, for example, to exclude any notion of 'God' or supernatural power from their attributional framework; and to suppose that (despite Levenson's original formulation) the influence of medicine would always be viewed in a positive light. Moreover, like Rotter's and his colleagues' work before them, they completely ignored (presumably were ignorant of) the possibility that locating influence in 'external control' might be a realistic appraisal of structural factors such as poverty, oppression or the impact of capitalism. Consequently their research was vulnerable to the criticism expressed by Harré about psychometric methodology more generally:

> The use of questionnaires with limited range questions ... which effectively preclude elaborations and reinterpretations ... means that the concepts deployed ... are predetermined. The effect of this is to produce not a representation of the social world being studied, but the representation of the shadow cast upon the social world by the prior conceptual apparatus deployed by the person who constructed the questionnaire. (1979: 115)

I.I. In other words, psychometric research is prey to the same troubles as experimentation?

Is is and it isn't. The problem of Harré's 'shadow cast' certainly applies to both. Over some of the other troubles of experimentation, these stem from its siting in hypothetico-deductive method. Some psychometrics is not – it takes a pragmatic or 'probabilistic' position (cf. Chapter 6). However, whenever it gets to assuming it can explain or even predict the coincidence between its measures by recourse to 'latent processes' or 'inner essences' (such as attitudes, or intelligence, or personality), it gets into the experimenter's trap. And the same critique applies – it only 'works' (that is, when it does work!) because researchers can draw on the same system of the cultural knowledge of interrogation as their subjects.

Dissolution

It was the above kinds of analysis which underpinned the first wave of 'climate of perturbation' attacks on hypothetico-deductive method. This initial critique centred on an acknowledgement that people are not passive puppets of their 'inner drives' but 'active organisms'. They are, according to this argument, socially intelligent and aware beings, whose behaviour is not lawful in a mechanistic sense but lawful because they are persons-in-culture who act out the roles and follow rules that their culture has taught them (cf. Harré and Secord, 1972). Hence, the argument went, it is the roles and rules that we should be studying – not hypothetical 'essences in the head'.

Around the same time, even those who hung on to the experimental paradigm in social psychology were forced to recognize that it was riddled with 'artefacts' (e.g. Jung, 1971) which undermined the experimental manipulations and created the 'experimenter's dilemma'. Subjects' behaviour was found, for example, to be strongly mediated by such things as: 'self-presentation' (Abelson, 1968), 'awareness' (Page, 1970), 'social desirability' (Crowne and Marlow, 1964), 'demand characteristics' (Orne, 1962), and 'impression management' (Tedeschi, Schlenker and Bonoma, 1971).

A turn to 'softer' methods

The difficulty faced around this time was a simple one. It was one thing to recognize that hypothetico-deductive methods are pretty hopeless for researching into the social aspects of people's behaviour and experience. It was quite another to suss out a way forward. A number of laboratory-based alternatives were proposed, including role-playing (Freedman, 1969; Greenberg, 1967; Mixon, 1972) and simulation (Bem, 1965, 1967). But it soon became clear that they raised exactly the same kinds of problems as the experiments they were intended to replace. So long as one hangs on to the hypothetico-deductive way of thinking, then any experimental method used will still be subject to the same artefactual problems, since all social situations give rise to demand characteristics or impression management. The same argument goes for psychometrics – to 'work', a scale must be comprehensible and any comprehensible scale can be 'faked' (cf. Semin and Rogers, 1973).

I.I. Was this one of social psychology's famous crises?

It certainly was (cf. Elms, 1975)! Once it was recognized that there was nothing in the mainstream's menu of methods to resolve it, early critical social psychologists started to turn outside the discipline for alternatives. It was here that the strange location of social psychology as a branch of both psychology and sociology came in very useful.

BOX 11.1   Where the Action Is

Contemporary with the focus on the 'experimenter's dilemma' and the emergence of an 'active organism' social psychology that emerged in psychological social psychology from the mid-1960s, US sociological psychologists were developing research based on notions of human agency, human action and human meaning-making, under such (not always helpful) labels as cognitive sociology (Cicourel, 1973), existential sociology (Douglas and Johnson, 1977), and qualitative sociology (cf.

Sarbin and Kitsuse, 1994). It was, to a very considerable extent, to this tradition – of social psychological research outwith psychology the discipline – that the early generation of critical social psychologists turned to look for alternative methods and alternative models. These were, on the whole 'soft' (qualitative) formulations. For a period, a turn to an interdisciplinary 'interpretational social psychology' (in which psychological and sociological 'social psychology' were merged) seemed a real possibility (cf. Lindesmith, Strauss and Denzin, 1975; Sampson, 1971).

I.I. But that's not how it's turned out?

That would be over-simplifying things. But there were serious difficulties, and critical social psychologists (cf. Henriques et al., 1984) started to take in other ideas from the 'climate of perturbation' which caused them to question whether efforts to conjoin psychological and sociological approaches might not be doubling up on old problems rather than generating new alternatives.

The interrogation interminable

For some critical social psychologists, the move to what are usually called 'qualitative' methods (i.e. those which seek to parallel 'ordinary social life' more closely and generate data in the form of people's descriptions of their thinking and actions rather than 'objective measures') contained a hidden pitfall. The fundamental approach was really no different. We have elsewhere described this as the 'interrogation interminable' – the inevitably always-incomplete endeavour of trying to extract data from subjects. We argued that this resembles the cultural melodrama of interrogation – the 'nice guy/nasty guy' routine beloved of police and intelligence work (and their reproduction as entertainment).

The 'nasty guy' backs the target into a corner of the interview-room and demands 'just the facts ma'am' and simple . . . 'yes' or 'no' (quantifiable) answers. The 'nice guy' operator then offers a cup of tea and a cigarette, and empathizes with the participant, even to the extent of appearing to defend her from the 'blow cold' operator – and draws out . . . (qualitative) information. Whichever approach to interrogation is taken, the purpose is still to break down the resistance of the subject – to get them to yield a testimony to the truth. (Curt, 1994: 113)

The experiment goes marching on!

Perhaps not surprisingly, the outcome of this 'crisis' was one that, with hindsight, was like that of other challenges to the experimental hegemony (e.g. Rosenzweig, 1933). The social psychology establishment did not recant and admit the error of its ways – there was no revolutionary overthrow of the old order. Instead, the majority of social psychologists remained within or rejoined the fold. The minority became a site of heresy – a fringe that could, for the most part, be comfortably ignored. Social psychology today remains a predominantly hypothetico-deductively-based discipline, the majority of whose studies make either a merely token bow to issues of social construction or none at all.

BOX 11.2   Social Psychology's 'Texts of Identity'

To show that this is the case, we have chosen at random a single issue of the *European Journal of Social Psychology* – volume 23 (1993). It begins with a study hypothesizing that people expect social class to influence an individual's life chances, and that these are well-founded expectations: social class is both seen to be associated with occupation, educational achievement, unemployment and personal relationships,and actually is related to them. The result? Yes they did and yes it did.

The next study in this edition of the journal took as its goal a simpler hypothesis – to test whether 'positive–negative asymmetry can be found in the strength of political attitudes'. Indeed it could – people were found to differ in the extent to which they felt strongly about political parties, with those positively endorsing them having greater strength of feelings.

The third study set out to test the theory that members of a group tend to see group members as more similar to each other when confronted by a dominant sub-group. This study was also 'successful' – women belonging to a sorority were shown to see each other as more 'feminine' and men from a fraternity as more 'masculine' when considered in relation to the other group. (It is worth – as we pointed out in Chapter 10 – noting the 'stereotypical' (*sic*) traits used in the instrument to measure this effect. For women they were 'gentle', 'dependent', 'shy', and 'reluctant to speak in class'. For men they were 'ambitious', 'opinionated', 'involved in intramurals' and 'believing wild parties are the best parties'.)

We could go on with our review of the way the hypothetico-deductive creed is still alive and kicking – perhaps it is kinder that we do not!

Discipline and publish – don't discipline and you won't get published!

The mainstream approach to research has not been – nor (in the foreseeable future) do we see it as being – 'overthrown' or discarded – critical approaches are not about to replace the mainstream approach. On the contrary, in its own terms, mainstream research is stronger than ever. As we mentioned in Chapter 1, the 'good ship' social psychology goes from strength to strength. Every year more mainstream journals get started, more mainstream research gets done, and more mainstream papers get published. Indeed in the UK this situation has recently been exacerbated by the introduction of a formal system of research assessment in which research funding is directly linked to performance ratings. The highest credit is awarded to peer-reviewed papers published in international journals of high reputation – for which read those journals which are endorsed and produced by the most powerful of mainstream academics and institutions.

This poses a serious problem for those of us seeking to pursue critical social psychology. In the research we do, an important element is its critique of the mainstream. This is not at all easy to get published – for obvious reasons. It would be naive to expect the establishment to co-operate actively with publicizing its own shortcomings. Likewise we can hardly expect them – fully committed as they are to 'doing scientific research' – to accept the premises upon which our critique is based (our refutation of their scientism).

One of us (WSR), for example, recently gave an invited seminar at one of the UK's most prestigious universities. In it she reported data which, she argued, exposed profound shortcomings of the 'locus of control scale' when used in research on people's health beliefs. In the discussion afterwards the question inevitably came (from somebody whose reputation had been carved out of research using this scale), 'So are you saying that all the research I have done over the last ten years has been a waste of time?' A 'Yes' answer would neither have been well received, nor was given. Another of us (PS) submitted a paper to a prestigious mainstream journal devoted to publishing research on the topic of 'personality'. Naturally his paper took a highly antagonistic stance to the very concept of 'personality'. Again not surprisingly, the paper was not accepted for publication – on the grounds that 'the study lacks the theoretical development of the underlying construct that we emphasize in this journal'.

I.I. (Ironically) Excuse me! This appears to be degenerating into special pleading – a moan session on how those nasty establishment hacks give you a hard time in seminars and won't publish your papers. Surely the answer is to set up conferences and journal production yourselves?

The Authors: Funny you should say that – watch out for the launch of our new international journals, and send off to us for a subscription to *Manifold*. As for conferences – we make our own, see you in Barcelona!

I.I. Hmph! And you complain about the establishment's marketing ploys!

Yes, but there is a serious point being made here, . . .

I.I. (Muttering) There always is.

. . . which is that the academic world is becoming an extremely hostile place in which to 'go critical'. Dissent is very effectively silenced by the gatekeepers of the mainstream. You will need to search very hard to find it in the textbooks and journals that constitute the main fodder on your library shelves.

I.I. Let me see if I'm catching your drift. You are saying that just because there is very little (if any) critical social psychology research published in the best-known and most established journals and textbooks, we mustn't assume that it is not being done or doesn't matter. It is being done, and you are convinced it does matter. But if we want to find out about it, we will have to track it down in more obscure places.

Yes, in those new journals which are expressly committed to providing a forum in which critical work can be addressed, and in books like this – which is why we wrote it. Possibly because book publishing – as a commercial business – has less at stake and more to gain from allowing dissenting voices, there are a growing number of counter-texts like ours, though you will still not find them prominent in your reading lists – certainly not if you are following a conventional social psychology course.

I.I. So why on earth do you expect students like me to bother reading them?

Well, unless you are following a course which takes a critical stance, the answer has to be that it depends on how you rate the significance of your own performance indicators (your assignment and exam gradings). If these are all that matter to you, we are surprised you are still with us so far into the book. Perhaps that you are still with us suggests that we are 'getting through' to you.

I.I. This is all beginning to come across as rather patronizing. For now assume I accept that there is more to life than exam grades, and let's get back to the subject of this chapter. I've waited long enough to find out what on earth all this 'fluff and froth' (as you put it) means in terms of research.

The 'good ship' experimental social psychology sails on

For these sorts of reasons, despite (indeed, in spite of) what is now building up to a fair body of critical unease on the fringes of social psychology about the whole scientific, hypothetico-deductive approach, this continues to be the *modus operandus* that the majority continue to adopt. This is, by the way, also true of the academic discipline of psychology as a whole (practitioners are another, if equally sorry, story but that is another book).

Considered as a site of power, experimental social psychology has shown, in purely practical terms, that it can continue to make a future for itself (and a living for its devotees), albeit one where critical ideas have been, to a degree, assimilated (in safely diluted form). There has been a partial assimilation of notions from the 'crisis' of the 1970s and, for all the reasons we have spelt out above, experiments continue to 'work'. While (indeed because) theory after theory moves through its cycle of fashion from innovation to troubled 'old hat', the institution itself is able to seem vital and ongoing – it shows no signs of going away, or even losing its status as 'the mainstream'.

Alternative methodologies

There are many ways in which, given the failure of the 'crisis' of the 1970s to produce a radical turn in social psychology as a whole, the subsequent track of the discipline can be narrated. Certainly the wider social context of the cultural (and economic) retrenchment that followed cannot be ignored as a contributory factor (cf. Henriques et al. 1984). Comforting as that attribution may be, it is also worth considering the internal problems that beset the 'crisis'. From the start (e.g. Armistead, 1974) it was never more than a forum of discontent, and its tensions were generally greater than its commonalities. Further, because it was trying to argue itself into being, much of its energy went into rhetoric and theorising rather than research.

Where empirical research was done, the overall impression, on hindsight, is of a not very successful struggle towards the 'meaning' that 'old methodology' (Harré, 1977, 1979) removed or dislodged. Too often 'alternative methods' boiled down to rehashings of approaches taken from humanistic psychology (e.g. Kelly's personal construct theory, 1955), microsociology (e.g. Garfinkel, 1967), phenomenological sociology (e.g. Lyman and Scott's accounting, 1968) and symbolic interactionism (e.g. Lindesmith, Strauss and Denzin, 1975) – to name but a few. Too often work was haunted by the dualistic dream that experimental and hermeneutic approaches might (ultimately) be mutually informative (cf. Antaki, 1988). (This concern is also voiced about social representations theory; see pp. 142–44 above.)

Hindsight is, of course, a cruel critic. One of us (RSR) himself has such a past to 'live down'. Others (such as Ken Gergen, Rom Harré, Tomás Ibáñez, Edward Sampson and John Shotter) in the vanguard of critical social psychology have also traced a personal history of discontent from the 1970s crisis to the present-day 'turn to textuality'. That turn owes a debt to the crisis of two decades ago, but it is also (and more importantly) a launchpad to the new. Critical social psychology today can point to a range of alternative methods that serve and service its agenda, much as experimentation serves and services mainstream social psychology. Critical social psychology has come of age, and to grasp that requires a recognition that it is a profoundly distinct venture at every level. Perhaps, though, what marks it off most of all is that it argues that what is salient to the way people act and see the world are 'not things hiding inside the person which a psychologist can then "discover" but are created by the language used to describe them. Psychological phenomena have a public and collective reality, and we are mistaken if we think that they have their origin in the private space of the individual' (Parker and Burman 1993: 1).

Asking different questions

Therefore what marks out the methodologies of critical social psychology is that they are all concerned with symbolic systems (mainly that of language) and how these are used to do things – to construct knowledge, to legitimate it, maintain and monger it. This implies a fundamentally different set of questions for enquiry to address.

The sociologist of science Michael Mulkay is good at summarizing the critical approach. No longer, he argues, can there be an assumption that 'there is a single coherent factual world which can be accurately and consistently represented by the application of a constant method' (1989:

27). Rather, there are 'many potential worlds of meaning that can be imaginatively entered and celebrated, in ways which are constantly changing' (1989: 27–8). '[E]very "social action" and every "cultural product" or "text" has to be treated as a source or an opportunity for creating multiple meanings or further texts' (Mulkay, 1985: 10). Consequently, there has been a move to 'abandon the notion, borrowed from natural science, that analysis must adopt a monologic, univocal form' (Mulkay, 1985: 75). What are needed instead are 'analytical texts containing multiple textual agents which can operate, to some extent, independently and thereby deal with different aspects of textuality' (1985: 75).

Box 11.3 What Makes a Methodology 'Alternative'?

In one way or another (even though different language may often be used) all critical methodologies exhibit at least some of the following:

- a focus not on discovering or elucidating psychological 'essences' or processes but on exploring textuality
- an acknowledgement of diversity – that there are always multiple ways in which any topic, issue or concern is constituted in textuality – is 'storied into being'
- viewing these alternative discourse as epistemologically equivalent – no one of them having any claim to epistemological superiority (i.e. to being 'the truth')
- recognizing, reflexively, that this applies to the textuality of the research endeavour itself – the discourse by which the research is told is just as much a 'story' as the 'stories' it seeks to elucidate
- developing taxonomies of these alternative discourses
- exploring the ways in which they have been constructed, their warrants and authorities
- looking to how they are used – to justify or prescribe certain forms of conduct; to promote certain ideologies.

I.I. I do worry that you call this a 'story'. How can anyone be expected to take that seriously?

It is perfectly 'serious' – what's missing (we hope) is any claim to special 'expert' knowledge. The key point is that made by Bruner (1986) which makes it clear that a move has been made from doing paradigmatic science (i.e. hypothesis-testing) to doing narrative science – the way of working *is* to tell a story.

Thus the central questions critical methodologies address are to do with how and why particular kinds of knowledge are made, are made to matter, and are made to work. Moreover (by implication, if not explicitly) a critical question always has to be – who is gaining what out of constructing the world in this way? We will now describe three main methodological approaches that have been adopted to pursue empirical research from a critical perspective: social representations research; discourse analysis; and Q-methodology.

Social representations research

Social representations theory (see Chapter 6), first proposed by Moscovici (1961), is often seen to be the key point of conceptual fracture which enabled a distinct European social psychology to separate from the Anglic (largely US) mainstream discipline. It was certainly one element in the 1970s crisis, and, while its critical credentials are now in question (cf. Parker, 1989; Potter and Wetherell, 1987; Stainton Rogers, 1991), it had an undoubted influence on the 'turn to textuality'. However, even though social representations theory is clearly innovative in conceptual terms, its research has generally stuck with conventional, 'soft' and 'hard', methodologies.

Herzlich's (1973) study of social representations of health and illness was conducted primarily by way of semi-structured interviews, which were subjected to a process of 'distillation' in order to identify and describe the representations which were being expressed and drawn upon. In this way Herzlich identified three main ones for health: a notion of 'equilibrium'; of health-in-a-vacuum; and reserve of health. With regard to illness, she writes of discovering three main metaphors: illness as 'destroyer'; as 'liberator'; and as 'occupation'. The main problem with this kind of approach is that its analytics are largely opaque – described only in vague terms, which obscure what it is that the researcher is doing in order to be able to arrive at the results which are reported. Thus it is beset by all the accusations generally thrown at ethnographic work – that what is reported is no more than the researcher's own insights and understandings, and these are far from 'objective'.

Where social representations theorists use psychometric methods, they usually subject the data obtained to forms of multi-variate analysis, in order to explore 'the links between collective and cognitive [read individual psychological] dynamics' (Doise et al., 1993). These, of course, are equally subject to the accusations usually laid against psychometrics by critical theorists.

Social representations work has also been criticized for taking an overly consensual view of social reality (see, for example, Potter and Wetherell, 1987; Stainton Rogers, 1991). Many of its best-known empirical works have focused on only a small number of alternative social representations (such as the Herzlich work described above), assuming that large conglomerates of people share a single, common social representation (indeed, in its most basic form, this is a central tenet of social representations theory).

Such a criticism is certainly less true of present day work in this field, as specifically argued by Doise et al. (1993). The multivariate statistical procedures which underpin psychometrics (most notably factor analysis) were originally designed to meet a nomothetic agenda. Specifically, they were employed to reduce complex intercorrelation matrices of relations between test items (e.g. of intelligence, of attitudes, of personality) into universal scales based upon test items of high inter-(co)covariance. Since the advent of computers (which post-dated the classic multivariate procedure – factor analysis – by decades) the field of multivariate analysis has expanded vastly. These newer techniques include cluster analysis, multi-dimensional scaling and correspondence factor analysis. It is now possible to find procedures suited not only to closed-ended scale items but also to coded open-ended responses and even raw text.

The most straightforward approach to non-consensuality is to assume that one's target responses vary by established 'demographics' (e.g. age, sex, social class, education, urban/rural location, ethnicity). Multivariate analyses which 'break' the analysis by one or an indexical set of several of these often reveal that target responses vary markedly by the 'break'. For example, separate factor analyses by segment can show quite contrasted factor structures for, say, young men, young women, older men and older women. In market research (where such techniques are widely employed) this is referred to as 'market segmentation'. This technique can identify, for example, a segment such as 'TwINCs' (couples with two incomes and no children) who tend to adopt a particular purchasing pattern different from other groups.

However, it is possible to be considerably more adventurous – for example, to hypothesize *a priori* as to the segmentation expected, and then to test that prediction on criterion groups. For instance, one might hypothesize that a 'goat and loom' lifestyle both exists and is practised in particular by those who support 'ecological' pressure groups. Doise et al. (1993) give a good digest of these techniques applied to academic research questions in the specific conceptual setting of social representations theory. An example given is of closed-ended survey data on 'mental illness'. Four student groups (medicine, nursing, psychology and sciences) and three professional groups (psychiatric nurses, psychiatrists and psychologists) were involved. The data analysis successfully revealed that there were indeed differences in the account given of mental illness. Professionals and students gave different accounts from each other, and, within students, psychology students gave different accounts from the rest.

Although it was orders of magnitude more subtle than first-generation multivariate work, at core, we view this social representations programme as still owing more to the 'old paradigm' than the new alternatives. It tends to segment by taken-for-granted criteria, and it remains couched in theory-language which hovers around (but never seems to make the leap into) the 'turn to textuality'. However, much as with Q methodology (See pp. 248–53), techniques like correspondence analysis can take more than one conceptual agenda. Informed by critical perspectives, it offers a useful grounding and adjunct to discourse analytical approaches. A good example in this new genre is Pujol's (1993) exploration of discourses concerned with reproductive technology – though here, while his analytical techniques are similar to those used by neo-social representationalists, his conceptual 'homeland' is very evidently in the 'critical camp'.

Discourse analytic approaches

It is some measure of the impact of the textual turn that 'discourse analysis' is in grave danger of becoming a buzz-term! Rather as students of language discover they have been grammarians all their lives without knowing it, it has now become *de rigueur* in many quarters to reinterpret interpretative research traditions (even, we have heard it claimed, high school rhetoric courses!) as actually involving discourse analysis in all but name. These retellings are made all the easier by the usefulness of the term itself – 'discourse' has much of the vacuous 'feel-good' factor for critical-social psychologists that 'cognitive' has for mainstreamers. For all that over-use of the term – which implies that 'discourse analysis' these days merits a 'health warning' (contains bromide, do not exceed the stated dose, abuse may seriously damage your understanding) – discourse analysis is a major (arguably the major site) of critical psychological work.

I.I. Hey! What happened to the suffix 'social'?

We deliberately dropped the word 'social' back there as many would deny that it is limited to or even uniquely salient to social psychology.

I.I. So tell me, given its ubiquity, what exactly is discourse analysis, other than the best thing since sliced bread?

Apart from the observation that we are not too keen on sliced bread, the trouble is that there's no agreed guide to or description of discourse analysis – it is a contested activity. Burman and Parker (1993) offer some way through the maze. They make a useful tripartite division of the 'reference points' (their term) in discourse analytic research. Their approach to the divide is itself quite discourse-analytic, and, apart from its heuristic value, can serve as a first introduction to the approach. Their 'analysis' is based upon a particular feature of the text of works in discourse analysis – specifically, the 'family', 'tribe' or 'tradition' (our words) to which the references and citations mainly belong and the research language in which they are sited. Reworking their divide slightly (but keeping their titles), we have:

- repertoires and dilemmas
- conversation and the making of sense
- structure and subject

Repertoires and dilemmas   The 'family' here is the largely UK-based tradition of Potter and Wetherell (1987) and Billig et al. (1988). The approach is sited within the 'climate of perturbation'; in that it is not hypothetico-deductive but rather (as we would describe it) 'critical-polytextual'. It is concerned with making readings of texts, in order to explore what purpose is being achieved by discursive labour. It examines this mainly with respect to 'talk' – 'naturalistic' utterances. That is, rather than doing interviews in the conventional manner, the approach is often to target settings where 'talk' is going on anyway – such as counselling sessions, case conferences and the like. Such 'talk' is seen as constructed from a pre-existing, shared (collective) manifold of linguistic or interpretative repertoires, and the analysis 'attempts to look systematically at the organization of phenomena which social psychologists have traditionally understood in terms of attitudes, beliefs and understandings.' (Potter and Wetherell, 1987: 146). An interpretive/linguistic repertoire (these terms are used interchangeably) is defined by Potter and Wetherell thus:

> Interpretative repertoires are recurrently used systems of terms used for characterizing and evaluating actions, events and other phenomena. A repertoire ... is constituted through a limited range of terms used in particular stylistic and grammatical constructions. Often a repertoire will

be organized around specific metaphors and figures of speech (tropes).
(1987: 149)

What this kind of discourse analysis is intended to 'reveal' is the
inconsistent, fragmentary character of talk, and with that 'revelation'
comes an argument against the mainstream psychologists' subject possessed of stable essences of attitude, belief or personality. The tendency is
to regard talk as predicated upon collective ideas (and hence as bounded
by them) but shaped by its users to shifting purposes and functions. The
main aim of this kind of research is to expose what people are doing with
– and achieving by – their discursive labour. And the main focus is upon
individual speech acts – as instruments through which the strategies of
'talk' (as a discursive activity) may be better understood.

BOX 11.4 Discourse Analysis: According to Potter and Wetherell

It is Jonathan Potter and Margaret Wetherell's work on discourse analysis
– particularly their 1987 book – which has done most to bring this
approach to the attention of social psychologists. Indeed, its influence has
spread widely – it is increasingly common to find 'discourse analysis'
mentioned under the 'methods' section of large numbers of research
proposals and reports across a diverse range of disciplines – economics,
computing, management studies, you name it, they are using it!
  This is something of a British phenomenon. Elsewhere – especially in
Europe – the term 'discourse' is more likely to hark back to Foucault, and
the meaning of 'discourse analysis' applies to rather different methods
(we will come on to these later).
  What, however, Potter and Wetherell did was to make a 'critical' (i.e. of
hypothetico-deductivism) method acceptable to the mainstream. Indeed,
in some quarters it is viewed as little more than a sophisticated version of
'content or structural analysis' (and hence not too threatening).
  A distinction – we believe – needs to be made between their theorization
and their method. Their book marked a crucial milestone in bringing to a
wide audience the recognition that hypothetico-deductive method is
flawed – and in promoting the application of social constructionist ideas to
psychology (alongside semiotics, hermeneutics and notions like reflexivity). Nearly ten years on, the early chapters of their book still offer one of
the best introductions around to this whole field.
  Over method, however, the shift is less radical. Their technique of
'discourse analysis' is very fine-grained, and seeks to locate the site of
the analysis primarily within the text under scrutiny. Their major research

question is usually 'what is going on – what is being achieved – by this person's "talk" at this point in the conversation (or whatever)?'. As such it has much more communality with traditional psychological approaches to research (and much less with approaches used in other disciplines – such as media and film studies) than other variants of discourse analytic work.

Both the theory and the methods of this dialect of discourse analysis have more recently been formulated into a formalised model (DAM – Discursive Action Model) by Edwards and Potter (1992). DAM is seen by some critical social psychologists as an old-style 'theory-machine' in new clothes (Lee, 1994).

Conversation and the making of sense   The 'tradition' here is more sociological, showing debts to ethnomethodology and phenomenological sociology. The approach is less analytic than the 'repertoires and dilemmas' tradition – more concerned with the craft of 'listening' to how sense is made by the account-giver and, through the research process, providing them with an opportunity to express their own views, experiences or meanings. There is considerably less 'effort after meaning' on the researcher's part, and more reliance on the talk itself (quoted 'thickly') to make the story for itself. Rather than seeking to identify the discursive resources (such as linguistic repertoires) being used and their function, the emphasis is shifted to explore 'meanings in the making', to how talk can operate as a creative dialogue.

Another term sometimes used here is 'reflexive methodology', which reflects a turn to a kind of neo-humanistic approach, which seeks especially to validate the experience of those under study. A good example of the whole alignment is provided by Shakespear, Atkinson and French, who state their commitment thus: 'An awareness of self is important in research; but, equally important, is an awareness of the "subjects" of one's research' (1993: 5). They go on to state, specifically, their concern not to overlook the power relations implicit in research:

The subjects of our research/writing are drawn primarily from oppressed, marginalized and otherwise vulnerable groups in this society. Authors testify to the importance, in this context, of developing an awareness of the potentially exploitative nature of face-to-face research. Other-awareness is a first step towards sensitive interviewing and an empathetic approach. . . . [W]e seek to 'give voice' to people otherwise rarely heard through documenting their (previously neglected or misrepresented) lives and experiences. . . . The legitimation of our research lies in its potential to empower the people about whom we write and with whom we research (1993: 5–6).

Thus the aim, here, is to 'tell it like it is' – to seek to recount (rather than analyse) discourse, and to ensure that the persons whose accounts are under scrutiny are 'given a voice'. Thus while the actual techniques used are not necessarily different in principle, their application is more informed by hermeneutic notions. There is less emphasis on what readings can be placed on talk, or on the ways those readings may have originated, and more emphasis on ensuring that the subjects' own readings are expressed.

Structure and subject   Here the term 'tribe' best captures the reference points. The work here is, of all the three variants, that most strongly located within the climate of perturbation, and post-structural/postmodern influences are strong. There is (as with the other variants) a clear commitment to a social constructionist stance over 'reality' and its constitution, but what sets this grouping apart is that its major concern is to 'disillusion' – to challenge, deconstruct, stir up and make mischief. There is a strong antagonism towards all foundationalist assumptions, which brings with it a language of texts and textuality (cf. Curt, 1994) and the use of narrative (story) metaphorics (seen, for example, in the work of Haraway and Mulkay). Similarly it is made explicit that the researcher can offer only a reading of talk or writing – there is no site of truth, not even in those who voice or inscribe an account (Game is expecially good on this).

Thus, unlike both the above variants, there is much less conviction that the analyst possesses any ability to discern intention or purpose; and the level of analysis is much more 'macro'. Individual examples of 'talk' and text are viewed merely as means to interrogate discursive labour operating at the collective level of culture. A drawing into the net of Foucault (e.g. 1980) and other French theorists broadens the approach further in the direction of transdisciplinarity and brings in an appreciation of how not only objectivity but also subjectivity is 'constructed'. In other words, this approach is as much concerned with tectonics as with textuality – how, in global terms, different discourses mould, shape and act upon each other; how they evolve, get sedimented, archived and represented.

Where we stand

It is the last of these which we see our own discourse-analytic work most matching, and we use the umbrella term 'critical polytextualism' to describe it (see Curt, 1994, for a fuller description of what this is used to mean). Indeed, it is a study into jealousy by Stenner (1993a) which Burman and Parker employ as one of their exemplars of the 'structure and subject' dialect. There are three main ways in which we would see ourselves as employing discourse-analytic research. The first of these (concursive analysis) will be covered under the next main heading. The second is the 'thematic decomposition' which, for example, Stenner (above) employed. Thematic decomposition is a reading craft – where 'reading' carries the dynamic sense of a relocated rewriting (cf. Game, 1991). It demands an active spectatorial location or subject-position (much as does critical film theory; cf. Mulvey, 1975). It does not claim to reveal what is 'really going on' in, say, an account or interview. Instead, researchers are clearly seen as account-givers themselves. As a result, there is a continual (tropic) reflection. Reading a 'thematic decomposition' offers the reader both the offered 'reading' and the possibility of engaging in a 'thematic decomposition' of the researcher's engagement with the topic and narrative devices. It is, in Stenner's words (1993a: 130) 'always-ever incomplete'.

The last of the critical-polytextual approaches we employ turns to the idea of cultural resources (not as fixed social essences, of course, but as located possibilities). The research question here addresses not the accounts people give but the simulations they find plausible. If we want to know what passes for, say, jealousy within a group we ask them to 'make it' in the form of (typically) a short play. This we call a 'seeded thematic' because once we have set the 'seed', the evolution and refinement of the development of the vignette in terms of plot, characterization and dialogue is in the hands of the group. Once produced, a seeded thematic can be subjected to whatever form of discourse analysis one wishes – from a statistical correspondence analysis to a thematic decomposition. Once again, the material is seen not as final but as open to endless rereading and rewriting.

Q methodology

Q methodology employs a particular form of multivariate analysis, in order to identify and describe the different 'stories' that can be told about a particular topic or issue. It usually does this by examining the way people respond in systematically different ways to propositional samples of discourse. They are given a set of such propositions, each one a separate card or piece of paper, and asked to sort them along a dimension – such as from 'strongly characteristic' to 'strongly uncharacteristic'. Examples of propositions might be:

Figure 11.1   Carrying out a Q sort

- is warm and affectionate
- cares about their appearance
- seems to live in a world of their own
- is full of energy.

These statements would be used to describe a person. For example O'Dell (1995) used such statements to gain descriptions of 'abused' and 'non-abused' children.

I.I. This sounds suspiciously like conventional psychometrics to me.

Well it's not. Curb your tongue, knave, and listen. What the analysis does is identify different sorting patterns. These are then examined, in order to infer what particular 'story' is being told by each one.

An effective Q study depends upon meticulous and thoughtful sampling of the propositions. People can 'tell a story' only if they have the appropriate statements with which to tell it. Thus the start of a Q study involves a careful and methodical review of the things people write and say about the topic or issue in question. This is not unlike a form of discourse analysis, although the texts on which it is applied are generally highly comprehensive. It is not unusual for a researcher to spend several months reading everything from scholarly journals to 'pulp' magazines, watching television documentaries and soaps, interviewing individuals and groups, and keeping a notebook of what is said in the pub and the hairdressers'. We usually call this a concourse analysis – as it is directed to the concourse (or confluence) of texts to which we are concerned ('concourse' is a term devised by Stephenson, the originator of Q methodology). In practical terms (i.e. to the satisfaction of participants) we have found that people find it easiest to carry out Q sorts when we divide them up into three main discursive domains:

1 representational propositions about what things (social objects such as persons) are like – for example, 'a mad person', 'an abused child', 'democracy'
2 theoretic propositions (understandings or explanations) about why things are the way they are – for example, explanations of addiction, of what causes illness
3 conductual, policy-directed or strategic propositions concerning what should be done about something – such as what we should do about mental illness, how democracy should be fostered.

In other words, while they can sort a set of propositions which include all of these, people find it 'makes more sense' if they do a Q sort which has only one of these kinds of statements in it (i.e. representations or understandings or conduct-prescriptions). When we want to study across this range (and indeed the discursive links and disjunctions between them), we usually ask people to sort two separate Q sets (e.g. one on understandings and one on policy-prescription). Whichever facet is selected for study, its concourse is usually sampled to yield a pool of between thirty and eighty propositions (in appearance rather like questionnaire items).

I.I. Hmph!

The sampling is checked with pilot participants for balance (i.e. roughly equal numbers of 'agree' and 'disagree' items), comprehension and clarity of expression, and comprehensiveness (ability to cover a good range of aspects of and positions on the issue at hand). What happens next makes Q methodology stand in contrast to the kinds of approaches covered above. It is a way of allowing participants to apply themselves to the sample. They are asked to form or configure them as a whole. This is called Q sorting and is achieved by providing them with a grid in which to 'make their story' (Figure 11.2). In this example, one item is to assigned to each of the '6' positions, two to each of the '5' positions, with eight items being placed in the neutral or null position. This accommodates fifty-six items in all; smaller Q samples may use an eleven- or nine-point distribution. Q sorting, from the participants' point of view, consists of first sorting the items into the pyramid structure and then recording the item number into a similar-shaped data grid.

Q methodology is ideal for addressing the critical kinds of research

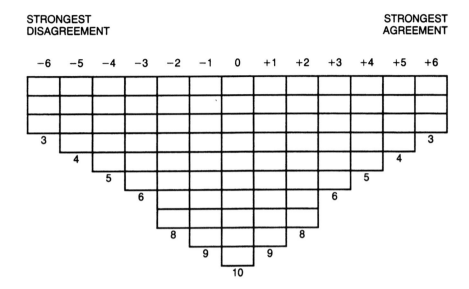

STRONGEST
DISAGREEMENT

STRONGEST
AGREEMENT

Figure 11.2 Q sort response form

questions which are concerned to hear 'many voices'. What makes it unique as a method lies in how those voices are allowed expression. Through Q sorting we obtain person-structured – but culturally informed – pen-pictures, impressions, compositions or manifestos. Unlike conventional (what we call R-methodological) forms of multivariate analysis, in Q methodological analysis the basic data are the pairwise intercorrelations between expressed Q sorts. It is these correlations which are then Q factor-analysed. This 'reduces' the matrix of correlations between the Q sorts by assuming that they reflect the action of a small set of independent factors or components (the finite diversity of interest).

The final stage of a Q methodological study is to give a reading to the emergent factors. This is done by making comparisons and contrasts between the positionings of items in the reconstructed Q sorts representing each factor. The readings may be aided by theoretic considerations, previous research and/or cultural knowledge. Considerable use is also made of the open-ended comments we ask participants to make in 'explaining' the position allotted to items. This too can be thought of as a form of discourse analysis. The credibility/plausibility of our readings can be checked further by re-presenting a digest to the exemplifying participants for their reflexive correction.

I.I. Look – I can't keep quiet any longer. Just tell me how this differs from a conventional psychometric approach?

Where do we start? Well, for one thing just because there are numbers involved and statistics does not make this in any way a 'mainstream' approach. For one thing, it is not based on hypothetico-deductive reasoning. There is no hypothesis that gets tested. Rather it is expressly speculative. For another thing, even unlike much work in the social representations tradition, we do not assume that we know how (or even if) alternative configurations are related to participant location. Biographical information about participants is used to explore whether or not this is the case – and if so what facets of location are important. Where it is, we can go on to argue why it might be that particular stories tend to be told in particular locations. But these are not prejudged.

I.I. Sorry, you've lost me. Give an example.

Well – let's think (there are so many to choose from). A good example is the study Stainton Rogers and Stainton Rogers did on addiction (1986). In it they found expressed an explanation of addiction which had a decidedly 'social-constructionist' flavour – seeing it as a cultural production (as opposed, say, to a biomedical explanation in terms of physiological vulnerability or a sociological explanation around notions of how oppressed groups use drugs, alcohol and tobacco as sources of solace – both of which were also expressed in the study). What was interesting was that the participants whose sorting patterns fitted most closely on to this explanatory discourse did not all give the same sorting pattern on the 'social policy' Q sort. Some of them proffered a libertarian, laissez-faire prescription – to deregulate all forms of 'addictive substances'. Others offered a prescription which favoured more regulation. However, their concern was not about 'hard drugs' but about tobacco and alcohol. These – they argued – were the 'real problems' society needs to address. This marked division into two alternative social policy prescriptions could be understood better by looking at the biographical locations of the two groups. The 'deregulators' were academics undertaking 'critical' research, who refused to accept any political or ideological location. The 'regulators', by contrast, although they too included 'critical' researchers, were explicit about their political affiliations – they identified themselves (variously and in combination) as 'Feminists', 'Marxists' and 'Vegetarians'. Not surprisingly also, the first group were all smokers who regularly drank alcohol, whereas the second group were non-smokers who drank alcohol, if at all, only in moderation.

I.I. The second group come over as decidedly 'puritanical' to me!

You may very well say that – we could not possibly (especially given that the former group included some of us and the latter some of our friends)! The point at issue, however, is not so much a personal agenda as to stress how this illustrates how Q methodology is not based on hypothetico-deductivism. When WSR and RSR did that study, they did not expect this result – though it made perfect sense once the data came out the way it did. In Will Stephenson's phrase, Q methodology is 'abductive' (a phrase he scavenged from Peirce, 1934). That is, it is exploratory, speculative – it makes no assumptions, *a priori*, about what the results of a study will be. Brown expresses this well:

> Q samples provide a launch pad for an investigation, an entrée into a phenomenon, the scientist's best initial guess as to how a particular administrative situation, social consciousness, or whatever operates. The data gathered with the Q sample may lead in quite different directions ... There is never any guarantee, in other words, that splash-down will occur in the same area as the point of departure. (1980: 39)

I.I. OK, I'm gradually getting hooked. So – are you going to tell me how to 'get into the Q'?

No, not here – there is not room in this book to describe the methodology in detail. If you want to know more then you can follow it up in Curt (1994), Kitzinger (1987) or Stainton Rogers (1991). All we wanted to do here is to give you some 'flavour' of what Q methodology has to offer as an 'alternative', critical approach. Also do bear something in mind. Q methodology is a lot more than using Q sorts. It involves a great deal of what would otherwise be called 'discourse analysis', both in the work done to arrive at the statements used to make up the Q set and in the detailed exposition and analysis of the accounts, explanations, representations (or whatever) obtained.

Conclusions

To describe 'critical' approaches to methodology could easily take up a whole book, if their diversity and subtlety were to receive appropriate attention. That is not what this book is about. What we hope to have done is to at least give you some impressions of what sorts of things they are up to – and how they differ from mainstream approaches.

If we are to leave you with a message, it is this. Mainstream social psychology looks to methods that test theories and which claim to tap into intra-personal and/or social essences that those theories take as axiomatic. Critical methods do not. They assume that as linguistic/

discursive practices construct reality with us, for us and through us, experimental methods can only ever reflect back to us the causes, forces, processes and effects their users put there – theorize there – in the first place. It is that which makes so much experimental social psychology appear commonsensical and which renders its myth of scientific understanding a dead-end.

Alternative methods address the textual, socially constructed world more directly and explicitly. They are concerned both with the 'process' (the discursive practices that construct the manifold that passes for reality) and the 'products' (the various forms in which social objects, subjectivity and our contested understandings are expressed.)

Unlike the way scientific methodologies are usually presented (as objective probes into the workings of a reality which does not understand itself), alternative methodologies accept that they are narrative – little different in kind to the accounts, talk, writings that they study. So too, of course, are the outputs of critical social psychologists, their presentations and their papers. Indeed, because they are making a space, rather than provisioning an already established market, critical social psychologists need to be, quite overtly, story-tellers. The recognition of critical social psychology as a craft of racontage and reportage, scription and scrivenage, is crucial to its appreciation both as medium and as message.

12 Inconclusions

Over the last eleven chapters we have sketched out one reading – our reading – of critical social psychology. It is a reading which is plural and diverse – but then so too is critical social psychology. Its textuality is rather like an irregular patchwork of varicoloured fabric – there are no simple directions, no clear markers that line up or shape our composition. In developing our reading we have inevitably (but usually knowingly) poached and scavenged from the work of other critical psychologists, and sewn them into our patchwork. But we hope the end-product has at least given you an overall impression of what criticality implies and what it has to offer.

We also hope that we have alerted you to the importance of scepticism over all stories – including ours. We hope that you will now be more prepared to make your own critical readings of the texts in the area, and to explore for yourself whether the collage of critical work adds up to something that matters to you. Clearly, it does to us, and one way of reviewing that 'something' is to seek to summarize our questioning of received social psychology.

I.I. Hang on there – you're not intending a mere regurgitation of what has gone before, I hope!

Beryl: Look, authors, there's only one way to deal with that kind of interruption and that's to let me loose on it. Besides, nobody's written for me in over six months and I'm getting rather lonely and not a little paranoid. You seem to have been going off on your own and leaving me very much on the sidelines of late.

I.I. Hang on, who are you?

Beryl: The author of *Textuality and Tectonics*, an earlier work the authors contributed to writing (cf. Curt, 1994). I'm good on scepticism, so I thought I could help out . . .

Authors: Curb your tongues, both of you. We're already pushing the word limit for this book as it is. If it's dialogics you want, then we'll write you some. But be warned, if you start acting like positivists at a seminar, then we'll write you both out.

The dialogue

I.I. Ms Curt – or Beryl, if I may – you probably know the authors better than anybody else – how would you sum up their message?

Beryl: First, I guess, it's that intellectual life has been radically stirred up over the past two decades or so. Many labels have been stuck on these tectonics – terms like postmodernism, post-structuralism and critical theory. The authors have used (well, sort of modified from me) the portmanteau term 'climate of perturbation' to express the challenge, the flux and the uncertainty involved in this movement, while avoiding coming across as just another 'grand theory'. What they've tried to do in this book is to offer, at an introductory and basic level, an account of how social psychology can be approached from within this climate of perturbation.

I.I. Or, to put it another way, they have set out to offer an account of critical social psychology as the radical alternative to traditional theory and method in mainstream social psychology?

Beryl: Pretty well, as long as you accept the dangers of too clear-cut a picture. Certainly whenever you detect a critical eye directed on to mainstream social psychology, you're likely to be seeing critical social psychology at work – or at least a dialect of it.

I.I. Though in places I get the distinct impression I've also been getting a history lesson.

Beryl: Because history matters – otherwise ideas come across as if they have sprung up out of nowhere, all neat and shiny new. It's important for anyone interested in what's shaking up social psychology right now to be aware of the staging-posts that have led to criticality.

I.I. Fair enough – that's consistent with their argument that all knowledge is constructed by somebody and for a purpose – it does not simply lie around, waiting to be discovered. At times, though, it has come over as a rather self-indulgent history lesson, not to say positively 'biased' (a term I know the authors have trouble with). I know they keep repeating 'this is just our story', but at times this seems rather disingenuous. There's something rather shifty, it seems to me, in, at one and the same time, accusing others of presenting rhetoric as if it were mere abstract knowledge, and lashing out reams of rhetoric yourself.

Beryl: (Somewhat ironically) But it's all right done from within the 'climate of perturbation' because in that context it's reflexive!

I.I. But is reflexivity anything more than a kind of verbal good-luck talisman for people in this area? It does seem to be a very trendy term, right now.

Beryl: Methinks you are now playing DA (Devil's Advocate, not Discourse Analyst, though one can be forgiven for sometimes thinking they are one and the same). I'm not going to pull out definitions for you – you can go back over the text and do that for yourself. Reflexivity is a lot more than a charm – although I admit some writers do come over as using it like that. In the book, however, the authors are, I think, using it for a number of serious purposes.

I.I. Like . . .

Beryl: Well, for turning analytics back on themselves. A case in point is the way the authors point out how mainstream social psychologists often seem to fall into the very 'errors' that they accuse 'ordinary people' of making. If you remember, for example, in Chapter 8 the authors described how social psychologists' theories on aggression tend to make the 'fundamental attribution error' described in Chapter 7 – they individualize it and ignore the social, economic and political contexts within which 'aggression' can also be understood. This gave the authors (or rather, they gave themselves) the opportunity to explore another standard critical device – irony.

I.I. I don't get the impression that such irony goes down a bundle with the mainstream. Aren't social psychologists supposed to be serious? They present themselves as having expert knowledge – which they expect others to take seriously.

Beryl: Dead right, at that level there is a 'battle' going on. Social psychology is not just a site of learning, but a site of action. For instance, it's a site of assessment. Take assessment . . .

I.I. You take assessment – I don't want it.

Authors: And you didn't get it – that section got cut in the re-drafting of the book some months ago. It's a pity, though. Applying a critical analysis to the whole edifice of how exams, essays and multiple-choice tests are used by psychology departments is a good way of showing that an attack on essentialism doesn't just hit at social psychology's theorization and research paradigms, it questions the very techniques it uses for perpetuating itself.

Beryl: I see what you're getting at. The same deconstructive logic that can be applied to psychometric tests applies just as much to the tests and examinations used in universities to assess students' performance. Once we accept that we cannot assess the person as essence (their 'actual' inner qualities), all we can do is lay attributions of quality upon their expressions (their expressed answers to our inquisitions); the whole enterprise of setting and marking examinations and awarding degree classes becomes distinctly dubious.

I.I. I suppose what you're saying is that it's one thing for, say, engineering departments to set and mark tests of performance. When they do so, this has no implications for how engineering is theorized. But when social psychologists do it, then they are, in concrete terms, going along with their own theory that people can be measured. Once you question that assumption, setting and marking tests and examinations becomes a very dubious enterprise indeed.

Beryl: Precisely. It could be argued that it is not just paradoxical but perverse to teach a critical social psychology which profoundly questions whether people can be measured, and then be prepared to set students essays on this precise topic, mark them and use the marks awarded as the basis for awarding grades and degree classes.

I.I. Now that really is making trouble! I can just imagine what would happen in the authors' own institutions if they refused to engage in conventional assessment procedures. I do remember, though, one of my tutors advising me that examination success was a matter not of actually being any good at psychology but of being able to weave an impression of excellence.

Beryl: It's by no means only 'critical' psychologists who are cynical over the system. But assessment does pose a very particular problem for critical social psychologists. The trouble is that adopting a critical stance does not, in itself, offer a way out – all the critical faculties in the world cannot provide a magic potion that will make the practical realities of the world in which we live disappear. They remain very much 'there' and we have very little choice but to go on living with them.

I.I. That's rather a weak answer, isn't it? Are you saying that all criticality has to offer is a new way of looking at the world – that it provides no means at all for actually doing anything about it?

Beryl: Not at all. Indeed, many critical theorists view political actions as the most important feature of criticality – criticality, for them, is just the starting-point for subverting praxes and systems that critical analysis expose as harmful or wrong.

I.I. But isn't there a paradox there too? How, from a critical perspective, can notions like 'harmful' or 'wrong' not themselves be matters of dispute? Isn't this a recipe for infinite regress? And isn't that the real problem with criticality – it leads to a situation where there are no foundational moral truths – and hence no justification for taking a moral stand on anything?

Beryl: Not at all. Being agnostic over 'truth' does not mean never taking a moral stand. What it does mean is being prepared to 'own' that moral stand, and not trying to justify it as being a 'given' (and hence not itself open to challenge).

I.I. But let's get back to the point. It strikes me that your position is decidedly impotent – you seem to be saying that in the hurly-burly of the 'real world' (or 'the practicaly realities' of the world in which we live, as the authors would put it) there is actually little choice over just colluding with it.

Beryl: You're using some markedly dubious and strong language there, but I'll admit you do have a point. Given that criticality is a distinctly marginalized activity and the mainstream is so powerful, there are (in practical terms) limits to what can be achieved. Let me give you another example, though, that will help to explain what criticality is about. A critical 'thought experiment' some of us have used is the notion of schooling as a form of enforced conscription. Where else (other than in the armed forces) are people required to wear uniforms, to comply unquestioningly to arbitrary authorty, and even today made to engage in compulsory team sports?

I.I. You're not seriously suggesting we disband the education system – are you?

Beryl: No, I – or at least the authors – wouldn't dare (you might find it instructive to ponder why). But we are suggesting that asking awkward questions is a worthwhile activity, and one way of doing that is to proffer subversive readings of taken-for-granted systems and structures. What we are doing is playing the establishment at its own game. That is what the mainstream social psychology mission is doing – using its claim to knowledge to persuade people to see the world in a particular way. All we are doing is introducing a little heresy – suggesting that there are other, quite different ways of seeing the world, and once that is done, it becomes a bit more possible to change the world. We are unlikely to dismember the school system simply by calling it 'conscription', but we can begin to get people to think somewhat differently, say, about 'problems' such as 'school phobia'.

Try another one. It used to be the case that children as young as eight could be hanged for stealing. Now (despite the best efforts of the tabloid press) such treatment is 'unthinkable'. The change is not just a matter of a few reformers suggesting that this is inhuman, but in the way society as a whole has (largely) changed its perceptions of children and how they should be treated. Making something 'unthinkable' is a first step to making it 'un-do-able'. We need to ask ourselves what forms of treatment of children will become 'unthinkable' and hence 'un-do-able' in the future. Or another way is to consider what are the actions that we take for granted that are seen as bizarre or cruel in other cultures. The trial of two ten-year-olds for the murder of Jamie Bulger is a good example – in most of mainland Europe this was seen as decidedly inhuman. A critical approach to this issue that we have used is to suggest that if it is legitimate to put a ten-year-old in the dock, surely it is just as legitimate to have ten-year-olds on juries? And not just for that particular trial, but all trials – why not? Most people baulk at that suggestion – but at least it makes them think!

In my book I used the term 'disenchantment' – in both its senses (to be freed from the 'enchantment' used to construct the taken-for-granted world; and to become cynical about outcomes and effects) – to describe what criticality involves. Being critical is all about being 'disenchanted'.

I.I. But aren't you going about it in a decidedly elitist manner? It's all very well to write scholarly arguments about ten-year-olds on juries, but this is not going to change very much is it – how much effect do you think this will have on the way the majority of British people think? Surely movie makers, journalists and political activists have a far better chance of actually making a difference?

Beryl: Actually, I rather agree. One of the questions the authors have been raising in this book is how far do (or can) psychologists have any impact upon the world – the answer seems to be 'not a lot'. It's worth considering why that is.

I.I. Well, for a start, I would point to the obscure language they use – and the authors have certainly used language which has been very impenetrable at times. I thought their intellectual hero, Michel Foucault, warned against the 'secret knowledge' of the Academy? Not much has been 'challenged' in this book in that respect?

Beryl: Agreed, but for new work, a new 'language' is required and it is bound to seem alien.

I.I. Over specific examples I don't have a problem, they were clear enough. But over this 'new language' I do wonder whether it just seems alien or that it is alien?

Beryl: 'Alien' is a matter of position, isn't it?

I.I. Yes, I can take that. But if I were to position myself as, say, a quantity surveyor, wouldn't social psychologists be right to see me as 'Other'?

Beryl: Neat. But let's look at your example. To suggest that we could think about social Being as usefully approached in terms of house bricks or wood planks isn't radical – it's just perverse. But it is radical, I think, to suggest that the social Being cannot be thought of as made up of 'things' at all.

I.I. Sometimes this book talks of being radical, sometimes critical. Is this just for more elegant writing, do you think – or is there something more lurking in those 'words'?

Beryl: I don't think it's so much lurking as there to be picked up. The questioning of mainstream social psychology has both a politically radical facet and a conceptually critical one. Crucial to both is a textual/discursive turn. Attention to language (in the broadest sense) informs both the critique of mainstream social psychology as theory and as practice, and the alternative forms of conceptualization and enquiry of critical social psychology.

I.I. I've certainly been aware of a lot of play with language. What worries me a bit is knowing how to be a good judge in all this. What makes for 'good' critical social psychology, for example? Can one have some confidence that it is a truly new 'story' rather than just an old story revamped? For instance, take the first thematic chapter which has the title

'From Personality to Textual Identities'. I could argue that (being literary for a moment) 'A rose by any other name would . . .'

Beryl: '. . . smell as sweet?' Well, I hardly think that the topic of personality comes up 'smelling of roses' after the authors have had a go at it. That's one criterion I would use to assess a new agenda – does it make you question? And does it make you question in new and alternative ways? Does it, in other words, help you to home in on what makes a particular form of knowledge 'taken-for-granted' rather than merely hitting its already established weak spots? To do that it must pursue a new narrative, reframe the issue in a fresh way . . .

I.I. That really is a politician's answer – one that doesn't deal with the original question set.

Beryl: I could say the same over the traditional study of personality! But that's just another rhetorical device. What matters is the presence, for a start, of a critical reframing – such as exposing how personality research was grounded on a psychology which divided up its territory. This is still there in the glossy textbook approach, fracturing sociality in terms of levels, starting at the individual, through interpersonal interaction, to the operation of psychological forces in the social world. So one thing that makes good critical work is a radical reframing . . .

I.I. That's the third time, I think, you've used that particular expression – don't mystify, explain.

Beryl: What I mean by 'reframing' is a sense of starting afresh by coming to a topic or an issue or a question from a different direction. The best photographers are those who take pictures of perfectly ordinary things, but, by 'framing' the shot in an innovative way, they make the object appear strange and unusual, and so they make us look at it in an active manner rather than just 'seeing' it. Artists do this sort of thing all the time. A good example is Serrano's 'Piss Christ' – an image of Christ viewed through a thin film of urine, which gives it sepia tones. The juxtaposition of the 'sacred and the profane' is deeply troubling – and, by troubling our sensibilities, makes us ask uncomfortable questions. An example of reframing as applied to personality is to expose the impossibility of studying the 'individual' in any way other than as embedded and enmeshed within the 'social', and thus troubling our notion of 'the self' as an individual outside of space and time.

I.I. That's better. But even if I accept what you say, that still leaves the question of how to judge that it is a 'truly' different story – that the new start doesn't lead back to the old finishing line.

Beryl: You can never be sure. But if you look back to what those early chapters offer, there is quite a detailed exposition of the 'new sights' and how to appreciate them . . .

I.I. Gone into the travel business, have we?

Beryl: That's not such a bad metaphor. Re-framed in the language of the travel brochure, I think the invitation to make a critical trek around social space would look something like this:

- Feast on a panorama of views of the textualized and socially constructed and positioned nature of 'identity' and the 'self'.
- Escape from the boring old package holiday tour around interpersonal relations. Wonder instead at the magic of 'between ourselves'. Listen to culturally narrated relationship-tales which we tell to each other and to ourselves. Be moved to hear how we construct locations for ourselves and each other within a context of stories. And, feel for yourself the conditions of power, ideology and reality-construction that operate within those tales.
- Stand in awe as critical dialecticians deconstruct the traditional conception of the person as a 'puppet' of social and biological determinations. Join in the experience of metaphors which stress the humanly organized and maintained nature of the social world. See people moving through time as you've never seen it before – as both constituted by and constitutors of the social and personal, both 'player and played'.
- Learn the dangers of regarding development as an unfolding individual process rather than an increasing engagement with an ongoingly constructed social world.

I could go on . . .

The Authors: Great stuff. Any chance we can quote it on the back cover?

I.I. Snap out of it all of you. That may be your version of reality, but I'm still making up my mind.

Beryl: Then you need to re-read Part III.

I.I. I guess I asked for that. But while we're on the subject, isn't there something very dangerous – anti-democratic even – in the argument that there's 'nothing behind' our words and our actions?

Beryl: Remember it is mainstream psychology that has given us models of the person wherein 'attitudes and behaviour' emerge from a learning machine, a psychodynamic battlefield, a face-saving actor or an information processing computer. There's not much space for 'free-will' in the theories it has offered for our words and actions, is there?

I.I. With respect, that's a weasel argument. What I asked was whether the approach you are offering is anti-democratic.

Beryl: Certainly we would caution against an over-individualized reading of personal powers, and we would point out the located, contingent and inequitably distributed constraints upon persons in culture when they 'make up their minds' on an issue. To that extent we are challenging the notion of uniquely individual powers. Is that what worries you? Let me ask you a question – what do you mean by 'anti-democratic?'

I.I. I guess the claim that what is going on when I'm in a ballot box placing my vote is discursive and collective rather than expressive of my own point of view.

Beryl: Then I think my point holds. If voting or ticking an attitude scale actually did express what was in someone's mind, the question then has to be asked – how did it get there in the first place? Mainstreamers tend to agree that attitudes are not innate but acquired. So, in their way of thinking, attitudes must be internalizations of environmental inputs. It's that mechanality – with its associated notion that all we have to do is 'tap' those internalizations and we can predict behaviour – that strikes me as decidedly anti-democratic.

I.I. What you seem to be saying is that the so-called post-Enlightenment project created a mechanical model of government.

Beryl: And its associated human science set out to reveal the workings of the machines involved? So that they could be 'humaneered'? Exactly.

I.I. Yet it came to see those machines as flawed, not able to process information effectively . . .

Beryl: You're moving on through the book to 'common-sense understanding' aren't you?

I.I. Well, it seems to go that way. But isn't the point the mainstream is making that, through having social science, there's a way out – that the scientific method can enable us to transcend our proneness to error?

Beryl: Like religious faith helps us to transcend our proneness to sin, you mean?

I.I. That's not altogether fair. Sin is always with us, science can claim a march of progress, a journey away from error to more accurate understanding.

Beryl: Certainly outside of social science, science can and does offer practical guidance in areas like, say, bridge-design or detecting genetic defects. In other words, it offers a technology and a conceptual system which provide practical benefits. But when we get into 'social science', it's not practical utility that's at issue. Medical science can tell us how to do a liver transplant on a three-week-old baby. But it can't tell us whether we should do this – whether, say, it's a sensible or morally justifiable use of scarce resources (which could, for example, be used to save the lives of literally thousands of children in a famine area dying from easily treated but less 'glamorous' diseases like dysentry). The question at issue, then, is whether the 'social' matches the notion of 'science' that works elsewhere. The critical argument is that it has not – that we need another way of going about asking and answering questions.

I.I. Which the book tries to tell me about . . .

Beryl: 'Science' is a human production – like everything else we do, it's an activity we undertake 'between ourselves'. It is not a set of laws given from the 'outside' to a special priesthood which can lead us to 'truth' about how we should resolve dilemmas about how to lead our lives. By making 'social science' a target for critical cultural analysis, its political sub-texts can be addressed.

I.I. Like when the authors point out its 'them' and 'us' stance, and you introduce us to your PLU principle?

Beryl: That's right. The critical cultural analysis of work on 'lay under-standing' has certainly seemed to be in the grip of that. But I think it is a much more general condition. The whole claim to humaneering relies upon it. To try to sum up, the nineteenth-century Academy dismembered knowledge into fields of enquiry and called them 'disciplines'. A critical reframing seeks to dissolve those boundaries – to see everything 'social' (including its study) as a manifold of competing narratives within which people express their accounts of reality and through which conduct is enabled and otherwise managed. This is part of what transdisciplinarity is about.

I.I. And critical polytextualism?

Beryl: It is my label for describing how to go about that endeavour – it's about exploring how people attempt to 'make sense' of their world by drawing upon the plurality of stories available to them within their culture, communities and social groups.

I.I. But isn't that also a way of putting yourself above the rest – just what you have been accusing mainstreamers of doing?

Beryl: Certainly that's the constant trap lurking to ambush critical work. Hence, the need for reflexivity, for seeing critical work itself as no different an endeavour in its contingencies from that which it studies.

I.I. Aren't we beginning to go round in circles?

Beryl: If you don't like where we are going, suggest an alternative tack.

I.I. All right, let's move on to Part IV on embodiment. You said that nineteenth-century psychology resulted from a dismembering of 'the human condition'. But it strikes me there is a different tale to tell. Psychology tried to link body and mind. Methinks over that it's the criticos who are trying to do the dismembering.

Beryl: There's something in that, but all is not what it seems.

I.I. Another of your so-called laws?

Beryl: More a 'pro-text' – a perturbating all-purpose proposition.

I.I. You're stalling.

Beryl: Body and mind were only conjoined in psychology in a textual sense. There never was a satisfactory theory as to how they interfaced with each other. Instead, vague notions of the 'biological bases of behaviour' or 'development' or 'maturation' were used rhetorically, to warrant the discipline, to give it a seeming grounding in 'real' science.

I.I. Are you trying to pretend that there's no biological reality? If you cut me, I bleed – if you shoot people they die – you can't 'critically reframe' them back to life again.

Beryl: Critical work is not trying to 'deny' embodiment, it is challenging a very particular reading of the body.

I.I. Which is?

Beryl: That we can read the body (and not just the human body but that of other animals) to find the wellsprings of troubled and troublesome behaviour. Specifically, critical social psychology suggests that the discipline has a residual 'foundationalism' in which behaviour is seen as grounded, in the individual, upon pre-given mechanisms like drives; propensities to be 'programmed' by learning; and upon developmentally unfolding faculties of information-processing.

I.I. Hence the working over of aggression, sexuality and emotion?

Beryl: Just so. They have been, over the last decade or so, areas where social-constructionist work has been very active.

I.I. Before we move on, can you refresh me as to the fine-grain differences between social construction, discourse analysis, cultural analysis and critical polytextualism?

Beryl: I doubt if a decent attempt to do that would refresh you – it would bore the pants off most people! My suggestion is that you take it by the texts, or from the texts . . .

I.I. From their texts, ye shall know them?

Beryl: It's the best way I know. They are very distinctive dialects, with lots of more local variety.

I.I. So the social construction of emotion . . .

Beryl: Tends to put the spotlight on exploring human emotion-talk and display in terms of socially constructed understandings, which are culturally and historically constituted. Some constructionists do, however, still see the emotion body as still 'there' all right, but obscured behind the view of discourse.

I.I. Can't see you relating to that given you don't have a body.

Beryl: Precisely my point – neither did Natasha Rostoff in *War and Peace* or Heathcliff in *Wuthering Heights* – which does not stop such fictional characters emoting like mad all over the place, without a hormone or limbic system in sight! More generally, let's say I'm agnostic over whether we can ever grasp the 'real', whether it's bodies we're talking about or anything else. But my main interest lies somewhere else and I'm glad to see it covered in this book – opening up new methods for exploring constituted knowledge. Rather than asking 'is this knowledge true?' (which I regard as unanswerable) it means asking more interesting questions, such as: 'What's the problem?', 'What's the issue?'.

I.I. Meaning?

Beryl: Just so. Meaning. If, say, aggression is 'socially constructed' – made, and made known between ourselves – it hardly fits the 'disease model' psychology often brings to it – which requires identifying a clear cause, course and effect. A consideration of the culturally and historically contingent nature of the available texts of aggression is crucial not just to its effective study but also to a critical stance on the use of psychology to 'give answers to' the 'problems of aggression'.

I.I. It sounds like you critical polytextualists want a slice of the action too – to get to pontificate on 'social problems'.

Beryl: It's more a matter of getting to challenge the kind of thinking that sees the world in terms of 'social problems' needing 'solutions' (providing, of course, a mandate for problem-solvers to earn their crust and interfere in other people's lives). The position we all take is that, first, notions like 'aggression' are variously socially constructed, so that they can never be tied down – except in a discourse (such as, to some extent, legal discourse) – in terms of objective, value-free definitions. And secondly, that so too are notions like 'social problems'. These also only get tied down in local, contingent usage.

I.I. Such as . . .

Beryl: Political agendas. Hence the argument that the discipline becomes 'politics by other means' when it gets into 'social problems'.

I.I. But sex and emotion aren't 'social problems' exactly.

Beryl: (Hamming up the tune): '. . . Jealous-eee . . .'

I.I. You mean we make 'problems' of them?

Beryl: Yes, because that's the way we are led to see them. We have inherited and are immersed in ways of thinking about these notions which invite a sense of trouble and problem. Put it another way, whenever we think about the human condition – and social psychology took this over unexamined – we tend to think in terms of culturally ingrained dichotomies that profoundly matter – such as thinking/feeling, body/mind, male/female, heterosexual/homosexual, sex/gender, and nature/nurture – and which carry with them the implication of there being 'problems' associated with them.

I.I. That worries me a bit. You seem to be saying, 'stop thinking in dichotomies and you can leave all your worries behind you'. Sounds like phoney evangelism, or, even worse, a kind of 1984-world in which, once 'thought crime' becomes impossible, all human horror and terror get neatly un-thought out of existence. Yet women are, in any sense of 'the real', really oppressed by patriarchy, homosexuals really are hounded by bigots. Un-thinking dichotomies does not alter these forms of prejudice and mistreatment one whit – they still go on, whatever reading we put on them.

Beryl: Did I say they don't? The point remains that the whole trap of utopianism or dystopianism is that it presumes a singularity. Even within dichotic thinking it is never like that, there is always endless argument based on different uses of the bipoles. What criticality tries to generate is not some global 'New Think' but a local moratorium on simplistic, unreflexive thinking – a space in which it becomes possible to reflect, to see things differently, to think 'Other'.

I.I. And, presumably, to do Other?

Beryl: Precisely – it is no mere call to reflect, but to act differently too . . .

I.I. Meaning that, like other dialects of critical social psychology, it argues for new ways of doing research?

Beryl: Well, not just research. We talked of other kinds of action earlier. But research is an important issue too. The critical turn is not just a matter of conceptualization, but of getting a new handle on methodology.

I.I. I wondered when we were going to get to your perverse preoccupation with Q methodology – an 'in group' activity if I ever saw one!

Beryl: More like polysemous perversity, perhaps. Certainly Q-method is an important part, but not the only part, of our methodological portfolio. We use it, quite simply, because we have found it serviceable for doing what we want to do – scrutinizing in ways intended not to reveal 'truths' but to explore how people make and monger and use knowledge.

I.I. Why this word 'methodology', what's the matter with 'methods'?

Beryl: What is this? Did you skip Chapter II? It's full of what's wrong with method – or more to the point, what goes wrong when we put it on a pedestal and worship it.

I.I. What you've called 'Methodolatry'.

Beryl: Indeed, it's my way of bringing home to people the trap that's set for the unwary when 'methods' get treated in psychology (indeed, in social science generally) as if they were no more than practical ways of going about finding out things.

I.I. You mean generating more 'creata' in the quest for performance ratings?

Beryl: Possibly that's over-cynical. While the press to publish – and never mind the value of the 'knowledge' so discovered – is strong (and growing stronger), I'm perfectly prepared to acknowledge that research-ers also do genuinely want to 'find out what makes people tick'. It's not (just) their motivation that worries us, it's the whole rotten edifice they have constructed in order to try to do so.

I.I. That's being a bit harsh, surely?

Beryl: I'm not using the term 'rotten' merely as invective, I mean it more literally than that – 'rotten' as crumbling and falling to bits. What I'm arguing is that there is something profoundly and seriously wrong with the whole endeavour. Ideas like 'reliability' and 'validity' have become ends in their own right. Unless you can wave them, like good-luck talismans, over your research activity, the mainstream dismisses what you are doing as 'not very good science'. In this they miss the point that we're not trying to 'do' science at all – indeed, we are challenging the foundational notion of science being 'do-able' in respect to the social.

I.I. So when you are accused of being 'unscientific' you take this not as a rebuke, but as a compliment?

Beryl: Yes and no. I'm in no doubt that it's meant as a criticism – it's an accusation that we are 'not playing the game by the rules'. What irks us is that this is used to justify ignoring what we do – dismissing it as a failed and flawed attempt. As 'true believers' of methodolatry, it seems not to occur to them that we are playing a different game, with different rules.

I.I. But you have to admit you can come over as defensive? Like when you argue 'never mind the replicability, look at the outcome' about a Q-methodological study. That certainly sounds like special pleading.

Beryl: True, but that's just how 'true believers' in any fundamentalist faith tend to respond to any challenge to their doctrine. Rather than being prepared to take the challenge seriously, they just go on chanting, mantra-like, the tenets of their creed – as though this, in itself, will make the challenge go away. My concern is not so much that this is how 'true believers' often behave but that this is how scientists behave – which is why I assume the authors have presented mainstream social psychology as missionary evangelism. Reframing it in this way draws our attention to the way they are acting more like acolytes of a 'true faith' than brave adventurers setting out on a journey of discovery (which is how they like to portray themselves).

I.I. You're implying that they are not really searching for 'truth' – as they purport to be – but merely seeking to reinforce what they 'know' already to be true (i.e. what their faith tells them is true).

Beryl: Well, doesn't that seem to be what most social psychological studies are doing? It's dressed up in the arcane language of 'hypothesis testing', but, stripped of its scientized credentials, it does look a lot more like re-affirming faith than exploration.

I.I. And Q method is 'the real thing', you say? Don't try to tell me you lot make no assumptions about what you are seeking to 'discover'.

Beryl: You could say, how else could we behave – we're only human. This may sound ironic, but there's a serious point. Social construction-ism is not a matter of assuming that once you are 'liberated' into seeing that all knowledge is person-made, you will be somehow 'set free' from the very local and contingent conditions that make it and monger it. We are always-ever 'persons of our time and place', deeply and inescapably enmeshed within the practical and very 'real-looking' everyday world. That's the whole point – there is no conceptual vacuum we can occupy where we can be 'outside' the pressing 'social facts' that constitute our understanding of the world. All we can ever do is become – somewhat – disillusioned: begin to recognize the illusions *which constitute our 'social realities'* as illusions and not as really-real realities.

We use Q-methodology because it helps in this process. While we can and do predict some of the stories or representations we expect to find in a study (and indeed, strategically seek out people to express them) we can be surprised – we can dis-cover stories that we did not predict, and which take some considerable effort to 'make sense of'. It's this abductive capacity to surprise and to set conundrums that we like about Q.

I.I. Slipped that one in – abductive – what's that?

Beryl: Hmph! Go back and read Chapter 11, it's all there.

I.I. So where does this leave us?

Beryl: Pretty well up to the authors' word limit, I'm afraid.

I.I. And where do we go now?'

Beryl: That's largely up to you. If I can sum up the message this book has been trying to get over, it is that you should by now be pretty 'disillusioned' – much more cynical, not just about how mainstream social psychology constitutes its 'knowledge' but about everything that anybody tries to pass off on you as 'truth' or 'knowledge' or 'facts'. Our 'mission' has been to convert you from a 'true believer' to an agnostic. Further, the aim of the book has been to convince you of the merits of 'making trouble' and 'taking trouble' and also to give you some ammu-nition in those tasks. So next time you look along the bookshelves at all those glossy tomes, don't be fooled. Beware, in other words, of false prophets offering you enlightenment – and equally salespersons 'selling' you their wares. Nothing is ever what it seems.

I.I. Even you, dear Beryl?

Beryl: (gradually fading away) Me? I'm no more than a figment of the imagination – but then, aren't we all?

Bibliography

Abelson, R. P. (1968) 'Simulation of social behaviour', in G. Lindzey and E. Aronson (eds) *Handbook of Social Psychology* (2nd ed). Reading, Mass.: Addison-Wesley.

Abelson, R. P. et al. (eds) (1969) *Theories of Cognitive Consistency: A Sourcebook*. Chicago: Rand McNally.

Abramson, I. Y., Seligman, M. P. P. and Teasdale, J. D. (1978) 'Learned helplessness in humans: critique and reformulation', *Journal of Abnormal Psychology*, 87, 349–74.

Adorno, T. W., Frenkel-Brunswik, E., Levison, D. J. and Sanford, R. N. (1950) *The Authoritarian Personality*. New York: Harper.

Ajzen, I. (1988) *Attitudes, Personality and Behavior*. Milton Keynes: Open University Press.

Ajzen, I. and Fishbein, M. (1973), 'Attitudes and normative beliefs as factors influencing behavioural intentions', *Journal of Personality and Social Psychology*, 21 (1), 401–15.

Ajzen, I. and Fishbein, M. (1980) *Understanding Attitudes and Predicting Social Behaviour*. Englewood-Cliffs, NJ: Prentice-Hall.

Ajzen, I. and Madden, T. J. (1986) 'Prediction of goal-directed behavior: attitudes, intentions and perceived behavioral control', *Journal of Experimental Social Psychology*, 22, 453–74.

Ajzen, I. and Timko, C. (1986) 'Correspondence between health attitudes and behavior', *Journal of Basic and Applied Social Psychology*, 7, 259–76.

Alexander, C. N. and Knight, G. W. (1971) 'Situated identities and social psychological experimentation', *Sociometry*, 34, 65–82.

Allport, G. W. (1954) 'The historical background of modern social psychology', in G. Lindzey (ed.) *Handbook of Social Psychology*, Vol. 1. Cambridge, Mass: Addison-Wesley.

Allport, G. W. and Postman, L. (1947) *The Psychology of Rumor*. New York: Holt, Rinehart & Winston.

Andersen, M. L. (1994) 'The many and varied social constructions of intelligence;' in T. R. Sarbin and J. I. Kitsuse (eds) *Constructing the Social*, London: Sage.

Antaki, C. (1988) *Analysing Everyday Explanation: A Case Book of Methods*. London: Sage

Antaki, C. and Fielding, G. (1981) 'Research on ordinary explanation', in C. Antaki (ed.) *The Psychology of Ordinary Explanations of Social Behaviour*. London: Academic Press.

Argyle, M. (1993) *The Social Psychology of Everyday Life*. London: Routledge.

Argyle, M., Shimoda, K. and Little, B. (1978) 'Varience due to persons and situations in England and Japan', *British Journal of Social and Clinical Psychology*, 9, 221–31.

Armistead, N. (ed.) (1974) *Reconstructing Social Psychology*. Harmondsworth: Penguin.

Armon-Jones, C. (1985) 'Prescription, explication and the social construction of emotion', *Journal for the Theory of Social Behaviour*, 15 (1), 1–21.

Aronson, E., (1988) *The Social Animal* (5th edn). New York: Freeman.

Aronson, E., Wilson, T. D. and Akert, R. M. (1994) *Social Psychology: The Heart and the Mind*. New York: HarperCollins.

Asch, S. E. (1951) 'Effects of group pressure upon the modification and distortion of judgements', in H. Guetzkow (ed.) *Groups, Leadership and Men*. Pittsburgh: Carnegie Press.

Asch, S. E. (1952) *Social Psychology*. Englewood Cliffs, NJ: Prentice-Hall.

Ash, S. E. (1956) 'Studies of independence and conformity: a minority of one against a unanimous majority', *Psychological Monographs*, 70 (9, whole No. 416).

Asch, S. E. (1959) 'A perspective on social psychology', in S. Koch (ed.) *Psychology: A Study of a Science* (vol. 3). New York: McGraw Hill.

Askenasy, H., (1978) *Are We All Nazis?* Secaucus, NJ: Lyle Stuart.

Austin Locke, J. (1990) 'Rashamon: a social anthropological model'. BASAPP Newsletter, No. 5, 9–11.

Averill, J. R. (1975) 'A semantic atlas of emotional concepts', *JSAS Catalog of Selected Documents in Psychology*, 5, 330.

Averill, J. R. (1982) *Anger and Aggression: An Essay on Emotion*. New York: Springer-Verlag.

Averill, J. R. (1986) 'The acquisition of emotions in adulthood', in R. Harré (ed.) *The Social Construction of Emotions*. Oxford: Blackwell.

Averill, J. (1990) 'Six metaphors of emotion', in D. Leary (ed.) *Metaphors in the History of Psychology*. Cambridge: Cambridge University Press.

Averill, J., Catlin, G. and Chon, K. K. (1990) *Rules of Hope*. London: Springer Verlag.

Baddeley, A. D. (1992) 'Is memory all talk?' *The Psychologist*, October, 447–8.

Bakhtin, M. (1975) *The Dialogical Imagination* (ed. M. Holquist). Minneapolis: University of Minnesota Press.

Bandura, A. (1977) *Social Learning Theory*. Englewood Cliffs, NJ.: Prentice-Hall.

Bandura, A. (1983) 'Psychological mechanisms of aggression', in R. G. Green and E. I. Donnerstein (eds) *Aggression: Theoretical and Empirical Reviews*, vol. 1: *Theoretical and Methodological Issues*. New York: Academic Press.

Bandura, A. (1986a) *Social Foundations of Thought and Action*. Englewood Cliffs, NJ: Prentice Hall.

Bandura, A. (1986b) *Social Learning Theory*. Prentice-Hall: Englewood Cliffs, NJ.

Bandura, A., Ross, D. and Ross, S. (1963) 'Imitation of film mediated aggressive models', *Journal of Abnormal and Social Psychology*, 66 (1), 3–11.

Bannister, D. and Fransella, F. (1971) *Inquiring Man: The Theory of Personal Constructs*. Harmondsworth: Penguin.

Barker, R., Dembo, T. and Lewin, K. (1941) 'Frustration and aggression: an experiment with young children', *University of Iowa Studies in Child Welfare*, 18, 1–314.

Barker, R. L. (1987) *Surviving Jealous Relationships: The Green Eyed Marriage*. Macmillan: New York.

Baron, R. A. (1972) 'Reducing the Influence of an Aggressive Model: the restraining effects of peer censure', *Journal of Experimental Social Psychology*, 8, 266–75.

Baron, R. A. (1977) *Human Aggression*. Plenum: New York.

Baron, R. A. and Byrne, D. (1984) *Social Psychology: Understanding Human Interaction*. (4th edn) Boston: Allyn & Bacon.

Barthes, R. (1972) *Mythologies* (Trans. A. Lavers). London: Jonathan Cape.

Bartlett, F. C. (1932) *Remembering*. Cambridge: Cambridge University Press.

Baumgart, H. (1990) *Jealousy: Experiences and Solutions*. Chicago: University of Chicago Press.

Bell, A. P. and Weinberg, M. S. (1978) *Homosexualities*. New York: Simon & Schuster.

Bell, A. P., Weinberg, M. S. and Hammersmith, S. K. (1981) *Sexual Preference: Its Development in Men and Women*. Bloomington, Ind: Indiana University Press.

Bell, P. A. and Baron, R. A. (1976) 'Aggression and heat: the mediating role of negative affect', *Journal of Applied Social Psychology*, 6, 18–30.

Bem, D. J. (1965) 'An experimental analysis of self-persuasion', *Journal of Experimental Social Psychology*, 1, 199–218.

Bem, D. J. (1967) 'Self-perception: an alternative interpretation of cognitive dissonance phenomena', *Psychological Review*, 74, 183–200.

Bem, S. (1977) 'On the utility of alternative procedures for assessing psychological androgeny', *Journal of Consulting and Clinical Psychology*, 45, 196–205.

Bem, S. (1978) 'Beyond androgeny: some presumptuous prescriptions for a liberated sexual identity', in J. Sherman and F. Denmark (eds.) *Psychology of Women: Future Directions in Research*. New York: Psychological Dimensions.

Berger, P. L. and Luckmann, T. (1967) *The Social Construction of Reality*. Harmondsworth: Penguin.

Berkowitz, L. (1972) 'Social norms, feelings, and other factors affecting helping and altruism', in L. Berkowitz (ed.) *Advances in Experimental Social Psychology*, vol. 6. New York: Academic Press.

Berkowitz, L. (1993) *Aggression*. New York: McGraw Hill.

Bhaskar, R. (1978a) *A Realist Theory of Science*. Hemel Hempstead: Harvester Wheatsheaf.

Bhaskar, R. (1978b) *The Possibility of Naturalism*. Hemel Hempstead: Harvester Wheatsheaf.

Bhaskar, R. (1989) *Reclaiming Reality: A Critical Introduction to Contemporary Philosophy*. London: Verso.

Bhavnani, K. K. (1990) 'What's power got to do with it? Empowerment and social research', in I. Parker and J. Shotter (eds) *Deconstructing Social Psychology*. London: Routledge.

Billig, M. (1976) *Social Psychology and Intergroup Relations*. London: Academic Press.

Billig, M. (1978) *Fascists: A Social Psychological View of the National Front*. London: Harcourt, Brace Jovanovich.

Billig, M. (1982) *Ideology and Social Psychology*. Oxford: Blackwell.

Billig, M. (1987) *Arguing and Thinking: A Rhetorical Approach to Social Psychology*. Cambridge: Cambridge University Press.

Billig, M. (1989) [Original authored material] in D. Howitt et al. *Social Psychology Conflicts and Continuities*. Milton Keynes: Open University Press.

Billig, M., Condor, S., Edwards, D., Gane, M., Middleton, D. and Radley, A. (1988) *Ideological Dilemmas*. London: Sage.

Bless, H. (1993) 'Affect and its impact on social cognition and behaviour', symposium in *Social Psychology in Europe*, abstracts book, European Society of Experimental Social Psychology, Ediçòes Cosmos: Lisbon.

Bourdieu, P. (1977) *Outline for a Theory of Practice*. Cambridge: Cambridge University Press.

Boyne, R. and Ratansi, A. (eds) (1900) *Postmodernism and Society*. Basingstoke: Macmillan.

Brehm, S. S. and Kassin, S. M. (1990) *Social Psychology*. Boston: Houghton Mifflin.

Broverman, I. K., Vogel, S. R., Broverman, D. M., Clarkson, F. E. and Rosenkrantz, P. S. (1972) 'Sex role stereotypes: a current appraisal', *Journal of Social Issues*, 28, 59–78.

Brown, P. (1974) *Towards a Marxist Psychology*. New York: Harper & Row.

Brown, R. (1965) *Social Psychology*. New York: Free Press.

Brown, R. (1986) *Social Psychology* (2nd edn). New York: Free Press.

Brown, S. (1994) 'The missing bodies of constructionism', *Manifold*, 1, (1), 1–9

Brown, S. R. (1980) *Political Subjectivity: Applications of Q Methodology in Political Science*. New Haven: Yale University Press.

Bruner, J. (1986) *Actual Minds, Possible Worlds*. Cambridge, Mass.: Harvard University Press.

Burger, J. M. (1993) *Personality* (3rd edn). Pacific Grove, Cal: Brooks/Cole.

Burgoyne, J., Omrod, R. and Richards, M. (1987) *Divorce Matters*. Harmondsworth: Penguin.

Burkitt, I. (1991) *Social Selves*. London: Sage.

Burman, E. (1994) *Deconstructing Developmental Psychology*. London: Routledge.

Burman, E. and Parker, I. (eds) (1994) *Discourse Analytic Research: Repertoires and Readings of Texts in Action*. London: Routledge.

Buss, A. R. (1979) *A Dialectical Psychology*. New York: Invington.

Campbell, D. T. (1963) 'Social attitudes and other acquired behavioral dispositions' in S. Koch (ed.) *Psychology: A Study of a Science*, vol. 6. McGraw-Hill: New York.

Cancian, F. M. (1987) *Love in America: Gender and Self-Development*. Cambridge: University Press.

Cannon, W. B. (1927) 'The James-Lange theory of emotion: A critical examination and an alternative theory', *American Journal of Psychology*, 39, 106–24.

Cantrill, H. (1940) *The Invasion from Mars*. Princeton: Princeton University Press.

Carlsmith, J. M. et al. (1984) *Methods of Research in Social Psychology*. New York: Addison-Wesley.

Carlson, R. (1984) 'What's social about social psychology? Where's the person in personality research?', *Journal of Personality and Social Psychology*, 47, 1304–7.

Casling, D. (1993) 'Cobblers and song-birds: the language and imagery of disability', *Disability, Handicap and Society*, 8 (2), 203–10.

Cattell, R. B. (1967) *The Scientific Analysis of Personality* (revd edn). Harmondsworth: Penguin.

Chambers (1983) *Chambers 20th Century Dictionary*, ed. E. M. Kirkpatrick. Edinburgh: W. & R. Chambers.

Chesler, P. (1972) *Women and Madness*. New York: Avon.

Chodorow, N. (1978) *The Reproduction of Mothering*. Berkeley, Cal.: University of California Press.

Christie, J. R. R. and Orton, F. (1988) 'Writing a text on the life', *Art History*, 11 (4), 545–63.

Christie, R. (1954) 'Authoritarianism revisited', in R. Christie and M. Jahoda (eds) *Studies in the Scope and Method of 'The Authoritarian Personality'*. New York: Free Press.

Christie, R, and Cook, P. (1958) 'A guide to published literature relating to the authoritarian personality through 1956', *Journal of Personality*, 45, 171–99.

Christopher, F. S. and Cate, R. M. (1985) 'Premarital sexual pathways and relationship development', *Journal of Social and Personal Relationships*, 2, 271–88.

Cicourel, A. V. (1973) *Cognitive Sociology: Language and Meaning in Social Interaction*. Harmondsworth: Penguin.

Clanton, G. and Smith, L. G. (eds) (1977) *Jealousy*. Englewood Cliffs, NJ: Prentice-Hall.

Clark, D. and Haldane, D. (1990) *Wedlocked? Intervention and Research in Marriage*. Cambridge: Polity Press.

Clarke, A. C. (1973) *Profiles of the Future: An Inquiry into the Limits of the Possible*. London: Pan Books.

Cleckley, H. (1964) *The Mask of Insanity*. St Louis: Mosby.

Collin, F. (1985) *Theory and Understanding: A Critique of Interpretive Social Science*. Oxford: Blackwell.

Collins, B. E. (1974) 'Four components of the Rotter Internal-External scale: belief in a difficult world, a just world, a predictable world, and a politically responsive world', *Journal of Personality and Social Psychology*, 29 (3), 381–91.

Cottrell, N. N. (1972) 'Social facilitation', in C. G. McClintock (ed.) *Experimental Social Psychology*. New York: Holt.

Coulter, J. (1989) *Mind in Action*. Oxford: Polity Press.

Cozens, J. (1991) *OK to Talk Feelings*. London: BBC books.

Craib, I. (1986) Review of M. Mulkay, 'The World and the Word'. *Sociology*, 20, 483–4.

Crowne, D. P. and Marlow, D. (1964) *The Approval Motive: Studies in Evaluative Dependence*. New York: Wiley.

Curt, B. (1994) *Textuality and Tectonics: Troubling Social and Psychological Science*. Buckingham: Open University Press.

Daly, M., Wilson, M. and Weghorst, S. G. (1982) 'Male sexual jealousy', *Ethology and Sociobiology*, 3, 11–27.

Danzinger, K. (1990) *Constructing the Subject*. Cambridge: Cambridge University Press.

Darley, J. M. and Latané, B. (1968) 'Bystander intervention in emergencies: diffusion of responsibility', *Journal of Personality and Social Psychology*, 8, 377–83.

Darmon, P. (1985) *Trial by Impotence: Virility and Marriage in Pre-revolutionary France* (trans. P. Keegan). London: Chatto & Windus.

Davies, B. and Harré, R. (1990) 'Positioning: the discursive production of selves', *Journal for the Theory of Social Behaviour*, 20, 43–63.

Davies, C. (1975) *Permissive Britain: Social Change in the Sixties and Seventies*. London: Pitman & Sons Ltd.

De Fleur, M. L. and Westie, F. R. (1963) 'Attitude as a scientific concept', *Social Forces*, 42, 17–31.

De Rosa, A. (1987), 'The social representation of mental illness in children and adults', in W. Doise and S. Moscovici (eds) *Current Issues in European Social Psychology*, vol. 2. Cambridge: Cambridge University Press.

De Swaan, A. (1990) *The Management of Normality*. London: Routledge.

Deleuze, G. (1990) *Foucault*. Minneapolis: Univeristy of Minnesota Press.
Deleuze, G. and Guattari, F. (1992) *A Thousand Plateaus: Capitalism and Schizophrenia*. London: The Althane Press.
Denzin, N. K. (1977) *Childhood Socialisation*. San Francisco: Jossey-Bass.
Denzin, N. K. (1988) 'Blue velvet: postmodern contradictions', in M. Featherstone (ed.) *Theory, Culture and Society, special issue on postmodernism*, 5 (2 & 3).
Derrida, J. (1974) *Of Grammatology*. Baltimore: Johns Hopkins University Press.
Derrida, J. (1987) *The Post-Card: From Socrates to Freud and Beyond*. Chicago: University of Chicago Press.
Derrida, J. (1978/1990) *Writing and Difference* (trans. A. Bass). London: Routledge.
Deutsch, M. and Gerard, H. B. (1955) 'A study of normative and informational social influence upon individual judgement', *Journal of Abnormal and Social Psychology*, 51, 629–36.
Doane, M. A. (1992) 'Film and masquerade: theorising the female spectator', in *Screen, The Sexual Subject: a Screen Reader in Sexuality*. Routledge: London.
Doise, W. (1976) *L'Articulation psychosociologique et les relations entre groupes*. Brussels: De Broeck.
Doise, W., Clemence, A. and Lorenzi-Coldi (1993) *The Quantitative Analysis of Social Representations*. London: Harvester-Wheatsheaf.
Dollard, J., Doob, L. W., Miller, N. E., Mowrer, O. H. and Sears, R. R. (1939) *Frustration and Aggression*. New Haven, Conn.: Yale University Press.
Douglas, J. D. and Johnson, J. M. (1977) (eds) *Existential Sociology*. Cambridge: Cambridge University Press.
Douglas, M. (1966) *Purity and Danger*. New York: Routledge.
Duck, S. (1988) *Relating to Others*. Milton Keynes: Open University Press.
Duck, S. (1986) *Human Relationships: An Introduction to Social Psychology*. London: Sage.
Duck, S. (1992) *Human Relationships* (2nd edn.) London: Sage.
Durkheim, E. (1895/1982) *The Rules of Sociological Method*. London: Macmillan.
Dutton, D. G. and Aron, A. P. (1974) 'Some evidence for heightened sexual attraction under conditions of high anxiety', *Journal of Personality and Social Psychology*, 30, 510–17.

Eagley, A. H. and Kite, M. E. (1987) 'Are stereotypes of nationalities applied to both women and men?', *Journal of Personality and Social Psychology*, 53, 451–62.
Eco, U. (1992) *Interpretation and Overinterpretation*. Cambridge: Cambridge University Press.
Edwards, D., Ashmore, M. and Potter J. (1993) *Death and Furniture: The Rhetoric, Politics, and Theology of Bottom Line Arguments Against Relativism*. Mimeograph: Discourse and Rhetoric Group, Loughborough University.

Edwards, D. and Potter, J. (1992) *Discursive Psychology*. London: Sage.

Ehrenreich, J. (ed.) (1978) *The Cultural Crisis of Modern Medicine*. New York: Monthly Review Press.

Eisenstein, H. (1984) *Contemporary Feminist Thought*. London: Unwin.

Eiser, J. R. (1980) *Cognitive Social Psychology: A Guidebook to Theory and Research*. London: McGraw-Hill.

Ekman, P. (1982) *Emotion in the Human Face* (2nd edn). New York: Cambridge University Press.

Ekman P. and Friesen, W. V. (1974) 'Detecting deception from the body or face', *Journal of Personality and Social Psychology*, 29, 288–98.

Elms, A. C. (1975) 'The crisis in confidence in social psychology', *American Psychologist*, 30, 967–76.

Erikson, E. (1963) *Childhood and Society*. New York: Norton.

Essed, P. (1991) *Understanding Everyday Racism: an interdisciplinary study*. London: Sage.

Eysenck, H. J. (1952) *The Scientific Study of Personality*. London: Routledge.

Eysenck, H. J. (1957) *Sense and Nonsense in Psychology*. Harmondsworth: Penguin.

Eysenck, H. J. (1967) *The Biological Basis of Personality*. Springfield, Ill.: C. C. Thomas.

Eysenck, H. J. (ed.) (1970–1) *Readings in Extraversion-Introversion*, (vols 1–3). London: Staples.

Fairclough, N. (1992), *Discourse and Social Change*. Cambridge: Polity.

Fathali, M., Taylor, D. M. and Wright, S. C. (1993) *Social Psychology in Cross-cultural Perspective*. New York: Freeman & Co.

Festinger, L. (1957) *A Theory of Cognitive Dissonance*. Stanford Cal.: Stanford University Press.

Festinger, L. (1962) 'Cognitive dissonance', *Scientific American*, 207, 93–9.

Festinger, L. and Carlsmith, J. M. (1959) 'Cognitive consequences of forced compliance', *Journal of Abnormal and Social Psychology*, 58, 203–10.

Feyerabend, P. (1975) *Against Method*. London: New Left Books.

Fiske, S. T. and Taylor, S. E. (1984) *Social Cognition*. Reading, Mass: Addison Wesley.

Flugel, J. C. (1930/1971) *The Psychology of Clothes*. London: The Hogarth Press.

Ford, C. S. and Beach, F. A. (1952) *Patterns of Sexual Behaviour*. New York: Ace Books.

Foucault, M. (1970) *The Order of Things*. London: Tavistock.

Foucault, M. (1972) *The Archeology of Knowledge*. London: Tavistock.

Foucault, M. (1977) *Discipline and Punish: The Birth of the Prison*. Harmondsworth: Peregrine.

Foucault, M. (1978/1980) *Power/Knowledge*, ed. C. Gordon. Brighton: Harvester.

Foucault, M. (1979) 'Interview with Lucette Finas', in M. Morris and P. Patton (eds) *Michel Foucault: Power, Truth, Strategy*. Sydney: Feral.

Foucault, M. (1980, orig. 1976) *The History of Sexuality, Volume 1.* Harmond-sworth: Penguin.

Foucault, M. (1982) 'The subject and power', in H. Dreyfus and P. Rabinow, *Michel Foucault: Beyond structuralism and Hermeneutics.* Chicago: University of Chicago Press.

Foucault, M. (1984) 'What is enlightenment?', in P. Rabinow (ed.) *The Foucault Reader.* Peregrine: Harmondsworth.

Foucault, M. (1986) *The History of Sexuality,* vol. 2: *The Use of Pleasure.* Harmondsworth: Penguin.

Foucault, M. (1988) 'Technologies of the self', in L. H. Martin, H. Gutman and P. H. Hutton (eds) *Technologies of the Self.* Tavistock: London.

Fox, N. (1993) *Postmodernism, Sociology and Health.* Buckingham: Open University Press.

Fox, N. J. (1992) *The Social Meaning of Surgery.* Buckingham: Open University Press.

Freedman, J. L. (1969) 'Role playing: psychology by consensus', *Journal of Personality and Social Psychology,* 13, 107–14.

Freeman, M. (1993) *Re-writing the Self.* London: Routledge.

Freud, S. (1900/1953) 'The interpretatiuon of dreams', in J. Strachey (ed.) *The Standard Edition of the Complete Psychological Works,* vol. 4/5 London: Hogarth Press.

Freud, S. (1905/1953) 'Three essays on sexuality', in J. Strachey (ed.) *The Standard Edition of the Complete Psychological Works,* vol. 7. London: Hogarth Press.

Furnham, A. (1983) *Lay Theories – Everyday Understanding of Problems in the Social Sciences.* Oxford: Pergamon Press.

Gadamer, H. G. (1975) *Truth and Method.* London: Sheed & Ward.

Galbraith, J. K. (1976) *Money: Whence it Came, Where it Went.* Harmond-sworth: Pelican.

Game, A. (1991) *Undoing the Social.* Milton Keynes: Open University Press.

Garfinkel, H. (1967) *Studies in Ethnomethodology.* Prentice-Hall: Englewood Cliffs.

Gavey, N. (1992) 'Technologies and the effects of heterosexual coercion', *Feminism and Psychology,* 2 (3), 325–52.

Geertz, C. (1984) 'From the Native's point of view: on the nature of anthropol-ogical understanding', in R. A. Shweder and R. A. LeVine (eds) *Culture Theory: Essays on Mind, Self and Emotion.* Cambridge: Cambridge University Press.

Gergen, K. J. (1994) *Toward Transformation in Social Knowledge.* (2nd edn) London: Sage.

Gergen, K. J. and Gergen, M. M. (1988) 'Narrative and the self as relationship', in L. Berkowitz (ed.) *Advances in Experimental Social Psychology.* New York: Academic Press.

Giami, A. (1986) 'Les representations du Handicap: une approche psycho-sociale clinique', in G. Bellelli (ed.) *La Representation sociale de la maladie mentale.* Naples: EAESP & University of Naples.

Gilligan, C. (1977) 'In a different voice: women's concepts of self and morality', *Harvard Educational Review*, 47, 481–517.

Gillis, J. R. (1988) 'From ritual to romance: towards an alternative history of love', in C. Z. Stearns and P. N. Stearns, (eds) *Emotion and Social Change: Toward a New Psychohistory.* New York: Holmes and Meier.

Gilmartin, B. (1977) 'Jealousy among the swingers', in G. Clanton and L. G. Smith (eds) *Jealousy.* Englewood Cliffs, NJ: Prentice-Hall.

Gilroy, P. (1993) *The Promised Land.* Cambridge, Mass.: Harvard University Press.

Gleeson, K. (1991) 'Out of our minds: the deconstruction and reconstruction of madness', unpublished Ph.D. thesis: University of Reading.

Goffman, E. (1959) *The Presentation of Self in Everyday Life.* Garden City, NY: Doubleday.

Goffman, E. (1963) *Stigma.* Englewood Cliffs, NJ: Prentice-Hall.

Goldberg, S. (1977) *The Inevitability of Patriarchy.* London: Temple Smith.

Gonzalez-Crussi, M. (1988) *On the Nature of Things Erotic.* London: Picador.

Graham, E. (1992) 'Postmodernism and paradox', in J. Doherty, E. Graham and M. Malek, *Postmodernism and the Social Sciences.* Basingstoke: Macmillan.

Gray, J. A. (1981) 'A biological basis for the sex differences in achievement in science?', in A. Kelly (ed.) *The Missing Half: Girls and Science Education.* Manchester: Manchester University Press.

Greenberg, M. S. (1967) 'Role playing: an alternative to deception?' *Journal of Personality and Social Psychology*, 7, 151–60.

Greenwood, J. D. (1992) 'Realism, empiricism and social constructionism: psychological theory and the social dimensions of mind and action', *Theory and Psychology*, 2 (2), 131–53.

Griffin, C. (1993) *Representations of Youth: The Study of Youth and Adolescence in Britain and America.* Cambridge: Polity.

Grossberg, L., Nelson, C., and Treichler, P. (eds) (1992) *Cultural Studies.* London: Routledge.

Guerin, B. (1986) 'Mere presence effects in humans: a review', in *Journal of Experimental Social Psychology*, 22, 38–77.

Gunter, B. (1985) *Dimensions of Television Violence.* London: Gower.

Hall, S. and Held, D. (1989) 'Citizens and citizenship', in S. Hall and M. Jacques (eds) *New Times: The Changing Face of Politics in the 1990's.* London: Lawrence & Wishart.

Haney, C., Banks, C. and Zimbardo, P. G., (1973) 'Interpersonal dynamics in a simulated prison', *International Journal of Criminology and Penology*, 1, 69–97.

Haraway, D. (1989) *Primate Visions: Gender, Race, and Nature in the world of Modern Science.* London: Routledge.

Haraway, D. (1984) 'Primatology is politics by other means', in R. Bleier (ed.) *Feminist Approaches to Science*. London: Pergamon.

Harré, R. (1977) 'Rules and the explanation of social behaviour', in P. Collett (ed.) *Social Rule and Social Behaviour*. Oxford: Blackwell.

Harré, R. (1979) *Social Being: A Theory for Social Psychology*. Oxford: Blackwell.

Harré, R. (1983) *Personal Being: A Theory for Individual Psychology*. Oxford: Blackwell.

Harré, R. (1986) 'Social sources of mental content and order', in J. Margolis et al. (eds.) *Psychology: Designing the Discipline*. Oxford: Blackwell.

Harré, R. (1989) 'Language games and the texts of identity', in J. Shotter and K. J. Gergen (eds) *Texts of Identity*. London: Sage.

Harré, R. (1992) 'What is real in psychology: A plea for persons', *Theory and Psychology*, 2 (2), 153–9.

Harré, R. (1993) *Social Being* (2nd edn). Oxford: Blackwell.

Harré, R., Clarke, D. and De Carlo, N. (1985) *Motives and Mechanisms*. London: Methuen

Harré, R. and Gillett, G. (1994) *The Discursive Mind*. London: Sage.

Harré, R. and Secord, P. F. (1972) *The Explanation of Social Behaviour*. Oxford: Blackwell.

Harris, P. (1989) *Children and Emotion: The Developmental of Psychological Understanding*. Oxford: Blackwell.

Harris, M. (1974) 'Mediators between frustration and aggression in a field experiment', *Journal of Experimental and Social Psychology*, 10, 561–71.

Hartl, E. M., Monnelly, E. P. and Elderkin, R. D. (1982) *Physique and Delinquent Behavior: A 3 Year Follow up of William H. Sheldon's Varieties of Delinquent Youth*. New York: Academic Press.

Harvey, D. (1989) *The Condition of Postmodernity*. Oxford: Blackwell.

Hassan, I. (1987) *The Postmodern Turn: Essays in Postmodern Theory and Culture*. Ohio: Ohio State University Press.

Hauck, P. (1991) *Jealousy: Why it Happens and How to Overcome it*. London: Sheldon Press.

Heelas, P. (1986) 'Emotion talk across cultures', in Harré, R. (ed.) *The Social Construction of Emotions*. Oxford: Blackwell.

Heelas, P. and Lock, A. (eds) (1981) *Indigenous Psychologies* London: Academic Press.

Heidegger, M. (1962; orig. 1928) *Being and Time*. Oxford: Blackwell.

Heidegger, M. (1971) *Poetry, Language, Thought*. New York: Harper & Row.

Heider, F. (1944), 'Social perception and phenomenal causality', *Psychological Review*, 51, 358–74.

Heider, R. (1958) *The Psychology of Interpersonal Relations*, New York: Wiley.

Henriques, J., Hollway, W., Urwin, C., Venn, C. and Walkerdine, V. (1987) *Changing the Subject: Psychology, Social Regulation and Subjectivity*. London: Methuen.

Herzlich, C. (1973) *Health and Illness: A Social Psychological Analysis*. London: Academic Press.

Hill, M. and Lloyd-Jones M. (1970) *Sex Education: The Eroneous Zone*. London: National Secular Society.

Hilman, J. and Ventura, M. (1989) *We've Had a Hundred Years of Psychotherapy – and the World's Getting Worse*. San Francisco: Harper.

Hochschild, A. R. (1983) *The Managed Heart: Commercialization of Human Feeling*. Berkeley: University of California Press.

Hoffman, M. L. (1975) 'Developmental synthesis of affect and cognition and its implication for altruistic motivation', *Developmental Psychology*, 11, 607–22.

Hollway, W. (1989) *Subjectivity and Method in Psychology*. London: Sage.

Horton, P. B. (1972) *Sociology*. New York: McGraw-Hill.

Hovland, C. I. and Weiss, W. (1951) 'The influence of source credibility on communicative effectiveness', *Public Opinion Quarterly*, 15, 635–50.

Howitt, D. (1991) *Concerning Psychology: Psychology Applied to Social Issues*. Milton Keynes: Open University.

Howitt, D. et al. (1989) *Social Psychology: Conflicts and Continuities*. Milton Keynes: Open University Press.

Hoyles, M. (1979) *Changing Childhood*. London: Writers & Readers.

Hull, C. L. (1943) *Principles of Behaviour: An Introduction to Behaviour Theory*. New York: Appleton.

Humphrey, G. and Argyle, M. (1971)(eds) *Social Psychology through Experiment*. London: Methuen.

Hyman, H. H. and Sheatsley, P. B. (1954) ' "The authoritarian personality": a methodological critique', in R. Christie and M. Jahoda (eds) *Studies in the Scope and Method of 'The Authoritarian Personality'*. New York: Free Press.

Ibáñez, T. (ed.) (1989) *El conocimiento de la realidad social*. Barcelona: Sendia.

Ibáñez, T. (1991) 'Social psychology and the rhetoric of truth', *Theory and Psychology*, 2, 187–202.

Ibáñez, T. (1994) 'Constructing a representation or representing a construction?', *Theory and Psychology*, 4 (3), 363–83.

Ingleby, D. (1985), 'Professionals as socialisers: the "psy complex" ', in A. Scull and S. Spitzer (eds) *Research in Law, Deviance and Social Control*, Jai Press: New York.

Izard, C. (1971) *The Face of Emotion*. New York: Meridith.

Izard, C. (1977) *Human Emotions*. New York: Plenum Press.

Jacobs, R. C. and Campbell, D. T. (1961) 'The perpetuation of an arbitrary tradition through several generations of a laboratory microculture', *Journal of Abnormal and Social Psychology*, 62, 649–58.

James, W. (1890) *Principles of Psychology*, vols 1 and 2. London: Macmillan.

Jeffreys, S. (1990) *Anticlimax: A Feminist Perspective on the Sexual Revolution*. London: The Women's Press.

Jeffs, T. and Smith, M. K. (eds) *Social Work and Social Welfare Yearbook 3.* Buckingham: Open University Press.

Jenkins, P. (1992), *Intimate Enemies: Moral Panics in Contemporary Great Britain.* New York: Aldine de Gruyter.

Jodelet, D. (1984) 'Représentations sociales: phénomènes, concept et théorie', in S. Moscovici (ed.) *Psychologie Social.* Paris: Presses Universitaires de France.

Jodelet, D. (1991) *Madness and Social Representation.* Hemel Hempstead: Harvester Wheatsheaf.

Johnson, D. M. (1945) 'The "Open Phantom Anesthetist" of Mattoon: a field study of mass hysteria', *Journal of Abnormal and Social Psychology*, 40, 175–86.

Johnston, J. (1973) *Lesbian Nation: The Feminist Solution.* New York: Simon and Schuster.

Jones, E. E. and Davis, K. E. (1965) 'From acts to dispositions: the attribution process in person perception', in L. Berkowitz (ed.) *Advances in Experimental Social Psychology*, vol. 2. New York: Academic Press.

Jones, E. E. and Gerard, H. B. (1967) *Foundations of Social Psychology.* New York: Wiley.

Jourard, S. M. (1968) *Disclosing Man to Himself.* Princeton, NJ.: Van Nostrand.

Jung, K. (1971) *The Experimenter's Dilemma.* New York: Harper and Row.

Kakar, S. (1990) 'Stories from Indian psychoanalysis: content and text' in J. W. Stigler, R. A. Shweder and G. Herdt (eds) *Cultural Psychology: An essay on Comparative Human Development.* New York: Cambridge University Press.

Kamin, L. J. (1974) *The Science and Politics of IQ.* Potomac, Md: Erlbaum Associates.

Kamuf, P. (ed.) (1991) *A Derrida Reader: Between the Blinds.* Hemel Hempstead: Harvester-Wheatsheaf.

Kelley, H. H. (1967) 'Attribution theory in social psychology', in D. Levine (ed.), *Nebraska Symposium on Motivation*, vol. 15. Lincoln: University of Nebraska Press.

Kelly, G. A. (1955) *The Psychology of Personal Constructs.* New York: Norton.

Kemper, T. D. (1988) 'A Manichaean approach to the social construction of emotions', *Cognition and Emotion*, 2 (2), 353–65.

Kinsey, A. C., Pomeroy, W. B. and Martin, C. F. (1948) *Sexual Behavior in the Human Male.* Philadelphia: W. B. Saunders.

Kinsey, A. C., Pomeroy, W. B., Martin, C. F. and Gebhard, P. H. (1963) *Sexual Behavior in the Human Female.* Philadelphia: W. B. Saunders.

Kirscht, J. P. and Dillehay, R. C. (1967) *Dimensions of Authoritarianism.* Lexington, Ky.: University of Kentucky Press.

Kitzinger, C. (1987) *The Social Construction of Lesbianism.* London: Sage.

Kitzinger, C. (1989) 'The regulation of lesbian identities: liberal humanism as an ideology of social control', in J. Shotter and K. Gergen (eds) *Texts of Identity*. London: Sage.

Kitzinger, C. and Perkins, R., (1993) *Changing our Minds: Lesbian Feminism and Psychology*. London: Onlywomen Press.

Klandermans, P. G. (1983) 'Rotter's EI Scale and socio-political action taking: the balance of 20 years research' *European Journal of Social Psychology*, 13, 399–415.

Kline, P. (1988) *Psychology Exposed*. London: Routledge.

Kohlberg, I. A. (1966) 'Cognitive developmental analysis of children's sex role concepts and attitudes', in E. E. Maccoby (ed.) *The Development of Sex Differences*. Stanford, Calif.: Stanford University Press.

Kohlberg, I. A. (1969) 'Stage and sequence: the cognitive-developmental approach to socialization', in D. A. Gosling (ed.) *Handbook of Socialization Theory and Research*. Chicago: Rand McNally.

Kövecses, Z. (1989) *Emotion Concepts*. New York: Springer-Verlag.

Krech, D., Krutchfield, R. S., and Ballachey, E. L. (1962) *Individual in Society*. New York: McGraw-Hill.

Kretschmer, E. (1925) *Physique and Character*. New York: Harcourt.

Kuhn, T. C. (1970) *The Structure of Scientific Revolutions* (2nd edn). Chicago: University of Chicago Press.

Kvale, S. (1990) 'Postmodern psychology: a contradictio in adjecto?', *The Humanist Psychologist*, 18, 35–55.

Lange, N. (1888) 'Beiträge zur Theorie der sinnlichen Aufmerksamkeit unter der aktiven Apperception', *Philosophische Studien*, 4, 390–422.

Latané, B., Williams, K. and Harkins, S. (1979) 'Many hands make light the work: the causes and consequences of social loafing', *Journal of Personality and Social Psychology*, 37, 822–32.

Lather, P. (1990) 'Postmodernism and the human sciences', *The Humanistic Psychologist*, 18, 64–81.

Latour, B. (1988a) *The Pasteurisation of France*. Cambridge, Mass.: Harvard University Press.

Latour, B. (1988b) 'A relativist account of Einstein's relativity', *Social Studies in Science*, 18, 3–44.

Lawson, A. (1988) *Adultery: An Analysis of Love and Betrayal*. Oxford: Blackwell.

Lazarus, R. S. (1984) 'On the primacy of cognition', *American Psychologist*, 39, 124–9.

Le Bon, G. (1895) *Les Lois psychologiques de l'évolution des peuples*. Paris: Alcan.

Lee, N. (1993) 'Justice and care: a Q-methodological investigation into cooperation between police and social workers in the UK', European Association of Experimental Psychology. *Social Psychology in Europe*, Lisbon: Ediçòes Cosmos.

Lee, N. (1994) 'Xenomorph versus theory machine: can we get by without theory?', paper presented at Manchester Metropolitan University, May 1994.

Lefcourt, H. M. (1981) *Research with the Locus of Control Construct* vol. 1: *Assessment of Methods*. New York: Academic Press.

Lerner, M. (1980) *The Belief in a Just World: A Fundamental Delusion*. New York: Plenum.

Levenson, H. (1981) 'Differentiating between internality, powerful others and chance', in H. H. Lefcourt (ed.) *Research with the Locus of Control Construct*, vol. 1: *Assessment Methods*. New York: Academic Press.

Levenson, H. and Miller, J. (1976) 'Multi-dimensional locus of control in sociopolitical activists of conservative and liberal ideologies', *Journal of Personality and Social Psychology*, 33, 199–208.

Leventhal, H. and Hirshman, R. S. (1982) 'Social psychology and prevention' in G. S. Sanders and J. Suls (eds) *Social Psychology of Health and Illness*. Hillside, NJ: Earlbaum.

Lifton, R. J. (1961) *Thought Reform and the Psychology of Totalism*. New York: Vintage.

Lindesmith, A. R., Strauss, A. L. and Denzin, N. K. (1975) *Social Psychology* (4th edn). Hinsdale, Ill.: Dryden.

Litton, I. and Potter, J. (1985) 'Social representations in the ordinary explanation of a riot', *European Journal of Social Psychology*, 15, 371–88.

Lobsenz, N. M. (1977) 'Taming the green-eyed monster' – in G. Clanton, and L. G. Smith (eds) *Jealousy*. Prentice-Hall: Englewood Cliffs.

Lorber, J. and Farrell, S. A. (eds) (1991) *The Social Construction of Gender*. London: Sage.

Lorde, A. (1984) *Sister Outsider*. New York: Crossing Press.

Lorenz, K. (1966) *On Aggression*. New York: Harcourt, Brace & World.

Lyman, S. M. and Scott, M. B. (1968) 'Territoriality: a neglected sociological dimension', *Social Problems*, 15, 236–49.

Lyons, J. (1978) *The Invention of the Self*. Carbondale, Ill.: Southern Illinois University Press.

Lyotard, J. F. (1984) *The PostModern Condition: A Report on Knowledge*. Manchester: Manchester University Press.

MacDonald (1976) 'Homophobia: its roots and meanings', *Homosexual Counseling Journal*, 3, 23–33.

Macey, D. (1993) *The Lives of Michel Foucault*. London: Vintage.

MacIntyre, A. (1981) *After Virtue*. London: Duckworth.

Manstead, A. S. R. (1993) 'Cultural variation in children's understanding of display rules', in *Social Psychology in Europe*, abstracts book – European Association of Experimental Psychology. Lisbon: Ediçòes Cosmos.

Marcus, D. E. and Overton, W. F. (1978) 'The development of cognitive gender constancy and sex role preferences', *Child Development*, 49, 1119–34.

Markovà, I. (1982) *Paradigms, Though and Language*. New York: Wiley.

Markus, H. (1977) 'Self-schemata and processing information about the self', *Journal of Personality and Social Psychology*, 35, 63–78.

Marmor, J. (1980) *Homosexual Behaviour*. New York: Wiley.

Marsh, P. (1978) *Aggro: The Illusion of Violence*. London: Dent.

Marsh, P. E., Rosser, E. and Harré, R., (1977) *The Rules of Disorder*. London: Routledge & Kegan Paul.

Marx, K. (1978) 'Speech at the anniversary of the "People's Paper"', in R. C. Tucker (ed.) *The Marx-Engels Reader*, 2nd edn. New Jersey: Norton.

Maslow, A. H. (1968) *Towards a Psychology of Being* (2nd edn). Princeton: Van Nostrand.

Masters, W. and Johnson, V. (1966) *Human Sexual Response*. London: Churchill.

Mazur, R. (1977) 'Beyond jealousy and possessiveness', in G. Clanton and L. G. Smith (eds) *Jealousy*. Englewood Cliffs: Prentice-Hall.

McDougall, W. (1908) *An Introduction to Social Psychology*. Boston: Luce.

McDougall, W. (1928) 'Emotion and feeling distinguished', in M. C. Remert (ed.) *Feelings and Emotions*. Cambridge, Mass.: Clark University Press.

McDougall, W. (1935) *The Energies of Men* (3rd edn). London: Methuen.

McGuire, W. (1986) 'The vicissitudes of attitudes and similar representational constructs in twentieth century psychology', *European Journal of Social Psychology*, 16, 89–130.

McKinlay, A. and Potter, J. (1987) 'Social representations: a conceptual critique', *Journal for the Theory of Social Behaviour*, 17, 471–88.

McNeil E. B. (1973) *Being Human: The Psychological Experience*. San Francisco: Canfield.

Middlemist, R. D., Knowles, E. S. and Matter, C. F. (1976) 'Personal space invasions in the lavatory: suggestive evidence for arousal', *Journal of Personal and Social Psychology*, 33 (5) 541–6.

Milgram, S. (1963) 'Behavioural study of obedience', *Journal of Abnormal and Social Psychology*, 67, 371–8.

Milgram, S. (1974) *Obedience to Authority: An Experimental View*. New York: Harper & Row.

Miller, G. A., Galanter E. and Pribram, K. H., (1960) *Plans and the Structure of Behavior*. New York: Holt, Rinehart & Winston.

Miller, J. G. (1984) 'Culture and the development of everyday social explanation', *Journal of Personality and Social Psychology*, 46, 961–78.

Miller, N. E. (1941) 'The frustration-aggression hypothesis', *Psychological Review*, 48, 337–42.

Mitchell, J. (1974) *Psychoanalysis and Feminism*. London: Allen Lane.

Mixon, D. (1972) 'Instead of deception', *Journal for the Theory of Social Behaviour*, 2, 145–77.

Morin, S. F. (1977) 'Heterosexual bias in psychological research on lesbianism and male homosexuality', *American Psychologist*, 19, 629–37.

Morley, D. (1980) *The 'Nationwide' Audience*. London: British Film Institute.

Morris, D. (1967) *The Naked Ape*. London: Corgi.

Morss, J. R. (1990) *The Biologising of Childhood*. Hove: Lawrence Erlbaum.

Moscovici, S. (1961) *La Psychanalyse: Son image et son public*. Paris: Presses Universitaires de France.

Moscovici, S. (1976) *Social Influence and Social Change*. London: Academic Press.

Moscovici, S. (1981) 'Bewusste und unbewusste Einflusse in der Kommunikation', *Zeitschrift für Sozialpsychologie*, 23, 93–103.

Moscovici, S. (1982) 'The coming era of representations', in J. P. Codol and J. Leyens (eds) *Cognitive Approaches to Social Behaviour*. The Hague: Nijhoff.

Moscovici, S. (1988) 'Notes towards a description of social representation', *European Journal of Social Psychology*, 18, 211–50.

Moscovici, S. and Hewstone, M. (1983), 'Social representations and social explanations: From the "naive" to the "amateur" scientist', in M. Hewstone (ed.) *Attribution Theory: Social and Functional Extensions*, Oxford: Blackwell.

Mulkay, M. (1985), *The word and the World: Explorations in the Form of Sociological Analysis*, London: George Allen & Unwin.

Mulkay, M. (1989) 'Looking backward', *Science Technology and Human Values*, 14(4), 441–59.

Mulkay, M. (1991) *Sociology of Science: A Sociological Pilgrimage*. Milton Keynes: Open University Press.

Mulvey, L. (1975) 'Visual pleasure and narrative cinema', in *Visual and Other Pleasures*. London: Macmillan.

Murphy, G. (1929) *An Historical Introduction to Modern Psychology*. London: Kegan Paul.

Murray, H. A. (and coll.) (1938) *Exploration in Personality*. New York University Press: Oxford.

Nagel, T. (1970) *The Possibility of Altruism*. Oxford: Clarendon.

Nietzsche, F. W. (1918) *The Genealogy of Morals*. New York: Modern Library.

Nelson, S. (1987) *Incest, Fact and Myth*. Edinburgh: Stradmullion.

Nisbett, R. E., and Ross, L. (1980) *Human Inference: strategies and shortcomings of Social Judgment*. Englewood Cliffs, NJ: Prentice-Hall.

Oakley, J. (1992) *Morality and the Emotions*. London: Routledge.

O'Dell, L. (1993) 'The harm warrant: abusing the abused?', paper presented to the European Association of Experimental Social Psychology General Meeting, Lisbon.

O'Dell, L. (1995) *Child Sexual Abuse: An Investigation of the Epistemology of the 'Harm Warrant'*. Forthcoming doctoral dissertation, The Open University, Milton Keynes.

Orne, M. T. (1962) 'On the social psychology of the psychological experiment: with particular reference to demand characteristics and their implications', *American Psychologist*, 17, 776–83.

Ortner, S. and Whitehead, H. (eds) (1981) *Sexual Meanings: The Cultural Construction of Gender and Sexuality.* Cambridge University Press: New York.

Ortony, A., Clore, G. L. and Collins, A. (1990) *The Cognitive Structure of Emotions.* Cambridge: Cambridge University Press.

Ortony, A. and Turner T. J. (1990) 'What's basic abour basic emotions?', *Psychological Review,* 97 (3), 315–31.

Page, M. M. (1970) 'Role of demand awareness in the communicator credibility effect', *Journal of Social Psychology,* 82, 57–69.

Parker, I. (1988) *The Crisis in Modern Social Psychology, and How to End It.* London: Routledge.

Parker, I. (1992a) *Discourse Dynamics: Critical Analysis for Social and Individual Psychology.* Routledge: London.

Parker, I. (1992b) 'Discourse discourse: social psychology and postmodernity', in J. Doherty, E. Graham and M. Malek, *Postmodernism and the Social Sciences.* Basingstoke: Macmillan.

Parker, I., and Shotter, J. (eds) (1990) *Deconstructing Social Psychology.* London: Routledge.

Parton, N. (1992) *Governing the Family: Child Care, Child Protection and the State.* Basingstoke: Macmillan.

Passini, F. T. and Norman, W. T. (1966) 'A universal conception of personality structure?', *Journal of Abnormal and Social Psychology,* 47, 728–31.

Peirce, C. S. (1934) 'On selecting hypotheses', in C. Hartsgorn and P. Weiss, (eds) *Collected Papers of Charles Sanders Peirce,* vol. 5, *Pragmatism and Pragmatacism.* Cambridge, Mass.: Harvard University Press.

Piaget, J. (1952) *The Origins of Intelligence in the Child.* New York: International Universities Press.

Pickering, A. (1980) 'The role of interests in high energy physics: the choice between charm and colour', *Sociology of the Sciences,* 4, 107–38.

Pinch, T. (1986) *Confronting Nature: The Sociology of Neutrino Detection.* Dordrecht: Reidel.

Pines, A. and Aronson, E. (1981) 'Polyfidelity: an alternative lifestyle without jealousy?', *Alternative Lifestyles,* 4 (3), 373–91.

Plutchic, R. (1962) *The Emotions: Facts, Theories and New Models.* New York: Random House.

Pollock, G. (1988) *Vision and Difference: Femininity, Feminism and the Histories of Art.* London: Routledge.

Pollock, G. (1988) 'Modernity and the spaces of femininity', in *Vision and Difference: Femininity, Feminism and the History of Art.* London: Routledge.

Popper, K. R. (1959) *The Logic of Scientific Discovery.* New York: Basic Books.

Potter, J. and Edwards, D. (1992) *Discursive Psychology.* London: Sage.

Potter, J. and Litton, I. (1985) 'Some problems underlying the theory of social representation', *British Journal of Social Psychology,* 24, 81–90.

Potter, J. and Wetherell, M. (1987) *Discourse and Social Psychology: Beyond Attitudes and Behaviour*. London: Sage.

Press, I. (1980) 'Problems in the definition and classification of medical systems', *Social Science and Medicine*, 14b, 45–57.

Pujol, J. (1993) *Retórica technocientífica y técnicas de reproducción asistida*, unpublished doctoral dissertation, Universitat Autònoma de Barcelona, Spain.

Rachman, S. (1966) 'Sexual fetishism: an experimental analogue', *The Psychological Record*, 16, 293–6.

Raymond, J. G. (1979) *The Transexual Empire*. Boston: Beacon Press.

Reich, C. A. (1971) *The Greening of America*. New York: Bantam.

Reisenzein, R. (1983) 'The Schachter theory of emotion: two decades later', *Psychological Bulletin*, 94, (2), 239–64.

Rheingold, H. L. (1982) 'Little children's participation in the work of adults: a nascent prosocial behaviour', *Child Development*, 53, 114–25.

Rhinehart, L. (1972) *The Diceman*. London: Granada.

Ricci Bitti, P. E. (1993) 'Cultural similarities and differences in facial expression of emotions', in *Social Psychology in Europe*, abstracts book – European Association of Experimental Psychology. Lisbon: Edições Cosmos.

Rich, A. (1980) 'Compulsary heterosexuality and lesbian existence', *Signs: Journal of Women in Culture and Society*, 5 (4), 631–60.

Richards, M. P. M., (ed.) (1974) *The Integration of a Child into a Social World*. Cambridge: Cambridge University Press.

Ringelmann, M. (1913) 'Recherches sur les moteurs animés: Travail de l'homme' *Annales de l'Institut National Agronomique* (2e série), 12, 1–40.

Rogers, C. R. (1942) *Counselling and Psychotherapy: Newer Concepts in Practice*. Boston: Houghton Mifflin.

Rogers, R. S. (= Stainton Rogers, R.) (1974) *A Normative Approach to Attitudes and Cognitive Consistency*, unpublished doctoral thesis, University of London.

Rohrer, J. H., Baron, S. H., Hoffman, E. L. and Swander, D. V. (1954) 'The stability of autokinetic judgements', *Journal of Abnormal and Social Psychology*, 49, 595–97.

Rokeach, M. (1960) *The Open and Closed Mind*. New York: Basic Books.

Rosaldo, M. Z. (1980) *Knowledge and Passion: Illongot Notions of Self and Social Life*. New York: Cambridge University Press.

Rose, N. (1989) 'Individualizing psychology', in J. Shotter and K. J. Gergen (eds) *Texts of Identity*. London: Sage.

Rose, N. (1985) *The Psychological Complex*. London: Routledge.

Rose, N. (1991) *Governing the Soul: The Shaping of the Private Self*. London: Routledge.

Rosen, R. D. (1978) *Psychobabble: Fast Talk and Quick Cure in the Era of Feeling*, London: Wildwood House.

Rosenau, P. M. (1992) *Postmodernism and the Social Sciences: Insights, Inroads and Intrusions*. Princeton: Princeton University Press.

Rosenzweig, S. (1933) 'The experimental situation as a social problem', *Psychological Review*, 40, 337–54.

Ross, E. A. (1908) *Social Psychology*. New York: Macmillan.

Rossi, A. (1977) 'A biosocial perspective on parenting', *Daedalus*, 106, 1–32.

Rotter, J. B. (1966) 'Generalised expectancies for internal versus external control of reinforcement', *Psychological Monographs*, 80 (Whole No. 609).

Russell, D. E. H. (1988) 'Pornography and rape: A causal model', *Journal of Political Psychology*, 9(1), 41–73.

Ryle, G. (1949) *The Concept of Mind*. London: Hutchinson.

Sabini, J. and Silver, M. (1982) *Moralities of Everyday Life*. Oxford: Oxford University Press.

Said, E. (1978) *Orientalism*. New York: Panthenon.

Sampson, E. E. (1971) *Social Psychology and Contemporary Society*. New York: Wiley.

Sampson, E. E. (1985) 'The decentralization of identity: towards a revised concept of person and social order', *American Psychologist*, 43, 1203–11.

Sampson, E. E. (1989) 'The deconstruction of self', in J. Shotter and K. Gergen (eds) *Texts of identity'*. London: Sage.

Sampson, E. E. (1990) 'Social psychology and social control', in I. Parker and J. Shotter (eds) *Deconstructing Social Psychology*. London: Routledge.

Sampson, E. E. (1991) *Social Worlds, Personal Lives: An Introduction to Social Psychology*. London: Harcourt Brace Jovanovich.

Sampson, E. E. (1993) *Celebrating the Other*. Hemel Hempstead: Harvester-Wheatsheaf.

Sampson, E. E. and Insko, C. A. (1964) 'Cognitive consistency and performance in the autokinetic situation', *Journal of Abnormal and Social Psychology*, 68, 184–192.

Saraga, R. and Macleod, M. (1991) 'A feminist reading of recent literature on child sexual abuse', in P. Carter, T. Jeffs and M. K. Smith (eds) *Social Work and Social Welfare Yearbook*, 3. Buckingham: Open University Press.

Sarbin, T. (ed.) (1986) *Narrative Psychology: The Storied Nature of Human Conduct*. New York: Praeger.

Sarbin, T. and Kitsuse, J. (eds) (1994) *Constructing the Social*. London: Sage.

Sayer, J. (1987) 'Psychology and gender divisions', in G. Weiner and M. Arnot (eds) *Gender Under Scrutiny: New Inquiries in Education*. London: Unwin Hyman.

Sayers, J. (1982) 'Is the personal political? Psychoanalysis and feminism revisited', *International Journal of Women's Studies*, 6, 71–86.

Scaife, A. (1994) *Personal communication*.

Schachter, S. and Singer, J. (1962) 'Cognitive, social, and physiological determinants of the emotional state', *Psychological Review*, 69, 379–99.

Schank, R. C. and Abelson, R. P. (1977) 'Scripts plans and knowledge', in P. N. Johnson-Laird and P. C. Wason (eds) *Thinking: Readings in Cognitive Science*. New York: Cambridge University Press.

Schoeck, H. S. (1969) *Envy: A Theory of Social Behaviour*. Bristol: Western Printing Services.

Schofield, M. (1965) *The Sexual Behaviour of Young People*. London: Longman.

Schofield, M. (1973) *The Sexual Behaviour of Young Adults*. London: Allen Lane.

Schutz, A. and Luckmann, T. (1973) *The Structures of the Life-World*, vol. 1. Evanston: Northwest University Press.

Schutz, W. C. (1973) *Joy: Expanding Human Awareness*. Harmondsworth: Penguin.

Scully, D. and Bart, P. (1978) 'A funny thing happened on the way to the orifice: women in gynecology textbooks', in J. Ehrenreich (ed.) *The Cultural in Modern Medicine*. New York: Monthly Review Press.

Sedgewick, P. (1992) *Psychopolitics*. London: Pluto.

Segal, L. (1987) *Is the Future Female? Troubled Thoughts on Contemporary Feminism*. London: Virago.

Semin, G. R. (1987) 'On the relationship between representations of theories in psychology and ordinary language', In W. Doise and S. Moscovici (eds) *Current Issues in European Social Psychology*, vol. 2. Cambridge: Cambridge University Press.

Semin, G. R., and Manstead, A. S. R., (1983) *The Accountability of Conduct: A Social Psychological Analysis*. London: Academic Press.

Semin, G. R. and Rogers, R. S. (= Stainton Rogers, R.) (1973) 'The generation of descriptive-evaluative responses in scale answering behaviour: a model', *European Journal of Social Psychology*, 3, 311–28.

Shaffer, D. R. (1985) *Developmental Psychology: Theory, Research and Applications*. Monterey, Cal.: Brooks/Cole.

Shah, I. (1994) *Exploits of the Incomparable Mullah Nazrudin*. London: Octagon Press.

Shakespear, P., Atkinson, D. and French, S. (eds) (1993) *Reflecting on Research Practice*. Buckingham: Open University Press.

Sheldon, W. H. (coll. S. S. Stevens) (1942) *The Varieties of Temperament*. New York: Harper.

Sherif, M. (1935, repr. 1966) *The Psychology of Social Norms*. New York: Harper & Row.

Shotter, J. and Gergen, K. (eds) (1989) *Texts of Identity*. London: Sage.

Shotter, J. (1984) *Social Accountability and Selfhood*. Oxford: Blackwell.

Shotter, J. (1992) 'Social constructionism and realism: adequacy and accuracy', *Theory and Psychology*, 2 (2) 175–182.

Shotter, J. (1993a) *Conversational Realities: Constructing Life through Language*. Sage: London.

Shotter, J. (1993b) *Cultural Politics of Everyday Life*. Buckingham: Open University Press.

Shulman, A. K. (ed.) (1979) *Red Emma Speaks: The Selected Speeches and Writings of the Anarchist and Feminist Emma Goldman*. London: Guildford Press.

Siann, G. (1985) *Accounting for Aggression: perspectives on aggression and violence*. New York: Allen and Unwin.

Sighele (1898) *La Foule criminelle* Paris: Alcan.

Skinner, B. F. (1938) *The Behaviour of Organisms*. New York: Appleton-Century-Crofts.

Smart, B. (1993) *Postmodernity*. London: Routledge

Smith, R. (1981) *Trial by Medicine: Insanity and Responsibility in Victorian Trials*. Edinburgh: Edinburgh University Press.

Sokoloff, B. (1948) *Jealousy: A Psychological Study*. London: Staples.

Soyland, A. J. (1994) *Psychology as Metaphor*. London: Sage.

Sperling, H. G. (1946) *An Experimental Study of Psychological Factors in Judgement*, unpublished master's theseis, NSSR.

Stainton Rogers, R. and Stainton Rogers, W. (1990a) 'What the Brits got out of the Q: and why their work may not line up with the US way of getting into it!', *Electronic Journal of Communication/La Revue Electronique de Communication*, Troy: New York, Computer file, access via Email 'Send ROGERS VIN190' COMSERVE@RPIECS

Stainton Rogers, R. and Stainton Rogers, W. (1990b) 'Radical social constructionism: Q methodology and the post modernist treatment of beliefs, values and ideologies as cultural texts', paper presented to the Third Europe-Israel Conference on Beliefs, Values and Ideology, The Jacob Blaustein Institute for Desert Research, Mitzpe Ramon, Israel.

Stainton Rogers, R. and Stainton Rogers, W. (1990c) 'Social constructionists as raconteurs: reflections on the telling of stories', paper given to the General Meeting of the EAESP, Budapest, Hungary.

Stainton Rogers, R. and Stainton Rogers, W. (1992a), *Stories of Childhood: Shifting Agendas of Child Concern*. Hemel Hempstead: Harvester-Wheatsheaf.

Stainton Rogers, R. and Stainton Rogers, W. (1992b) 'Textuality and tectonics: Social Psychology, the millennium and construction of homo narrans narratur', paper presented to the Czecho-Slovak Medium Size meeting of the EAESP, Smolenice, Slovakia.

Stainton Rogers, W. (1986) 'Cultural representations of "addiction": links and disjunctions between perspectives', paper given to the Special Theme Meeting of the EAESP, Lisbon, Portugal.

Stainton Rogers, W. (1991) *Explaining Health and Illness*. Hemel Hempstead: Harvester-Wheatsheaf.

Stainton Rogers, W. and Stainton Rogers, R. (1986) 'Social issues and participant democracy', paper prescnted to the Second Annual Conference for the Scientific Study of Subjectivity, Missouri, USA.

Stainton Rogers, W. and Stainton Rogers, R. (1989), 'Taking the child abuse debate apart', in Stainton Rogers, W., Hevey, D. and Ash, E. (eds), *Child Abuse and Neglect: Facing the Challenge*. London: Batsford.

Stainton, Rogers, W., Stainton Rogers, R. Lowe, I and Kitzinger, C. (1986) 'When social issues are multiplexly represented: Q methodology, social policy and participant democracy', paper given to the Special Theme Meeting of the EAESP, Lisbon, Portugal.

Stearns, C. Z. and Stearns, P. N. (1986). *Anger: The Struggle for Emotional Control in America's History*. Chicago: University of Chicago Press.

Stearns, C. Z. and Stearns, P. (1988) *Emotion and Social Change: Toward a New Psychohistory*. New York: Holmes & Meier.

Stearns, P. N. (1989) *Jealousy: The Evolution of an Emotion in American History*. New York: New York University Press.

Stenner, P. (1992) 'Feeling deconstructed?: With particular reference to jealousy', unpublished Ph.D. Thesis, University of Reading.

Stenner, P. (1993a) 'Discoursing jealousy', in E. Burman and I. Parker (eds) *Discourse Analytic Research: Repertoires and Readings of Texts in Action*. London: Routledge.

Stenner, P. (1993b) 'Wittgenstein and the textuality of emotion', *Practice*, 9 (2), 29–35.

Stenner, P. (1994) 'Theo-ry is dead', paper presented at Manchester Metropolitan University, May 1994.

Stenner, P. and Eccleston, C. (1994) 'On the textuality of being: towards an invigorated social constructionism', *Theory and Psychology*, 4 (1), 85–103.

Stenner, P. and Marshall, H. (1995) 'A Q methodological study of rebelliousness', *The European Journal of Social Psychology*, 25 (6), 621–36.

Stephenson, W. (1953) *The Study of Behaviour: Q-technique and its Methodology*. Chicago: University of Chicago Press.

Stephenson, W. (1961) 'Scientific creed: 1', *Psychological Record*, 11, 1–26.

Storms, M. D. (1979) 'Sex role identity and relationships to sex role attributes and sex role stereotypes', *Journal of Personality and Social Psychology*, 38, 783–92.

Sullivan, T. (1992) *Sexual Abuse and the Rights of Children: Reforming Canadian law*. Toronto: University of Toronto Press.

Sully, J. (1901) *The Teachers Handbook of Psychology*. London: Longmans Green.

Sutherland, E. H. and Cressey, D. R. (1974) *Principals of Criminology* (9th edn). New York: Lippincott.

Tajfel, H. and Turner, J. C. (1979) 'An integrative theory of intergroup conflict', in W. C. Worchel and F. G. Austin (eds) *The Social Psychology of Intergroup Relations*. Monterey, Calif.: Brookes/Cole.

Tajfel, H. and Turner, J. C. (1986) 'The social identity theory of intergroup behavior', in S. Worchel and E. G. Austin (eds) *The Psychology of Intergroup Relations* (2nd edn). Chicago, Ill: Nelson Hall.

Taussig, M. (1986) 'The nervous system', paper presented to the British Medical Anthropology Society Conference, Cambridge.

Taylor, C. (1989) *Sources of the Self*. Cambridge: Cambridge University Press.

Taylor, M. C. and Hall, J. A. (1982) 'Psychological androgeny: theories, methods and conclusions', *Psychological Bulletin*, 92, 347–66.

Tedeschi, J. C., Schlenker, B. R. and Bonoma, T. V. (1971) 'Cognitive dissonance: private ratiocination or public spectacle?', *American Psychologist*, 26, 685–95.

Terman, L. M. and Miles, C. C. (1936) *Sex and Personality*. New York: McGraw-Hill.

Thomas, A. (1987), 'The Social Construction of Gender: A Psychological Study', unpublished Ph.D. thesis, University of Reading.

Thomas, A. and Chess, S. (1980) *The Dynamics of Psychological Development*. New York: Brunner/Mazel.

Thomas, E. M. (1985) *Comparing Theories of Child Development* (2nd edn). Belmont, Cal.: Wadsworth.

Thomas, M. H., Horton, R., Lippincott, E., and Drabman, R. (1977) 'Desensitization to portrayals of real-life aggression as a function of exposure to television violence', *Journal of Personality and Social Psychology*, 35, 450–8.

Tiffin, J., Knight, F. B. and Josey, C. C. (1940) *The Psychology of Normal People*. Boston: Heath.

Townsend, P. (1969), 'Foreword', in P. Morris, (ed.) *Put Away: A Sociological Study of Institutions for the Mentally Retarded*. London: Routledge & Kegan Paul.

Triandis, H. C. (1971) *Attitude and Attitude Change*. New York: Wiley.

Triplett, N. (1898) 'The dynamogenic factors in pace making and competition', *American Journal of Psychology*, 9, 507–33.

Van Dyke, T. (1992) 'Discourse and the denial of racism', *Discourse and Society*, 3 (1), 87–118.

Varela, J. A. (1975) 'Can social psychology be applied?', in M. Deutsh and H. A. Hornstien (eds) *Applying Social Psychology*. Hillside, NJ: Lawrence Erlbaum.

Vollmer, H. (1977) 'Jealousy in children', in G. Clanton and L. G. Smith (eds) *Jealousy*. Englewood Cliffs: Prentice-Hall.

Walkerdine, V. (1988) *The Mastery of Reason*. London: Routledge.

Walkerdine, V. (1990) *Schoolgirl Fictions*. London: Verso.

Walkerdine, V. and Lucey, H. (1989) *Democracy in the Kitchen*. London: Virago.

Walling, W. H. (ed.) (1909) *Sexology*. Philadelphia: Puritan.

Wallston, B. S. and Wallston, K. A. (1981) 'Health locus of control scales', in H. M. Lefcourt (ed.) *Research with the Locus of Control Construct*, (vol. 1). New York: Academic Press.

Walster, F. and Walster, G. W. (1978) *Love*. Reading, Mass.: Addison-Wesley.

Warner, C. T. (1986) 'Anger and similar delusions', in R. Harré (ed.) *The Social Construction of Emotions*. Oxford: Blackwell.

Warren, C. A. B. (1987), *Madwives: Schizophrenic Women in the 1950's*, New York and London: Rutgers University Press.

Wason, P. (1977) 'The theory of Formal Operations – a critique', in B. Geber (ed.) *Piaget and Knowing: Studies in Genetic Epistemology*. London: Routledge.

Weber, M. (1978), *Economy and Society: An Outline of Interperative Sociology*, 2 vols. Berkeley: University of California Press.

Weinberg, T. S. (1973) *Society and the Healthy Homosexual*. New York: Anchor.

Weiner, B. (1986) *An attribution Theory of Emotion and Motivation*. New York: Springer-Verlag.

Weldon, F. (1971) *Down Among the Women*. Harmondsworth: Penguin.

West, C. and Zimmerman, D. H. (1991) 'Doing gender', in J. Lorber and S. A. Farrell (eds) *The Social Construction of Gender*. London: Sage.

Wetherell, M. and Potter, J. (1992) *Mapping the Language of Racism: Discourse and the Legitimation of Exploitation*. London: Harvester-Wheatsheaf.

White, G. L. and Mullen, P. E. (1989) *Jealousy: Theory, Research and Clinical Strategies*. London: The Guildford Press.

Wicker, A. W. (1969) 'Attitudes versus actions: The relationship between verbal and overt behavioural response to attitude objects', *Journal of Social Issues*, 25, 41–78.

Wiggins, J. S., Wiggins, S. N. and Conger, J. C. (1968) 'Correlates of heterosexual somatic preference', *Journal of Personality and Social Psychology*, 10, 82–98.

Wilkinson, S. (ed.) (1986) *Feminist Social Psychology: Developing Theory and Practice*. Milton Keynes: Open University Press.

Wilson, E. O. (1975) *Sociobiology*. Cambridge, Mass.: Harvard University Press.

Wilson, E. O. (1978) *On Human Nature*. Cambridge, Mass.: Harvard University Press.

Wilson, T. D. and Linville, P. W. (1982) 'Improving the academic performance of college freshmen: attribution therapy revisited', *Journal of Personality and Social Psychology*, 42, 367–76.

Wittgenstein, L. (1958) *Philosophical Investigations* (2nd edn. ed. G. E. M. Anscombe, trans. G. E. M. Anscombe and R. Rhees). Oxford: Blackwell.

Wittgenstein, L. (1961) *Tractatus Logico-philosophicus*. London: Routledge.

Wittgenstein, L. (1965) *The Blue and Brown Books*. New York: Harper & Row.

Wittgenstein, L. (1980) 'Remarks on the philosophy of psychology', in *Collected Works*, vol. 1 (trans. G. E. M. Anscombe, G. E. M. Anscombe and G. H. Von Wright). Oxford: Blackwell.

Wittgenstein, L. (1981) *Zettel* (2nd edn. ed. trans. G. E. M. Anscombe, G. E. M. Anscombe and G. H. Von Wright). Oxford: Blackwell.

Woolgar, S. (1988a) *Science: The Very Idea*. Chichester: Ellis Horwood Limited.

Woolgar, S. (1988b) *Knowledge and Reflexivity: New Frontiers in the Sociology of Knowledge*. London: Sage.

Worrell, M. and Stainton Rogers, W. (1992) 'Child concern: discourses of predation, protection and paternalism', *Proceedings of the International Excellence in Training Conference*, University of Dundee.

Wright, D. (1971) *The Psychology of Moral Behavior*. Harmondsworth: Penguin.

Young, A. (1980), 'The discourse on stress and reproduction of conventional knowledge', *Social Science and Medicine*, 14b, 133–46.

Yuval-Davis, N. (1994) 'Women, ethnicity and empowerment', *Feminism and Psychology*, 4 (1) 179–80.

Zajonc, R. B. (1984) 'On the primacy of affect', *American Psychologist*, 39, 117–23.

Zajonc, R. B., Heingartner, A. and Herman, E. M. (1969) 'Social enhancement and impairment of performance in the cockroach', *Journal of Personality and Social Psychology*, 13, 83–92.

Zajonc, R. B. (1965) 'Social facilitation', *Science*, 149: 269–74.

Zammuner, V. (1993) 'Factors associated with adhesion to display rules in Italian children', in *Social Psychology in Europe*, abstracts book – European Association of Experimental Psychology. Lisbon: Ediçòes Cosmos.

Zimbardo, P. G. (1970) 'The human choice: Individuation, reason, and order versus deindividuation, impulse and chaos', in W. J. Arnold and D. Levine (eds) *Nebraska Symposium on Motivation: 1969* (vol. 17, 237–307). Lincoln: University of Nebraska Press.

Zimbardo, P. G. (1976) *Psychology and Life* (brief 9th edn) Glenview, Ill.: Scott, Foresman & Company.

Zimbardo, P. G. (1977) *Shyness: What is it, What to Do about It*. Reading, Mass.: Addison-Wesley.

Index

abductive approach, 253, 271
Academy, The 226, 261, 265
addiction, 252
adolescence, 107
Adorno, T. D., 118–19
adrenaline, 180
ageism, 223
aggression, 14, 26
    critical polytextual theory of, 170–1
    as cultural drama, 165–6
    drive-based, 160
    as frustration, 155–7
    phenomenological theory of, 165
    politics of, 166–70
    situational explanations, 160
    social learning theory of, 161–3
    socially constructed, 170–2
Ajzen, I., 127–8
aliens, 195
Amnesty International, 81
analysis,
    cluster, 242
    concursive, 249–50
    correspondence, 242, 245, 248
    factor, 49–50, 242
    multivariate, 241–2, 248
    of variance, 136
androgeny, 205
animality, 107
    as domestication, 107
anthropology, 11, 12
    sexual, 221
anti-semitism, 118
anxiety, 53

Anything Goes, 219
APA, 6, 44
apartheid, 86
Aronson, E., 5, 43, 93–4, 150, 227–9
arousal, 73–4
Asch, S. E., 80–1
assessment, 258–9
attitudes, 11, 13, 25, 111–12
    and behaviour, 126
    centrality of, 112
    change, 11, 123–6, 229
    as personality, 120
    problems, 122
    scales, 25, 112, 122
    as 'set', 120
attribution,
    pessimistic, 140
    re-attributed, 141–2
    theory see under theory
Authoritarian Personality, The, 117–19
auto-kinetic effect, 79
Averill, J., 35

Baby books, 107
Bandura, A., 164
Bannister, D., 133
Bartlett, F. C., 142–3
behaviourism, 113
    radical, 113
Being, 35, 38, 45–6, 55, 65–7, 78
belief in a just world, 139
Bem, S., 200–1, 205–6
Beryl Curt, 3, 255–72
Beryl's Laws

first, 22
second, 30
third, 56
fourth, 112
fifth, 119
sixth, 206
Bhaskar, R., 36
bias, self-serving, 116, 212
Billig, M., 87, 110, 135, 159, 170, 244
biology, 11, 12
    as discursive resource, 195
bio-social science, 12, 16, 174
blooper, 138
Bobo doll, 162
boots, thigh-length, 223
Bourdieu, P., 58, 210
BPS., 6, 44
brainwashing, 115
Brown, R., 25, 117, 203
Brown, S. R., 253
Bulger case, 260
Burman, E., 103, 244
bystander apathy, 106, 108

Cattell, R. B., 43, 47, 49–50
censorship, 211
central processing mechanism, 27
child,
    rearing, 106
    sexual abuse, 22
    theory of mind, 105
    wolf, 95
circumstance, 56–7, 63–5
circumstantial ontology, 65
citizenship, 28
civilization, frailty of, 75
climate of perturbation, 3, 4, 32, 35, 36, 97,
        108, 126, 175, 202, 209, 232, 234, 247
CND, 17
cognitive,
    algebra, 113
    approach, 113
    dissonance, 35, 53
    misers, 133
    overload, 152
    science, 27
    social psychology, 134–5
common-sense, 14
    icality, 128, 162, 171, 2202, 229
    and science, 130
    social, 143
communicator credibility, 228–30
complex,
    Electra, 105, 174

Oedipus, 105, 174
concourse, 249
concursive, 248, 249
conditioning, 106
    sexual, 223
conduct, 112
conformity, 76, 78, 80–1
conservatism, 39
convergence effect, 79
conversation, 35, 36
    dangling, 272
Craib, I., 37
creata, 50
crisis in social psychology,
    as condition of social psychology, 22, 108
    in 1970s, 238
    and sexism, 205
critical polytextualism, 170–1, 244, 247, 265
crowd behaviour, 74–5, 173–4
cultural studies, 33, 208
Curt, B. 97, 110, 146, 154, 169, 234, 264
cyborg, 223

Darwinism,
    biological, 101
    intellectual, 16
    social, 102
'death and furniture' argument, 38
deindividuation, 76, 85
democracy, 90
desire, 209
detemporalizing, 58
development,
    cognitive, 105
    as theory of civilization, 16
developmentalism, 101
deviance, 168, 193
dialogics, 256
disability, 96
    social construction of, 96
discourse, 243–8, 257
    self-serving, 61
    singularizing, 41
discourse analysis, 87–8, 243–7
    reference points, 244–7
    and social constructionism, 245
discursive,
    action model (DAM), 246
    agnostics, 36
    domains, 250
    labour, 4
    mind, 36
    phenomena, 31
    practice, 46

production, 116
psychology, 33
resources, 194
disenchantment, 125, 260
disillusion, 247
Doise, W., 242
Down's syndrome, 100
dramaturgical research, 57
dynamogenics, 72–3
dyslexia, 100

Eccleston, C., 35, 65
economics, 11, 12, 16
eco-terrorism, 169
Edwards, D., 130, 246
electric shocks, 82, 157, 160, 170
embodiment, 14, 100, 109, 192, 220
emotion, 13
    as always-ever social, 188–91
    as animal passions, 189
    as attribution, 179–82
    as communication, 177
    ethological models of, 189
    James Langer theory of, 175
    mainstream approach to, 176–82
    moral concern over, 178
    psychometric approach to, 177–9
    social construction of, 182–90
    as ways of Being, 183
empowerment, 88, 96, 112
enlightenment, 16, 24
epistemology, 240
    lay-, 151–2, 171
Erikson, E., 101
eroticization, 219–21
errors,
    as bloopers, 138–9
    comedy of, 34
    commonsense, 134
    fundamental attribution, 159
essences, 28, 30
essentialism, 28
ethnocentrism, 17, 118, 195
ethnography, 26
ethogenics, 22, 26–7, 165
ethology, 108
eugenics, 82, 102
experimenter's dilemma, 233
experiments, 227–9
    artefacts of, 232–3
    critique of, 229–31
extraversion/intraversion, 48–50
Eysenck, H. J., 48, 49–50, 113

faking, 233
falsifiability, 22
    canon of, 21
fascism, 86, 89
feeble-mindedness, 28
feminism, 102
    its appropriation of psychoanalysis, 208
    and critical social psychology, 207
    see also under film-theory; theory
Festinger, L., 124–6
fetishism, 221, 223
film-theory, 33, 208, 248
    feminist, 194
    and psychoanalysis, 208
Fishbein, M., 127–8
footing, 64–6, 187
Foucault, M., 26, 27–9, 46, 77, 126, 199,
    210–12
foundationalism, 259, 266, 270
    rejection of, 247
Frankfurt school, 118
Fransella, F., 133
free-will, 64
frustration, 155–7
    -aggression hypothesis, 156
F-scale, 119
Furnham, A., 134

G spot, 224
Game, A., 248
gaze, 195
    male, 108, 194, 216
Geertz, C., 45–6
gender, 14
    biological basis of, 200
    cognitive development theory of, 200
    differences, 202–6
    disturbances, 217
    identity, 205
    and mental health, 204
    and power, 205
    psychodynamic theory of, 201
    roles, 118
    social learning theory of, 200
Gergen, K., 103, 107
Gergen, M., 103
Gilligan, C., 108
Gleeson, K., 155
goal plans, 27
Goffman, I., 56–7
governmentality, 28, 39, 45–6, 211–12
    and resistance, 212
Great Depression, 115
Griffin, C., 168
groups,

in-, 197
marginalized, 246
minority, 86
norms, 79
out-, 86
pressure, 81, 242

Häagen Daz ice cream, 218
Haraway, D., 108, 194
Harré, R., 24, 31, 36, 56, 57, 64, 122, 126, 166, 186, 232
Heidegger, M., 56
Henriques, J., 86, 88, 110, 234
HIV, 215
Hollway, W., 86, 110, 234
homo narrans naratur, 36
homophobia, 62, 209–10
humaneering, 2, 18, 21, 29, 31, 46, 114–15, 159, 175, 195
humanism *see* liberal humanism
humanity, 28
hypothetico-deductivism, 7, 25, 26, 113, 225, 238
critique of, 232
hystericization, 211

'I' and 'me', 63
Ibañez, T., 97, 100
identity,
biological warrant for, 198
lesbian, 62
politics of, 69
situated, 51–3
texts of, 169, 197
textual, 60–1
ideology, 26, 159
impression management, 57
incest, 222
individual differences, 14, 54
individualism, 24
self-contained, 76, 102
individualization, 28
information processing, 109
instinct, 57
intellectual imperialism, 17
intelligence, 28
tests of, 103
internalization, 107
interpersonal,
interaction, 14
relations, 16
interpretative repertoires, 244–5
interrogation interminable, 146, 234
izzat, 154

jealousy, 89, 186–7
Josey, C. C., 21

Kelley, H. H., 136–7
Kelly, G., 135
Kent State Massacre, 13
Kline, P., 23, 128
Knight, F. B., 21
Knowing of Third Kind, 110
knowledge,
expert and lay, 133, 144, 151
hierarchies of, 33
lay epistemic, 132
in relation to power, 212
social, 146

Le Bon, G. 74–5, 78–9
learned helplessness, 140
lesbian,
identity, 62
politics, 96
sadomasochistic, 220
separatism, 207
liberal humanism, 5, 39, 54, 83, 85
and emancipation, 96
literary theory, 33
locus of control, 120–1, 231
health, 119
looks, 185
body-, 186
in-, 185
out-, 185
Lorenz, K., 165

Machiavellianism, 51
madness, 155
March of Civilization tale, 17–18, 22
March of Progress tale, 32
'marked' categories, 194
market segmentation, 242
Marxism, 78, 102
neo-, 110
Maslow, A. H., 101
masturbation, 28, 91, 210, 213–15, 224
mutual, 222
maternal deprivation, 21
McCarthyism, 115
McNaughten Rules, 104
Mead, M., 63
Mensa, 103
mental,

health, 204–5
  illness, 243
metaphor, 35, 241, 245
methodology,
  alternative, 238–47
methods,
  experimental, 27
  qualitative, 234
  in relation to theory, 29
  scientific, 20, 42
Milgram, S., 82–3
mission,
  -ary agenda of social psychology, 1
  and attribution, 132
  and social cognition, 131
  statement, 2
modelling, 164, 200
Modernism, 4, 15, 16, 22, 28–9, 37, 77, 84,
  90, 93
  of the self, 97
monologism, 109
moralization, 103–6
  mainstream theories of, 105
  male orientation of, 108
Morss, J., 103, 105
Moscovici, S., 78, 143, 151
Mulkay, M., 141, 239–40
Mulvey, L., 208
mysogeny *see* sexism

narrative,
  metaphorics, 247
  psychology, 36
  science, 241
nature/nurture theorization, 94–6, 107–8
  in relation to gender, 200
  as sexual alchemy, 202
Nazis, 82
need(s), 35
  achievement, 51
  consistency, 116
  narrative, 202
  paradigmatic, 202
New Deal, 115
nymphomania, 224

object-ing, 45
ontology, 153
  circumstantial, 65
opinion polls, 70, 111
opinionation, 114, 129, 231
Other, 63, 115, 222
  a bit of the, 193–5

  sexual, 222
  significant, 63

paedophilia, 193
paradigm
  new, 26, 28, 31
  old, 28
  shift, 23
paradigmatic science, 241
Paris Commune, 75, 174
Parker, I., 22, 36, 37, 57, 110, 130, 142
participant observation, 116, 166
patriarchy, 39, 40, 62, 206, 207
pedagogization, 211, 215
permissiveness, 221–2
person perception, 67
personality, 13
  16 PF scale of, 50
  authoritarian, 86
  biological theories of, 48–52
  Catell's approach to, 49–50
  as character language, 68
  Eysenck's theory of, 48–50
  implicity theory of, 50
  moral agenda around, 68
  as physiology, 48
  psychometric approach to, 49
  social learning theories of, 52
personhood, 29, 44
  reification as personality, 47–51
phenomenology, 55, 165
phereomones, 218
philosophy, 25
  anti-, 110
Piss Christ, 262
pleasure,
  perverse, 212
PLU principle, 206
policing, 28
political correctness, 87, 224
politics, 37, 38, 39–40, 96, 97
  and power, 163
  of the self, 68–9
post structuralism, 33
post-Enlightenment project, 15, 97, 167
  moral philosophy of, 106
postmodern, carnival, 37
postmodernism, 9, 32–3, 192
  see also climate of perturbation
Potter, J., 88, 122, 130, 143, 145, 210, 215,
  244, 246
power, 26, 163, 246
  gay, 216
  and gender, 205

and knowledge *see* knowledge
/knowledge synarchy, 78
and politics, 163
regulatory, 168
relations, 246
practical/expressive distinction, 57
prejudice, 86–8, 116
presencing, 59
primatology, 108, 193
prison,
    psychologists, 85
    simulated, 84
Prisoner's Dilemma, 83
professionalization,
    of concern, 46
pro-social behaviour, 19, 20
pro-text, 266
psychiatrization, 271
psychoanalysis, 86
psychobabble, 21, 91, 101
psychologism, 4
psychology,
    applied, 39
    child, 101
    departments of, 39
    as a discipline, 31
    discursive, 33
    Gestalt, 197
    humanistic, 27
    implicit, 133
    its self-serving bias, 44
    social developmental, 94–5, 106
    the subject of, 19
    see also social psychology
psychometrics, 49, 113, 116, 203, 231–3
psychopathology, 62
psychotherapy, 93–4, 102
psy-complex, 104, 210
Pujol, J., 243
Puritanism, 115, 252

Q methodology, 248–53
    versus psychometrics, 249–52
Q samples, 250
Q sorts, 250
questionnaires, 232

R methodology, 251
racism, 86
    institutionalized, 86
radicalism, 39
rape,
    date, 224
realism, 25–6

biological, 25
critical, 36
disputed, 77
new, 37
reality,
    contested, 67
    negotiated, 145
    social, 167
reasoned action, 127
reflexivity, 89–90, 240, 245, 246, 248, 251,
    257–66
    of methodology 246
reframing, 262–3, 265
reification, 58, 77
relationships,
    intimate, 91
    kinship, 90
    personal, 91–4
    romantic, 90
    sick, 94
relativism, 37
religion, 42, 104
repertory grids, 26
representational labour, 116
reproductive technology, 243
resistance, 8, 159, 212
resisting the discipline, 85–6
revolution,
    sexual, 216
rhetoric, 3
    political, 87
role,
    playing, 26
    theory, 58
Rome, 100
Romulus and Remus, 94, 202
Rose, N., 28, 93
Rotter, 120–1, 139–40

sadomasochism, 212
    lesbian, 220
Sampson, E. E., 78, 109
Schachter, S., 180
Schadenfreude, 183
science,
    as discourse, 141
    as story-telling, 34–5
scientific method, 20
scientism, 23–5, 28
    and sex, 217
scientist,
    naive, 133
scopophilia, 217, 221
scripts, 27

of identity, 197
seeded thematics, 185, 248
self,
  -abuse, 213
  as a compound, 46
  -control, 168, 193, 207
  -esteem, 205
  experimental social psychology of, 66
  -exposure, 220
  looking-glass, 63
  -presentation, 233
  -schemas, 142
  social construction of, 45–6, 60
  -talk, 61
  technologies of, 46
  textuality and tectonics of, 60
sex, 193, 195–7
  categorization, 195–6
  chromasomal, 196
  differences, 198
  education, 193
  hormones, 198
  identity, 196
  as not 'natural', 199
  play, 222
sexism, 86
  in theorizing, 108–9
sexuality, 14
  bi-, 193
  childhood, 213
  as discourse, 212
  Foucauldian analysis of, 210–12
  genital, 196
  hetero-, 92, 102, 216
  homo-, 47, 53, 92, 193, 209, 212, 216,
    224
  liberal discourse on, 216
  liberation, 215–17
  pomo-, 192
  signification, 211–12
  trans-, 217
  see also lesbian
Shaffer, D. R., 42
shell-shock, 28
Shemin, G., 232
Sherif, M., 78–9
Shotter, J., 36, 68, 93, 97, 110
Singer, J., 180
singularization, 38
situationism, 52, 54
  and social problems, 52
social,
  always-ever, 95
  determinism, 64

economy, 116
facilitation, 72–4
hygiene, 104, 108, 115, 142–5
influence, 81
interaction, 70–1
learning, 162–3
loafing, 76
perceptual systems, 116
policy, 72
practice, 168
representations, 113, 124–43
repression, 28
rules, 230
science, 8
see also social constructionism; social
  psychology; theory
social constructionism, 9, 29, 35, 53, 71
  of disability, 96
  and discourse analysis, 246
  of emotion, 182–90
  versus social learning, 162–3
social psychology,
  applied, 139
  as art, 43
  cognitive, 134–5, 137
  defined, 89
  as discipline, 31
  excess of theories in, 29–30
  experimental, 65–6
  grounding assumptions of, 31
  interpretational, 234
  its market niche, 10–11
  as Mission, 2–4, 83
  as narrative, 34
  problem orientated, 5, 39, 89
  its product range, 7–9
  in relation to socio-linguistics, 188
  sociological, 234
  subject matter, 31
  see also crisis in social psychology
socialism,
  old style, 39
socialization, 107, 98–100
  deconstructed, 99–100, 107–8
sociobiology, 39, 99
sociology, 11, 12
  cognitive, 233
  ethnomethodological, 246
  existential, 233
  micro, 239
  phenomenological, 239–46
  qualitative, 233
  of scientific knowledge, 145, 239
Stainton Rogers, R., 95, 137, 202, 233, 252

Stainton Rogers, W., 95, 121, 137, 202, 229, 231, 252
Stenner, P., 31, 36, 65, 66, 155
stereotyping, 86–7, 117
   sex-role, 217
subversion, 260
suggestibility, 79
Sully, J., 105
Superman, 202
symbolic interactionism, 55
synaesthenia, 117

Tarzan, 95
taxonomies, 240
tecton, 36
   as 'hot spot', 210
tectonics, 18, 36, 97, 110, 247
   power, 210
textuality, 65, 110, 116, 240, 247
thematic decomposition, 213, 248
theory,
   attitude, 135
   attribution, 131, 135–42
   cognitive dissonance, 137
   cognitive social learning, 120
   correspondence inference, 136
   covariation, 136
   critical, 256
   is dead, 29–32
   feminist, 206–9
   Freudian, 143
   grand, 256
   humanistic, 103
   of influence, 78
   of learned helplessness, 140
   learning, 113
   machines, 245
   personal construct, 135
   of planned action, 127
   of reasoned action, 127
   schema, 131, 135, 142–4
   social identity, 197
   social learning, 120
   social representations, 142–4
therapy, 94
   client centred, 102
   see also psychotherapy
Tiffin, J., 21

time, 57–9, 231
totalizing,
   theories, 32, 74, 88, 96
trait/state distinction, 53
transdisciplinarity, 33, 209
   and sexuality, 209
Triandis, H. C., 11
turn,
   discursive, 122
   Foucauldian, 27
   humanistic, 135
   to 'softer' methods, 233
   textuality, 54–9, 239

unconscious, 208
UNESCO, 102
urinals,
   shared, 73
Urwin, C., 86, 110

variable,
   dependent, 71, 114, 228
   independent, 71, 228
vegetarians, 252
Velvet Underground (The), 223
Victorian values, 213
virginity, 222
Volkerpsychologie, 16

Walkerdine, V., 86, 110, 198, 221
Walling, W. H., 231–15
wanking *see* masturbation
war,
   cold, 82, 83, 115
   of the Ghosts, 143
   second world, 115
   Vietnam, 115
   of the Worlds, 75
warrant,
   biological, 198, 218
   of scientificality, 82
Wetherell, M., 88, 122, 130, 143, 145, 210, 215, 237, 244
Wild Boy of Aveyon, 95

Zajonc, R. B., 73–4
Zeitgeist, 191
Zimbardo, P. G., 84, 167, 215
Zimbardo Prison Study, 84

Printed in the United Kingdom by
Lightning Source UK Ltd., Milton Keynes
139475UK00001B/7/P

9 780745 611839